2nd Edition

Boatbuilding with Aluminum

2nd Edition

Boatbuilding with Aluminum

A COMPLETE GUIDE FOR THE AMATEUR AND SMALL SHOP

STEPHEN F. POLLARD

International Marine / McGraw-Hill
Camden, Maine • New York • Chicago • San Francisco • Lisbon • London • Madrid
• Mexico City • Milan • New Delhi • San Juan • Seoul • Singapore • Sydney • Toronto

The McGraw·Hill Companies

1 2 3 4 5 6 7 8 9 DOC DOC 0 9 8 7 6

© 1993, 2007 by International Marine

All rights reserved. The publisher takes no responsibility for the use of any of the materials or methods described in this book, nor for the products thereof. The name "International Marine" and the International Marine logo are trademarks of The McGraw-Hill Companies.

Library of Congress Cataloging-in-Publication Data
Pollard, Stephen F.
  Boatbuilding with aluminum: a complete guide for the amateur and small shop / Stephen F. Pollard. — 2nd ed.
    p. cm.
  ISBN 0-07-144318-5 (hardcover)
    1. Aluminum boats—Design and construction—Amateurs' manuals. 2. Aluminum work—Amateurs' manuals. I. Title. II. Title: Boatbuilding with aluminum.
  VM321.P56 2006
  623.82'07—dc22   2006012686

ISBN-13: 978-1-265-81124-2
ISBN-10: 1-26-581124-5

Questions regarding the content of this book should be addressed to
International Marine
P.O. Box 220
Camden, ME 04843
www.internationalmarine.com

Questions regarding the ordering of this book should be addressed to
The McGraw-Hill Companies
Customer Service Department
P.O. Box 547
Blacklick, OH 43004
Retail customers: 1-800-262-4729
Bookstores: 1-800-722-4726

Unless noted below, all photos and illustrations are by the author.

Photos courtesy: Unimet, Inc (p. 6); Ocean Alloys (p.7); Northwind Marine (pp. i–iii, 8, 10, 16, 40); Lake Assault Custom Boats (p. 9); Hoestead Skiffs (p. 10); Titan Boats (p. 11); Plate Master Boats (vii, chapter openers); Precision Boat (p.14); O & W Enterprises (p. 19); Sovereign Yachts (p. 33, 274); Northwest Plasma Cutting (p. 72); Miller (pp. 89, 94); Aliboats (p. 160); Vortec (p. 210); Maritime Outfitters (p. 258).

*To those boatbuilders and designers who
constantly strive to produce a better aluminum boat.*

CONTENTS

Acknowledgments   ix
Preface to the Second Edition   1
Introduction   3

1. **Introduction to Aluminum**   5
2. **Characteristics of Marine Aluminum**   21
3. **Designing for Aluminum**   29
4. **Fabricating Techniques**   69
5. **Welding Aluminum**   89
6. **Aluminum Boat Lofting**   123
7. **Aluminum Boat Construction Sequence**   159
8. **Sailboats**   181
9. **Propulsion Systems and Controls**   205
10. **Fuel Systems**   233
11. **The Electrical System**   245
12. **Woodwork and Insulation**   257
13. **Aluminum Painting Systems**   271

Appendix A   Laying Out a Camber Curve   277
Appendix B   Calculating Material Stretch-Out for Brake Bending   281
Appendix C   Modifying the Lines for a Developable Surface   287
Appendix D   Line Fairing with a Flexible Batten   296
Appendix E   Conventional Drivetrain Installation   299
Appendix F   Leveling a Structure Using a Water Level   304
Glossary   307
Index   317

ACKNOWLEDGMENTS

I wish to thank Raymond H. Richards of Newport Beach, California and Richard W. Etsell of Anacortes, Washington—both highly respected naval architects, marine engineers, longtime business associates, brilliant designers, and very good friends—for their assistance with my continual technical questioning.

Many thanks to Tim Hill of J & H Boat Works, Astoria, Oregon; Mike Sandeman of Almar, Tacoma, Washington; Ken Baker of Allen Marine and Mat Stromer of Pacificskiffs, Sitka, Alaska; Oly Whitethorn of O & W Enterprises, Petersburg, Alaska; Russ Shivers of T & S Welding, Juneau, Alaska; Mike Bullock of Aliboats, Botswana; Rodney Dredge, Queensland, Australia; Chris Smith of Working Boats UK, United Kingdom; and any others whom I may have unintentionally omitted, who have generously shared data with me to make this book possible.

PREFACE TO THE SECOND EDITION

Until fairly recently, readily available information on aluminum hull construction had been lacking, posing a dilemma for aluminum boatbuilders, both at the amateur level and in small professional shops. This need was the catalyst for the original publication of *Boatbuilding with Aluminum* in 1993. And while much of the original information is still current, the industry has seen significant changes since then—most of them computer related; for example, computer-aided design (CAD) and computer-guided cutting machines, as well as the use of the Internet for transferring files between designer, builder, and cutting service.

Designers of welded-aluminum boats now commonly use boat design and 3D-CAD software, rather than the traditional manual techniques of ducks and splines that were still in common use in 1993. A computer-generated surface model, in three-dimensional space, has replaced the conventional lines drawing as the primary lofting reference. Using this surface model, designers load data for hydrostatic calculations directly into ship design software. This surface model then becomes the master loft from which a designer can rapidly and accurately determine the shape of frames and girders. Once the shape of a part is determined, the next step is usually detailing the part in 2D, using an off-the-shelf CAD program. Then the parts are grouped according to thickness, nested on stock-size material sheets, and sent, via the Internet, to a computer-guided cutting facility, which could be anywhere in the world. At the cutting facility, the sheets are put on a cutting table, and parts are cut out and marked with layout lines.

CAD is simple in theory, but not necessarily simple in application. Thus, in this second edition, I have attempted to provide you with an overview of the interface between the personal computer, the Internet, and the boat designer/builder.

However, before you can effectively use the computer as a design tool, you must have a clear understanding of the basics of the design, lofting, and construction of a welded-aluminum vessel. For this reason, the material included in the first edition of this book is still relevant and has only been edited to make the data as clear and current as possible. This book still takes a hands-on approach, with steps to follow for lofting and constructing a welded-aluminum boat using manual cutting methods, along with some of my own procedures for computer lofting and preparing computer files for automatic cutting of parts.

As a boatbuilding material, welded aluminum has great versatility. A number of boat types can be constructed with it: power and sailing recreational craft, rigid inflatable boat hulls, landing craft for both recreational and commercial use, and vessels for law-enforcement and military applications. Since the 9/11 attacks, U.S. government agencies have accelerated the procurement of welded-aluminum, harbor patrol boats to an unprecedented level. These small, extremely fast, and rugged boats are now our front line of defense in our harbors and shores, accentuating the desirability of welded-aluminum craft.

As was the case with the original publication of this book, construction of welded-aluminum boats in the United States still tends to be regionalized. Most boats built in Oregon, Washington, and Alaska are welded aluminum, with a good number of welded-aluminum boats in the Gulf states. Other regions, including the Great Lakes and Atlantic seaboard, are still waiting to discover the full potential of welded-aluminum boats.

It has been my pleasure to work with builders in a large number of countries. Boat styles and aluminum alloy selection differ to some degree by country and region, but wherever rugged and tough boats are required, aluminum seems to lead the pack.

INTRODUCTION

The characteristics of the material used to construct a boat hull are of primary interest to both boatbuilders and boatowners. There has long been a lack of readily available data on aluminum hull construction, a dilemma for potential builders and owners of aluminum boats. Questions as to aluminum's resistance to corrosion and its compatibility with other boatbuilding materials are common. The lack of knowledge about aluminum hull characteristics and fabrication techniques can result in a reluctance to either buy or construct an aluminum boat. I believe that once an individual becomes knowledgeable about aluminum boatbuilding, he or she will give serious consideration to the use of welded aluminum over other building materials. The simple fact is aluminum boats have so many positive aspects that it's difficult not to make aluminum the material of choice.

This book takes a hands-on approach to the construction of a welded-aluminum boat—from basic conceptual needs through sea trials—from the perspective of the boatbuilder. It is a how-to book and includes information on the characteristics of aluminum, fabrication techniques, boat propulsion, fuel and electrical systems, insulation, woodwork, and fairing and painting. Many procedures involve the use of materials that aren't compatible with aluminum, and you will learn how to make suitable accommodations between them. You will also find a chapter devoted to laying out, or lofting, and a discussion of computer-assisted design (CAD) and lofting, with special emphasis on developable surfaces as it pertains to hard-chine boats.

This book will guide you in selecting a construction method for a welded-aluminum boat and detail the steps you will need to actually build your boat. The appendices at the back of the book contain information necessary to fully cover the scope of aluminum boatbuilding, but which does not fit neatly into the body of the manuscript. I have also sprinkled helpful tips throughout to help you evaluate quality and speed production.

While I realize that potential boatbuilders and owners have varied interests regarding boat types, in general, I have not segregated this book into sections devoted exclusively to sail or power, or to the split between recreational and commercial boats. The same fabricating techniques and installation procedures are common to most aluminum boats. The majority of welded-aluminum boats currently being produced are small planing boats, and this boat type has been my primary emphasis. However, I have devoted a chapter to sailboat construction that includes such topics as aluminum spars and lead ballast keels. And I have used a drift boat as the primary example for the discussion of lofting because of the simplicity of this hull's form and construction.

I also include a brief history of how small welded-aluminum boats have evolved, including the development of special extrusions and of design features that are currently employed. Since this evolution in design and techniques has resulted in the present style of the small welded-aluminum boat, I believe this information will be useful.

Limited-production boatbuilding with aluminum can be faster, simpler, and more economical than with other hull materials. The manufacturing technology has been simplified to such an extent that a high-quality welded-aluminum hull can be constructed rapidly, even by a novice. Since the introduction of economical computer-guided cutting, the need for special skills has been even further diminished. I have worked with this lightweight metal for more than three decades and am often pleasantly reminded of just how easily it can be fabricated. The peculiar workability of aluminum, specifically the ability to cut it with woodworking tools, reduces the need for special metalworking skills.

The proliferation of boatbuilders capable of producing welded-aluminum boats and marketing them successfully is quite obvious in the Pacific Northwest of the United States. Every weekend it appears that about half the trailer boats heading toward the Oregon coast—or inland to whitewater rivers—are welded aluminum and have been constructed locally. The Pacific Northwest coast, including the infamous Columbia River bar and Alaska, has some of the most treacherous waters in the world. Aluminum boats routinely operate in these waters with safety and confidence, and many of these boats are constructed by local builders using the techniques found in this book.

CHAPTER 1

Introduction to Aluminum

EVOLUTION OF THE ALUMINUM HULL FORM

A number of factors influence and contribute to a boat's hull form and final lines. They include boat type, intended operating environment, consumer style preferences, design innovations, propulsion systems, manufacturing costs, and building materials. Aluminum boat design is no exception; in fact, changes in many of these factors spurred the evolution of the welded-aluminum boat.

Building Materials

Looking back over the history of boatbuilding materials, from wood to aluminum, we can see how the introduction of new materials influenced the evolution of hull design and form.

Wooden planks, one of the earliest building materials for boats, were a flexible medium available in long, slender lengths. Builders installed the planks longitudinally by gently curving around a boat's framing. Because the planks were relatively narrow, they could also follow the transverse contour of the framing to obtain a hull surface consisting of many planks, which were then planed and sanded into a rounded hull surface. This type of finished hull surface is considered a nondevelopable, compound curvature surface since large sheets of a material, such as metal, could not easily fit the hull contour.

After World War II, there was an explosion of plywood boat construction. These boats were economically constructed from large, flat sheets that could easily wrap around a structure. (If you can wrap a sheet of plywood, or other material, around a boat's hull framing in large pieces, then the boat's hull is considered *developable*.) The resulting designs evolved to take advantage of the plywood material, starting the trend that changed the traditional hull form from nondevelopable wood plank construction to developable surfaces.

Boatbuilders began using aluminum for small aluminum boats about the same time as fiberglass boats entered the market after WWII. Initially, they built both riveted and welded-aluminum boats to planked-wood boat designs, attempting to copy their graceful curves, rounded chines, and hull forms. But what was easily constructed of wood turned out to be much more difficult to construct in metal. The nondevelopable surfaces of a wood-planked hull were difficult to imitate in metal and were very labor intensive. Because of the higher labor costs associated with nondevelopable hull surfaces, aluminum hull design evolved to use developable surfaces, resembling hull designs for plywood.

An artistic boat designer can produce a very attractive hull and outboard profile for a welded-aluminum boat using fully developable surfaces. Carefully joining developable plates (see Figure 1-1) gives the illusion of compound curvature. Designs intended specifically for aluminum construction with developable surfaces can yield attractive and functional boats in their own right. The 24-foot

Figure 1-1. Boats built from fully developable surfaces, if carefully designed and nicely faired—like this Raymond H. Richards–designed quarter-ton racer *Tar Bucket*—can be as shapely and attractive as boats built with compound curvature.

sportfishing center-console boat shown in Figure 1-2 is a good example of such a design.

Driven primarily by economics, the evolution of aluminum hull forms is likely to continue, resulting in more and more distinctive looks.

Aluminum Boat Builders

Figure 1-2. This 24-foot welded-aluminum sportfisher, constructed by Ocean Alloys of Boynton Beach, Florida, is an example of the elegant lines that can be obtained using developable surfaces.

Early builders of small welded-aluminum boats were almost all small, informal operations employing fewer than half a dozen workers. Each boat shop developed its own techniques as well as blatantly "borrowed" design and construction methods from each other. With little professional design work involved, approaches to boat design were often quite innovative—some successful, some not. Because expensive molds and fancy tooling were not required for aluminum boat construction, financial investment and risks were reduced. Designers had more freedom to try new designs, and take advantage of aluminum's design flexibility, without the worry of major financial loss if a design was ineffective. Design innovations that did work were exchanged among builders, often by movement of key personnel from one shop to another through normal layoff and hiring. The result is that today a large number of current designs look similar, with only minor design variations apparent among major manufacturers.

ALUMINUM BOAT OWNERS

Early purchasers of small welded-aluminum boats were serious commercial boat operators or, to a more limited extent, experienced sportsmen on their third or fourth boat. These buyers wanted a robust boat capable of achieving high speeds and carrying heavy loads while providing superior maneuverability even when fully loaded. That small aluminum boats could be built without large set-up costs made aluminum the logical choice for custom commercial boats. These boats were intended to be functional, and their finish was a secondary consideration.

These early owners pioneered the development of welded-aluminum boats and introduced them to the public. The superior performance, rugged construction, and simplicity of aluminum boats resulted in a rapid acceptance by the boating public.

Figure 1-3. Welded-aluminum 17-foot RIB designed by Specmar, Inc., and constructed by Northwind Marine, Seattle, Washington.

THE IMPACT OF WATER-JET PROPULSION

In the Pacific Northwest, the explosion in welded-aluminum boatbuilding can be directly linked to the introduction of water-jet propulsion. Aluminum's high strength-to-weight ratio and its ability to withstand impact made its marriage with the water-jet drive ideal for river whitewater boating and resulted in a whole new concept in boatbuilding technology.

The small aluminum "jet sled" has proved to be the single most popular boat for river running in the Pacific Northwest over the past 30 years. The remarkable maneuverability and shallow-draft capability of the water jet, combined with an extremely tough and lightweight aluminum hull, provides a thrilling whitewater ride. Welded-aluminum jet boats have become a standard off-the-shelf item, as exemplified by the well-built water-jet-powered rigid inflatable boat, or RIB (Figure 1-3).

Impact of Extrusions

Of the common boatbuilding materials, only aluminum can be extruded, a characteristic designers have used to their advantage. Extruding is a manufacturing process that forces the material through a die to form it into the desired shape, such as angle, channel, pipe, and other structural shapes. Modern production-built small welded-aluminum boats are using more and more aluminum special *extrusions* to expedite production and improve appearance. The widespread use of special extrusions at the chine and gunwale (see Figure 1-4) has been a major contributor to design evolution and allows manufacturers to greatly speed production. Special extrusions also allow a loose tolerance for plate cutting and expedite the welding process by providing a consistently tight and uniform fit-up.

Usually the extrusions used at the chine and gunwale are very sturdy, resulting in an exceptionally strong joint. Many boat manufacturers weld the extrusions to the plates 100 percent on the inside of the hull, with either no welding or very light intermittent welding on the outside. This technique avoids weld spatter on the outside surface of the shell plate, maintaining the original high-quality finish of the aluminum sheet, and it makes the extrusions at the chine and gunwale areas appear to be trim strips.

WELDED-ALUMINUM BOAT CONSTRUCTION

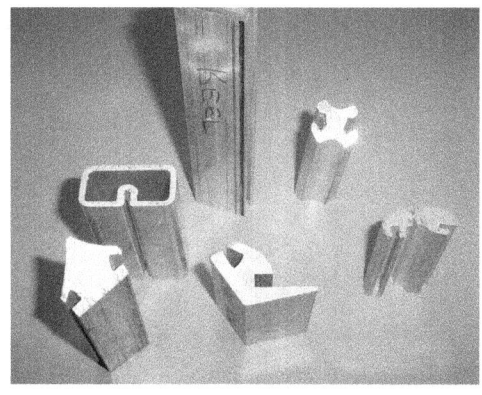

Figure 1-4. Typical small-boat chine, keel, and gunwale extrusions.

Welded-aluminum boats fall into three distinct groups:

- Smaller production boats manufactured in large quantities by production builders and assembled upright using special extrusions at the plate joints
- Conventional welded large boats (and limited-production small ones) with both transverse and longitudinal framing—often constructed inverted
- Precut boats constructed upright using minimum fixtures

The differences between the three groups are primarily in the manufacturing methods, but the hulls' structural designs can also be significantly different.

Small production boats are usually planing powerboats constructed in the upright position on some type of a *jig*. Each developable shell plate is formed from a single large sheet of aluminum and joined at the corners by the use of special extrusions. An example showing the use of extrusions is the deep-V lake-fishing boat shown in Figure 1-5.

Larger boats and some custom small boats are often constructed over an inverted aluminum framework of *transverse* and *longitudinal* members. Joint extrusions are rarely used; plates are

Figure 1-5. Production-built 18-foot fishing boat constructed using chine extrusions, by Lake Assault Custom Boats, Elk River, Minnesota.

Figure 1-6. Inverted construction of a 42-foot landing craft.

welded edge to edge at chines and deck to side seams. The inverted construction method (shown in Figure 1-6) is rapidly being replaced by upright construction due to the inception of the *computer-guided cutting* of parts. Upright construction is shown in Figure 1-7, and the products of this method include the open sport boats shown in Figure 1-8. In both cases, all parts, including shell plate, were precut using computer-guided equipment.

Small Production Boats

The hull form of small production boats built in aluminum has evolved to suit the material. Specialized extrusions and the availability of aluminum sheets in large sizes have contributed to the present-day look of welded-aluminum boats. Powerboat hulls typically exhibit hard chines, straight sheerlines, flat sloping transoms, and fully developable hull surfaces. Designs for small welded-aluminum sailboats have not yet evolved suitably for economical production, although a few, such as the *Tar Bucket* (Figure 1-1), have been constructed in limited quantities. Smaller boats are constructed without butt welding the shell

Figure 1-7. One example of upright construction is the 49-foot custom yacht *Eventide*. Upright construction is replacing the inverted method with the growing use of computer-guided cutting of parts. (*Eventide,* designed by Pat Bray and constructed by Northwind Marine Inc., Seattle, Washington.)

Figure 1-8. These 23-foot skiffs are also products of upright construction and computer-guided cutting, which speeds production and accuracy of smaller production boats. (Designed by Specmar, Inc., and built by Homestead Skiffs, Ketchikan, Alaska.)

plating (see Chapter 6), so their width, length, and depth are primarily determined by the size of available aluminum sheet. It's not uncommon for a small-boat manufacturer to advertise a "5-foot bottom" or a "6-foot bottom," indicating the width of the original aluminum sheet used to construct the bottom shell plate.

The high cost of marine-grade aluminum has encouraged builders to maximize the size boats that can be built from readily available and more economically priced 5-foot and 6-foot material (width). During the cutting operation, approximately 35 percent of the hull material will become remnants, even with careful layout and nesting of parts on stock sheets. These material remnants are not wasted though, because in most cases remnants are used for other miscellaneous boat components, such as brackets or windshield supports.

Aluminum extrusions at the chine, keel, and gunwale greatly speed production and improve exterior appearance. The framing using special extrusions is almost all longitudinal, with most transverse members intentionally not in contact with the shell plates. Small boats are usually built upright in a construction fixture, allowing the assembly of precut bottom and side panels with special extrusions at the seams before the interior framing is installed. In effect, the shell is constructed first, then the boat is framed to fit the shell—directly opposite to conventional construction practices. This method is best suited to production operations turning out large quantities of a similar design, allowing small aluminum hulls to be built very quickly once the templates and tooling are in place.

The upper size limit of boats currently constructed with corner extrusions is about 26 feet. Small-boat manufacturers have been reluctant to try larger sizes, believing that the big-boat market will require customization to the extent that small-boat building techniques will be unusable and production costs will soar. Once again the method of construction and consequent boat style are determined by economics.

McKenzie River Drift Boat

Aluminum has become a popular choice for the double-ended drift boats used for fishing the fast flowing rivers of the western United States. One example is the McKenzie River drift boat shown in Figure 1-9. These small production boats exploit aluminum's dual advantages of toughness and light weight. Given a drift boat's high incidence

Figure 1-9. Fourteen-foot McKenzie River drift boat constructed by Titan Boats, Albany, Oregon.

of grounding on rocks, the damage resistance of aluminum makes it a superior hull material to the traditional plywood, and the light weight of an aluminum boat eases launch and recovery.

Larger Boats

Larger aluminum boats—generally more than 26 feet—are constructed in the more traditional method: over a rigid framework of transverse frames, bulkheads, and longitudinal members. Transverse framing is often spaced at large intervals, with heavy longitudinal members (such as T-bars) used to fully develop the form and give structural strength (see Figure 1-10). This method of framing allows a greater latitude in hull form and is commonly used to construct sailboat hulls comprising many small parts that together approximate *compound curvature*. A large number of butt-welded seams are usually required.

The availability of large sheets of aluminum has encouraged fully developable hull surfaces—free of compound curvature—on the larger boats. Traditional bow flare, for example, is eliminated from large powerboats. Large sailboats with tra-

Figure 1-10. Longitudinally framed 48-foot sailboat.

ditionally round bilges are redesigned to allow use of large, flat sheets of material on large sections of the hull, limiting nondevelopable areas (see Chapter 4). If carefully designed, changes in hull appearance resulting from developable surfaces can be subtle, with little to no effect on performance.

Precut Boats

With the introduction of computer-guided cutting, many limited-production small boats have been drawn using CAD and are then cut using computer-controlled plasma arc, water jet, or router. This process results in substantial cost savings since the cost of the design and CAD work is spread over a number of boats. A small number of firms now provide precut kits, or the CAD data to cut boats automatically, to take advantage of this lower engineering cost. (Search the Internet for "aluminum kit boats," or visit my firm's site at www.specmar.com for sources.)

TRENDS

The trend in aluminum boats is toward larger and better-finished boats, including the application of paints for cosmetic purposes. As welded-aluminum boats have moved from the purely functional to the pleasure category, improved paint systems (such as the polyurethanes) have found wide acceptance with aluminum boat buyers. Decorative paint schemes, including stripes and contrasting patterns, are becoming much more popular. The sanded, swirled pattern on the hull side is a thing of the past; buyers now demand a high degree of surface luster in bare metal or a paint scheme applied in good taste.

As the small aluminum boat continues to evolve, more attention is being paid to the methods of propulsion. The once-reigning water-jet unit, though still immensely popular, is slowly losing its river dominance because of increasing restrictions on its operation. Wake, noise, damage to gravel spawning beds, and general nuisance level are all contributing factors to the gradual but ultimately significant reduction in popularity of the river-running water jet. Conversely, the water jet is gaining in popularity in larger diesel-powered boats to take advantage of simplicity of design, construction, maneuverability, and excellent shoal-draft capability—required for landing craft.

Large, high-horsepower, four-cycle outboard motors have taken the market by storm, and several new boats have been designed specifically to use these fuel-efficient and powerful engines. Figure 1-11 features a 42-by-12-foot landing craft that operates out of Sitka, Alaska. Powered by twin 220 hp four-stroke outboards, it is capable of a top speed approaching 31 knots empty and 21 knots with 7,000 pounds of cargo aboard. Figure 1-12 shows a popular 30-by-10 ½-foot charter salmon-fishing boat that is capable of 45 knots with twin 225 hp outboard motors.

The increase in popularity of offshore sportfishing along the Pacific Coast has resulted in a creeping growth in boat size. Welded-aluminum boats larger than those used for whitewater work have evolved for sportfishing in the open ocean and in semi-protected bays and sounds. These larger, beamier boats offer more security, fuel capacity, and accommodation.

Boatowners may still want to trailer boats in the 26- to 30-foot range yet not be required to obtain special oversize-load permits. The maximum legal width in most states is 8 feet 6 inches. Boats over the size limits may require a special permit that usually restricts their movement to daylight hours. Towing weight also becomes a significant factor for these larger vessels, pointing out another advantage of the lightweight aluminum boat.

Figure 1-11. Dual 220 hp four-stroke outboards power this 42-by-12-foot landing craft to more than 30 knots. Designed by Specmar and constructed by Precision Boat, Sitka, Alaska, this is the same boat shown under construction in Figure 1-6.

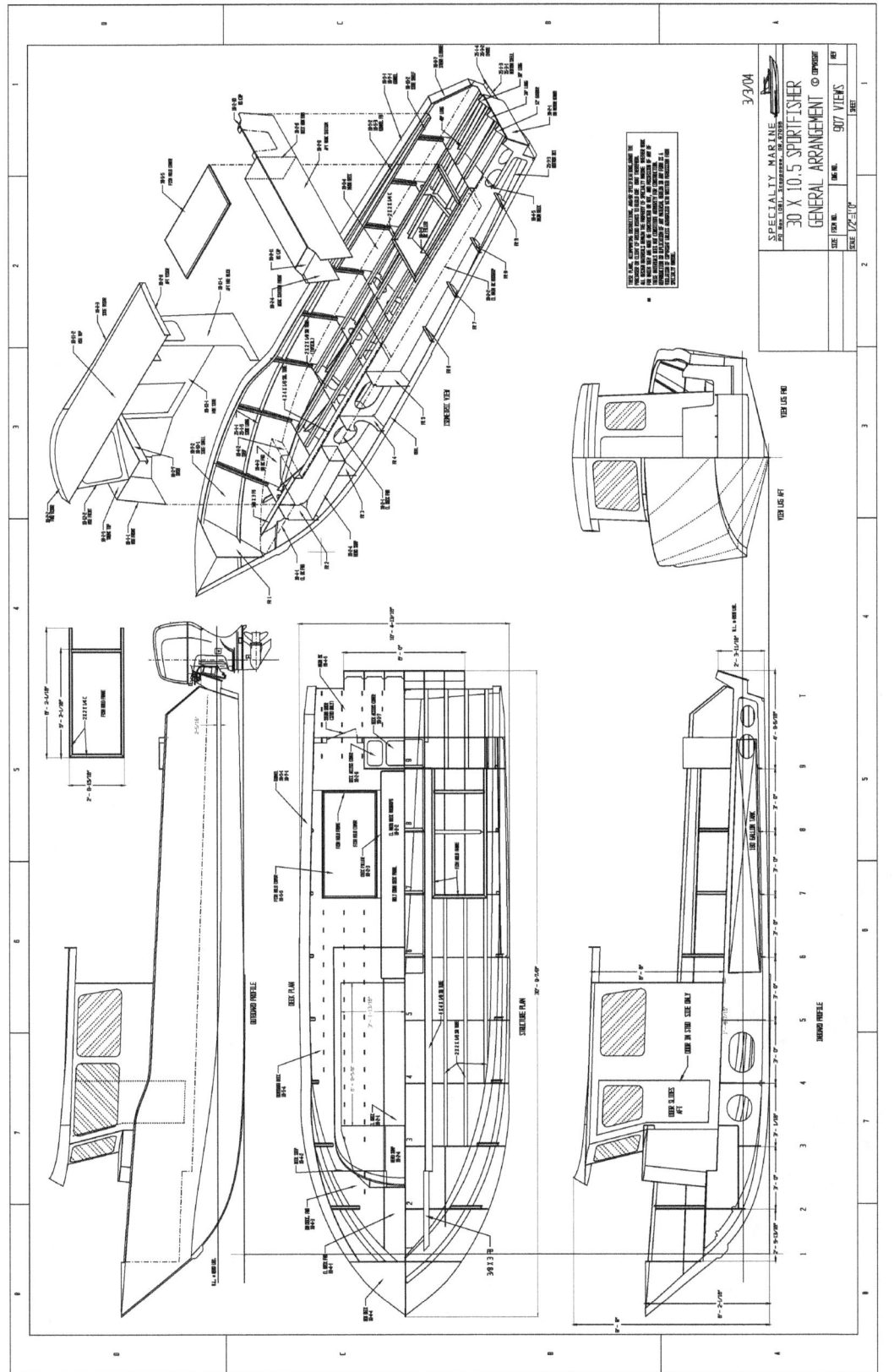

Figure 1-12. A 30-by-10½-foot sportfisher with twin 225 hp outboard motors. (Specmar, Inc., Design 907)

The dual requirements of reliability and ease of maintenance suggest that aluminum will continue to gain popularity for serious fishing machines.

ADVANTAGES OF ALUMINUM BOAT CONSTRUCTION

Boatbuilding with aluminum can be faster and simpler, when compared with other hull materials. When considering limited production, aluminum can also be the least expensive. The manufacturing technology has been refined and simplified to such an extent as to allow rapid and efficient construction of an aluminum hull, even by a novice. In fact, the virtues of aluminum are so numerous that it's difficult not to make it the material of choice for a new boat.

Lighter weight tops the list of advantages in favor of aluminum-hull construction. Appreciation of this attribute begins with the ease of handling the material during construction and continues through to the operational efficiency demonstrated by the finished boat. Movement of mass requires energy; the less the mass, the less energy is required. The resultant cost savings are readily apparent when you consider the high cost of fuel.

Minimal hull maintenance is another significant advantage. Aluminum doesn't need painting. It's nearly impervious to seawater corrosion; it isn't affected by ultraviolet light; it doesn't rot or attract worms; it doesn't rust. The time and cost savings realized with a boat that doesn't require routine hull maintenance are significant.

Figure 1-13 is an example of a finished, unpainted welded-aluminum yacht.

Figure 1-13. Aluminum yacht *Eventide* is an attractive boat even without paint. (This is the same boat shown under construction in Fig. 1-7.)

Strength-to-Weight Ratio

One primary advantage of aluminum is its high *strength-to-weight ratio*, which is a comparison of the dead weight of the material to its mechanical properties. In simplest terms, the higher the strength-to-weight ratio of the hull material, the lighter the boat can be constructed while maintaining a given level of strength. An equivalent hull constructed from a material with a lower strength-to-weight ratio will be heavier. For example, a welded-aluminum hull can be designed to weigh approximately one half the weight of a steel hull of equivalent strength and deflection. The strength-to-weight ratio of 5086-H116 marine aluminum alloy (ultimate tensile strength divided by weight in lbs/in^3) is 416, whereas that of hot-rolled steel ASTM-A36 is 205. The higher strength-to-weight ratio improves all aspects of the vessel efficiency.

This favorable ratio allows aluminum sailboats to have a higher percentage of ballast in the keel, making them stiffer and enabling them to carry more sail than sailboats constructed of a heavier hull material. This single factor caused a great surge in the construction of large aluminum racing sailboats in the 1960s and 1970s. (Racing-sailboat hulls constructed after the 1970s consisted mostly of high-tech composites, which have an even more favorable strength-to-weight ratio, but at considerably higher cost.)

Aluminum's high strength-to-weight ratio also makes it an excellent material for planing hulls. The simplest method of increasing boat speed in a planing hull is to reduce the weight of the boat. When speed is increased without increasing horsepower, obviously the boat's operational efficiency has been improved. This results in lower fuel cost for the same distance traveled and longer engine life (fewer engine revolutions) for equivalent speed.

The speed/displacement monogram, shown in Figure 1-14, was developed by Caterpillar as a quick method of estimating planing hull speed. This nomograph uses the boat's *displacement weight* (the boat's dead weight) and *shaft horsepower* (shp) to estimate speed in knots. In the example, a sample boat of 8,000 pounds displacement and 400 shp will reach 45 knots, as shown by the dashed line. If the same boat's displacement is reduced to 6,000 pounds by utilizing a hull material with a higher

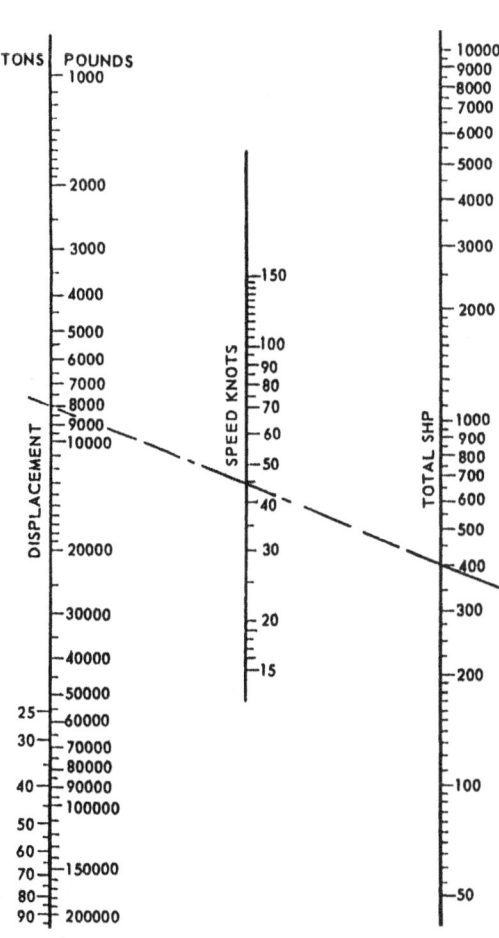

Figure 1-14. Speed/displacement nomograph for planing hulls.

strength-to-weight ratio, such as aluminum, the projected speed increases to 50 knots.

The high strength-to-weight ratio of aluminum is beneficial to all boat types. Weight savings result in reduced draft, lower power requirements to drive the boat, lower fuel consumption, bigger payload capacity, and reduced engine operating hours—meaning less frequent overhauls.

Ease of Building

Few special skills are required for working with aluminum. While it is similar to working with steel, aluminum is much lighter and can be cut and fabricated faster. (Although builders experienced in steel fabrication will need to rethink fabricating techniques.) Aluminum can be sawed, planed, and drilled with standard woodworking power tools. Special blades for aluminum will improve efficiency, but less expensive carbide-tipped woodworking blades will almost always suffice.

The fastest and most practical method of welding aluminum (described in detail in Chapter 6) is the semiautomatic MIG process, which uses a consumable aluminum electrode and an inert shielding gas. Experience has shown that a learning welder can become proficient with aluminum welding quicker than with steel. And the speed of aluminum weld metal deposit is a faster rate than equivalent steel welding simply because aluminum fusion requires considerably less heat than steel.

Durability

In addition to light weight and high strength, aluminum is also durable and very ductile (able to be bent or drawn out without breaking), and is more impact-resistant than steel or fiberglass. In fact, aluminum has about three times the elasticity of ship steel and five times the elasticity of reinforced polyester laminates in the working-stress range.

When compared to other boatbuilding materials, aluminum has a higher degree of *elasticity*. The energy of impact is dissipated more gradually and is absorbed as the plate deflects, which reduces the potential of rupture.

Because of the high resistance to impact damage, aluminum is a natural for operations in rivers where rocks are a continuous hazard. Water-jet-powered riverboats, including RIBs, have proven aluminum's worth in this environment. Small landing craft that are frequently grounded—like the one shown in Figure 1-15—also benefit from aluminum construction.

Low Maintenance

Low maintenance is a major advantage of aluminum hulls. An aluminum hull will last indefinitely with a minimum of care. Marine alloys in the 5000 series and structural alloys in the 6000 series are almost impervious to atmospheric and seawater corrosion. A clear, ceramic-like oxide that forms almost immediately on the metal's surface serves as a tough surface protectant. Since the aluminum oxide resulting from initial atmospheric corrosion protects the surface from further corrosion, painting isn't necessary. This factor alone often makes an aluminum hull less expensive to maintain than a comparable steel hull.

Figure 1-15. Because of its impact resistance, aluminum proves itself invaluable for boats that may often run aground, such as this 32-foot landing craft. (Constructed by O & W Enterprises, Petersburg, Alaska.)

Ease of Repair

Repairing an aluminum hull is simple. Normally, the damaged area is cut out and a new section is welded in. Almost any sheet-metal shop will have aluminum-welding capability and can do the repair quickly and cheaply. Compare the time and costs required to fix similar damage to a fiberglass, and you'll see substantial savings.

Cost Effectiveness

The advantages of building a welded-aluminum boat may be somewhat tempered by the higher initial costs. The raw materials needed to build an aluminum hull may cost more than the materials for a comparable steel hull, and working with aluminum might be more time-intensive than working with fiberglass and a mold. But in both cases, money will be saved in the long run.

A steel hull, for instance, requires sandblasting and painting. Not so for aluminum. You'll save time and money by eliminating these steps.

Additionally, aluminum parts weigh about half as much as steel; therefore, the job will require about 20 percent less labor to construct.

Building a welded-aluminum hull is more labor intensive than building a boat constructed in a mold. The skilled labor required for welded-hull construction, aluminum or steel, results in a higher unit hull cost than fiberglass. However, when you consider the longevity of aluminum and the long-term cost savings, aluminum can be more attractive than other boatbuilding materials. In addition, as mentioned earlier, low maintenance and high operational efficiency significantly add to long-term savings.

Fuel costs and low maintenance savings are realized faster if the boat is used frequently. Commercial operators, for example, have for a number of years selected aluminum boats for both their ruggedness and their economy of operation.

Resale Value

Aluminum boats manufactured by known professional builders generally have an extremely high resale value. A properly maintained three-year-old boat in good condition can return nearly 90 percent of the original purchase price. Jet boats and outboards command the best resale. Interestingly, the values are somewhat regionalized; in other words, a boat constructed in southern Oregon will have a higher resale value in southern Oregon than in Seattle. This is because buyers of aluminum boats often shop for a particular brand in a certain geographic area that are designed to suit local water conditions and style preference.

In some cases, particularly with jet sleds, 10-year-old boats have sold for more than their original cost. Such potential appreciation can make a well-designed aluminum boat a good investment.

Another interesting aspect is the salvage value of the basic aluminum. Few aluminum boats will be abandoned and left to deteriorate on some sandbar; they will be cut up for scrap. Aluminum in a clean condition will scrap for a significant amount of money. Beyond economics, this reduces the visual and/or environmental impact associated with abandoned boats.

Trailering

For a boat that will be trailered, the overall light weight of an aluminum boat reduces the tow vehicle requirements and allows the use of a smaller and lighter boat trailer. It also provides for more economical operation of the tow vehicle, which, for a boat often towed long distances, can generate significant savings.

CHAPTER 2

Characteristics of Marine Aluminum

Various aluminum alloys have been developed for both high-welded strength and resistance to saltwater corrosion. These alloys are commonly found in the 5000 series and 6000 series. (Aluminum alloys with high copper content, such as aircraft alloys in the 2000 series, are not recommended for saltwater usage.)

Selection of the proper aluminum alloy for boat construction must take into consideration the metal's fundamental characteristics:

- Strength—both in the welded and unwelded condition
- Corrosion resistance (both atmospheric and saltwater)
- Weld ability
- Forming ability
- Availability
- Price

ALLOYING

In its pure state, aluminum is much too soft to be of any practical commercial use. To obtain the high welded strength and corrosion resistance necessary in a marine environment, *alloying elements*—manganese, magnesium, silicon, and others—are introduced into the aluminum during its manufacture. (The relative compositions of the four alloys used in boat construction are shown in Table 2-1.)

TABLE 2-1 — Alloying element upper limits for five aluminum alloys.

Alloying element upper limits (unless shown as a range) for five aluminum alloys, percent by weight

Alloy	Si	Fe	Cu	Mn	Mg	Cr	Zn	Ti	Other	Aluminum
5052	0.25	0.40	0.10	0.10	2.2–2.8	0.15–0.35	0.10	–	0.15	Remainder
5083	0.40	0.40	0.10	0.40–1.0	4.0–4.9	0.05–0.25	0.25	0.15	0.15	Remainder
5086	0.40	0.50	0.10	0.20–0.7	3.5–4.5	0.05–0.25	0.25	0.15	0.15	Remainder
6061	0.80	0.70	0.15–0.4	0.15	0.8–1.20	0.04–0.35	0.25	0.15	0.15	Remainder
6063	0.60	0.35	0.10	0.10	0.45–.90	0.10	0.10	0.10	0.15	Remainder

Aluminum in the nontempered condition is classified as fully annealed and is identified by a "-0" following the alloy identification number. This is the softest material available in the designated alloy.

With a heat-treatment process, the aluminum alloy is first heated then rapidly cooled by immersing it in water. This is followed by aging at room temperature. After the initial tempering, artificial aging, involving slightly elevated temperatures, is used to increase strength. Heat-treatable alloys, such as 6061 and 6063, show considerable increase in strength with this tempering process.

Non-heat-treatable alloys (e.g., the 5000 series) are tempered by cold working, such as rolling and stretching, to improve strength. After cold working, alloys that have a high percentage of magnesium are often given a final low-temperature heating—called stabilizing—to ensure stability of properties. This treatment slightly reduces strength but increases ductility.

Heat treatment is designated by a "-T" following the alloy designation (e.g., 6061-T6); cold working or strain hardening is identified by a -H (e.g., 5052-H32). Numbers that follow the "-T" or "-H" designations indicate the degree of hardness and other properties of the material.

The various aluminum alloys and tempers used in welded boat construction provide a wide range of strengths, as shown in Table 2-2. Corrosion resistance and workability are shown in Table 2-3. After careful review of alloy and temper characteristics, the data in the tables shows that the 5000 series aluminum alloys are best suited to the requirements for sheet and plate in welded-boat construction. (Note: Although 5000 series aluminum alloy extrusions offer superior performance in many respects, alloy 6061-T6 is a common choice for interior members because of its lower price and greater availability.)

TABLE 2-2	Mechanical properties of various unwelded aluminum alloys.		
Unwelded mechanical properties of aluminum alloys			
Alloy & Temper	Tensile (psi)*	Yield (psi)**	Elong. (% in 2")***
5052-0	25,000	9,500	30
5052-H32	31,000	23,000	12
5083-H116	44,000	31,000	16
5086-0	35,000	14,000	17
5086-H116	40,000	28,000	12
5086-H32	40,000	28,000	12
6061-T6	42,000	35,000	12
6063-T5	21,000	15,000	12
6063-T6	30,000	25,000	12
Mechanical properties of aluminum alloys in the welded condition			
Alloy & Temper	Tensile (psi)*	Yield (psi)**	Elong. (% in 2")***
5052-H32	25,000	13,000	12
5083-H116	40,000	24,000	16
5086-H116, H32	35,000	19,000	10
6061-T5, T6	24,000	20,000	12
6063-T6	17,000	11,000	12

* Ultimate tensile strength before rupture
** Yield strength is that which produces a permanent set of 0.2 percent of gauge length
*** Elongation percent is for a test specimen 1/16 inch thick or in the range of 0.051 to 0.113 inch. Elongation percent tends to increase as thickness of the sample increases.

USE OF THE 5000 SERIES ALLOYS

The most commonly used aluminum alloys for marine applications are found in the 5000 series, which use magnesium as their primary alloying element. Their resistance to saltwater corrosion is excellent, they have high welded strength, and they're fairly ductile. As indicated by the -H temper designation, the 5000 series alloys are strain hardened for strength. Because they are strain hardened instead of heat treated, they will retain their high strength when heated by welding.

TABLE 2-3	Characteristics of various aluminum alloys, with "A" being excellent and "D" being poor.				
	Resistance to Corrosion		Workability		
Alloy	Atmospheric	Marine	Welding	Forming	Machining
5052-0	A	A	A	A	D
5052-H32	A	A	A	B	D
5083-H113	A	A	A	C	D
5086-0	A	A	A	A	D
5086-H116	A	A	A	B	D
5086-H32	A	A	A	B	D
6061-0	A	B	A	A	D
6061-T4	A	B	A	C	C
6061-T6	A	B	A	C	C
6063-0	A	B	A	A	D
6063-T4	A	B	A	B	C
6063-T5	A	B	A	B	C

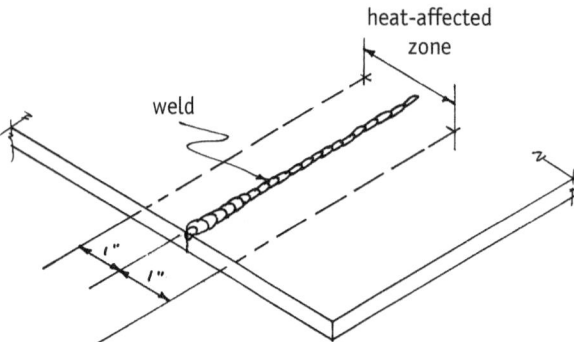

Figure 2-1. The heat-affected zone in welded aluminum.

The heat-affected zone is generally considered to be within 1 inch of the weld bead, as shown in Figure 2-1. Heat-treated material, such as 6061-T6, can become partially annealed within this zone by the heat of welding and lose considerable strength, but with strain-hardened alloys, such as 5086-H116, the resulting strength loss is minimal.

Applications

For boatbuilding it is almost always safe to select aluminum alloy 5086-H116. This alloy is available in a large assortment of thicknesses and plate sizes, has good weld strength, and is fairly ductile. Its only negative is that it is usually comparatively expensive.

Alloys 5086 or 5083 are used for critical high-strength areas requiring welding, such as all bottom plating and fabricated structural framing that require high strength, and which are cut from plate or sheet. Both of these alloys can be extruded into special shapes and, after tempering, are usually designated H112. Extrusions made from 5086 and 5083 alloys cost much more than comparable shapes in 6061; therefore, their use is generally limited to applications calling for maximum welded strength or other specific performance-related factors. The U.S. Navy usually specifies that all hull material, including extrusions, must be alloy 5086.

One of the most popular alloys for building small boats is 5052-H32. This is the common aluminum sheet for forming and for areas where you need less than maximum strength, such as for the sides. It's very ductile and has good strength in the welded condition. Available in a large number of sizes, 5052 costs considerably less than 5086 or 5083. This material can be used for fuel tanks, formed hatch covers, and applications not requiring high strength. Many builders of small welded-aluminum boats use this alloy for internal framing, sides, and decks to reduce cost.

USE OF 6000 SERIES ALUMINUM ALLOYS

The 6000 series alloys, specifically 6061 and 6063, are commonly used in areas that do not require high strength in the weld zone. These alloys are commonly found on the vessel interior in the form of bar, angle, and T-bar shapes. The 6000 series alloys are readily available in many shapes and sizes, which is not the case for the 5000 series. Cost is another factor. The 6000 series alloy extrusions are considerably less expensive than similar extrusions in the 5000 series alloys.

Applications

Essentially a structural alloy, 6061 has magnesium and silicon as its primary alloying elements. It exhibits very good resistance to saltwater corrosion and can be used effectively in boat construction for such things as cabin sole framing and longitudinal T members—almost any application not requiring high weld strength. A wide selection of standard structural shapes—angle, T-bar, pipe, etc.—as well as numerous special extrusions are available in 6061-T6 aluminum alloy. However, don't use 6061-T6 in critical welded areas, because welding heat can reduce its strength up to 57 percent in the heat-affected zone. Careful design, with welds located outside critical sections, will allow wide use of 6061-T6 in welded applications (see Figure 2-2).

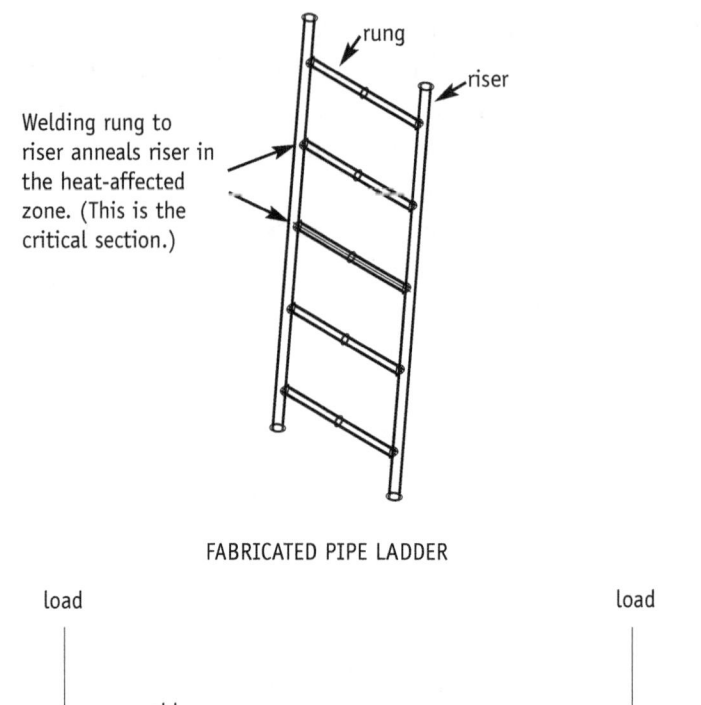

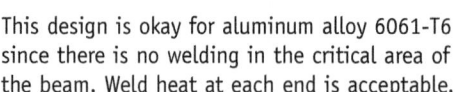

Poor design for aluminum alloy 6061-T6 since weld heat will anneal the aluminum in the weld zone in the critical area at center of span.

This design is okay for aluminum alloy 6061-T6 since there is no welding in the critical area of the beam. Weld heat at each end is acceptable.

Figure 2-2. Careful design (as shown lower right) will allow the use of 6061-T6 in welded applications.

Alloy 6061 and 6063 chine extrusions are widely used in small welded-aluminum powerboats and drift boats. Since the chine of a boat is often submerged, it requires 100 percent welding on at least one side of each seam to ensure a watertight hull. The heating of the extrusion during welding causes annealing of the metal, resulting in loss of strength. This loss of strength is not a problem in a typical chine extrusion. Chine extrusions are usually designed with a rather massive cross section compared with the cross-sectional area of the abutting boat bottom and sides. Because there will be a loss of strength in the extrusion caused by the heat of welding, the extrusion is designed with increased cross-sectional area to compensate for loss of strength.

The 6061-T6 alloy is one of the least expensive boatbuilding aluminums for structural shapes, but may fracture with excessive cold bending. Most boatyards will not attempt to make formed handrail from 6061-T6 pipe for this reason. Check in Appendix B (Table B-1) for the minimum bend radii before attempting to form 6061-T6.

In contrast, alloy 6063-T4 forms quite easily. Commonly, small-boat manufacturers will select this material for pipe that requires bending—such as handrail. 6063-T4 is about 50 percent as strong in yield as 6061-T6. However, with careful consideration of the mechanical characteristics of 6063, you can find applications in small boat construction.

STOCK SIZES OF MARINE ALUMINUM

You can readily obtain aluminum plates and sheets in the 5000 series and in lengths up to 20 feet from most aluminum suppliers. (One supplier in the Seattle area is now stocking 25-foot lengths.) If the material is available in coil stock, it can be cut to any length that is practical to handle. (Coil cutting also incorporates flattening since the coiled material does have a memory.) Stock widths up to 8 feet are available; wider material can be special ordered. Upon request, suppliers can give the surface of the aluminum a thin, Teflon-sheet, protective covering that is easily removed if you want to reduce the possibility of damage to the material surface during handling. However, because of the problem associated with weld heat melting the Teflon cover, it is not recommend using this under normal shop conditions. (Welding in close proximity to the Teflon sheet will cause it to melt and fuse to the aluminum. It will then be extremely difficult to remove.)

Most standard structural shapes, such as angle, channel, I-beam, pipe, and flat bar, are available in 6061 and 6063, and to a much more limited extent, in 5083 and 5086. In addition to standard structural shapes, a number of sharp-corner shapes are available, including square and rectangular tubing, angle, and channel. Lengths range from 12 to 25 feet, depending on the shape, alloy, and manufacturer.

SPECIAL ALUMINUM EXTRUSIONS

On most small planing aluminum boats, special proprietary extrusions are commonly found on the chine and gunwale and along the keel. Such extrusions are

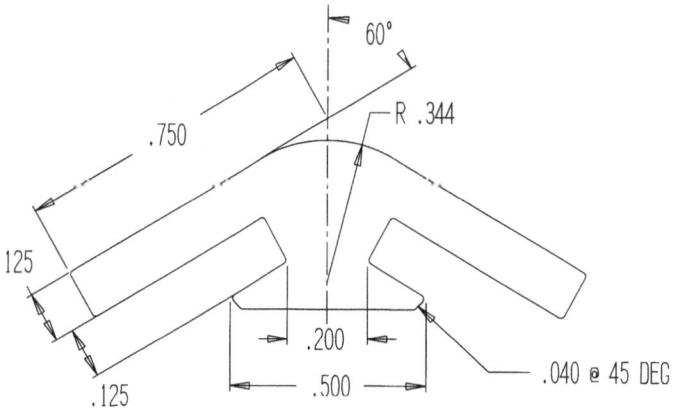

Figure 2-3. Drift-boat chine extrusion, die number 285954, available from Pacific Metals, Portland, Oregon.

usually manufactured in special mill runs for a specific customer and are not economical to produce for orders of less than 500 pounds. For this reason, large manufacturers have a considerable advantage over the small boatbuilding shops by virtue of their greater purchasing power. However, a few suppliers do carry a limited stock of common small-boat extrusions. Call aluminum suppliers to determine what's available.

The extrusion in Figure 2-3 is used to join the plates at the chine of a McKenzie River drift boat and is currently available from Pacific Metals Company in Portland, Oregon. Some other special extrusions designed for boat manufacturers are shown in Figure 1-4.

PURCHASING ALUMINUM

The costs of the different aluminum alloys and the thicknesses of plates in the same alloy vary considerably. Suppliers' price books will have numerous price breaks based upon the quantity of material purchased. Quoted prices may be based upon total poundage for the order or separated into the different material sizes and alloys. When purchasing aluminum, shop around until you find a supplier who can provide all of the sizes you need, and who will give you the appropriate price breaks for the quantities you purchase.

References

Kaiser Aluminum and Chemical Sales, Inc. *Aluminum Boats,* 2nd ed. Oakland, Calif.: Kaiser Aluminum and Chemical Sales, Inc., 1978.
———. *Welding Kaiser Aluminum.* Oakland, Calif.: Kaiser Aluminum and Chemical Sales, Inc., 1978.

CHAPTER 3

Designing for Aluminum

What follows is an overview of the design reasoning that today's aluminum boat builders commonly employ—in concert with established boat design criteria—to develop functional and economical boats. Although certain design principles are discussed, this chapter is not a comprehensive examination of all aspects of aluminum hull design. Nor should it be construed as a design guide. Rather it is a discussion of design options currently favored by boatbuilders. Anyone contemplating the construction of a new boat should become familiar with these design options, then discuss them with the designer.

For reasonable assurance of achieving the desired design criteria, check the credentials of the designer to make sure he (or she) is familiar with aluminum hull construction and experienced in the type of boat you want. For small boats that are not subject to any regulatory society requirements, a boat or yacht designer or a plan service can provide excellent designs. Projects that come under a regulatory agency, such as the U.S. Coast Guard (usually associated with commercial vessels), require some type of regulatory endorsement and should be designed by a professional naval architect.

Good hull design takes numerous criteria into consideration:

- Appearance
- Intended use
- Stability
- Performance

- Seaworthiness
- Structural integrity
- Safety standards
- Compliance with state and federal regulations

Usually, however, the single biggest factor in the design of a welded-aluminum boat is economic feasibility. It's nice to dream about the ideal boat, but no matter how wonderful the design, if the boat can't be built within your required budget, the design is of little value. To keep construction cost down, the design of every detail must take both labor and material costs into consideration.

Even with careful attention to cost, you still may be faced with a choice between quality and cost savings. A gray area divides the need to keep down cost and the need to maintain an acceptable standard of quality. In boatbuilding vernacular, the term "good boatbuilding practice" characterizes an acceptable quality standard for the type of product being produced. While this term has no clear definition, it generally means a standard of quality commonly accepted by boatbuilders and boatowners, based on experience and tradition.

One of the best publications to assist you (whether you are a novice or professional boatbuilder) with the design and quality standards for a pleasure boat is *Standards and Recommended Practices for Small Craft* by the American Boat and Yacht Council (ABYC). The ABYC's *Standards and Practices* is actually made up of individual standards for more than 60 areas of boat design and construction. By following the ABYC recommendations, even if you are a novice, you will achieve quality in those areas covered. You can purchase the publication as a complete set or by individual sections; review the available standards on the ABYC website, www.abycinc.org; or get it on CD-ROM.

Some techniques and materials that are used, even by professional builders, are highly suspect as to the resulting quality. Others, although not up to the purists' standards, may certainly be adequate for a trailer boat that will spend 99 percent of its life out of the water. The techniques and materials I recommend in this book reflect reasonable compromises between quality and cost. If serious questions arise, discuss them with your boat designer.

DESIGN PARAMETERS

Boat design usually starts with the intended use of the boat. Other considerations are the desired size, performance, style, and cost of the boat. As each of these is broken down into specific parameters, a design begins to evolve.

Use

The intended use might be sportfishing, waterskiing, whitewater running, drifting, cruising, commercial fishing, hauling, or some combination of these or other uses. Keep in mind, there is no ideal, all-purpose boat design. The features that suit a boat for one application are often the very features that make it less suitable for a different use.

Size

Size is usually dictated by intended usage—and by the budget of the buyer. A boat that is to be trailered on U.S. highways must not exceed 8 feet 6 inches in width. Boats intended for use offshore usually have wider beams, requiring an oversize permit to travel on highways.

Performance

Performance criteria include speed, quality of ride, fuel economy, pulling power, and reliability. Speed is determined by the combination of horsepower and boat design. One method of estimating the performance of a planing boat is to measure the angle at the stern between a horizontal plane and the bottom of the hull, as shown in Figure 3-1. This angle is called the *deadrise*. Figure 3-1 shows only the deadrise at the extreme stern of the boat. In most cases, the deadrise will remain constant over the aft third of the bottom, then gradually increase as it approaches the bow.

Deadrise is a good indicator of boat speed, quality of ride, and fuel consumption. Since a boat rises up out of the water to plane, the flatter the bottom, the easier it will be for the boat to get on the plane—which translates into higher speed (with given horsepower) and lower fuel consumption. Unfortunately, the flatter the bottom, the harder the on-plane ride will be in a chop.

For the smoothest ride at planing speed in a choppy seaway, the true deep-V hull

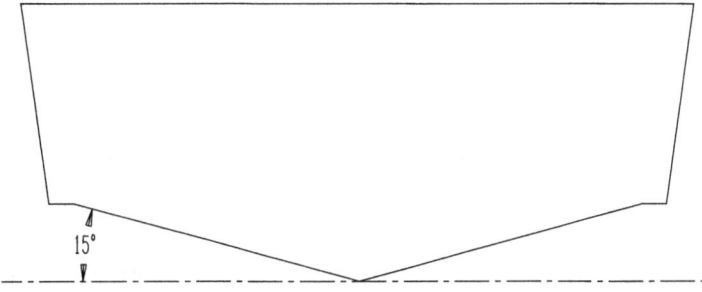

Figure 3-1. Deadrise of 15 degrees as viewed at the stern.

form—20 degrees or more deadrise at the stern—is hard to beat. But the advantages of the deep-V hull are likely to be offset by higher power requirements, greater fuel consumption, and decreased stability. Another objection to the deep-V hull is that it tends to "flop over" excessively, both at rest and during a turn reversal. The semi-deep-V hull form, with about a 15-degree deadrise at the transom, offers a good compromise. A typical semi-deep-V hull form is as shown in Figure 3-1. Although it isn't as smooth in rough water as the true deep-V, the higher speed, better fuel economy, and level ride the semi-V hull provides make it a good compromise.

Cost

The cost of a boat is generally a function of its size, but the relationship between length and cost is closer to exponential than direct. As a boat increases in length, its width and depth, and the thickness of the materials used in its construction, also increase.

This results in a rapid increase in the mass of the boat and an equally dramatic rise in the cost. Occasionally a small-boat design can be stretched somewhat without a large increase in cost if the propulsion system is unaffected.

Style

Style is strictly a matter of taste, but some styles can be built rapidly and efficiently in aluminum and some can't. It's important to understand early on that if the design isn't conducive to construction in aluminum, costs skyrocket. Hull designs requiring the aluminum to be formed into nondevelopable surfaces are always more expensive to construct than those with developable surfaces (shell surfaces made from flat plate).

Putting It Together

Considering the vast array of design possibilities, determining specific design criteria requires a logical approach. This can be accomplished by making two lists, the first of the mandatory design requirements and the second of the desired additional features. Review the second list for features that provide the greatest utility or the best compromise in value or performance without compromising the mandatory requirements. Combining these two lists will establish the final design requirements.

DEVELOPABLE SURFACES

To easily form large, flat sheets of rigid material, such as aluminum, into a hull shape free of twists, the hull form must consist of *developable surfaces*. A developable surface consists of flat areas, sections of cylinders, and sections of cones. Each of these surfaces individually can be developed from a flat sheet of material. When they abut each other on a hull surface, a smooth transition from one form to another allows the composite surface to be formed from a single flat sheet.

Conversely, a *nondevelopable surface* cannot be made from a flat sheet without stretching or wrinkling. Picture laying a flat sheet of paper over a ball—you can't conform it to the ball shape without manipulating it. This is because a nondevelopable surface has *compound curvature*, i.e., the surface is curved in more

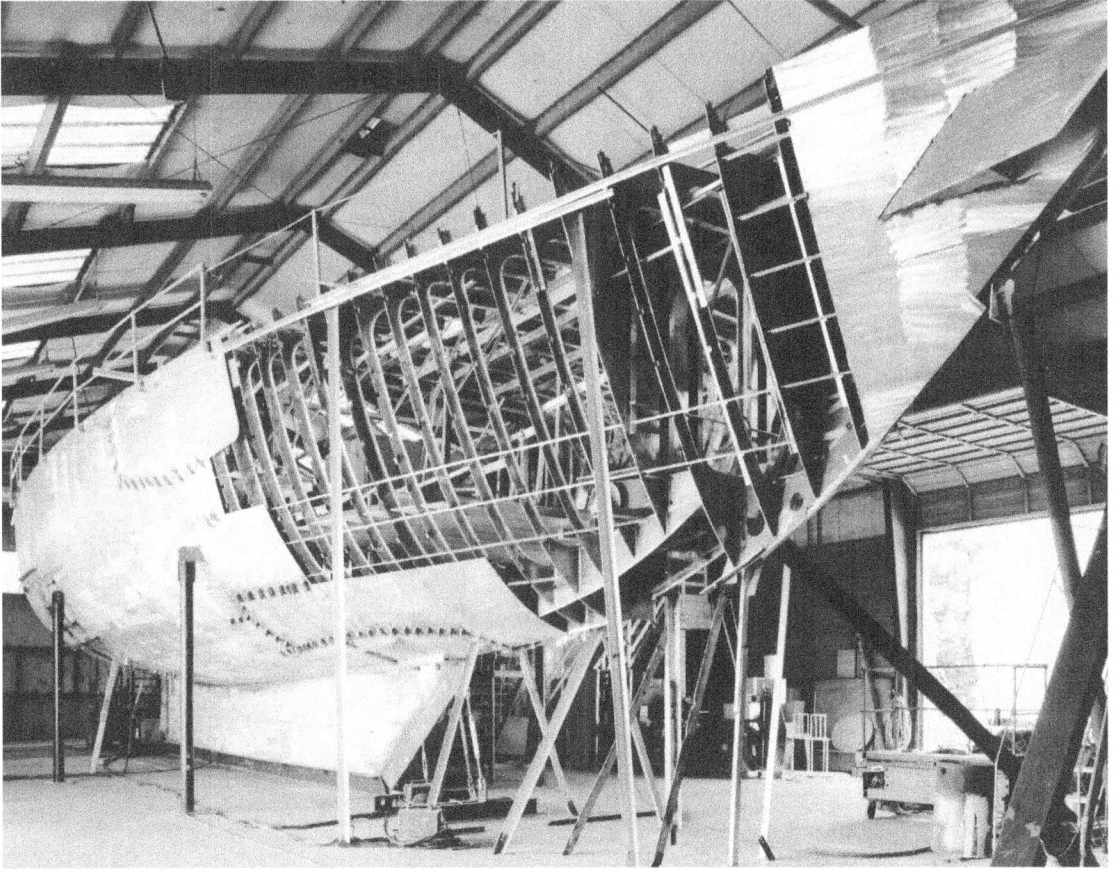

Figure 3-2. Fitting a large number of small plates to the hull of the *Venturosa* results in a close approximation of a true round bilge hull. Constructed by Sovereign Yachts, Seattle, Washington.

than one direction in space. Compound curvature is sometimes essential to conform to the boat's design lines—for example, as in a round bilge sailboat—forcing a compromise between price and style. (See Appendix C for a discussion of modifications to developable surfaces.)

Flats, cylinders, and cones are the basic developable surfaces. The simplest developable surface to lay out is the flat panel with no twist. When the panel requires some curvature, then the panel becomes a section of either a cylinder or a cone. (Picture draping a flat panel over a cylinder or cone to achieve that desired shape.) The technique used to develop a surface from a cylinder is termed *cylindrical development*, and the development of surfaces from cones is called *conical development*.

A surface is also developable if it consists of a combination of these surfaces with a fair transition between them. Most developable hull surfaces are developed from a majority of conical sections, and although they may also contain flat or cylindrical sections, they are often considered *conically developed*. Once a surface is carefully analyzed to ensure it is developable, then the shell plate for that surface can be unwrapped into a flat pattern.

Flat-pattern development of nondevelopable surfaces (i.e., surfaces that curve in more than one axis), as commonly found on sailboats, is not usually attempted with aluminum boats. Some nondevelopable surfaces approximate a developable surface by having large areas developable, and limiting nondevelopable surfaces to narrow sections at the turn of the bilge. These double-curvature sections are usually hand fit by cold working the sheets in small sections and using a large number of weld seams to approximate double curvature, as shown in Figure 3-2.

Ruling Lines

A hull with an abrupt transition from the bottom plate to the side plate at the chine, defined as a *hard-chine hull*, often can be designed with developable hull surfaces. This can be a major cost savings. By careful design, the shell plate can be curved in only one direction and still be in 100 percent contact with structural members. In order to design a boat with developable surfaces, certain parameters must be met.

In descriptive geometry, this type of hull surface is called a *ruled surface*. A straightedge can be placed on a ruled surface and oriented—in only one direction—so that it contacts the surface over the entire length of the straightedge. A line drawn along this straightedge is properly called an element of the generatrix (see Appendix C), but in the marine industry, it's usually referred to as a *ruling*.

To better visualize a ruled surface and a ruling, hold a pencil horizontally by one end and drape a piece of paper gently over it. The natural curve the paper assumes is a ruled surface, and it should be easy enough to see that a line drawn on the paper where it's in contact with the pencil would be straight and would run from edge to edge of the paper, normal to the direction of curvature. This line would be a ruling.

Not all surfaces are developable, so one method of designing a developable hull surface is to locate a fairly uniform spread of approximately 20 straight ruling lines that will span the hull bottom between keel and chine, and the side between the chine and sheer. By definition, a ruling must:

1. Be a straight line spanning the entire width of the developable surface
2. Be in contact with the surface over its entire length

The most common problem with designing a developable surface is finding the location of a number of ruling lines that will correctly define the surface. Ruling lines can not be located at random, but must be on the hull surface that is a portion of a cone, cylinder, or flat. Some hull surfaces can be constructed from a portion of a single cone, called a conical surface. More commonly, hull surfaces are *multiconic*, consisting of multiple abutting cones, flats, and cylinders. This type of surface usually defines the hull bottom or side on hard-chine boats. The process of designing a multiconic hull form that is fully developable usually requires some adjustment to the keel, chine, or sheer lines to obtain a satisfactory spread of ruling lines.

Cylinders

The surface of a cylinder is a developable surface. It can be compared to a roll of paper that is easily unrolled. A straight line, or ruling, can only be drawn on the surface of the cylinder parallel to the center line of the cylinder. Therefore all other straight lines on the cylinder's surface must also be parallel to each other. Conversely, if a surface is drawn through parallel ruling lines in space, the surface is cylindrical.

A cylindrical shape can be other than a round tube, and in fact can be elliptical or any shape where the straight-line ruling elements are parallel in three-dimensional space. This principle is often used to rapidly lay out a simple developable shape, such as the sides of a McKenzie River drift boat, as shown in

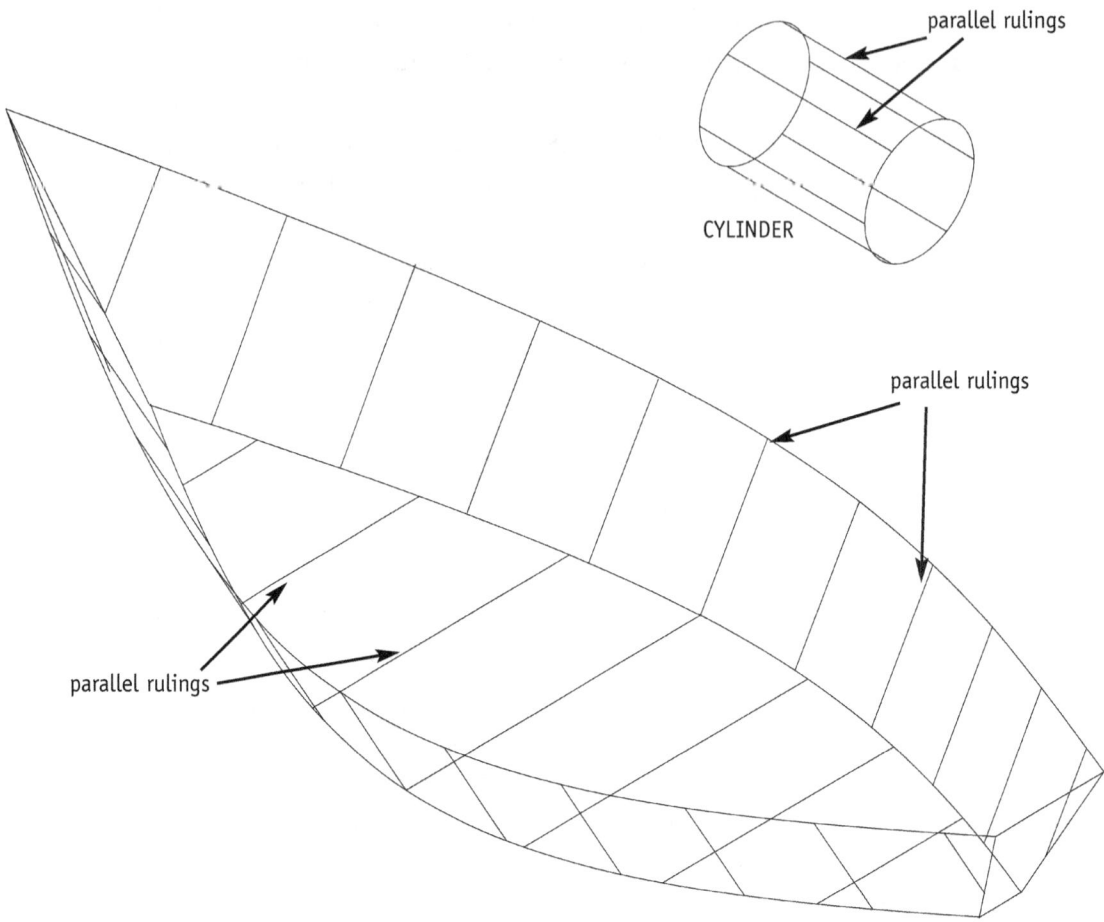

Figure 3-3. Cylindrical development—note the parallel rulings on both the cylinder and the drift boat.

Figure 3-3. Note that the rulings on each surface are parallel in three-dimensional space, thus insuring a cylindrical developable surface.

Conical Development

Conical development differs from cylindrical development in that a common apex of a cone is used for one end of a ruling, and a point on the base of the cone is used for the other end of the ruling. Visualize sweeping this ruling line around the base of the cone, holding one end at the cone's apex, to generate a conical surface, as shown in Figure 3-4. The base of the cone is not limited to a circle—it can be almost any shape as long as straight line elements radiate out from a

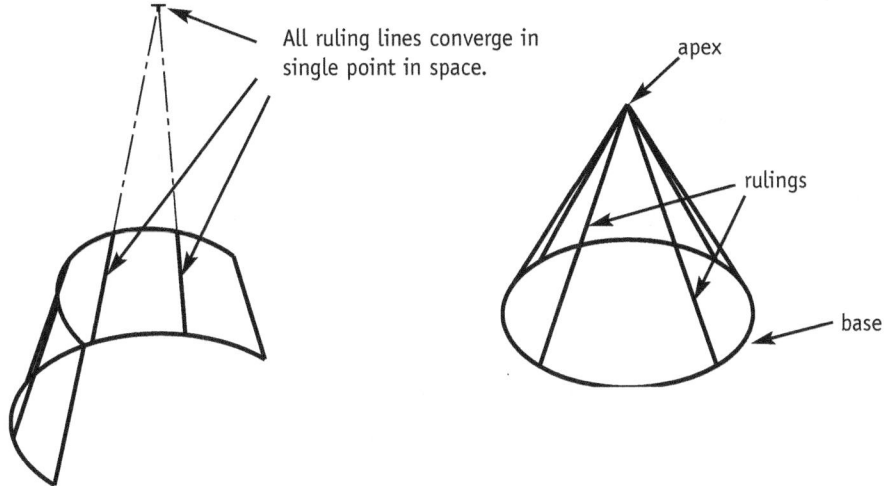

Figure 3-4. Conical development of a flying bridge.

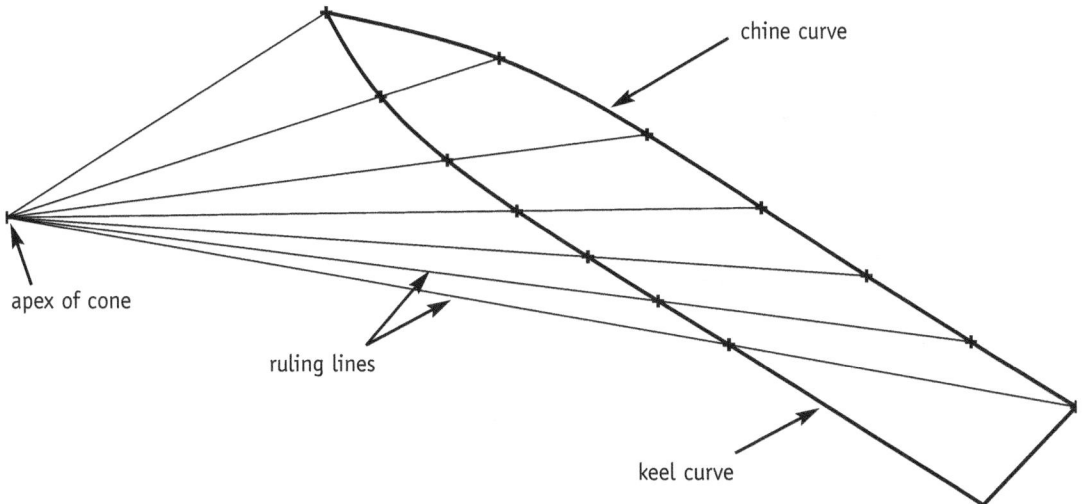

Figure 3-5. Conical hull bottom plate with a single cone apex.

common apex. As a practical matter, a full cone is rarely a required boat surface, but some conical shape that can be defined as a portion of a cone is one of the most common boat surfaces, as shown in Figure 3-5. To locate rulings for this shape, a theoretical apex of the cone may be projected into space to anchor one end of the ruling lines.

Combination of Surfaces

Usually the bottom and sides of a boat hull cannot be adequately represented with a single cylindrical surface, or with a single cone constructed with only one apex. Surfaces that appear to be multiconic may or may not be developable. The safest method to ensure the surface is a developable one is to locate ruling lines on the hull surfaces. The fastest and simplest method to develop the multiconic surface is to use ship-design software. Figure 3-6 is a hull with multiconic bottom and sides, with ruling lines located by the use of a ship-design program.

When designing a surface, whether a simple one or a complicated combination of cones and cylinders, it is important to remember that not every surface of single curvature can be easily plated. In any conical surface the curvature is sharper near the apex than it is farther away. This does not necessarily mean that

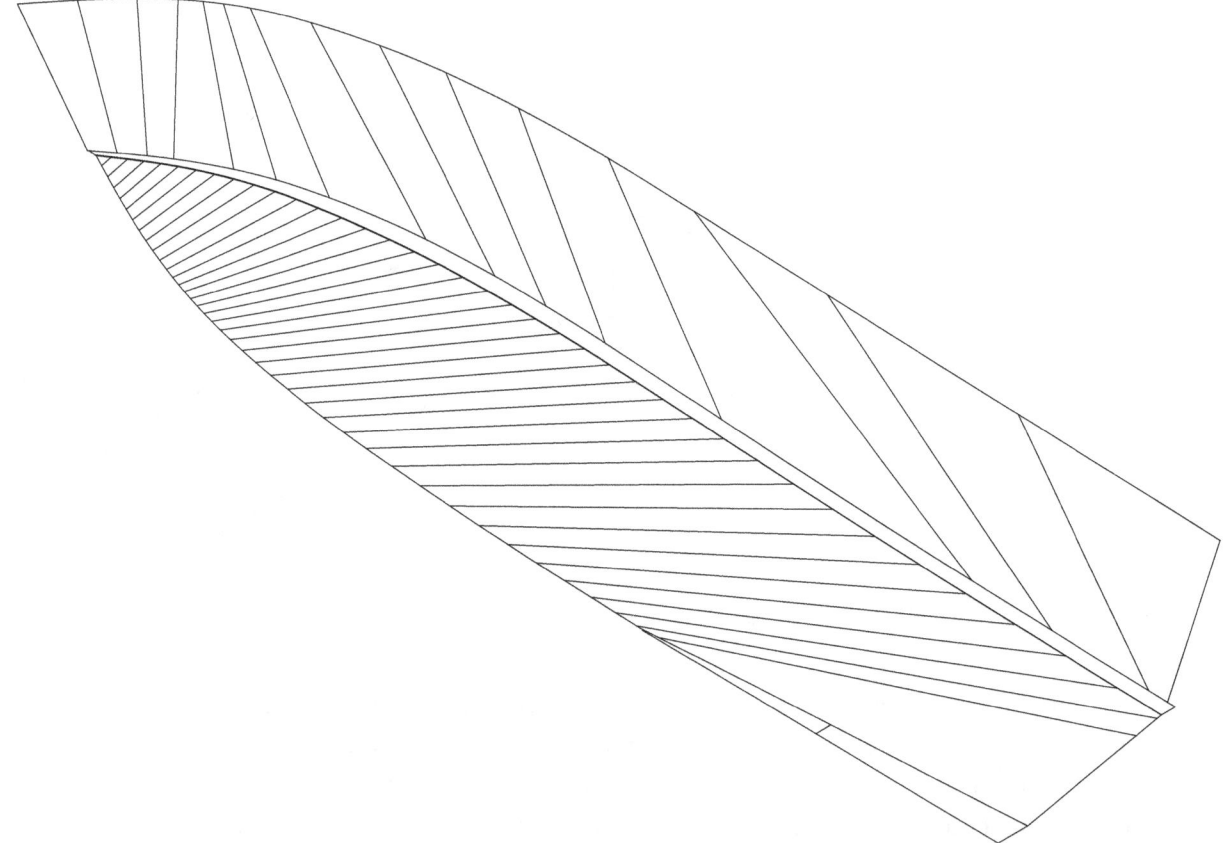

Figure 3-6. Multiconic developable hull surfaces.

an apex cannot be located near the edge of the plate, but if it is, the radius of curvature and the fairness of the plate in that region must be checked more carefully. In the same way, the transitions between the cones and cylinders must be smooth. When the whole development is finished, the assembly of all the pieces must form a single fair hull surface.

COST OF MATERIALS

Often the price of materials can influence the basic boat design. Consider first the availability and per-pound price of aluminum sheets in the sizes needed. Economical sizes for marine alloy plates are commonly stocked by suppliers. These typically include 4- and 5-foot widths, and 8-, 10-, 12-, and 20-foot lengths (and sometimes 25-foot lengths). Other lengths, particularly very long sheets, will usually cost more per pound. However, this doesn't necessarily rule out very long or wide plates since their use may provide a net cost saving by eliminating butt welding and its associated problems. Some suppliers stock aluminum sheet in coil form, allowing custom cutting to any practical length, but there is usually a set-up cost to run coil, so large orders are normally needed to justify the cutting cost.

The choice of alloys is also an economic consideration. Appropriate selections generally include 5052 and either 5086 or 5083 marine sheet and plate alloys as well as 6061-T6 and 6063-T4 structural alloys. The per-pound price of each alloy will vary. (Note: Sheet materials are less than 0.25-inch thick; plate is 0.25-inch and greater.)

DESIGN DRAWINGS

Although this chapter deals with design, amateur boatbuilders are strongly urged to obtain professionally developed boat drawings, particularly for their first boat.

The scope of the drawings needed to construct a boat is in direct relationship to the boat's size and complexity. Small outboard-powered boats require only a few drawings, while the construction of a yacht, power or sail, requires drawings that provide considerably more detail.

Drawings provided by a plan service are usually a bare minimum. These are typically accompanied by a set of construction guidelines, or specifications, that describe specific details that may not be shown on the drawings. The amount of detail on the drawings is in direct relationship to the plan costs: Highly detailed plans for a late-model design generally are considerably more expensive than an off-the-shelf set of plans intended for the novice builder. Plans are available drawn using a CAD system and often include detailed part drawings that can be used to automatically cut parts on computer-guided machinery, eliminating the need to manually loft the boat. One source for these plans is Specmar, Inc., at www.specmar.com.

Before starting any layout or boat construction, carefully review all of the provided drawings, specifications, and assembly instructions. The drawing review process starts with the *contract drawings*, which are the drawings provided by the designer to the boatbuilder. For boats that are to be constructed in the traditional manner—that is, requiring full-size *lofting* and *template* making—your next step is to study the lines drawing and the associated *table of offsets*. The contract drawings usually fall short of being the completely detailed drawings needed to construct all parts of the boat, so some basic boat structure often needs further development by the builder.

Planned production methods or the boatowner's requirements may necessitate actual design changes. Such alterations can be made (at an additional cost) by the original designer or, if minor, by the builder. One example of a modification is the side door modification shown in Figure 3-7. Keep in mind that seemingly minor alterations to a design can have serious consequences, so be cautious when revising plans. It's always best to consult a boat designer prior to finalizing any design changes.

Figure 3-7. Hinged side door gate for diver access.

The contract drawing package may also include detailed construction specifications for materials, machinery, and other items needing clarification and not shown on the drawings themselves. A careful examination of both the drawings and the specifications will reveal the exact shape, style, machinery, construction details, and accommodations of the subject boat.

Lines Drawing and Table of Offsets

A traditional *lines drawing* shows only the outline of the boat and includes very little construction information. Its primary use to the builder is to determine the shape and size of a boat and its parts. Historically, lines drawings were drawn full size on a loft floor where the lines could be used to make templates for fabricating parts. If the boat is to be computer lofted, then coordinates are taken from the lines drawings and table of offsets for input into a CAD lofting program. (We will go into this topic in more detail in Chapter 6.)

For those unfamiliar with lines drawings, the first view can be confusing. The meaning of the lines will be easier to visualize if the lines drawing (Figure 3-8) is compared with the *construction drawing* (Figure 3-9) of the same boat. The construction drawing shows the boat in sufficient detail to allow fabrication—except for the absence of critical dimensions defining the shape of the hull. Those essential dimensions are found on the lines drawing.

The lines drawing shows only a boat's geometry. The designer draws the *profile* (side elevation) and *plan view* (looking down from above) of the lines drawing first, then divides them into conveniently spaced, equal longitudinal intervals along the boat's design waterline. Each *station* is a "cut" through the boat in the transverse axis and is represented by a *station line* drawn at 90 degrees to the baseline in the profile view and 90 degrees to the centerline in the plan view. In the United States, station lines are numbered from the forward end of the boat. The relatively simple boat in Figure 3-8 has only four stations, numbered 1 through 4 on the lines drawing. (Most lines drawings will have ten transverse stations, with station 0 at the forward end of the design waterline and station 10 at the aft end. This makes manual calculations much simpler.) As is common practice with metal boats (and many wooden ones as well), the lines are lofted to the *inside* face of the hull plate. In other words, the thickness of the metal shell plate is ignored.

Taking the dimensions from the profile and plan views, the designer projects the station lines onto a body plan view, positioning them from the centerline of the boat and connecting them by the sheer and chine lines. The body plan usually

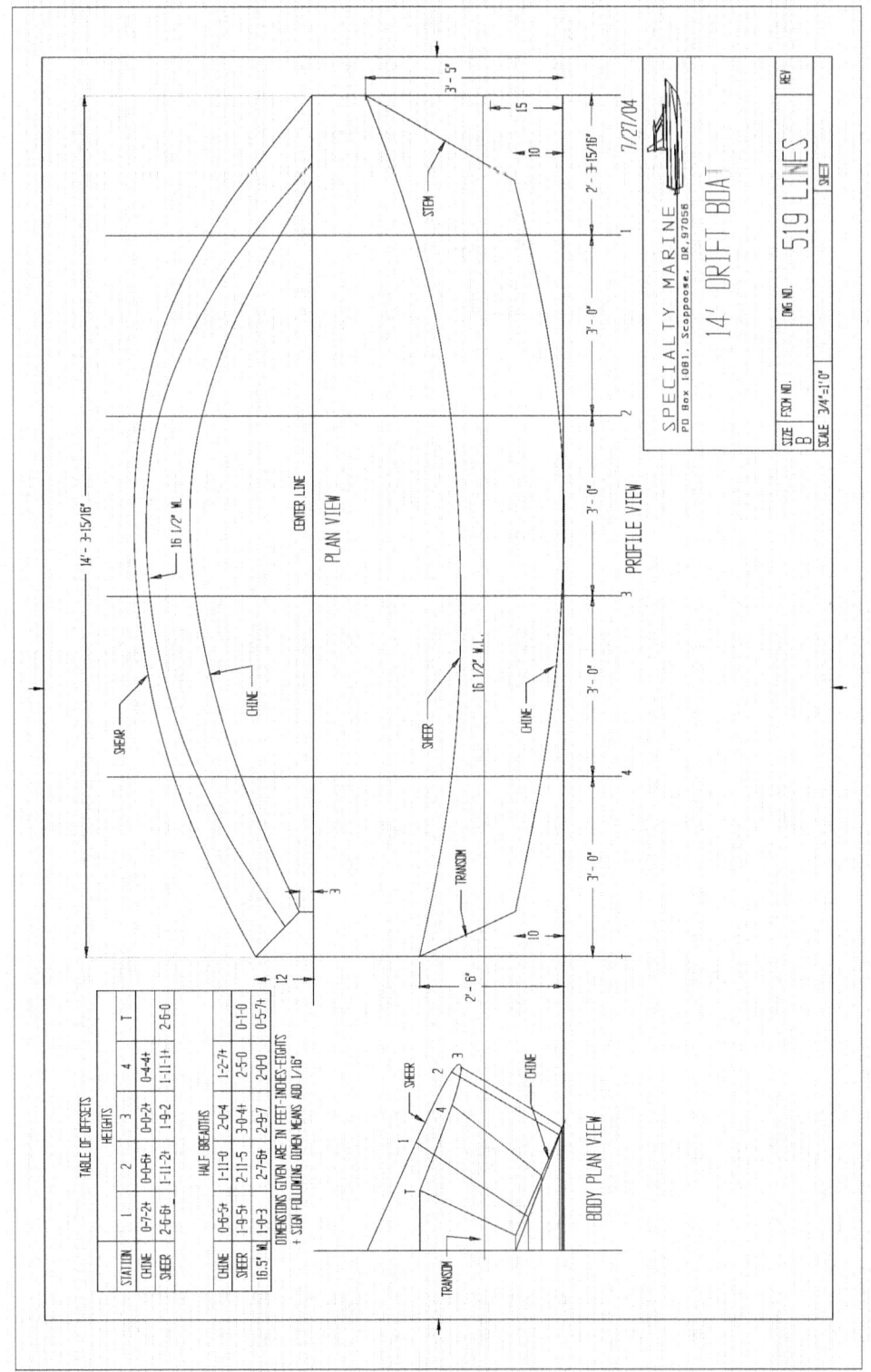

Figure 3-8. Preliminary lines drawing for a McKenzie River drift boat.

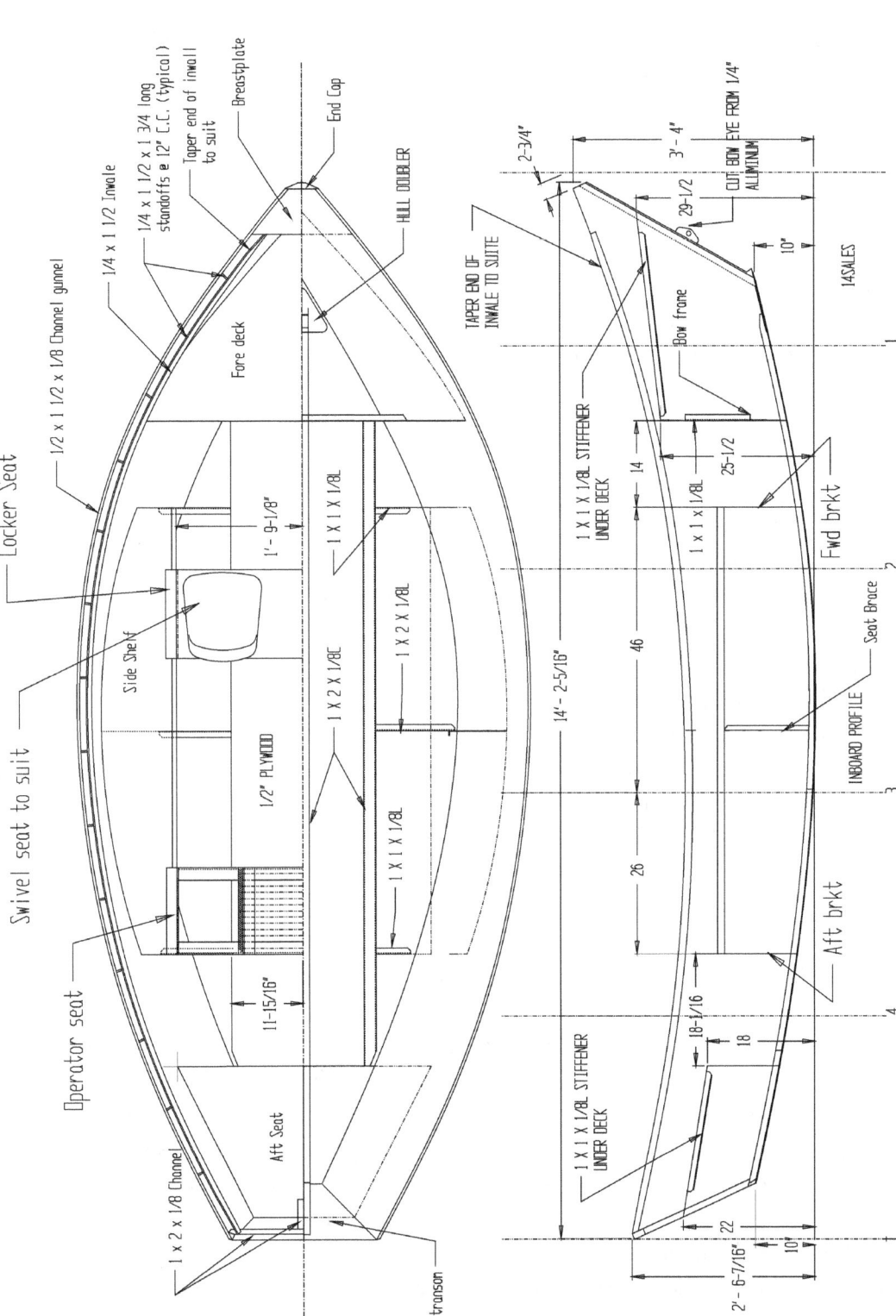

Figure 3-9. Inboard profile and plan view of a McKenzie River drift boat.

shows the half-side station outline on the right side from midships forward, and a half-side station outline on the left side from midships aft. In Figure 3-8, the body plan is all on one side of the center line for clarity. The body plan will become the primary view to develop the actual shape of transverse frames.

The designer can further define the hull shape by the use of waterlines, buttock lines, and diagonals. *Waterlines* are drawn parallel to the smooth surface of the water on which the boat floats. This flotation plane is called the design waterline, or DWL. Waterlines depict level planes that cut the boat at various vertical intervals. Usually, waterlines are identified by the vertical distance above the baseline. The *baseline* is the common reference line for all elevations, parallel with the DWL and generally the lowest point of the keel. The 16½-inch waterline shown in Figure 3-10 represents a horizontal plane 16½ inches above the baseline. Waterlines appear as straight lines in the profile and body plan views.

Buttock lines are drawn parallel to the boat's centerline plane and represent vertical cuts through the boat. Buttock lines appear in the plan and body plan views as straight lines parallel to the centerline.

Diagonals also appear as straight lines in the body plan view, but they are not parallel to the DWL or the centerline since they represent planes cut through the boat that are not level or vertical. Diagonals are often used to better define round-bilge hulls. Diagonals are usually not used on developable hull surfaces, but they are commonly found on round-bilge boats, such as sailboats. (Note: Figure 3-8 shows neither buttock lines nor diagonals.)

Lines drawings will sometimes be presented in the manner shown in Figure 3-10. Note that the plan view is superimposed over the profile view with the same line serving as the profile baseline and the plan centerline. The body plan has been moved to midships and uses station 3 in the profile view as its centerline. This arrangement not only reduces the size of the drawing (and/or the loft floor if doing manual lofting), but the shared baseline/centerline reduces the chance of error.

The lines drawing (Figure 3-10) usually includes a table of offsets that gives dimensions at critical points. The dimensions are divided into heights, which are measured vertically above the baseline, and half-breadths, which are measured transversely from the centerline. The columns give the dimensions in feet, inches, and eighths of an inch. A notation of a + or - following an offset adds or subtracts $\frac{1}{16}$ inch. For example, 1-10-6+ represents 1 foot $10\frac{13}{16}$ inches. (To obtain $\frac{13}{16}$ from 6+, $\frac{6}{8}$ths = $\frac{12}{16}$ths, plus $\frac{1}{16}$" for the "−+" notation, equals $\frac{13}{16}$.) The dimensions found in the table of offsets are scaled very carefully from the completed lines drawing by the boat designer and are used to lay out a full-size drawing of

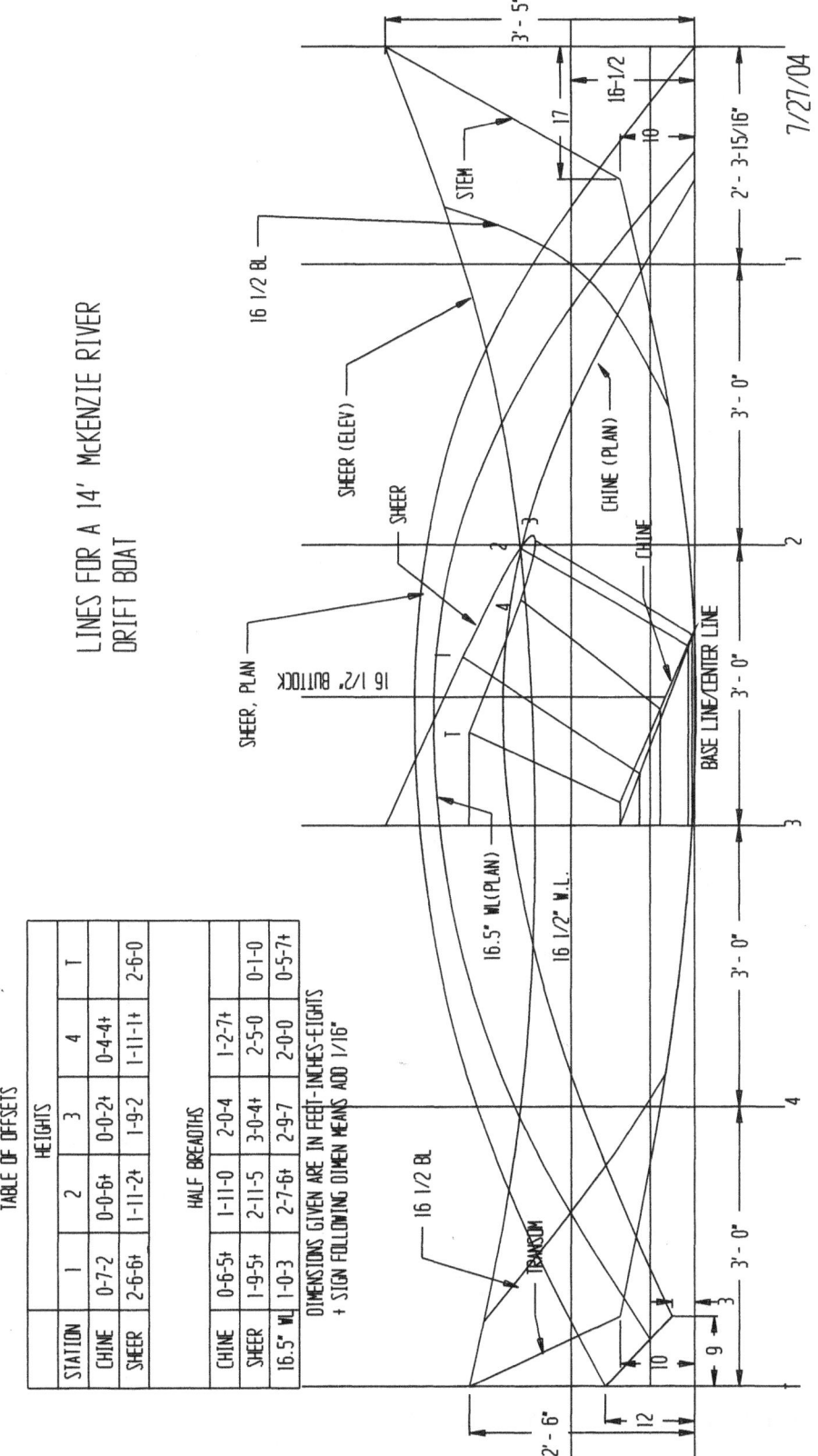

Figure 3-10. Finished lines drawing with a table of offsets for a 14-foot McKenzie River drift boat. (Illustration by author)

the boat on the loft floor. Hull lines for metal boats are usually drawn to the inside of the *shell plate* and the underside of decks and flats, except on the rare occasion when the outside measurement is critical. Drawing lofted lines to the inside of the shell plate and underside of flats speeds lofting by eliminating the need to consider shell plate thickness when laying out internal framing.

Construction Drawings

A basic construction drawing (Figure 3-9) includes an *inboard profile*, a *deck plan*, and a *midships section*. (Because of the small scale factor, the midships section is shown on a separate drawing, Figure 3-11.) An inboard profile is an elevation (side) view of the boat and shown as if it had been cut at the centerline to reveal

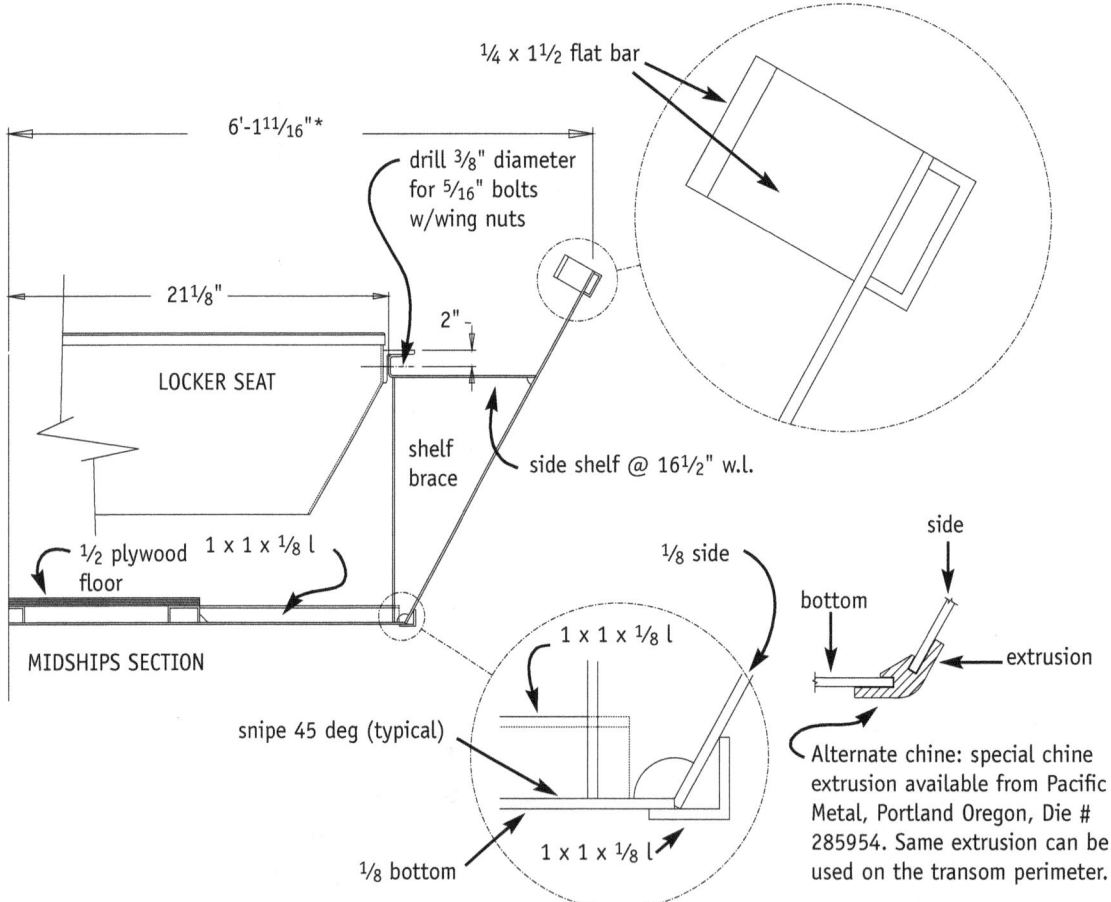

Figure 3-11. Midships section cut and details for a McKenzie River drift boat.

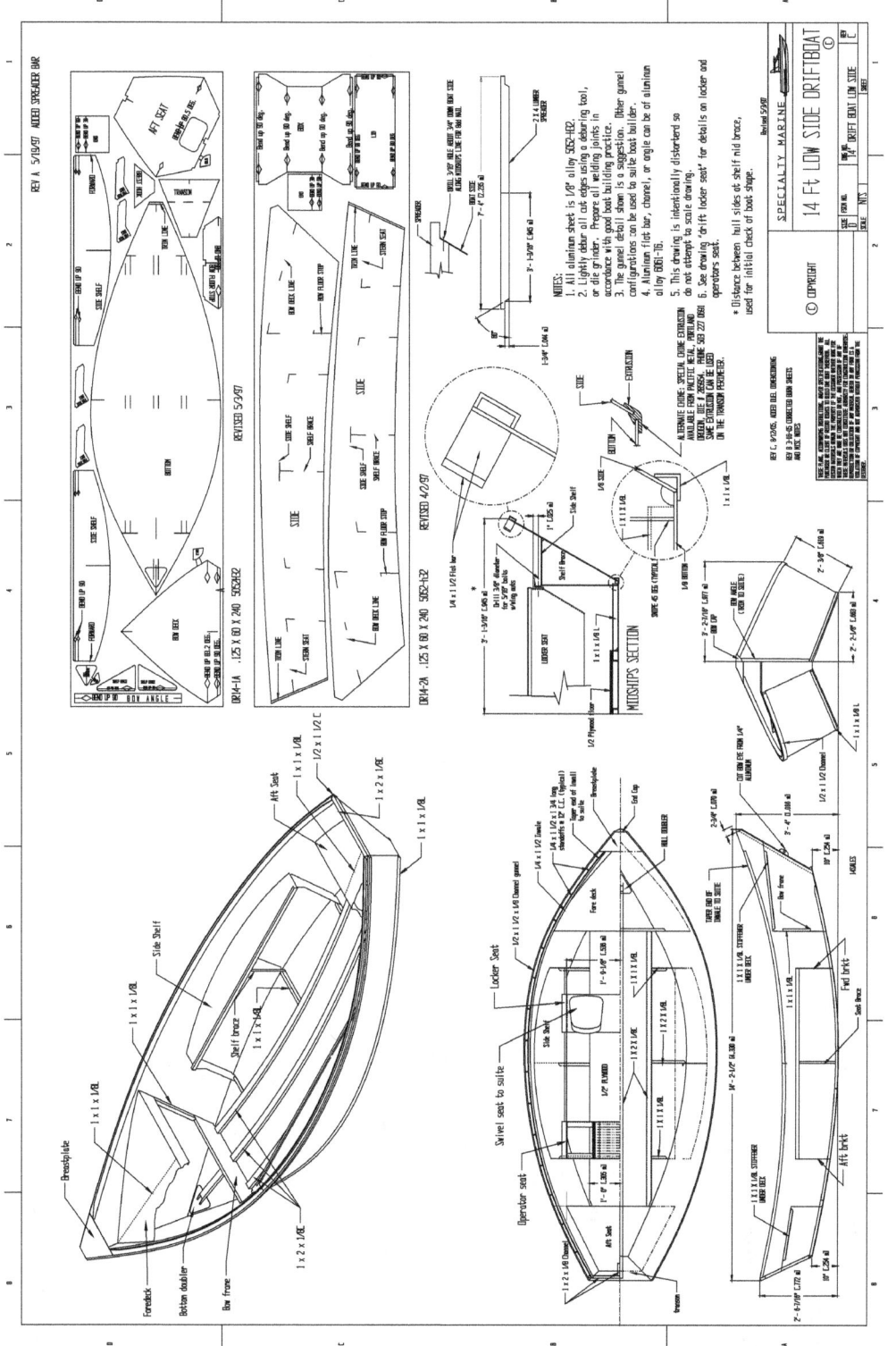

Figure 3-12. Construction assembly plans for a precut McKenzie River drift boat by Specmar, Inc., Scappoose, Oregon.

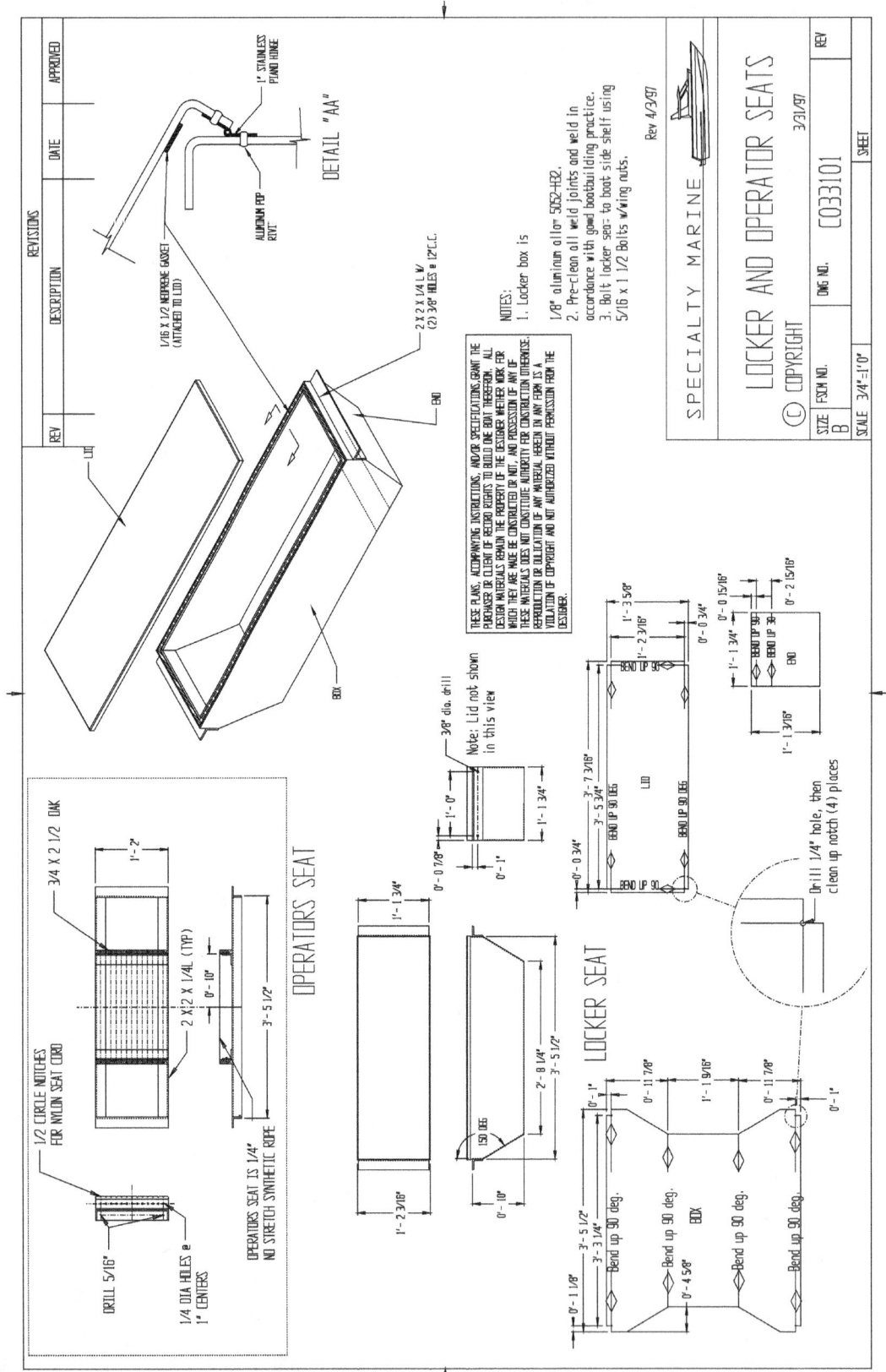

Figure 3-13. Locker and oarsman's seats for a McKenzie River drift boat, Specmar, Inc., Scappoose, Oregon.

the interior structure. A deck plan is a view from above looking down at the deck or, in the case of an open boat, at the interior. A midships section is a transverse view of the boat at about midships showing structural details. (See Figure 3-11.)

The actual drawings provided by Specmar, Inc. (www.specmar.com) to construct a computer-cut, 14-foot drift boat are shown in Figures 3-12 and 3-13. Note the material cutting layout in the upper right-hand corner of Figure 3-12. This is how the layout of this boat looks on the computer cutting file. Because this boat is designed for computer-guided cutting, a lines drawing with a table of offsets is not needed.

For larger boats, each drawing will probably be on an individual sheet; for small boats they are likely to be combined on single sheet or possibly two sheets. It's common to show split views in the plan view, such as a deck plan from centerline to starboard and the interior layout from centerline to port. It's also common to show only a half of a view through a bulkhead or frame location since they are usually symmetrical.

SUPERSTRUCTURE

Small boats, say less than 20 feet, don't normally have any structure above the gunwale except a windshield and perhaps a convertible soft top. Larger boats, such as sportfishing boats or cruising yachts, will have some type of enclosure for the operator and often a cabin of some kind. It's not unusual for the boat designer to leave the design of the deckhouse structure incomplete, requiring the builder to fill in the structural details.

DESIGN MODIFICATIONS

After review of the contract drawings, and prior to lofting, required modifications are incorporated into the design. Modifications might be alterations to the interior layout, different construction details, or any other change the boatowner desires. In small boat shops, modifications often are simply red-pencil marks on the contract drawings, requiring the loftsman to incorporate the changes in the lofting process. It is preferable to develop construction or working drawings before the lofting process that reflect the desired changes.

As the builder, you should review the drawings to identify areas of the design that need revisions to minimize production costs. This is particularly important when bending (with a press brake) can be substituted for welding. Modifications to the original contract drawings are customarily reviewed with the boat designer prior to the start of construction.

MODIFYING THE LINES FOR A DEVELOPABLE SURFACE

The design challenge for a hull that is to be constructed using flat-plate development is ensuring that the hull surfaces are all ruled surfaces, not compound-curved ones. Straight-line rulings must be located on the surfaces. When a number of rulings have been located, the station lines, buttock lines, and waterlines on the lines drawing are corrected to these rulings, ensuring a surface that can be formed from flat plate. (See Appendix C for a manual method of finding rulings and fairing the lines to these rulings.) The interior framing of the boat is then designed to conform to the corrected lines drawing and the natural development of the hull surface.

Small aluminum hulls are often constructed using large sheets of material, typically eliminating the need to confirm that the hull is a ruled surface prior to construction. The bottom and side plates are precut to size by estimating the correct shape, and then they are joined together so the edges are either in contact or within a special extrusion. The result is that the plates curve naturally into a ruled surface. After the plates are joined at the keel and chine to form the shell, the framing is fitted into the interior.

In a sense, the small-boat builder designs developable surfaces by utilizing a full-size mock-up. This full-size mock-up technique results in a boat that may or may not have the desired shape, usually requiring a number of trial-and-error mock-ups before the desired configuration is obtained. An approach that is much more cost effective is to use a scale model to find the ruling lines for a developable surface, as shown in Appendix C. Current practice is to use a special hull design computer program to insure a fully developable hull surface.

SMALL-BOAT VERSUS LARGE-BOAT DESIGN

As noted in Chapter 1, aluminum hulls may be plated and framed in two distinctly different ways, with the method selected usually depending on the size of the boat. For the purposes of this book, large boats are defined as those having a conventional framing system; that is, the transverse and longitudinal framing is constructed first, followed by the installation of shell plate. Conversely, small boats have the shell assembled first and the interior framing added afterward.

The working drawings and specifications for a large boat are prepared by a boat designer and provided to the builder. Combined with the specifications, these drawings will include sufficient structural details to allow construction of the boat. Design details not covered by the drawings but called out in the specifications—engine beds, fuel tanks, etc.—are developed by the boatbuilder.

The design of a small aluminum boat should conform with small-boat, welded-aluminum construction techniques, requiring the designer to make numerous decisions about the boat's structure. The remainder of this chapter deals primarily with designing the small welded-aluminum hull, but potential builders of large boats should find that similarities between small and large aluminum boats make much of what follows useful for them as well.

Engineering for Small Welded-Aluminum Boats

A common method of selecting a small welded-aluminum boat is to start with a stock design. One can obtain stock plans for small boats from a number of sources often found on the Internet. The stock design firms typically have catalogs and websites containing a number of stock designs for aluminum boats, and they can provide—for a fee—study plans for some of the larger boat designs. But since few stock designs meet all of a potential owner's requirements, they are often modified.

The various engineering considerations and calculations required to properly evaluate a design modification for aluminum construction are often beyond the capability of the potential owner or builder, so a boat designer, preferably one with experience in small aluminum boats, should be retained. However, small-boat engineering is occasionally accomplished by trial and error, without professional help. As an example, a prototype boat may be constructed based solely on the boatbuilder's experience with specific geometric shapes, framing styles, plate thicknesses, and propulsion systems. The prototype is operated throughout its entire *performance envelope* (speed, loading, and sea condition) to determine problem areas, and remedies are developed and tried until the boat operates without apparent problems.

The trial-and-error approach to small-boat design has many advocates, but to be effective, it can involve a great deal of time. So in the final analysis, you usually get what you pay for, and a professionally prepared design often turns out to be the less-expensive route to a satisfactory small boat.

STRUCTURAL CONSIDERATIONS

Structural considerations include plate thicknesses and framing sizes (*scantlings*) and their arrangement for adequate strength to meet the expected loads. The location of welds, the deflection of structural members under load, the effects of vibration, and the potential for buckling or fatigue should all be analyzed. An explanation of the engineering required for each of these is available in Kaiser Aluminum's book *Aluminum Boats*. (Unfortunately, this book is out of print but should be available in libraries.) Since the determination of actual scantlings is a very complicated process that involves considerable engineering expertise, empirical methods are commonly used, as found in *The Elements of Boat Strength* by Dave Gerr. On larger boats, classification societies such as the American Bureau of Shipping or Lloyds Register provide design guidelines.

Since most small welded-aluminum boat construction involves fast planing boats, and these boats are subject to much higher stress than strictly displacement boats, our emphasis is placed on the planing boat hull.

When a planing boat rises up on a plane, a large portion of the forward hull is actually out of the water. This overhang causes considerable hull stress as the bow impacts with waves. These impacts place high positive g-loads on the bow, resulting in high compressive stresses that tend to buckle the bottom plates of the hull. (Acceleration is measured in g units, one g being equal to the force of gravity.)

If a planing boat has longitudinal framing, buckling of the bottom plates is not usually a problem because the slamming-induced g-loads are absorbed by the longitudinal members. But designs with little or no longitudinal framing can experience buckling of the bottom and the sides under severe loading conditions. Stress damage from slamming also occurs in the gunwale area. Thicker plates will improve the bottom's resistance to buckling, and giving adequate cross section to the gunwale will avoid failure there.

Potential Structural Problem Areas

Welded-aluminum boats have historically exhibited structural failures in a number of specific areas. These problem areas require special design accommodations.

Center-mounted consoles. Center-mounted consoles frequently tear loose during a rough ride, causing significant damage and often injuring the boat operator. This problem can be prevented by securely anchoring the center consoles to the boat's structural framing, preferably by through-bolting or welding.

Motor wells. Weld cracks often occur between the members forming the well for the outboard motor. They are the result of metal fatigue due primarily to engine vibrations. Long, continuous members through the motor support area reduce the likelihood of this kind of failure.

Hull seams welded from only one side. Aluminum welds break more easily if welded from only one side. This is caused in part by defects on the nonaccessible side of the weld that allow cracks to start. Unless there is a compelling reason not to, weld both sides of all plate seams. (Most small-boat manufacturers that use chine extrusion weld the plates to the extrusion on the inside surface only. While this appears contrary to recommended practice, there are a large number of boats in service that have been welded in this manner and have had no apparent problems—probably because the extrusion itself actually provides the strength at the chine, reducing the stress on the weld. However, omitting the weld on one side is not good boatbuilding practice and is not recommended.)

Stitch-welded longitudinal members. Longitudinal members that are intermittently welded (see Figure 5-19) to the bottom shell plate will often break loose from the shell plate in the forward half of the boat. On boats 30 feet LOA (length overall) or less, weld all bottom longitudinal and transverse members using a chain welding sequence. On larger boats, I recommend using double continuous welding between the longitudinal bottom framing and shell plate in the forward half of the hull, and intermittent chain welding in the aft portion.

Bottom plating. The forward third to half of the bottom of a planing boat is subject to severe slamming impact. Be sure the bottom plates are of adequate thickness or sufficiently framed, or they may fracture.

Entrapped water. The alloys commonly used in boat construction are nearly impervious to corrosion from either fresh or salt water in a free-flowing state. However, entrapped water, such as that found between two overlapping layers of aluminum, loses its oxygen and becomes corrosive. This makes the practice of welding a doubler plate to the shell plate (to increase thickness in a local area) a bad idea, since moisture is trapped between the shell plate and the doubler plate. If you need increased thickness in a local area, such as an equipment foundation, insert a plate of thicker material. Slotted extrusions, commonly found on small production boats, are susceptible to corrosion from entrapped water. Repeated wetting by salt water, followed by evaporation, will cause the salinity of the entrapped water to increase dramatically, which can result in serious corrosion.

Hard spots. Hull stiffeners and other structural members that lie against the shell and do not terminate on a crossing structural member create hard spots. A hard spot will eventually result in a fracture of the shell plate at the unsupported end of the stiffener. To avoid this, taper the ends of the stiffener to reduce the abrupt change in the cross-sectional area to a minimum. As shown in Figure 7-13, this usually means trimming the stiffeners to a height of about ½ inch at the terminal end.

HULL DESIGN

Ideally, every hull design must meet a combination of engineering principles. The ultimate configuration of a hull depends to a great extent upon the desired performance criteria and the propulsion system to be used. A boat can have a *displacement* or *planing* hull. It can be hard-chined or have rounded bilges. It can be designed for speed or for comfort. But note that in each case, the choice is between one form or another—no single hull can excel in all areas of performance.

Hull Bottom

A planing boat is designed to run with the keel line higher in the bow, rising at about 1½ to 2 degrees in relation to the design waterline. This ensures that the boat will ride rather flat when on the plane, yet not so flat to cause bow-keeling, or broaching (the tendency for the forward part of the keel to submerge and act as a rudder, causing erratic directional control). For optimum performance, the after third portion of the bottom plate, on each side of the centerline, must be free of twist. This hull form has a constant deadrise in approximately the after third portion of the hull bottom. This hull form is called a *monohedron* hull and requires that the buttock lines be parallel in this area. A monohedron hull form is usually a fully developable surface.

The chine line rises fairly high as it approaches the bow. Allowing the chine line to rise increases the bottom deadrise and the twist in the bottom plate, with more deadrise forward than aft. For a developable bottom surface, this twist is usually gradual. Since the forward portion of the bottom plate is actually a portion of a developable cone, the bottom plate can be installed on a boat without undue force. On aluminum boats, the shape of transverse frames should be designed to conform to the shape of developable plating (see Appendix C).

The plate thickness on a small hull often seems to be excessive, but it is selected for ease of workability rather than minimum structural requirements. A bottom plate that is ¼-inch thick on a 22-foot boat may seem excessive, but the thicker material allows greater spacing between frames, reducing the number of parts as well as the labor costs to make and install them. As a compromise between cost of material, required hull strength, and labor savings, 3/16 inch is about the minimum bottom thickness on small welded-aluminum planing boats.

The additional strength of a thicker bottom plate allows the elimination of some longitudinal stiffeners. Even given the fact that economics are the primary driving force behind small-boat design, the slightly heavier boat that results from the thicker bottom plate is acceptable.

On small boats, similar logic applies to the side panels, which are normally 1/8 inch. This thickness is selected because it's about the minimum thickness that can be efficiently welded using the MIG production welding process. Transverse framing that was once common between the chine and the gunwale is no longer used in most newer designs. An aluminum angle with the flange turned up (see Figure 3-14) is typically used on the inside face of the side plate as longitudinal framing,

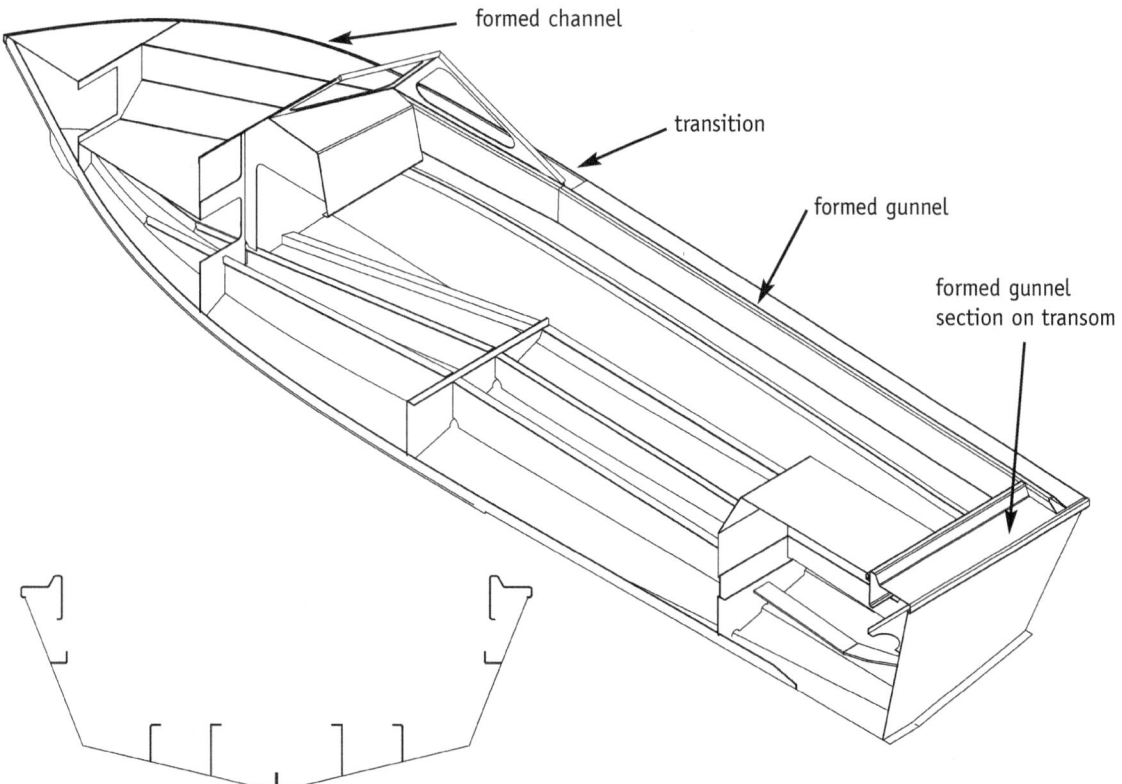

Figure 3-14. A 20-foot Specmar, Inc., Sportster showing formed sections.

running from the stern to a point about two-thirds distance to the bow. (This also serves as a stowage shelf for small tools and fishing tackle.) On some larger boats (more than 20 feet), side panels are of 5/32-inch material, allowing for higher freeboard without additional stiffeners.

Delta Pad

A number of aluminum planing boats have a flat area, sometimes called the delta pad or ski, along the keel on the aft portion of the hull. A delta pad on the bottom provides additional lift for rapid acceleration, allows the boat to plane at a lower speed, reduces draft when on plane, and provides a base to mount a water-jet intake. On smaller boats, this flat is typically about 16 to 20 inches wide at the transom, on the centerline of the hull, and extends forward one-half to two-thirds the waterline length of the boat, terminating in a point at the keel.

Strakes

Contrary to common belief, strakes, the angle shapes usually found running in the longitudinal axis on the bottom of a hull, are not for additional lift. Such strakes add stiffness to the bottom and reduce drag by knocking down spray when the boat is on plane.

Strakes on an aluminum hull are often cut down angle shapes, or they may be special extrusions. They should be 100 percent welded to minimize the potential of coming off. Strakes are often left open at the aft end to allow water to freely exit.

Chine

The intersection of the bottom of the hull and the side is called the chine—typically characterized as either hard or soft. A hard-chine hull has its bottom and side plates meeting at a relatively sharp angle, a hull shape commonly associated with planing powerboats. Soft chine suggests a more gradual, rounded transition between the bottom of the hull and the side.

To minimize the wetness often associated with a high-speed boat, a narrow chine flat (see Figure 3-15) may be used. In addition to knocking down the spray considerably, the chine flat reinforces the chine area. Special chine extrusions have replaced the chine flat in many small production hard-chine boats.

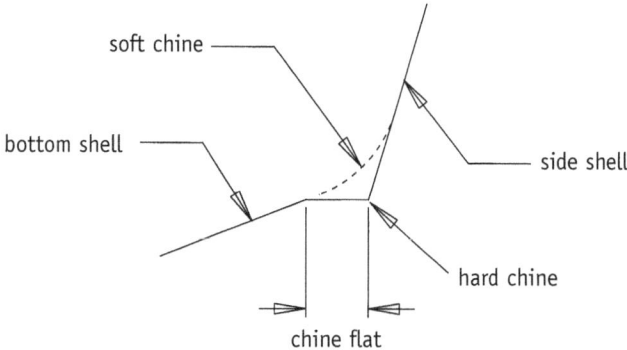

Figure 3-15. A narrow flat chine minimizes wetness associated with a high-speed boat.

The widespread use of chine extrusions on small, production-built, welded-aluminum boats has increased production efficiency. Chine extrusions eliminate the need for a precise fit between adjacent plates because adjustments can be made in the extrusion slots. And they also provide the option of welding only on the inside of the hull, eliminating unsightly weld spatter from exterior surfaces of the boat. If chine extrusions are kept small, they can be bent by hand around a jig or over a precut side or bottom plate, greatly simplifying their installation.

A number of special chine, gunwale, and keel extrusions are shown in Figure 1-4. The extrusion shown in Figure 2-3 is designed for the constant angle (120 degrees) between the bottom and the sides of a McKenzie River drift boat (figures 1-9 and 3-12) and provides little allowance for any twist to develop in the plates. But most hard-chine boats do have some bottom shape, and the angle between bottom and hull side isn't constant. This requires an extrusion with a bottom and side plate slot opening approximating the hull bottom and side material thickness, but with a wider chamber inside the extrusion that will allow some twist of the bottom or side plate as shown in Figure 1-4.

Transom

On small-planing-boat designs, the transom usually rakes aft at a minimum of 14 degrees, plus or minus 2 degrees, as specified in American Boat and Yacht Council standard S-12 (ABYC S-12). Additional slope, up to 19 degrees, is not uncommon for outboard-powered boats, since this allows the boat to be trimmed bow-down if necessary. The 14-degree transom angle will fit most inboard/outboard and water jet propulsion units.

Gunwale

Formed gunwales and gunwale sections made up of extrusions and sheet sections, like those shown in Figure 3-16, have evolved for welded-aluminum boat construction. Aside from providing sufficient strength to handle anticipated forces in this area of the hull, formed or built-up gunwale members also serve as conduits for control cables and wiring, cavities for upright flotation material, and in some cases rain flashing surfaces to which canvas tops can be attached.

The straight section of gunwale from the transom to the foredeck can be composed of sheet aluminum, which, with the use of a press-brake, has been formed into a shape similar to Figure 3-16A. A formed channel or gunwale extrusion from the forward end of the formed gunwale to the bow completes the gunwale, providing a smooth transition and a simple method of attaching the deck to the hull side, as shown in Figure 3-16B.

Note that the top of the side shell on the left side of Figure 3-16A extends above the bottom flange of the formed gunwale section. This allows a loose tolerance for cutting and fitting the side shell plate, thus expediting production. The disadvan-

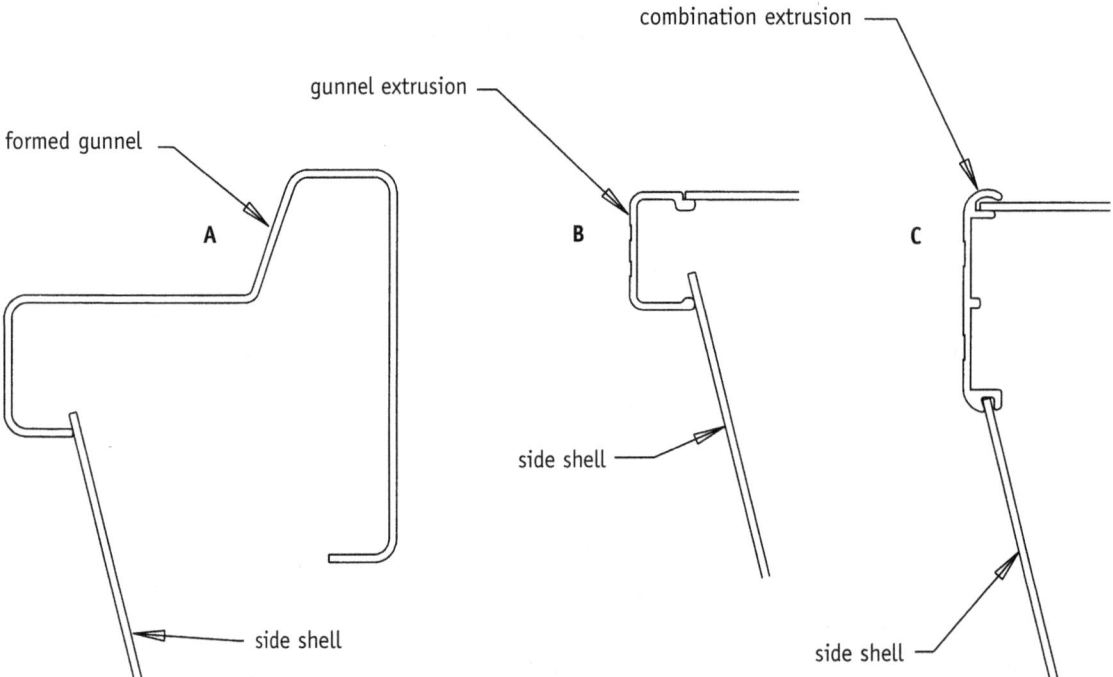

Figure 3-16. Typical formed gunwale (A) and gunwale sections constructed out of special extrusions (B and C).

tage of this is that the side-to-gunwale joint is inaccessible on the inside for welding, although as a practical matter, this has had no apparent ill effects. Figure 3-16C also illustrates an alternative configuration employing a special gunwale extrusion.

Framing

The framing in small welded-aluminum boats has evolved into bottom longitudinal frames and some transverse framing under the floorboards. In some cases, particularly in water-jet boats, longitudinal frames, or girders, are designed to not be in contact with the bottom plate in order to minimize bottom damage when grounding on rocks. Jet boat builders have known for some time that a grounding on rocks in a moving boat will cause the bottom shell plate to shear over transverse frames, while it will usually only crease along longitudinal framing. However, the downside to this technique is the use of a "floating" transverse frame, which is a poor support for the bottom plate, as all of the pressure on the bottom plate is through a small portion of the floating frame located at the longitudinal (see Figure 3-17). Additional transverse framing may be located in the area of a bow deck, and the sides of the hull normally have one large structural angle longitudinal located about midspan, which also serves as a storage shelf.

Decks

Small boats (smaller than 20 feet) normally have ¾-inch plywood main decks over aluminum angle subframing. Such decks are not watertight. They are secured with self-tapping, oval-head screws and stainless steel finish washers to transverse and longitudinal framing. The wood decking is usually well painted and often covered with some type of non-skid material.

Some builders have attempted to install watertight wooden weather decks, which are usually

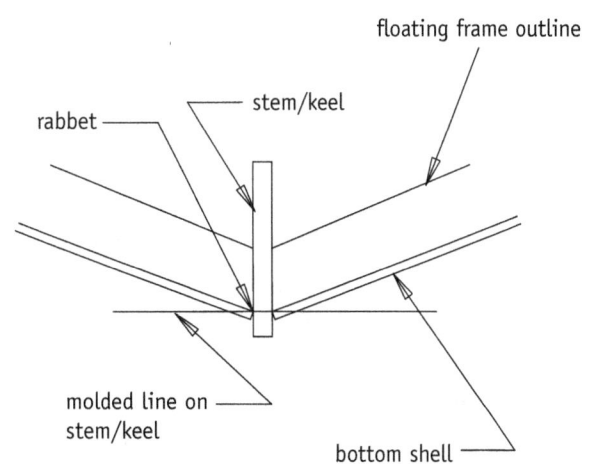

Figure 3-17. Section through the keel showing "floating" frame construction.

bolted to aluminum margin plates welded to the sides of the shell. Although wood has been used with some success for decks on steel hulls, aluminum expands and contracts and "works" much more than steel, so the attachment bolts are sure to egg-out their holes and leak. For a watertight deck, use aluminum.

Welded-aluminum decks can be as light as 1/8 inch plate on small boats, but under-deck stiffeners, on 12-inch centers or closer, will be needed to prevent excessive deflection underfoot. Even with closely spaced stiffeners, the deck may still be springy. Sprayed-in-place polyurethane foam under the deck will greatly reduce the tendency of the deck to move under the weight of walking. A good camber will also help stiffen the deck plate. On larger boats, the minimum deck plate thickness is 3/16 inch.

Aluminum decks are usually welded 100 percent to the shell on the outside to be watertight but intermittently welded on the underside to minimize the weld *shrink mark,* a slight ridge on the side plate, similar to that shown in Figure 5-22. Careful placement of rub rails and decorative paint schemes can help hide the deck-weld ridge.

Engine Bed

The general layout of the engine bed is usually called out by the boat designer, but engine-bed details are often developed by the boatbuilder. As a general rule, an engine bed consists of longitudinal girders within the engine compartment, welded to the bottom shell plate and adjacent framing similar to that shown in Figures 3-14 and 12-12. The girder ends can extend into adjacent areas. On boats with an aft-mounted engine, the aft ends of the engine-bed girders usually terminate at the transom. The forward end of the girders should taper uniformly to match continuing bottom longitudinal members so that an abrupt change of cross-sectional area does not occur.

The web of the longitudinal engine-bed girder is often constructed from aluminum material one standard thickness greater than the shell plate. (For example, with 3/16-inch bottom shell plate, use 1/4-inch material for the longitudinal engine-bed girder web.) The engine girder cap is one standard thickness thicker than the engine girder web; it is welded to the top of the girder into an L or T shape.

Engine-bed girders for aluminum boats are often spaced apart slightly less than the distance between the engine mounts. Most standard V-8 gasoline marine engines have their forward engine mount bolts located at 11 1/4 inches off centerline—port and starboard. Engine-bed girder spacing will often be 10 1/4 inches from centerline of the engine to the inboard faces of the girders—port and starboard—with the engine girder flange turned outboard for ease of access to the mount bolt nuts. Large-diameter holes, called lightening holes, are cut through the girder web, both to reduce weight and to allow access to the underside of the engine. Large limber holes should be cut through the aft end of the engine-bed girders at the transom and bottom plate intersection to facilitate drainage to the bilge. Since the engine girders are subject to high stresses, they are usually double continuous welded to the shell plate and adjoining boat hull structure.

Design considerations for engine-bed location and geometry must consider access to the underside of the engine for oil change and service (at least 1½ inches of clearance between the shell plate and the engine is desired), and access to the mounting bolts and nuts used to mount the engine.

When using flexible isolation mounts, set the top flange of the engine girder at the anticipated height of the base of the isolation mounts so that when the engine and gear are set in position on the engine bed, the shaft angle will be correct and the engine's output-gear flange will align with the propeller-shaft flange. If isolation mounts will not be used, set the engine-bed top flanges slightly lower than the anticipated location of the engine mounts to allow for some vertical adjustment during engine and shaft alignment.

Superstructure

The superstructure on an aluminum hull should be aluminum—⅛-inch material on small boats and 5/32- or 3/16-inch plate on larger ones.

Superstructure styles vary widely, depending on the owner's preference. On larger boats, the windshield may slope forward or aft. In northern, wet climates, a forward-sloping windshield fitted with a visor is popular because rain doesn't run down the glass, which translates into a clearer view when at anchor. The forward-sloping windshield also gives more headroom in the cabin.

The sides of any superstructure must tilt inward at the top, or an optical illusion will make them appear to be sloping outboard, disrupting the appearance of the boat. The proper term for this tilting inboard of side panels is *tumblehome*. The superstructure sides on commercial boats tilt inboard about 2½ degrees (2 to 3 inches from top to bottom on 7-foot high sides) to appear to be plumb; on yachts, the *tumblehome* is up to 8 degrees. Tumblehome is also needed on wide cabins to prevent damage to the cabin when the boat is rocked by waves when alongside a pier.

DESIGNING FOR EASE OF CONSTRUCTION

A boat that is designed to improve and simplify construction practices saves a lot of shop time and man-hours and also improves quality. As a general rule, use the largest piece of material that is practical. Try to minimize the amount of welding. Use a press brake to preform members, which will save welding time and improve quality (see Chapter 4, Fabricating Techniques). Design to allow for loose fit-up tolerance. Think out each joint and use a lap instead of a butt, when possible. Allow access for welding.

A number of proven time-saving practices merit consideration:

- Use offsets where practical to act as a built-in backing bar on ⅛-inch or thinner material (Figure 3-18A).

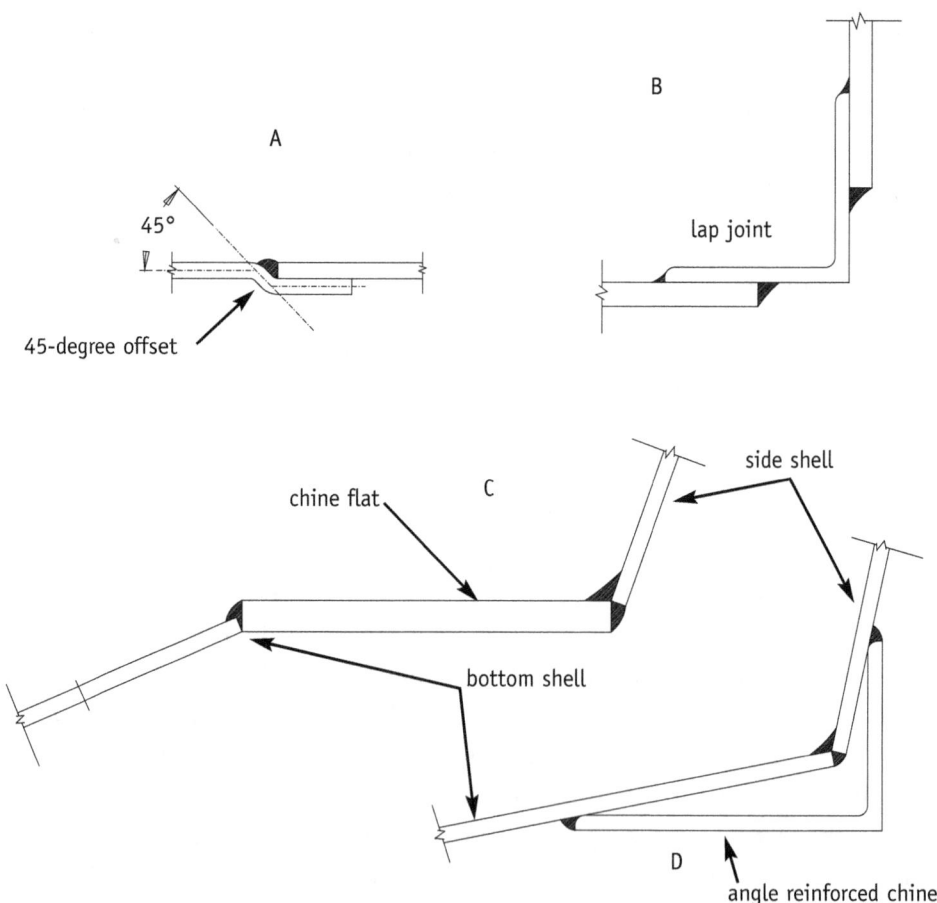

Figure 3-18. Hull and chine construction details.

Designing for Aluminum

- Lap joints (Figure 3-18B) allow very loose fit-up tolerances compared to butt joints and are much quicker.
- Figure 3-18C illustrates a typical large-boat chine using a separate cut member for the chine flat. This joint requires a good fit-up, but a chine using a standard angle for the chine flat (Figure 3-18D) can often be substituted. This substitution allows for a looser tolerance between the bottom and side plates since this joint is covered by the chine angle. And because the angle is fillet-welded, it's usually faster

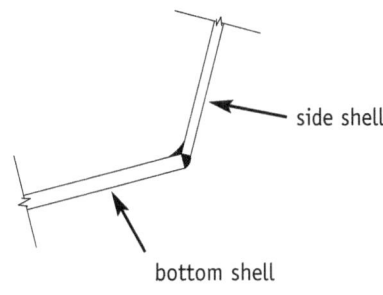

A. Plate edge-to-edge joint at chine (gunnel similar).

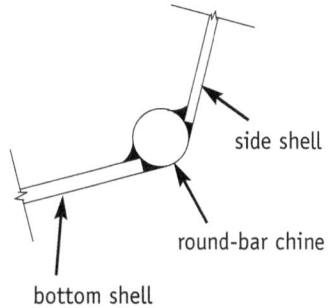

B. Round bar at chine.

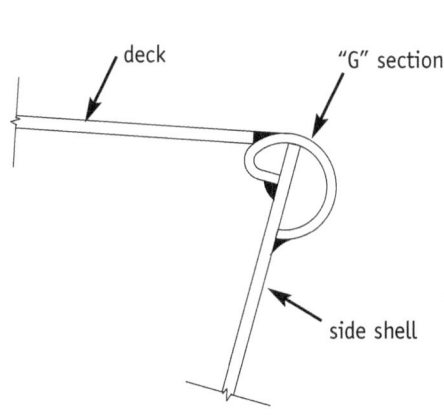

C. Special "G" section at gunnel.

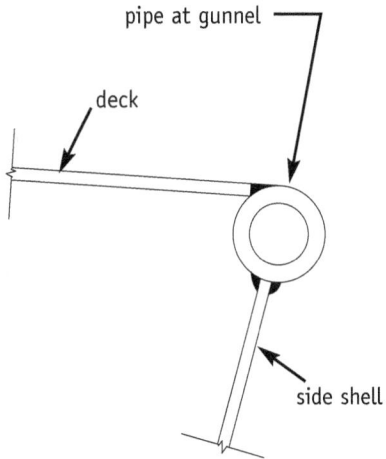

D. Pipe at gunnel.

Figure 3-19. Typical chine and deck edge details for a small boat.

and simpler than the butt welds required with a plate chine bar (Figure 3-18C). A round-bar chine (Figure 3-19B) isn't a good selection, because it's very difficult to maintain a fair line to the round bar. A flat plate chine or an angle over the chine, as shown in Figures 3-18C and 3-18D, is a much better solution.

- The plate edge-to-edge gunwale configuration illustrated in Figure 3-19A is much more difficult to fit up and maintain a fair line than the various formed gunwales detailed earlier (see Figure 3-16). A pipe or "G" section at the gunwale, as shown in Figures 3-19C and 3-19D, makes a more uniform gunwale than an edge-to-edge joint. A formed gunwale or channel allows the side plate to be cut to a much looser tolerance than edge-to-edge fit-up.
- Letting one member run slightly past another transforms a corner weld into fillet weld (Figure 3-20). This is commonly done where the transom attaches to the bottom and sides of the hull. Another advantage of letting the bottom plate extend slightly past the transom is that it can be bent down, if needed, for a trim tab.

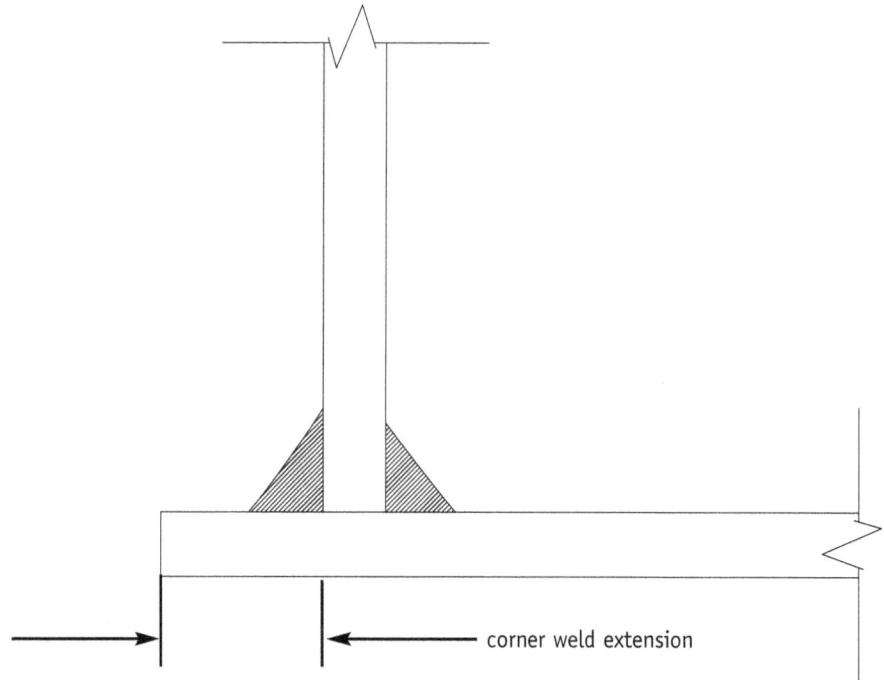

Figure 3-20. Extending one plate for a simpler fit and weld.

DESIGNING FOR USE OF PREFORMING

A press brake is a powerful, multipurpose machine. It can be used to bend metal into straight and uniform creases, and with the use of various dies, to form different bend radii. Well-thought-out use of the press brake will both speed production and greatly improve quality. For example, complex shapes can be developed from parts formed from flat patterns. Simple formed parts, designed to interconnect, are welded together to develop complex shapes, yet still stay within the parameters of flat-plate development. Chapter 4 contains more detailed information on the press brake.

While a helpful machine, it is not a common one for an amateur boatbuilder. Even many professional boatbuilders don't have press brakes, choosing instead to subcontract their forming work to sheet-metal shops.

Preforming is not limited just to the press brake. Other methods of bending or rolling aluminum are available, such as pyramid rolls for cylinders, angle bend rolls for forming angle and flat bars into curved shapes, the English wheel for stretching material, pipe benders, and other special tools for special operations. To take full advantage of preforming, the boat designer must be familiar with forming equipment procedures, capabilities, and limitations.

SEA TRIALS

A sea trial is the actual operation of a boat on the type of waters it was designed for. During the sea trial, an experienced boatbuilder will look for potential operational problems associated with the boat's design. Should any be found, the remedy is often minor modifications, easily accomplished on an aluminum boat by cutting, fitting, and rewelding. Once an acceptable level of performance is achieved, structural problems that may have shown up are isolated and solved.

The boatbuilder's sea trial should test the boat's maximum performance under various sea conditions. ABYC Section H-26, Powering of Boats, includes sea-trial tests for small boats. These tests are conducted using the maximum allowable horsepower for the boat, as determined by U.S. Coast Guard regulations, and as further defined by ABYC H-26.

ABYC test guidelines recommend quick-turn tests under specified conditions, but they don't include slamming tests. Slamming tests are necessary to test the hull's structural integrity and can best be accomplished by actually running fast in rough water. A reasonable structural test under slamming conditions for a pleasure boat would be 4 g's at the bow, and 2 g's at the center of gravity. This is generally lower than the likely design criteria for military or racing boats, which can be subject to extreme slamming conditions. (Tests conducted on the U.S. Navy YP-110 recorded 11.3 g's at the bow, 4.8 g's at the center of gravity, and 2 g's at the stern.)

One method of determining g forces is to use a bathroom scale with a known test weight, then subject the scale and weight to slamming forces. Divide the highest scale reading by the weight of the test weight, and you will obtain the g force. Another simple method to measure g forces is by the use of an aircraft type of g meter, available from an aircraft parts dealer.

After sea trials, thoroughly inspect the entire boat. If you discover broken welds, a change in the welding design, sequence, or location will usually solve the problem.

Aluminum is subject to fatigue failure, but whether this will become a problem in a particular design can't be adequately determined until the boat has had extensive running time. Most fatigue problems will be associated with vibrations originating from the propulsion system, so carefully watch the area around an outboard-motor mount (or in the vicinity of the propeller blades on inboard boats) for cracks caused by fatigue. Fatigue-related structural problems can be corrected—usually by design changes—as the areas are determined.

Panel vibrations can result in a buzzing or zinging sound. Locate such vibrations by touching the buzzing member with your hand. Relocating panel stiffeners, or simply altering the affected panel by placement of pads, insulation, or other means to disturb the frequency, will often eliminate such vibrations.

REGULATIONS

The only U.S. mandatory regulations for small pleasure boats are the USCG safety requirements, essentially limited to flotation, gasoline fuel systems, horsepower rating, and people-carrying capacity. There are no U.S. mandatory regulations pertaining to small-boat structural integrity. The boat's ability to withstand structural loads that may be imposed during operation is entirely in the hands of the boat designer and boatbuilder.

On inboard and inboard-outboard boats, the USCG regulations require basic flotation, i.e., flotation that ensures some portion of the boat will be above water. Level flotation is required for outboard-powered boats less than 20' long. In addition, boats less than 20 feet must display a plaque that shows safe loading and capacity and, if the boat is outboard-powered, the maximum horsepower rating.

All boats, no matter what the length, must meet USCG safety standards for ventilation of gasoline fumes and must have a hull identification number.

The USCG regulations apply to boats both professionally built and home built, and they are readily available from the USCG website, www.uscgboating.org/regulations/fedreg.htm. ABYC expands and clarifies the USCG regulations in a number of areas. If you follow the current revisions of ABYC, you should be in compliance with the USCG requirements for small pleasure boats. The ABYC web site is www.abycinc.org.

If your boat is to be used for purposes other than pleasure, such as carrying passengers, other regulations may apply. Contact the nearest USCG office for Subchapter T—Small Passenger Vessels (Under 100 Gross Tons). Subchapter T is a part of the *Code of Federal Regulation* (CFR), Title 46, Parts 166–199, and is available from the U.S. Government Printing Office, Washington, D.C. You can also review the Subchapter T regulations by clicking on the link at the bottom of the USCG web page called out in the previous paragraph.

Commercial passenger-carrying boats, such as charter fishermen, with six or fewer paying passengers, are not subject to "T" boat regulations. (Thus the term "six pack" for the license required to operate such a vessel.) If the boat will carry more than six paying passengers, then full compliance with Subchapter T is required.

Passenger-carrying vessels subject to Subchapter T regulations require plan approval prior to the start of construction and in-process inspections during boat construction. Plan approval is granted after a review by the USCG of all required plans for the vessel. Although not required, a professional engineer's stamp on the drawings will greatly expedite plan approval. It is recommended that a professional naval architect, familiar with Subchapter T requirements for aluminum boats, be retained to obtain plan approval.

Welding procedures and welding-machine operators should be certified for the welding process and the type of material welded. This certification can be obtained by following the guidelines specified in the U.S. Navy standard for qualification of welders (MIL-STD-248) or other USCG-approved guidelines (contact your local USCG inspection office to determine welder qualifications and guideline requirements). To meet the criteria of MIL-STD-248, each individual welder must demonstrate skill in welding in various positions by making weld test plates with the weld beads running in the vertical (upward), horizontal (on a vertical surface), overhead, and flat positions. A welder is certified for the welding process, material, and welding position for which he was successfully tested.

References

American Boat and Yacht Council, Inc. *Standards and Recommended Practices for Small Craft.* Millersville, Md.: American Boat and Yacht Council, Inc., 1991.

Kaiser Aluminum & Chemical Sales, Inc. *Aluminum Boats,* 2nd ed. Oakland, Calif.: Kaiser Aluminum & Chemical Sales, Inc., 1978.

Lord, Lindsay. *Naval Architecture of Planing Hulls.* New York: Cornell Maritime Press, 1946.

U.S. Coast Guard Boating Safety. "Boatbuilder's Handbook." U.S. Coast Guard. http://www.uscgboating.org/regulations/fedreg.htm.

U.S. Department of Transportation. *Code of Federal Regulation.* Title 46, Parts 166–199. Washington, D.C.: U.S. Department of Transportation (U.S. Coast Guard), 1988.

Gerr, Dave. *The Elements of Boat Strength.* Camden, Maine: International Marine/McGraw-Hill, 2000.

CHAPTER 4

Fabricating Techniques

Working with aluminum is similar to working with wood. Most standard power woodworking tools can saw, plane, and drill aluminum. Special blades designed for aluminum improve efficiency, but in most cases, less-expensive woodworking blades will suffice. An inexpensive, hardware-store, carbide-tipped woodcutting blade in a 7¼-inch handheld power circular saw (almost universally known as a Skilsaw, the most well-known trademark) is adequate for cutting aluminum. A heavy-duty power hand plane—the Porter Cable Versa-Plane, for example—that comes with a spiral carbide-tipped cutter can easily plane aluminum to obtain a professional-looking finish.

Larger professional boatbuilding shops will have handheld plasma-arc cutters, which are both fast and safe. Some shops are equipped with automatic plasma or water-jet cutters that can cut out parts to conform to computer cutting files. But all the parts needed to construct a 40-foot aluminum powerboat hull can be cut out with a circular saw and a band saw. The circular saw is one of the most versatile aluminum-cutting tools. It can make straight and large-radius cuts in flat plate; in fact, almost all plate cuts for framing and shell plate can be circular-saw cut. A vertical band saw is safer and quieter than a circular saw, but the throat depth (the distance from the blade to the frame) restricts the size of the piece that may be cut.

The fastest and most accurate method of cutting straight strips is with a power shear. Routers, nibblers, hand grinders, reciprocating saws, and jigsaws will also cut aluminum.

SHOP SIZE

The size of the boat you plan to construct determines the size shop you need. A two-car garage is easily big enough for the construction of a small boat—about 14 feet or smaller—provided there's access to 230-volt, single-phase electrical power (normally available in most modern homes) for welding. For larger boats, consider overhead room, working space around the hull, and adequate space to turn the inverted hull over once it's nearly complete. It's also nice to be able to get the boat out the door without tearing down the shop.

Aluminum doesn't like temperatures colder than 55 degrees Fahrenheit when welding, so in a cold climate, you need a facility providing at least a partially controlled environment.

Boats with shell plate thickness of ¼ inch and greater should be welded with 230-volt or 460-volt three-phase welding machines, which usually means a shop that can provide industrial three-phase power. Aluminum plate 3/16 inch thick or less can be welded on household 230-volt single-phase power.

Cutting aluminum with a hand power circular saw is noisy, but since the bulk of the saw cutting is done early on in the project, exposure to high noise levels is shortened. If you're working in a residential neighborhood, take noise control into account. (Sharp saw blades cut much quieter than dull ones.)

TOOLS

Any well-equipped home workshop will contain almost all the tools necessary to construct a small welded-aluminum boat. Below are a few additional tools (if not already in your workshop):

- A worm-gear drive, 7¼-inch handheld power saw (Skilsaw #HD77 or similar) equipped with a carbide-tipped blade for saw. (You can use a direct-drive saw, but it will not stand up to the heavy demand of aluminum sawing.)
- A right-angle grinder, preferably a 4½-inch (Makita or equivalent) with an aluminum grinding disc (4½-inch by ⅛-inch Brilliant T27) and a stainless-steel cup (Weiler M10 1.25 S.S., #13182).
- A 230-volt single-phase welding power supply compatible with MIG 1-pound spool welding gun, an argon bottle, flow meter, and adequate power and ground welding leads. (Note: you can rent an aluminum

Fabricating Techniques

MIG welding outfit on a daily, weekly, or monthly basis.)
- A 14-inch vertical band saw (Rockwell-Delta or equivalent) with a ½-inch-wide, eight-tooth blade.
- Six 4-inch forged steel C-clamps.

A few additional tools will make the job a lot easier:

- A high-speed die grinder (Makita GE0600 or equivalent), fitted with a cone-shaped carbide cutter (Brilliant 7D13956, similar to the one shown in Figure 4-1).
- A 7-inch angle grinder (Makita GA7001L or equivalent), with aluminum grinding disc (Brilliant T27) and a rubber backing pad and abrasive discs for sanding.
- A handheld power plane (Porter Cable Versa-Plane) with a spiral carbide cutter.
- A reciprocating saw (Makita or equivalent) with extra blades.

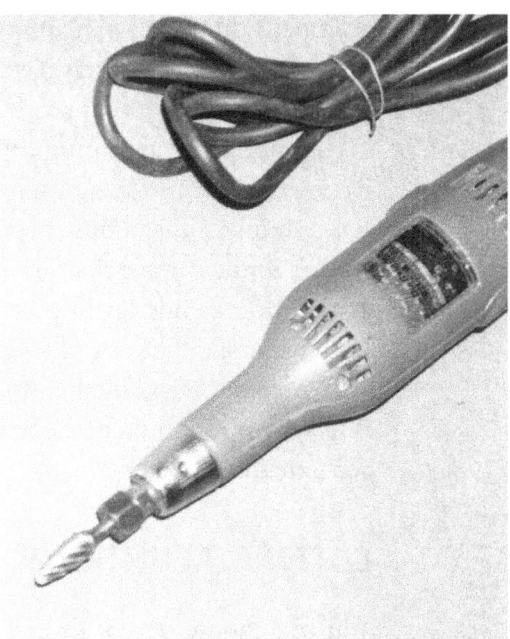

Figure 4-1. Electric die grinder with cone-shaped cutter.

MARKING ALUMINUM FOR CUTTING

The shiny surface of aluminum can be very reflective, making *layout lines* difficult to see. Combined with poor lighting, this can make layout marks almost impossible to follow with a cutting tool. The importance of clear and distinct layout lines requires an appropriate marking method and a location with good lighting.

Lay out the cutting lines on aluminum with an ink pencil or felt-tip marker—black, blue, and red are good colors. However, felt-tip markers don't last long when used to mark aluminum; a thin coat of oil on the surface of the aluminum collects dirt, and this dirty oil film damages the tips of the markers. An ink pencil (Noblot ink pencil 705) will last considerably longer than a felt-tip marker and makes a very distinct line that can be seen even in poor light.

On the hull exterior and anywhere the mark will show, use a water-soluble marker. Most felt-tip markers wash off aluminum easily with a little water, but some don't wash off at all, not even with standard industrial solvents such as acetone. While a permanent mark may be desirable in some instances, improperly removed felt-tip markings have been known to show through finish paint. A little experimenting with markers will determine which one to use.

Do not *scribe* aluminum by making a deliberate scratch in the work surface; it's too easy to mistake an unintentional scratch on the surface for the scribed line. For example, a metal burr between the circular saw and work being cut can put a scratch in the surface that, in poor light, might be taken for a scribed line. And if a scribed line ends up in a bent or high-stress area, it causes a notch effect that will encourage the start of a crack.

For computer-guided, automatically cut parts, a zinc pencil on a plasma cutting system, or an etched line on a water-jet cutting outfit, makes a distinct and accurate line.

CUTTING ALUMINUM

You can choose one of several cutting systems for aluminum: plasma arc, water jet, laser, sawing, shear, or router. The cutting method depends on available tooling and efficiency.

Figure 4-2. Plasma arc wet cutting table at Northwest Plasma Cutting, Seattle, Washington.

Plasma Arc Cutter

Plasma arc cutting has been around since the 1950s, but only in the past 10 to 15 years has it become a primary method to cut bulk materials for aluminum boats. Some boat shops have handheld portable plasma cutters that cut parts much more rapidly than mechanical tools. Figure 4-2 shows a 40-foot-long water table fitted with a single cutting torch. Included in the system is a zinc pencil, which is an automatic marking tool. The water table is advantageous to reduce heat-induced warping of cut parts.

Water Jet

Water-jet cutting is a more recent technology that provides extremely clean cuts. Both plasma arc and water-jet cutting are available from aluminum suppliers or through independent cutting facilities.

Laser Cutter

Laser cutting makes a very accurate and clean cut, but its use is limited to lighter-gauge materials that are not commonly used in welded-aluminum boat construction.

Power Saw

You can saw through aluminum quite easily with power woodworking tools using carbide-tipped blades. Because aluminum tends to adhere to the saw blade and plug the gap between the teeth, select a blade with large, widely spaced teeth and a wide set, similar to a rough-cut blade for wood. The past practice of using wax to stop aluminum buildup on saw blades isn't necessary, and it's a bad practice when welding is anticipated: the wax is difficult to remove thoroughly and will cause welding problems.

Circular Saw

On the West Coast, many small boat shops use the 7¼-inch worm-drive circular saw as their primary method of cutting aluminum. This saw is one of the most versatile aluminum-cutting tools, capable of almost all framing and shell plate cuts.

But first, a few words of caution about cutting aluminum with a circular saw are in order. Always wear a face shield; safety glasses alone are not sufficient. Both

Figure 4-3. A safe entry cut using a circular saw.

Figure 4-4. Plunge cutting with a circular saw allows a safe cut to the edge when the angle of the cut is less than 15 degrees from the perpendicular.

safety glasses and a full-face shield are recommended when sawing any metal because the chips thrown off by the blade sometimes stick to the skin, and they're hot enough to cause a mild burn. Wear a long-sleeved shirt or coveralls to protect your arms. Snug-fitting leather work gloves are a nice plus, both as hot-metal protection and protection from the razor-sharp fresh-cut edge. A lot of hand power-saw cutting is accomplished while kneeling on the material, so wearing nonmarking knee pads will help prevent the sharp saw chips from penetrating your knees, and they'll add to your kneeling comfort.

The noise level associated with cutting aluminum with a circular saw is loud enough to cause ear damage. Always wear ear protectors or plugs, both for protection from noise and to prevent cutting chips from entering the ear. The aluminum oxide present in aluminum welds is highly abrasive and will quickly dull saw blades, which slows the cutting rate and increases the noise level substantially. Both problems are solved by changing blades.

When using a circular saw to cut aluminum plate thinner than $3/16$ inch, the initial entry cut direction is important. Entering the material at a shallow angle to the edge produces a thin metal sliver on one side of the entry cut. This sliver can catch and bend into the rotating saw blade, resulting in a loud bang as the blade leaps out of the cut. To avoid this problem, always enter the material at no more than 15 degrees off a square (perpendicular) entry to the edge (see Figure 4-3).

When you require a shallower entry cut, avoid the potential kickback and resulting damage to the aluminum by simply turning the saw around 180 degrees and making a plunge cut (Figure 4-4). Hold back the blade guard and rest the front edge of the saw's sole or bottom plate firmly against the workpiece with the blade elevated above the plate. Start the saw and lower the back of the sole so that the blade gradually comes in contact with the aluminum, plunge-cutting an entry inside the plate edges. Then saw out to the edge (Figure 4-5). When plunge cutting, always be alert for kickback, and hold the saw firmly with both hands. Set the blade for maximum depth, but only allow a small portion of the blade to protrude through the metal until a sufficiently long cut is established. Then you can lower the saw so that the sole is in full contact with the aluminum. Once you've established the cut, reduce the saw blade depth.

Don't let these safety precautions eliminate or reduce your use of the circular saw—it's fast and safe when used properly. Psychological resistance to cutting metal with a circular saw is only overcome by actually trying it. With a little practice, your cuts will be straight and accurate. Use a ⅛-inch kerf allowance (the width of the saw blade cut) when laying out material. If you anticipate a lot of cutting, then get a blade designed for aluminum cutting, one with a zero-degree tooth-face rake angle (Figure 4-6). This blade will produce a smoother and quieter cut, but it costs more and isn't as readily available as a wood-cutting blade.

You can use a circular saw for large-radius cuts (1 foot and larger) on flat plate. Make an outside cut by a series of short, straight cuts, as shown in Figure 4-7.

You can also do inside-radius cuts, but you must allow ample blade room for the start and reentry cuts. Cut an inside curve by setting the circular saw blade depth very shallow—not much deeper than the thickness of the material. By cutting with the blade barely breaking through the material, you can easily cut an inside radius as tight as 12 inches. The start and reentry technique for circle cutting involves a kind of pumping motion. Keep the sole of the saw in contact with the aluminum at the front end of the saw, and rotate the saw up and down slightly. Leave the forward tip of the saw sole in contact with the aluminum at all times to allow the saw to follow the arc of the circle being cut. A proficient circular-saw operator can make a rapid circular cut in aluminum plate with barely perceptible vertical movement of the saw.

When cutting flat material with the circular saw, always consider what's under the material you're cutting. To ensure adequate blade-tip clearance, position the

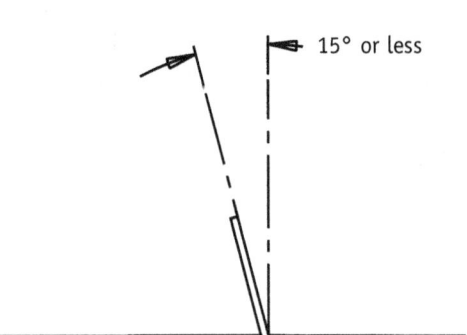
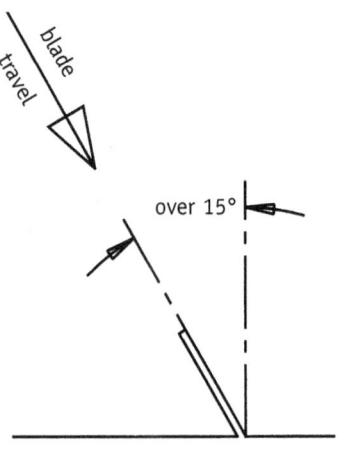
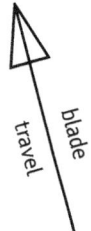

A. When entering plate from edge, do not exceed 15 degrees to normal for 1/8-inch aluminum or lighter. Angles greater than 15 degrees are okay for aluminum thicker than 1/8 inch.

B. Entry cut is made inside plate perimeter. Cut progresses out to edge.

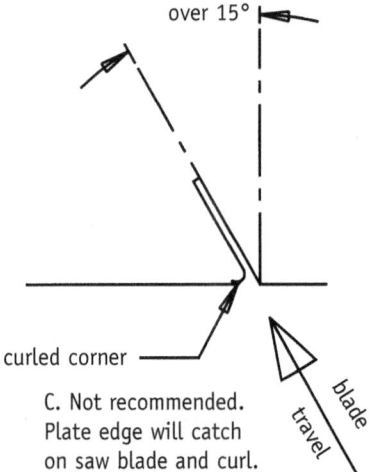

C. Not recommended. Plate edge will catch on saw blade and curl.

Figure 4-5. Circular-saw cutting procedures for thin plate.

material on a wooden cutting grid or lay two-by-fours flat on the floor, about 18 inches apart, and place your work on top of them. You must have adequate support and clearance under the aluminum to keep the saw blade from contacting the floor when you kneel on the material during cutting.

Keep in mind that sawing metal generates a considerable amount of heat. A little WD-40 squirted periodically on the saw blade will reduce the heat, as well as speed cutting and hold down the noise level.

A carbide-tipped blade with one or two missing tips is still usable, but when a blade loses a carbide tip that sticks in the metal, all of the tips will probably be knocked out with the

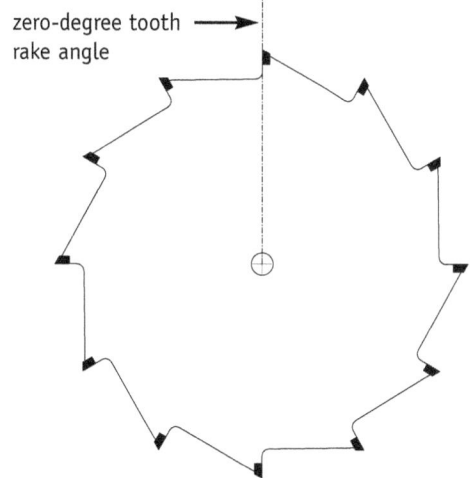

Figure 4-6. Aluminum-cutting blade with zero-degree tooth rake angle.

next rotation. More than two missing tips requires a blade replacement. Always have a few spare blades available.

The chips generated from sawing aluminum will collect in trouser cuffs and other areas of clothing. And these small, sharp chips are very difficult to remove

Figure 4-7. Circle cutting using a "plunge" cutting technique.

from carpet. Thoroughly empty your cuffs and pockets of aluminum chips before leaving the workplace.

Vertical Band Saw

A vertical band saw is safer and quieter than a handheld circular saw, but its throat depth limits the size of the piece that it can cut. It is the preferred cutting tool for small parts. A 14-inch (throat depth) woodworker's band saw commonly has a ½ hp motor, but a band saw equipped with a ¾ hp motor will have a substantially faster cutting rate in aluminum.

Use a ½-inch-wide, eight-tooth-per-inch blade for general cutting. This blade will cut alloys 5052, 5086, or 6061 without loading up between the teeth, and it will provide many cutting hours. When cutting softer alloys, such as 6063, the eight-tooth blade may load up; switch to a four-tooth-per-inch, skip-tooth, plywood-cutting blade. Allow approximately 1/16 inch for a band saw kerf.

The single most common problem with a band saw is that it may not track true. This is usually the result of loose blade guides, so keep the guides properly adjusted.

Blade width determines the minimum radius you can cut. For most purposes, the ½-inch blade works well, but you may need ⅜- and ¼-inch blades for special applications. It may be difficult to adjust the guides so that these narrower blades track true.

Use a constant pressure to hand-feed a band saw. To ensure a true cut, watch both the blade and the mark on the material. If the cut doesn't appear to be in line with the centerline of the table, check the guides for proper adjustment. A little WD-40 on the blade will ease cutting, reduce heat, and lengthen blade life.

Typically, a miter gauge is provided with a wood-cutting band saw. However, it has little application for aluminum; my experience has shown that the use of a gauge has little effect on an aluminum cut.

A word of caution when cutting round pipe on a band saw: the saw will tend to grab the pipe and rotate it. When this happens, the blade usually jams, then

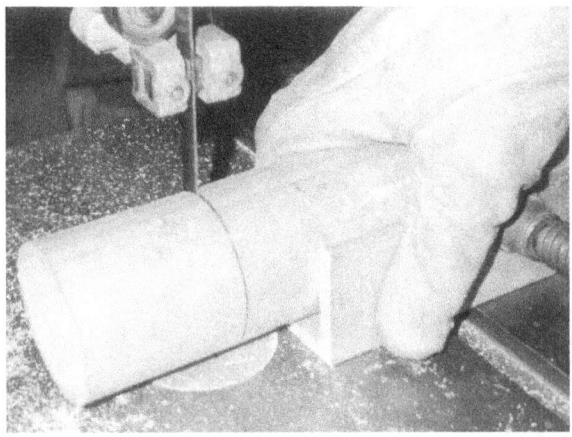

Figure 4-8. To prevent pipe from rotating when cutting with a band saw, clamp it to a piece of angle stock.

Fabricating Techniques

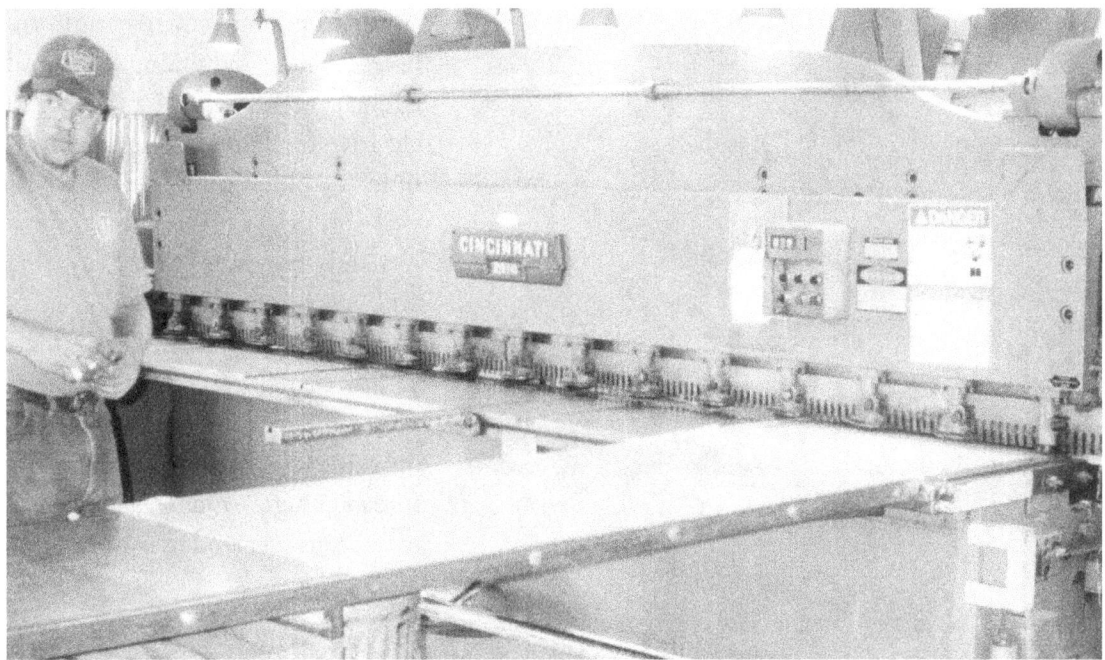

Figure 4-9. A power shear allows for fast and accurate straight cuts.

either breaks or kinks. Clamp round pipe to another piece of material (see Figure 4-8) so it can't rotate during the cut.

Power Shear

The fastest and most accurate method of making straight cuts is with a power shear (Figure 4-9). A local sheet-metal shop should be able to provide this service. Shear cuts are true and uniform, and in addition to the excellent appearance, there's no waste and no need for a kerf allowance. Shearing is economical if the sheet-metal shop doesn't have to do the layout. Layout consumes man-hours, and man-hours consume dollars. Limit the sheet-metal shop's time to shearing by laying out the parts to be sheared prior to delivery to the shear operator.

Other Cutting Methods

A number of other power woodworking tools can perform their functions equally well on aluminum, and in most cases, the wood-cutting blade will be adequate.

Figure 4-10. Use a router for cutting uniform holes.

Router. For cutting uniform holes, such as lightening holes and circular access holes, a handheld electric router fitted with a single-flute, carbide-tipped cutter works well. A circle-cutting guide, which is a slide-mounted center pin that attaches to the router with a pair of threaded ¼-inch rods, is commercially available. You will need longer guide arms on a number of boatbuilding applications; simply thread longer rods (usually NF thread), as pictured in Figure 4-10.

You can also use a handheld router for freehand work, but you must hold it very securely. Cutting notches in frames for through-passing, longitudinal T-bar is a good application for the handheld router. First drill ¼-inch holes at the corners of the notch, then saw-cut the sides of the notch to the holes. Complete the notch by using the router to plunge-cut between the two saw cuts, forming the bottom of the notch (Figure 4-11). Aluminum will tend to load up in the cutter if it's allowed to get too hot. For sustained cutting, use WD-40 on the cutter to help keep it cool.

Die grinder. A small electric or air router called a die grinder is a must. This handy tool can reach into areas not accessible to other tools. Fit it with a conical cutter, and you can use a die grinder to deburr, enlarge holes, chamfer sides of cut members, and gouge out hard-to-reach welds for repair. Grinder bits intended for aluminum have large, open flukes that resist loading up (Figure 4-1).

The high-speed saw shown in Figure 4-12 is a pneumatic die grinder fitted with a right-angle attachment. It is a very fast and easy-to-use tool for back-chipping.

Reciprocating saw. The reciprocating saw (recipro saw) is useful

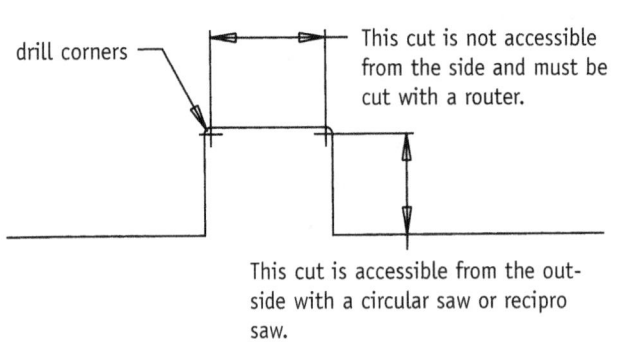

Figure 4-11. Notching a frame member can be accomplished with a saw and a handheld router.

when you need a narrow kerf or where you have limited accessibility to the part being cut. It cuts rapidly, making cuts comparable to those made by a band saw. The recipro saw is often used to cut shell plate already fitted to the boat structure to mate it with adjoining plate.

Angle grinder. Use an angle grinder, or sander, fitted with an aluminum-grinding disc to cut items such as temporary lifting eyes and strong-backs flush with a surface. You can also use the perimeter of the grinding disc as a cutting wheel (making a wide kerf). The grinding disc will wear very rapidly, and in some cases, pieces will slough off during the cutting process, making a full-face shield a must.

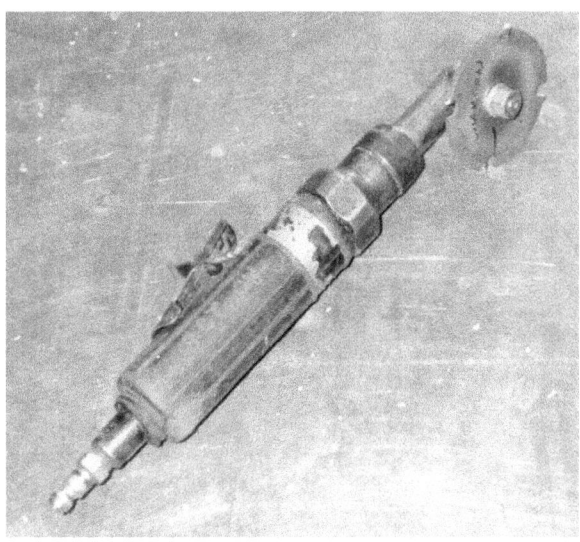

Figure 4-12. Right-angle attachment and saw blade on an air-powered die grinder.

Some boat shops use a 4½-inch angle grinder fitted with a saw blade for weld-bead removal. The bead-removal rate is very high, and in some shops, this blade-fitted grinder is a primary back-chipping tool. This is obviously a very dangerous tool, and in one large Northwest boatyard it has acquired the nickname of "meat axe." As a safety precaution, use snug fitting leather gloves and a full face shield.

Hand nibbler. The electric nibbler is used primarily for light gauge (⅛ inch and less) material requiring neat cuts, such as electrical panels. The nibbler is a common sheet-metal-shop tool.

PLANING ALUMINUM

The electric hand plane with a spiral carbide-tipped cutter (Figure 4-13), such as the Versa-Plane manufactured by Porter Cable, works very well on aluminum. This tool easily planes aluminum in a similar manner to wood, as shown in Figure 4-14. Cuts of 1/32 inch per pass on the edge of a ¼-inch plate are rapid and don't overwork the plane.

Plane any sawed edge that will show in the finished boat to enhance the appearance. The power plane prepares an edge very nicely, including beveling for welding. However, it will tend to grab as you pass off the material being planed. To counteract this, maintain firm downward pressure on the heel of the plane

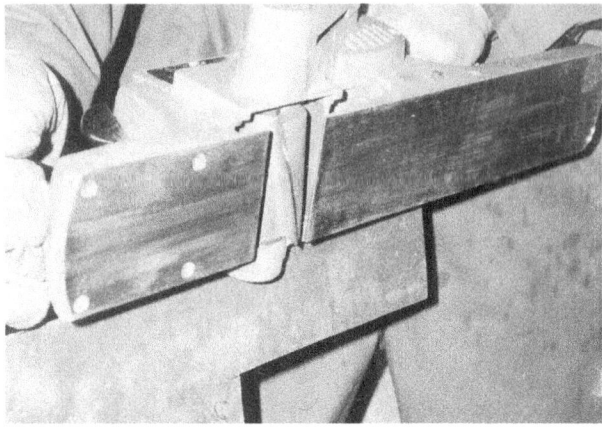

Figure 4-13. Hand-powered plane with spiral cutters.

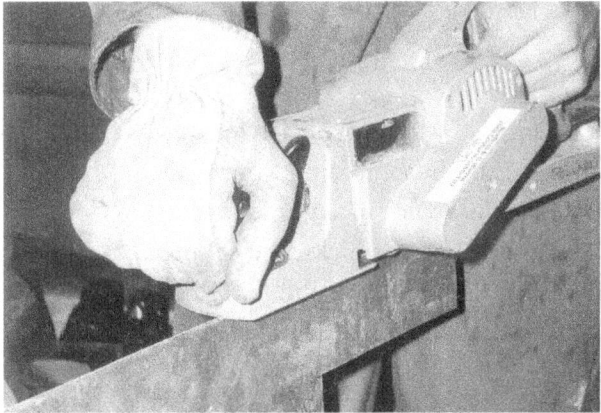

Figure 4-14. Planing aluminum with a power plane.

when ending a cut at the end of the material. Keep in mind that the chips the plane generates are hot and can cause a mild burn; use the same safety equipment when power planing as you use with the handheld circular saw.

FORMING ALUMINUM

A number of forming techniques can be employed on aluminum, including the press brake, the bending roll, and the pipe bender. A large number of sheet-metal and fabrication shops have adequate tooling to do a nice job of preforming aluminum.

One concern is the cleanliness of the forming tools. Most sheet-metal shops are likely to have clean tooling that will form or roll aluminum with minimum marking. Structural-steel shops, on the other hand, can be very rough with aluminum and don't usually consider the surface finish. Be aware of this and address the surface finish during preliminary discussions with your forming shop. Plate-forming rolls in steel fabrication shops are often oily and have numerous "dings" on the roll surfaces that will damage the aluminum finish. Determine how much surface damage you can accept prior to starting the forming operation.

Press Brake

A press brake is a powerful forming machine used to crease or bend metal (Figure 4-15). It can be mechanically or hydraulically powered and comes in a large assortment of sizes and capacities. Those typically found in modern sheet-metal shops can accommodate most bending requirements for small aluminum-boat construction. For heavier bending needs, larger brakes are available at metal fabrication shops.

Wherever practical, use press-brake forming to reduce welding and improve appearance. A brake-formed plate crease is a straight line, free of weld distortion, and smooth and pleasing to the eye. There are many areas of the boat where wise use of the press brake can make a definite difference in the quality of the finished product.

Figure 4-15. An example of a press brake, a forming machine that creases or bends metal.

Press brakes require bending dies. These are used in pairs, with the female, or lower, die fixed and the male die attached to the movable upper portion of the brake (Figure 4-16). Various bend diameters can be obtained by varying the die geometry. Angle bends, from small bend radii approaching zero to large radius bends, can be accomplished on the press brake.

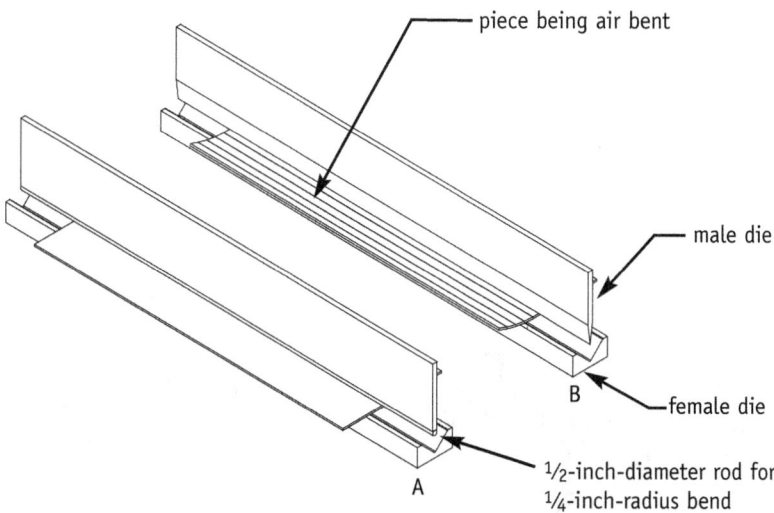

Figure 4-16. Press-brake dies—male and female—allow for various bend diameters.

Press-brake dies can be constructed to form large radius bends. However, when large radius bends or conical forming is required, it is more common to form a series of small angle bends spaced closely together, resulting in a series of adjoining flats that approximate a curved surface. This type of forming is called air bending because the male die of the press brake usually does not bottom out in the female die. The quality of a bend is directly related to the condition of the equipment and the skill of the press-brake operator. Examples of air bends are shown in Figures 4-17 and 4-18.

One area that almost always requires forming are cabin-window mullions. Welding this narrow strip will result in distortion that may not be acceptable. If the mullion is creased with the press brake where it changes direction (knuckles), a lot of problems are solved. There are many other areas on a superstructure where a smooth, distortion-free bend from a press brake can be used to advantage.

In place of welded-on flanges, brake-form flanges on frames and equipment foundations will eliminate both weld time and weld distortion. The forming of steps, cockpits, superstructure items, visors, metal doors, fuel tanks, rudder parts, and the leading edge of hollow keels are all ideal for press-brake work. The whole trick is to lay them out accurately.

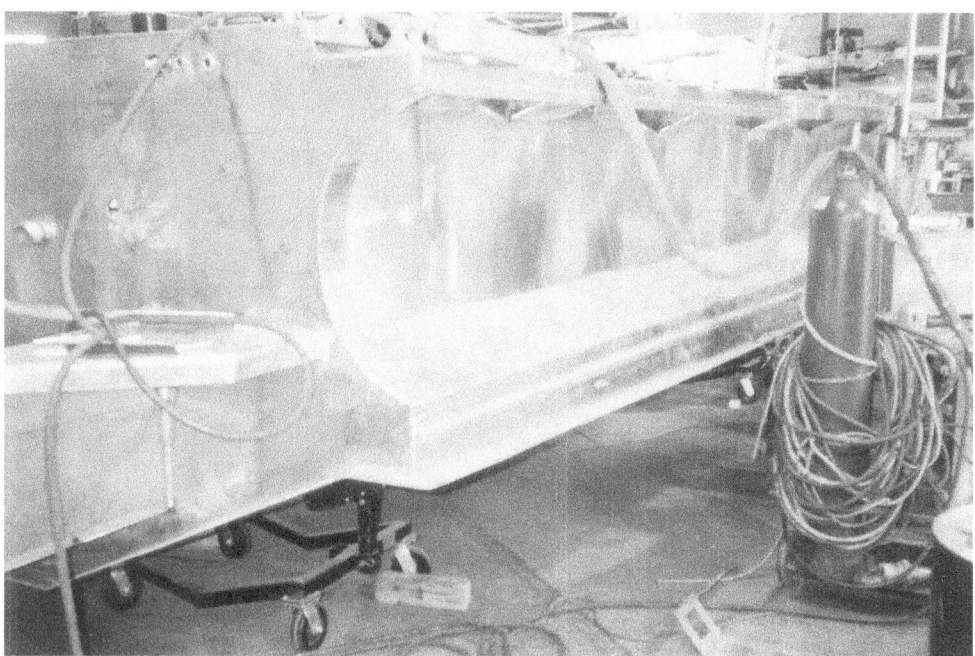

Figure 4-17. A large-radius air bend was used to form the outer edge of this RIB transom.

The prevailing opinion in some small-boat shops is that press-brake work is too expensive. Any work that is highly labor-intensive is expensive, but placing the material in the brake and operating the controls isn't time-consuming at all; in fact, it's very fast. It's the layout that consumes the man-hours. To save dollars, don't leave this function up to the press-brake shop. Lay out all the bends prior to delivering the material to the press-brake shop. This requires some time but is well worth the effort when the end cost is considered. (See Appendix B for press-brake layout specifics.)

Figure 4-18. Air bending was used to form the bow cone and lower hull sections of this SWATH vessel.

When a batch of material is laid out and ready for forming, take it to the press-brake shop. Explain your markings to the shop foreman so there won't be any misunderstanding. Provide angle-of-bend templates if bends other than 30, 45, 60, or 90 degrees are required. Be sure to note on the material whether each bend is up or down and the inside radius of the bend. (For the minimum bend radius to prevent cracking, see Appendix B, Table B-1.) Mark each piece with the appropriate identification. Provide sketches of the "as formed" pieces if you can. If possible, have someone present during the forming to answer any questions; it will save a lot of shop time if they can be answered on the spot.

Bending Rolls

A bending roll is used to put permanent curvature into flat plate. It can also be used, to a limited extent, to put a gentle curve in pipe (such as handrail) and T-bar. Sheet-metal shops usually have small bending rolls for light-gauge metal. Larger rolls suitable for rolling ¼-inch plate or heavier are commonly available at steel fabricators.

A typical plate roll (Figure 4-19) consists of two lower power-driven rolls and one adjustable upper idler roll. This configuration is called a pyramid roll. In operation, the end of the plate to be formed is placed between the upper and lower

Figure 4-19. A pyramid bending roll.

rolls, and the idler-roll adjustment screws are tightened to clamp down on the material and engage the power-roll drive. The plate is drawn into the machine between the top and bottom rolls, forcing curvature into the plate in proportion to the pressure exerted by the upper roll. The rolled plate curves upward as it travels through the roll. A very small vertical adjustment to the idler roll makes a large difference in the curvature diameter of the rolled plate.

One drawback of the pyramid roll is a flat spot at the start and stop of each piece that is rolled. The width of this flat is equal to half the distance between the drive rolls. To compensate for this, material can be intentionally left long, rolled, then trimmed to remove the flat areas. Another option is to put curvature in the start and end of the bend with a press brake. As a practical matter, trimming the flat from the plate after it is rolled is the usual choice.

The pyramid roll turns slowly and its safety is sometimes taken for granted, but it can easily pull a person into the roll. Never wear loose clothing around a roll, and stay constantly alert to danger. Never work alone on this machine; an operator should be at the controls at all times in the event of mishap. This is one piece of equipment where rapid reaction to danger could save a life.

Pipe Bending

For handrail and structural trim, bent pipe is often specified. Specialty fabricators can bend pipe to almost any radius, but by far the easiest and least expensive way to bend aluminum tubing is to rent or borrow an electrician's hydraulic conduit bender, like the one manufactured by Enerpac. A standard heavy-wall-conduit bender has fixed-radius bending shoes for bending pipe sizes from ½ to 4 inches in diameter. For accurate layout of pipe bends, obtain radii at the center of the bends from manufacturers' data or by experimentation.

FORMING COMPOUND CURVATURE IN SHELL PLATE

For round-bilge hulls, as associated with sailboats, the shell plate must be given compound curvature (see Chapter 3). This requires actually stretching or shrinking the metal. The usual technique for introducing compound curvature into flat plate requires large presses and special forming dies so that the material can be pressed into the desired shape. Another method, used by the aircraft industry to form relatively thin aluminum, is the stretch-forming process. This process also requires large dies.

Figure 4-20 shows a special forming roll for forming long, narrow strips of aluminum into gentle double curvature sheets. This roll was fabricated and used during the construction of the sailboat shown in Figure 4-21. Long, narrow longitudinal strips of shell plate had a small amount of compound curvature rolled into flat strips that were used to obtain a very close approximation of a compound curvature.

Small hulls have been successfully produced using presses and stretch forming. Larger boats, however, require presses and stretch-forming equipment too large to be economical, so the common practice is to construct the hull from a number of pieces. These are first preformed using rolls or a brake, then welded together over a rigid framework to approximate a compound curvature surface. Weld beads are ground flush, and

Figure 4-20. A pinch roll designed for putting a small compound curvature in long, thin strips.

Figure 4-21. Robert Derecktor plated this 50-foot sailboat hull with long, narrow strips of compound-curved shell plate.

judicious use of mallets on the weld seams bring the surface closer to the shape desired. An inert filler, similar to body putty, is finally used to fair any imperfections on painted surfaces.

References

Aluminum Company of America. *Forming Alcoa Aluminum.* Pittsburgh, Pa.: Aluminum Company of America, 1962.

CHAPTER 5

Welding Aluminum

A commercial welding shop with 440-volt three-phase electrical power has a number of aluminum arc welding processes available, but few of these processes will operate on the 220-volt single-phase electrical power commonly available in a home workshop. Fortunately, there are relatively inexpensive compact machines available, such as the Millermatic 251 (Figure 5-1). This is a lightweight, powerful welding power source operating on 208/230-volt, single-phase, 50-Hz electrical power—i.e., compatible with standard 220 single-phase household power. Another compact machine is an AC inverter, such as the Miller XMT 200. With this equipment, a novice boatbuilder can do professional-quality aluminum welding in a home workshop. However, the aluminum that you can consistently weld with this equipment is limited to thicknesses of 3/16 inch or less. For aluminum greater than 3/16 inch, you'll need three-phase power.

Figure 5-1. Millermatic GMAW 251 welding machine.

In addition to the power source, you will also need an aluminum welding gun, either a self-contained 1-pound spool unit or a canister-fed push-pull gun.

MIG, TIG, and pulse-arc are three typical electric-arc aluminum-welding processes. All three use an inert shielding gas, usually 100 percent argon, to cover the weld zone. The gas flows over the weld area to create a gas envelope that protects the molten weld puddle from contamination by the atmosphere.

Each welding process has a particular application. The TIG (tungsten inert gas) process is similar to an electric brazing operation, where the filler metal is hand-fed into the weld puddle. TIG is very slow compared with other aluminum welding processes and allows high heat buildup, but because it is slow, it gives the welder more time to carefully deposit the weld metal, resulting in very high-quality welds. TIG welding is often used for items that require a *weld bead* that will be the finished product without further dressing—handrails and fuel tanks, for example.

Gas metal arc welding (GMAW), more commonly referred to as MIG (metal inert gas) welding, is a semiautomatic welding process that utilizes a welding-wire feeder unit and a welding gun, in addition to the welding power source. It is very fast and is the primary production welding process for aluminum boat building. The MIG process works well on aluminum ⅛ inch and thicker, but on lighter gauge metals it requires such a high rate of speed to keep the weld heat under control that few welders can keep up, and poor-quality welds result.

Pulse-arc is a refinement of the MIG process. Pulse-arc welding sequences and controls the amount of current, the frequency, and the duration of the welding arc, allowing the welder to better control the weld heat. It's used to weld very thin metal—from 0.060 inch to 0.160 inch—and a welder of average skills can use it to produce consistent, high-quality, spatter-free welds. Pulse-arc equipment is expensive and usually requires industrial three-phase power.

The best welding process for amateur and small-shop production of aluminum boats is the MIG process using 100 percent argon shielding gas and a push/pull wire feeder. The MIG process is the most versatile, the fastest, the most economical, and the easiest to learn of the commercial aluminum-welding processes. The Millermatic 251, wired for 208/230-volt single-phase 50-Hz input power, fitted with either a 1-pound-spool gun or wire feeder canister, is not a toy but a sturdy commercial welding machine used in many metal-fabricating shops.

To operate this equipment in your home workshop, first check your circuit-breaker panel for the amperage available to the 220-volt outlet you plan to use. A 200–250 amp MIG welding machine operating on 220-volt, single-phase, input power can draw up to 55 amps under full load. A typical 220 circuit for a clothes dryer or a kitchen range that is rated at 50 amps will usually be adequate, since the maximum draw of 55 amps is rarely required. If in doubt, check with your local welding-equipment supplier and a licensed electrician.

You can rent aluminum-welding equipment, a course worth considering if you don't already have the required welding equipment. Your local welding-supply house should be able to provide rental equipment compatible with your needs. A MIG welding outfit that utilizes a 1-pound spool of welding wire is often a good choice for a small boat.

DIRECT CURRENT MIG WELDING EQUIPMENT

MIG welding uses a consumable aluminum wire (electrode) to transfer metal to the joint and an inert gas to shield the weld area from the atmosphere. The process uses direct current (positive electrode), and the ground clamp is negative. MIG equipment is designed to automatically feed filler wire and shielding gas through the gun and into the weld area. With the tip of the filler wire in near proximity to the work, pull the trigger on the welding gun to start the wire feed and activate the welding current and inert gas flow. When the wire makes contact with the item to be welded, the arc is established.

MIG welding equipment consists of the following:

- DC power source is the main welding machine.
- Welding wire feeder feeds welding electrode to the welding gun.
- Welding gun deposits electrode into the weld puddle.
- Shielding gas, usually argon, compressed and in a bottle that is connected to the feeder. The gas flows from the bottle to the wire feeder to the welding gun.
- Regulator/flow meter controls the rate of gas flow and is attached to the bottle.
- A *stretch* is the bundle of electrical wires that provide welding current and welding-machine electronic information from the power source to the feeder; sometimes the argon gas tube is included in the stretch.
- A *whip* is the bundle of conduit, tubes, and electrical cables that provide filler wire, shielding gas, electrical power, and electronic information to the welding gun from the wire feeder.
- A ground lead with a ground clamp provides a current path from the work back to the welding power source. Often the ground clamp is

attached to a convenient position on the boat hull close to the welding power source, effectively using the new hull as a portion of the ground circuit. This eliminates the need for a long ground lead.
- Power cord connects the welding power source to the electrical outlet.

Power Source

A good choice for the home workshop is the Millermatic 251 MIG welding machine. The Millermatic 251 can operate on normal 220-volt, single-phase household power and produce a high-quality weld for aluminum up to 3/16 inch thick. (For welding thicker aluminum consult the Miller Welding web site at www.millerwelds.com/products/mig/) Your welding equipment supplier can fit the power supply cord with a special plug to fit a household 220-volt dryer or stove outlet. The unit is equipped with digital meters to allow presetting of voltage and wire feed speed (amperage).

The predetermined machine settings for specific welding circumstances are listed in Table 5-1. As you gain experience with your welding system, you can fine-tune these settings through trial and error. You can make fine adjustments to the welding machine settings when welding in different positions.

Whatever your welding power source, it should have a power cord and ground lead long enough to locate it anywhere in your workshop area and be capable of producing consistent, high-quality aluminum welds.

Welding Wire Feeder and Welding Gun

Two types of welding wire feeders are commonly used by small boat shops: (1) the 1-pound-spool gun (such as the one manufactured by Miller) and (2) the production feeder with the wire canister separate from the gun (available from a number of sources).

The 1-pound-spool gun (Figure 5-2) has a small spool of aluminum welding (filler) wire mounted on the gun itself. The elimination of a separate welding-wire canister makes the spool-gun feeder the least expensive of the two. The spool gun is mobile and popular for tack-welding. It's often found in shops that do occasional aluminum welding. The price per pound for 1-pound spools of welding wire is considerably more than for the larger welding-wire spools, but despite this, some professional aluminum boat builders use the 1-pound-spool gun exclusively because of the high degree of mobility.

Welding Aluminum

Weld Type	Stock Thickness, Inches	Position*	Passes/ Weld	Speed Inches/ Min/Pass	Welding Arc		Argon		Electrode		
					Current Amps DC	Voltage Volts	Flow Ft³/ Hr	Used Ft³/ 100 ft	Diameter, Inches	Speed, Inch/ Min	Used per 10 ft Weld, lb
Butt weld	1/8	Flat	1	24	110	20	30	34	3/64	175	2
		H & V			100		30	35		170	2
		OVHD			105		40	38		170	2.5
	3/16	Flat	1	24	170	20	30	57	3/64	235	4.5
		H & V		20	150		35	75		215	4.5
		OVHD		18	160		40	80		225	5
Fillet weld	1/8	Flat	1	30	125	20	30	55	3/64	190	2
		H & V		24	115		30	70		180	
		OVHD		24	110		40	75		175	
	3/16	Flat	1	24	190	20	30	55	3/64	255	4.5
		H & V		20	165		35	70		230	
		OVHD		20	180		40	75		245	
Corner weld	1/8	Flat	1	30	110	20	30	34	3/64	175	2
		H & V		24	100		30	35		170	
		OVHD		24	100		40	38		170	
	3/16	Flat	1	30	170	20	30	57	3/64	235	4.5
		H & V		24	150		35	75		215	
		OVHD		24	160		35	80		225	

For welding material more than 3/16 inch thick, consult the Aluminum Association's *Aluminum Welder's Training Manual*.
*H & V = horizontal and vertical; OVHD = overhea. See Fig. 5-3.

The most popular production aluminum-welding wire feeder uses a 10-pound spool of welding wire mounted in a separate canister unit. The unit feeds wire (from 0.035- to 3/64-inch diameter) through a conduit to the gun. Similar systems for welding steel have a push-only feeder, but aluminum, because of its high coefficient of friction, requires a push/pull type of wire feeder. This requires feed rollers in both the feeder unit and at the welding gun. Although a push-only wire

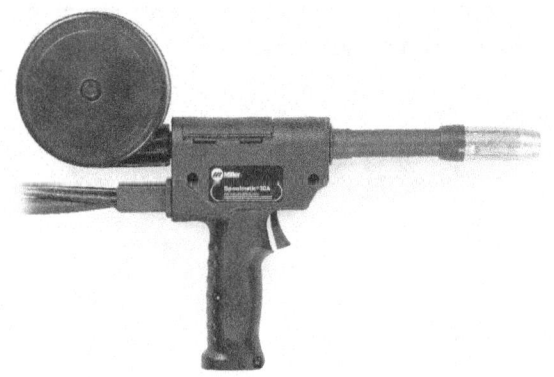

Figure 5-2. Miller Spoolmatic 1-pound-spool gun.

feeder can be used with aluminum, the length of the whip, the cable connecting the feeder to the gun, is often too short to be of practical use for boatbuilding.

There are a number of styles and manufacturers of push/pull feeders and guns. MIG guns are either air- or water-cooled. For small-boat building, an air-cooled welding gun is preferred because of its simplicity and lower maintenance requirements. Your local welding-equipment supplier can show you the various systems available.

The whip between the wire feeder and the welding gun should be at least 15 feet long. A conduit inside the whip delivers the welding wire from the feeder to the gun. The whip also contains the electric power lead, the shielding-gas tube, and, for guns that are water cooled, the tubing for the water.

The welding gun itself can have either a pistol-grip or gooseneck configuration. The gooseneck gun provides better access to tight areas; access to tight spots when using a pistol-grip welding gun is gained through the use of special, readily installed and removable tip attachments. Despite this inconvenience, many welders still prefer the pistol-grip gun.

The welding gun incorporates a set of rollers, preferably electrically powered, that pull the weld wire through the whip. (Some older welding guns have air-driven feed rollers that have been known to allow small amounts of lubricating oil on the filler wire, resulting in weld porosity.) The rollers are sized for the welding wire being used, and proper tension between the rollers and the welding wire is important. A feed control on the gun adjusts the speed of the wire feed.

MIG welding guns have a removable contact tip that provides the electrical contact between the power source and the welding wire. Tips usually are copper and sized for the welding wire being used. Have a few spare contact tips available while you're learning because they're easily destroyed by improper welding technique.

Stretch

The *stretch* is the electrical cable connecting the DC power source to the welding wire feeder. When building a small boat and using a production feeder, you need the stretch to be at least 20 feet long. With this length, you can locate the feeder at almost any location around the boat, allowing you to use the gun to weld all parts of the boat without having to move the power source. The combined lengths of the power cord, whip, and stretch set the maximum reach for the welding gun from the electrical outlet supplying the DC power.

Because the feeder on a 1-pound-spool gun is attached to the gun, the stretch connects the gun directly to the power source and to the gas bottle; there isn't a whip. For the spool gun, I recommend at least 30 feet of stretch, which will allow you to reach all parts of a 20-foot boat without moving the power source.

Inert Shielding Gas

Integral with the MIG welding process is the use of an *inert shielding gas*, normally argon (although helium is sometimes used, and mixtures of gases may be recommended for special applications). The shielding gas provides two functions: (1) a better path than air for current transfer, and (2) a gas envelope at the weld zone that protects the molten weld puddle from contamination from the atmosphere. In addition, argon partially removes aluminum oxide from the weld area, although the reason for this oxide removal is not well understood.

The shielding gas envelope must be protected from wind, which can blow the gas away from the weld zone, resulting in contamination of the weld puddle. This is one of the primary reasons why MIG welding of aluminum should be done indoors, free from drafts. If working outside, avoid windy days, and shield the work area from the wind with tarps or by other means.

Argon (100 percent) is preferred by most boatbuilders for MIG-welding aluminum since it provides additional cleaning action, a more stable arc, and less weld spatter than helium. Helium is preferred when using fully automatic welding, for heavy weldments, and in some overhead applications because of the gas density. Mixtures of helium and argon, with improved characteristics for certain applications, are available from welding suppliers.

Gas flow is started and stopped with the gun's trigger-switch. Some welding machines have a post-flow timer, allowing shielding gas to continue to flow for a brief period after the release of the trigger-switch, thus providing shielding gas to the weld until it solidifies.

The flow rate must be adequate to protect the weld puddle—see Table 5-1 for some recommended flow rates. Since shielding gases are expensive, excessive flow rates are not recommended. Common practice is to experiment by turning down the flow rate until weld contamination is evident, then turning the flow rate back up slightly for a safety margin.

Welding Filler Wire

MIG welding filler wire is available in either 1- or 10-pound spools. As noted earlier, the more popular production aluminum-wire feeder uses the 10-pound spool; the special 1-pound-spool gun uses the smaller spool. The cost of the welding wire is considerably more if purchased in 1-pound spools.

Welding-wire sizes vary, depending upon the application. For most aluminum boat building applications, a wire diameter of 0.035 to 0.045 inch is a good choice. The maximum size that can be used with 220-volt single-phase MIG welding systems is about 0.045.

The most common welding filler wire is alloy 5356, which is compatible with a wide range of aluminum alloys commonly used in boatbuilding. It can be used to join alloys 5052, 5086, 6061, or 6063 to themselves or to dissimilar alloys. Recently, some boatbuilders have been using 4043 filler wire, since it is easier to weld and looks nice. This wire is rated excellent for corrosion but has poor tensile strength. Use it for alloy 6061 or 5052 welding, but not for welding alloys 5083 or 5086, or in areas requiring high weld strength.

Welding wire should be clean and of high quality. The best method of insuring quality wire is to use it as soon as possible after removal from the package. Other methods and tips follow:

- Keep the wire clean and dry, free from dirt, water, oils, or other surface contaminants.
- Prevent contamination of your welding wire by cleaning weld-wire feeders, conduits, and drive rollers.
- Check the drive rollers in feeders and welding guns that have been used to weld steel. Oils are often present and must be removed prior to loading aluminum filler wire.
- Keep the welding spool covered during welding to prevent dirt buildup.
- Visually inspect your welding wire before using it; this is usually adequate to ensure cleanliness.
- If the wire appears dirty, remove and discard about two full wraps from the spool prior to attempting any welding.

SETTING UP YOUR WELDING SHOP

Estimated Costs

For a home workshop, or a shop anticipating only occasional aluminum welding, an aluminum-welding power supply such as the Millermatic 251 is a good setup, costing approximately $1,800. Add to this, a 1-pound-spool gun setup at $875. Welding wire sells by the pound, with wire on a 10-pound spool costing approximately 50 percent less than wire on 1-pound spools. Argon gas sells by the 100-cubic-foot unit (prices vary regionally and by the amount you purchase).

Since the price and capability of welding equipment vary, you should contact a welding-equipment supplier for suggestions on the type of equipment best suited to your needs. If you are building only one boat, then renting equipment may be a better option.

Equipment

To assemble a fully functional MIG aluminum-welding outfit operating on 220-volt single-phase input power, as described above, you need the following components:

- A DC power source set for 208/230-volt single-phase 50-Hz input, with a power cord of adequate length and fitted with a male plug compatible with the electrical outlet to be used.
- A welding-wire feeder and a welding gun configured as one of the following:
  1. A 1-pound-spool gun, fitted with a contact tip and drive rollers for 0.035 and 0.045-inch-diameter (3/64") filler wire and having a stretch at least 30 feet long, or
  2. A push/pull canister-type wire feeder having a stretch of at least 20 feet and a whip of at least 15 feet. Both the feeder and the gun should have drive rollers for both 0.035 and 0.045-inch-diameter (3/64") filler wire. The gun should be equipped with contact tips for the same wire.
- A ground clamp on a lead at least 20 feet long to provide the negative ground.
- A compressed-gas bottle filled with argon, preferably at least 150 cubic feet.

- A gas regulator and flow meter with fittings compatible with those on the stretch.
- Six 1-pound spools of alloy-5356 filler wire or, if using a push/pull canister-type feeder, one 10-pound spool of filler wire.
- At least three spare contact tips for the welding gun.
- One spare welding-gun gas cup.
- If using a pistol-type welding gun, one gun-nozzle adapter kit for restricted-access welding and one spare curved contact tip.

WELDER'S GEAR

To use MIG welding equipment, you must wear a full-face welding hood with a #10 or #11 lens for welding at or below 200 amps. Welders often attach a leather flap to the bottom of the welding hood to protect the exposed skin on the neck from arc burn. This piece of leather is usually about 6 inches square and pop-riveted to the hood's base. Clear safety glasses worn under the hood provide eye protection when the hood is up. Welding gloves and leather sleeves round out the welder's safety gear. Lastly, you will need a clean stainless steel hand wire brush for removing contaminants and soot from the weld.

TESTING YOUR WELDING SYSTEM

Once you have your new welding equipment, you'll need to test it. The very best way to evaluate new equipment is to have a professional from the welding-supply house assist you with the start-up of the system and the initial test welding at your shop. This will reduce the time to debug the equipment.

Welding-supplier representatives are often highly qualified welders who can offer sound advice for both the operation and the care of the equipment. Such a representative will provide the needed expertise to get the equipment on line and will suggest machine settings for the best results. (In addition, see Table 5-1 listing recommended settings for voltage, amperage, gas flow, and travel speed for MIG welding 1/8-inch and 3/16-inch aluminum.)

Getting to Know Your Equipment

You've set up and tested the welding equipment; next, spend some time learning how to use it and practicing welds. If you have a friend who is an experienced aluminum welder, solicit his assistance. But keep in mind that a welder who does a professional job on his machine at his shop may be out of his element on your machine in your shop. See how your welder friend performs prior to asking him to do a critical weld for you. With practice, you may be able to do it better.

Select some small scrap pieces of aluminum, similar in thickness to what you'll be working with, and practice. Try different welding positions and various machine settings as shown in Figure 5-3.

Practice welding under different conditions. For example, try welding both aluminum you've carefully cleaned first and aluminum you haven't cleaned. See a difference? Also notice the difference between welding cold and hot metal. Look for crater cracks at the termination of your welds.

One of the most important factors contributing to good weld quality is operator comfort, achieved mainly by placing your material in the easiest welding position possible. It's usually easiest to weld when the work is lying flat and about workbench high. (This is called the "flat" position in welding terms.)

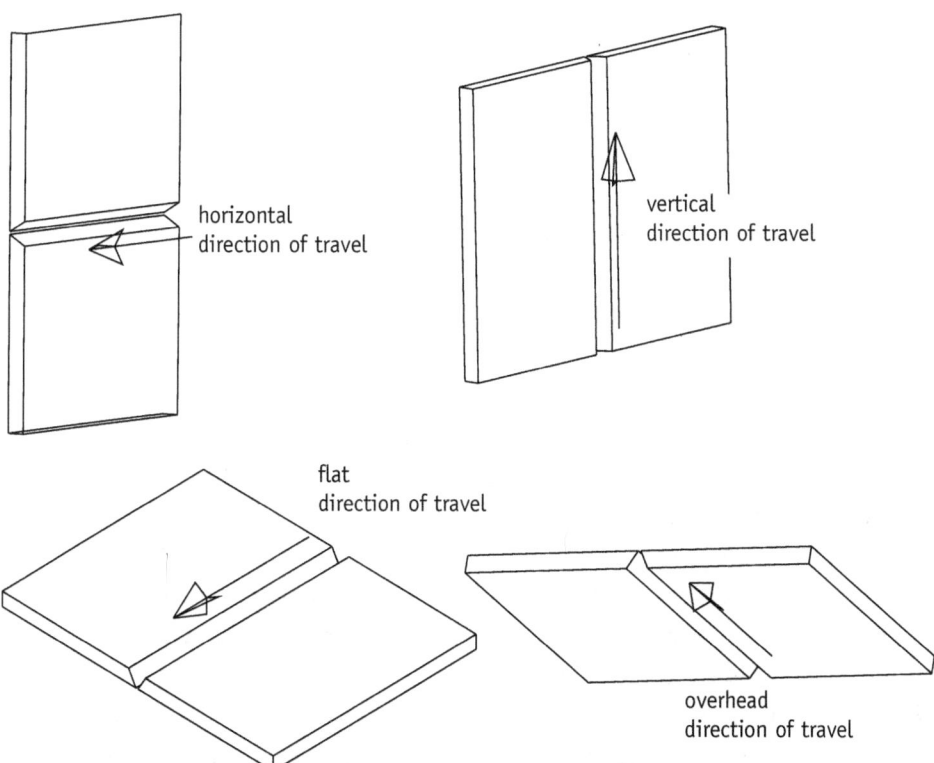

Figure 5-3. Welding positions.

You should have full visual access to the weld area with the welding hood down, and free motion of the gun over the entire area to be welded. Make a dry run of the weld beforehand to be sure that the equipment is located in the correct position and there aren't any restrictions to movement.

WELDING TECHNIQUE

Before you begin welding, be sure you have a full-face welding hood with a proper lens, safety glasses for under the hood, welding gloves, and welder's leather sleeve. Check the welding hood for light leaks and repair any you find. Put on the hood, gloves, and sleeves before starting a weld.

Assemble the welding power source, feeder, power and ground leads, argon bottle, and argon regulator into a complete welding system. Plug the welding power source into a 220-volt, single-phase outlet. Prepare for welding by testing the machine settings for the welding position and the thickness of the material to be welded. These steps follow:

1. Turn on the welding machine and set the amps and volts in accordance with Table 5-1.
2. Turn on the gas (argon) and adjust the rate of flow by turning on the power source and depressing the welding-gun trigger-switch, observing the rate of flow at the flow meter. Set the initial flow rate in accordance with Table 5-1. Adjust the flow rate later as necessary.
3. Set the feed rate on the welding gun to Fast.
4. Connect the ground clamp to a piece of scrap metal and try a welding pass. Then, when you've found a comfortable speed, you're ready to start welding on the boat.
5. The desired arc length is ⅛ to ⅜ inch between the work and the contact tip of the welding gun—visually check it during welding. Move the tip of the welding gun either closer to or farther from the work to adjust the arc length.
6. Weld a sample pass and observe the amperage draw on the meter. (A helper is handy here, in that he or she can observe the amperage draw while the weld bead is being placed.)
7. Keep running test passes and adjusting the power settings by turning the weld-power rheostat until the amperage shown on the meter is within the range of the specified amperage shown in Table 5-1.

8. When the amperage is okay, adjust the voltage reading to be in the range shown in Table 5-1.
9. Readjust amperage, voltage, gas flow, and wire feed as necessary, until the weld bead is being deposited at the desired gas flow, arc length, amperage, voltage, and rate of feed.
10. Listen to the sound of the welding process. It should be a consistent high-frequency buzzing with very little popping or crackling.
11. While testing the machine settings, practice post-weld purging and reversing the direction of travel for about 1 inch at the end of a weld bead. You will always have a crater crack at the end of a weld, and the reversing technique puts the crater over sound weld, eliminating the weak weld area. To properly complete the weld, remove the crack by chipping or sawing. (Word of caution: chances are that by the time you get the machine adjusted, your test plate will be very hot.)
12. Try your settings on a piece of material of about the same temperature as the part you wish to weld and the same thickness. If the bead looks good, you're ready to weld.

Back Chipping

When two plates are butt welded, the back side of the first weld pass is usually contaminated by exposure to the atmosphere, requiring removal of the contaminated weld from the weld zone. This contaminated material is usually removed by back chipping (sawing out the contaminated metal), most commonly done with a circular saw and a carbide tipped blade, or alternatively, with a small carbide-tipped saw blade mounted on a small angle grinder. You can also use a die grinder. The depth of the cut is only deep enough to remove all visible traces of porosity or visible contaminant. Use of an abrasive grinder for back chipping is not recommended because the abrasive residue from the grinding wheel is left in the groove.

For back chipping with a circular saw, retract the blade guard and lower the saw blade into the weld until it is sufficiently deep to gouge out the defective weld deposit and expose clean metal. This procedure is so simple that for most aluminum hulls, no other back-chipping technique is required on the exterior plates. To back chip welds in restricted areas, use a pneumatic chisel, die grinder, or small carbide-tipped circular-saw blade fitted to a die grinder equipped with a right-angle drive.

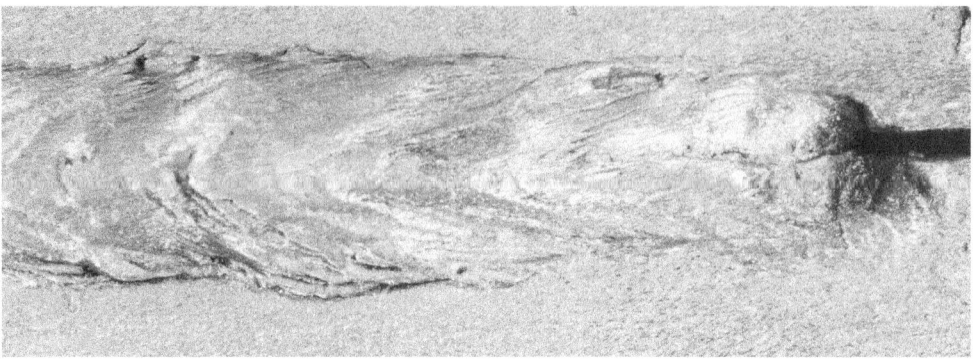

Figure 5-4. Crater crack at termination of a weld bead.

CRATER CRACKING

You've finished welding an aluminum tank, only to put a pressure test on it and find a leak at the start and stop of every weld pass. This is a common problem and is caused by crater cracking, cracks that form in the weld bead from the rapid cooling and contraction of the weld metal. Figure 5-4 shows a crater crack at the termination of a weld bead.

One method of resolving this problem is to back weld slightly at the end of a weld bead. Reverse the direction of travel and weld back over the new weld bead about 1 inch before breaking the arc, as shown in Figure 5-5. This should ensure

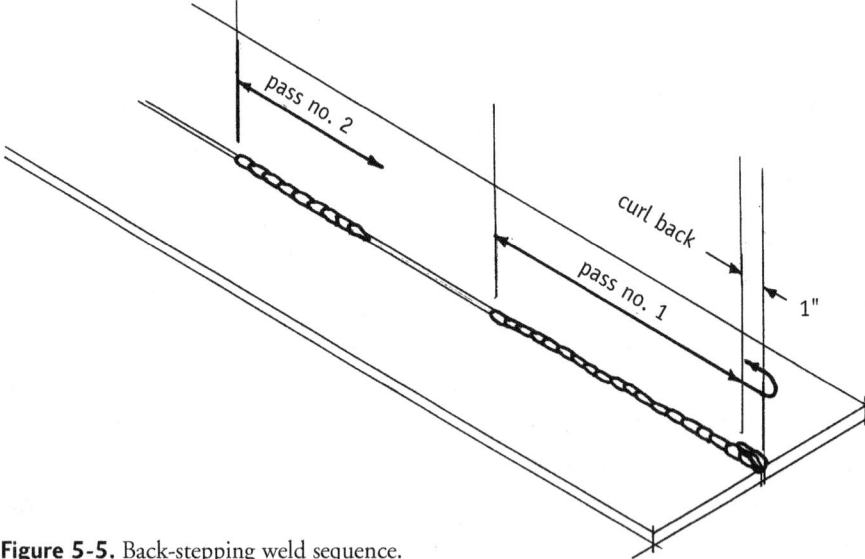

Figure 5-5. Back-stepping weld sequence.

that the crater crack will form over sound metal. After the weld cools, remove the cracked area by back chipping.

Because of crater cracking, you will always have to back chip at the termination of each weld bead to insure a sound weld.

Applying a Weld

The preferred way of applying a weld is to use a pushing motion while keeping the tip of the gun sloped at about 10 degrees away from the direction of travel (Figure 5-6). This is called pushing the weld bead. Applying the bead with a slight weaving motion will encourage good fusion and often gives a bead an excellent appearance.

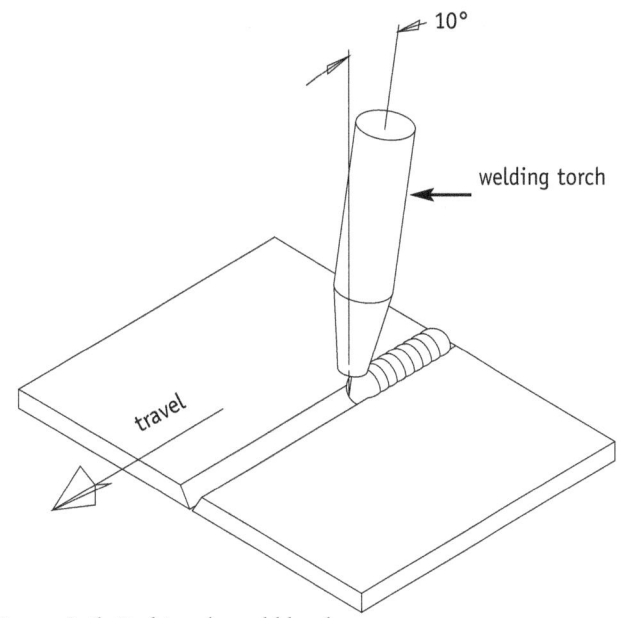

Figure 5-6. Pushing the weld bead.

Overcoming Heat Buildup

The high heat that builds up when laying down a continuous weld bead on aluminum can cause some problems. For example, when welding thin aluminum—1/8 inch or less—it's sometimes impossible to push the weld bead fast enough to prevent excessive melting of the parent metal. The result is often blow-through (just what it sounds like). In these cases, especially in the vertical and horizontal welding positions, the solution is to use a down-hand pass: keep the slope of the torch at about 10 degrees (see Figure 5-6) and reverse the direction of travel. The result is you are actually dragging the weld bead, allowing a much faster rate of travel and, consequently, less heat buildup.

Heat buildup can also cause welded material to warp. To avoid this, it's generally wise to use a back-stepping welding sequence:

1. Weld a bead between 6 and 12 inches long in a direction of travel away from you and terminate the bead with a 1-inch-long reverse (curl-back).

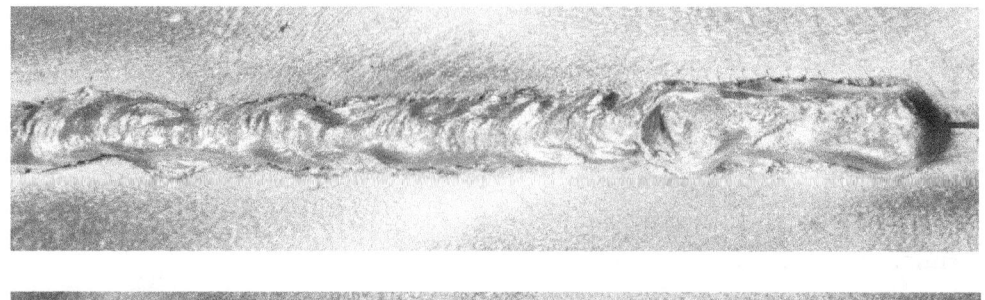
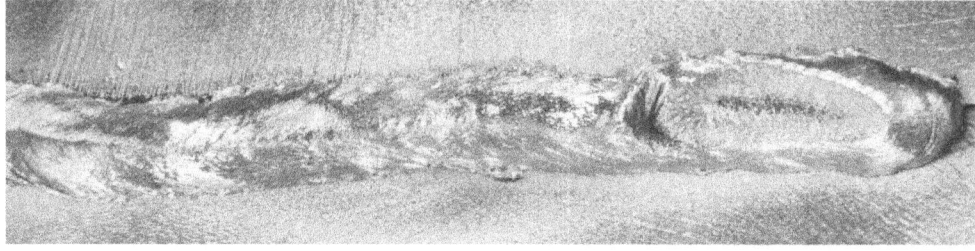
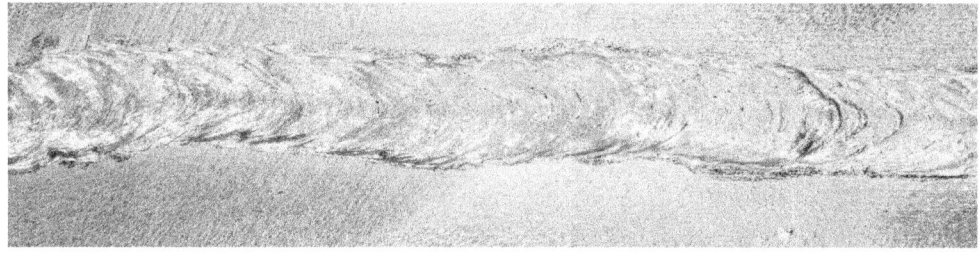

Figure 5-7. Weld bead appearance. Top: Cold. Center: Too hot. Bottom: Good.

2. Reposition the gun 6 to 12 inches from the start of this weld, and weld toward it (Figure 5-5).
3. Overlap the first weld slightly (1 inch) with the new bead. In effect, you're welding over the start of the first pass.
4. Start a third bead 6 to 12 inches from the second one, and so on, repeating this back-step sequence until the entire seam is welded.
5. Remove the slightly higher weld-bead crown at the overlaps, as well as crater cracks, by using an abrasive grinder, die grinder, or saw.

A high-crown weld bead is usually due to low heat, while flat, no-crown, or sunken weld beads are caused by too much heat. Figure 5-7 shows the difference in appearance between a cold and a hot weld bead. You can reduce weld heat slightly by turning down the amperage.

Welding Aluminum

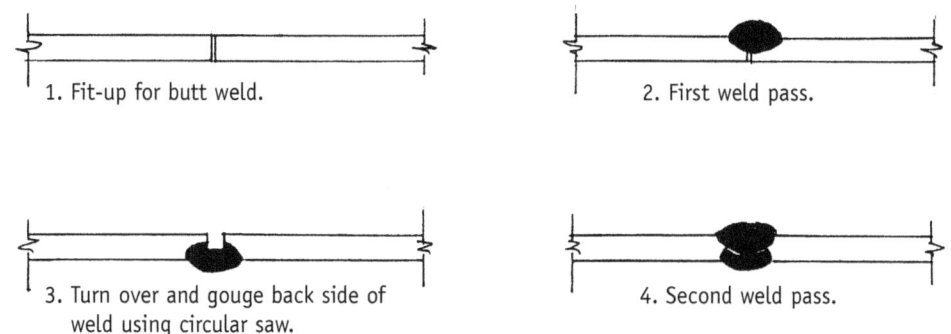

Figure 5-8. Butt-welding sequence.

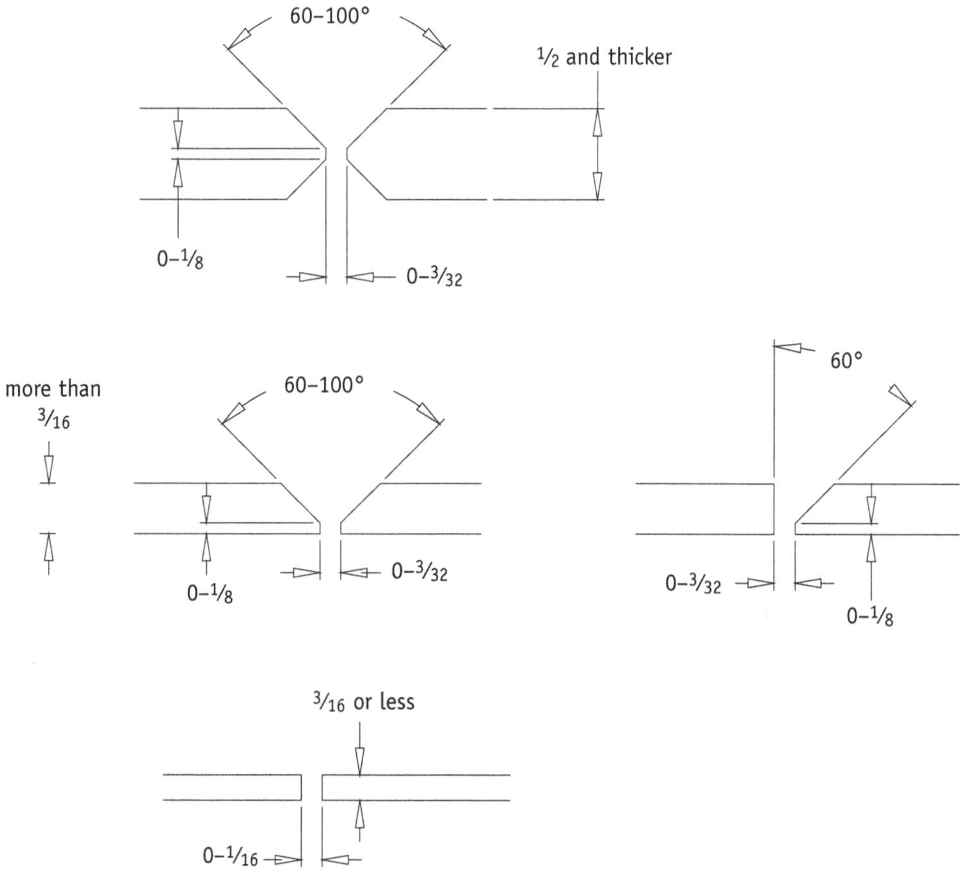

Figure 5-9. Weld groove preparation.

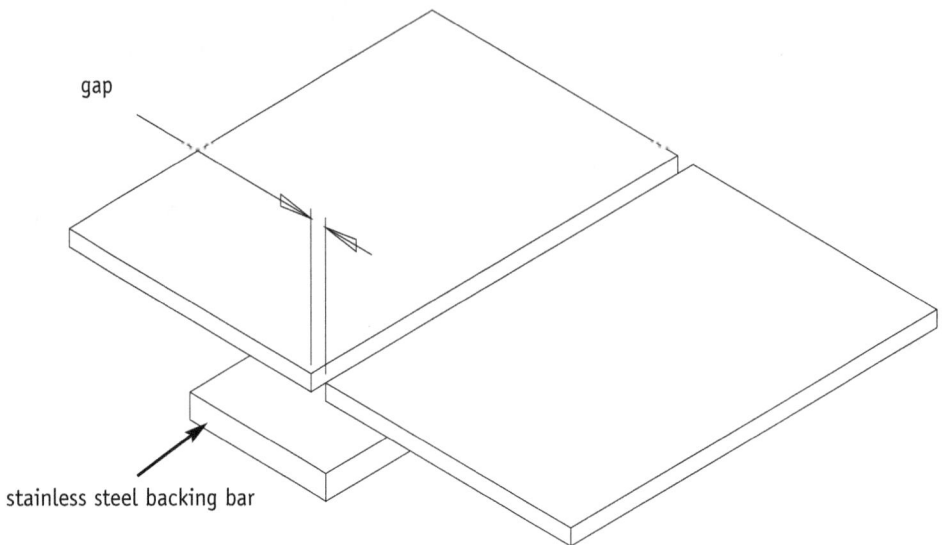

Figure 5-10. Stainless steel backing bar when filling a large gap in a critical area.

JOINT PREPARATION

Oxides and oils coat all unfinished aluminum, so before you begin welding, you must remove them from the area you plan to weld and up to 1 inch on each side of the weld. Do this initial surface cleaning with a power angle grinder fitted with a rubber backing pad and either an 80-grit sanding disc or a Scotch-Brite abrasive pad available from a welding supplier. Stainless steel wire brushes will rapidly remove aluminum oxide and dirt, but they load up with the oils from the aluminum surface and must be cleaned at regular intervals to avoid weld contamination.

The single biggest cause of weld contamination is oil on the work piece. Oils break down under the welding arc and create hydrogen bubbles that cause a very porous and weak weld. Solvent, such as acetone or alcohol, is a good degreaser for cleaning local areas for welding. (A word of caution: These solvents are very flammable.) Remove dirt and oxides by mechanical means, then wipe down the area with solvent and a clean rag just prior to welding. Dirt and other contaminants on poorly cleaned aluminum show up as dark spots in the weld.

It is rarely necessary on a small boat to bevel the edge of a plate for welding since the material is usually not more than 3/16 inch thick. All butt welds are straight butts, without a bevel. Where you need full penetration, butt weld the material from one side, back chip to sound metal from the opposite side, then reweld on the back-chipped side (Figure 5-8). Beveling plate edges before welding only becomes important when the aluminum is more than 3/16 inch thick, as shown in Figure 5-9.

When a large gap in a critical area must be filled, a stainless steel backing bar can help. Secure the bar in position against the back side of the weld joint (Figure 5-10) to help contain molten metal to the area of the weld joint. Remove the bar after you've completed the welding. Then back chip the back side of the weld area and reweld as necessary.

You could use an aluminum backing bar, but it will fuse to the weld joint. Then you will need to remove it after welding by sawing or grinding or leave it in place as part of the joint. Do not leave aluminum backing bars at critical welds since they can foster corrosion and cause high stress concentrations.

The welding procedures described above are the bare minimum requirements to effectively weld aluminum 3/16-inch or thinner using the MIG process. Thicker material requires full-penetration welding. The *Aluminum Welder's Training Manual and Exercises* (see reference listing at the end of this chapter) is an excellent guide to the additional requirements of full-penetration welding. More information on aluminum welding can be found in the other references listed at the end of this chapter.

FIT-UP FOR WELDING

Good fit-up (small weld gap) is a requirement for quality welding, just as it is for woodwork or pipe fitting. The size of the gap between adjoining surfaces to be welded will greatly affect the quality of the weld. Weld joints with very little gap (1/16 inch or less) are much easier and faster to weld than joints with a large gap, and a tight fit reduces weld heat and distortion. Neat, uniform gaps between surfaces to be welded will significantly contribute to the consistency and quality of the weld joint.

Butt welding requires close attention to fit-up, particularly between shell plates. The adjoining surfaces must be in close *alignment* to ensure a fair surface. One method of ensuring close alignment is to

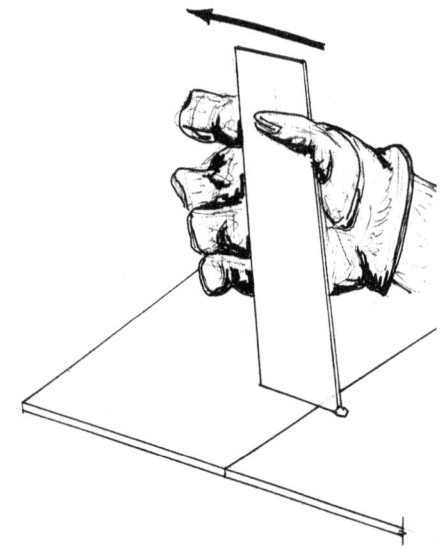

Figure 5-11. Using a flat bar to lever plates into alignment.

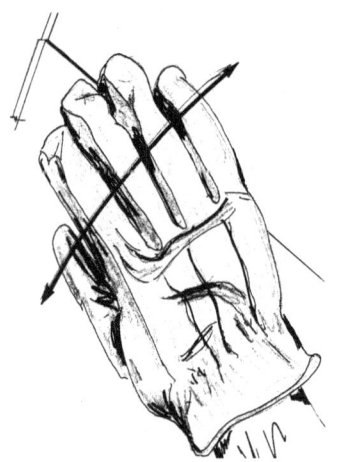

Figure 5-12. Checking plate alignment by feel, using a gloved hand.

place a flat bar on end, straddling the weld seam. Tack-weld one corner of the bar—just enough to hold it in place—to the lower of the two plates (Figure 5-11). Apply pressure to the top of the bar to force the two plates into alignment, with the tack-weld acting as a hinge. Look for any slight misalignments by running your gloved hand across the seam to be welded (Figure 5-12). After aligning the plate edges, tack-weld them together to sufficiently hold the alignment in the immediate area of the bar/lever. Then pull the bar in the opposite direction, away from the weld seam, to break the hinge tack-weld, and remove the bar. Reposition the bar as needed to continue the fairing process, tack-welding along the butt seam until it is in 100 percent alignment. When all alignment and tack-welding is completed, grind off the remains of the hinge tack-welds and sand the areas to restore the surface fairness of the aluminum plate.

When you need more pressure than a simple flat-bar-and-tack-hinge arrangement can provide, use saddles or dogs, with wedges (Figure 5-13). And for maximum alignment pressure, use a hydraulic jack in place of wedges. All of these procedures result in some damage to the plate surface, so use only when necessary.

Plates to be welded must not only be the same height, they must be in the same plane (Figure 5-14). Temporary structural members called *strongbacks* (see Figure 5-15) can be tack-welded to the plates to hold them in alignment. Once the material is aligned, weld the seam securely, remove any saddles or other tem-

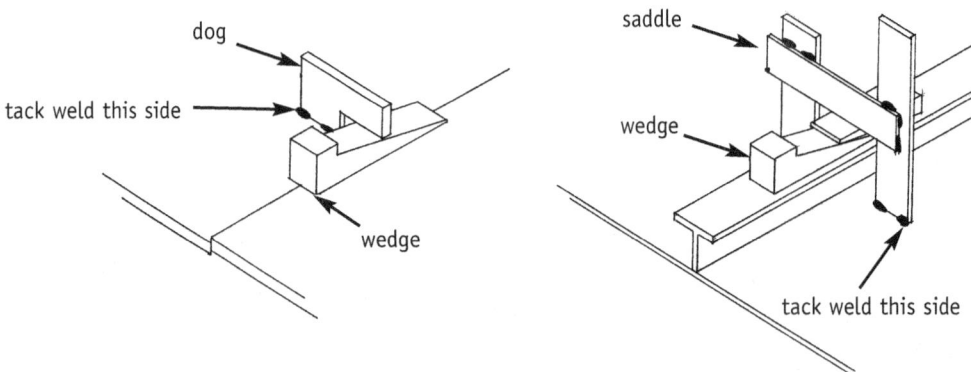

Figure 5-13. Saddle and wedge alignment.

porary alignment aids, and grind the temporary weld beads flush.

Butt Welding

Welding of plates together to produce a larger plate is called *butt welding*. The location of butt joints is influenced by the size of the plate available, the required levels of strength, and the fairness in the welded structure. Avoid locating butt joints in highly stressed areas since there is a small loss of strength in the heat-affected zone of welding, as shown in Figure 2-1.

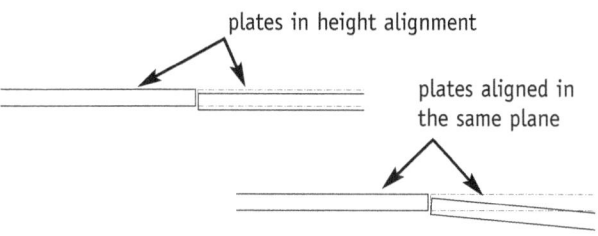

Figure 5-14. Aligning plates in the same plane.

Mechanical stiffening of the panel, provided by framing in close proximity to the weld seam, can reduce distortion in the panel. This often results in butt welds being located approximately 3 inches from a framing member.

Materials 3/16 inch or less in thickness, and sometimes up to 1/4 inch thick, are butt welded from one side without pre-beveling. Full-penetration welding is

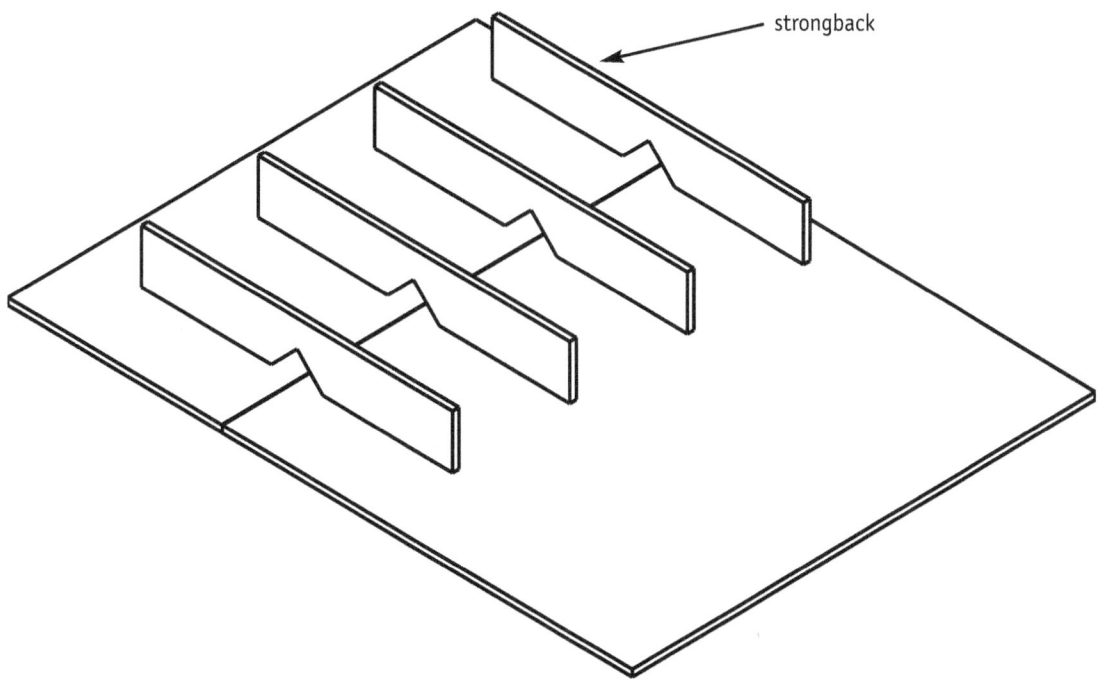

Figure 5-15. Temporary strongbacks.

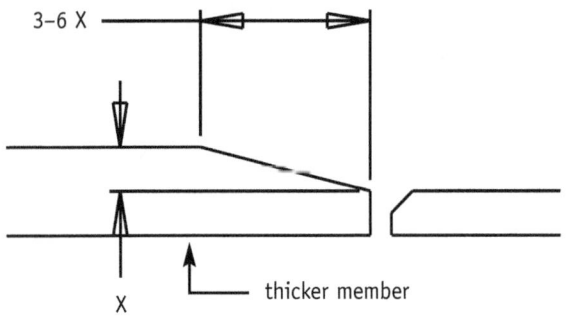

Figure 5-16. Edge preparation for butt welding plates of different thicknesses.

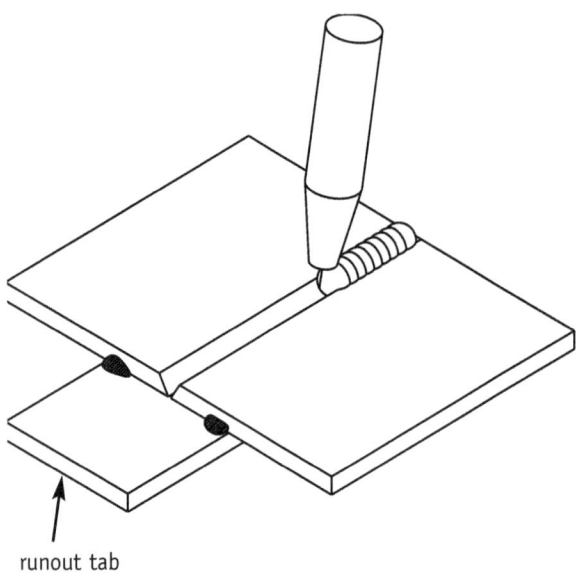

Figure 5-17. Butt welding to the edge of two plates using a runout tab.

accomplished by back-chipping then welding up the back-chipped groove. The result is similar to pre-beveling. The back-chipping process is therefore sometimes used on thicker plates to prepare the joint without pre-beveling, but pre-beveling thicker materials is usually preferred.

Preparation of plate for butt welding, if the material thickness of the thinner member is greater than 3/16 inch, requires beveling of at least one member to ensure full fusion in the weld zone. Figure 5-9 shows a number of weld preparation configurations for different material thicknesses.

Preparation for butt joints between plates of two different thicknesses when the difference is more than 1/8 inch should include beveling the thicker member at a slope of three to six times the difference in thickness (Figure 5-16).

Runout Tabs

To insure full fusion that is free from crater cracking at the exposed ends of plate butt welds, use *runout tabs*. Runout tabs are made from aluminum and used in a similar manner as backing bars (Figure 5-17).

Fillet Welds

Use *fillet welding* to join two members in a lapped joint or at approximately right angles to each other, in an "L" or "T" configuration, similar to Figure 5-18. Fillet welding can be either intermittent or continuous:

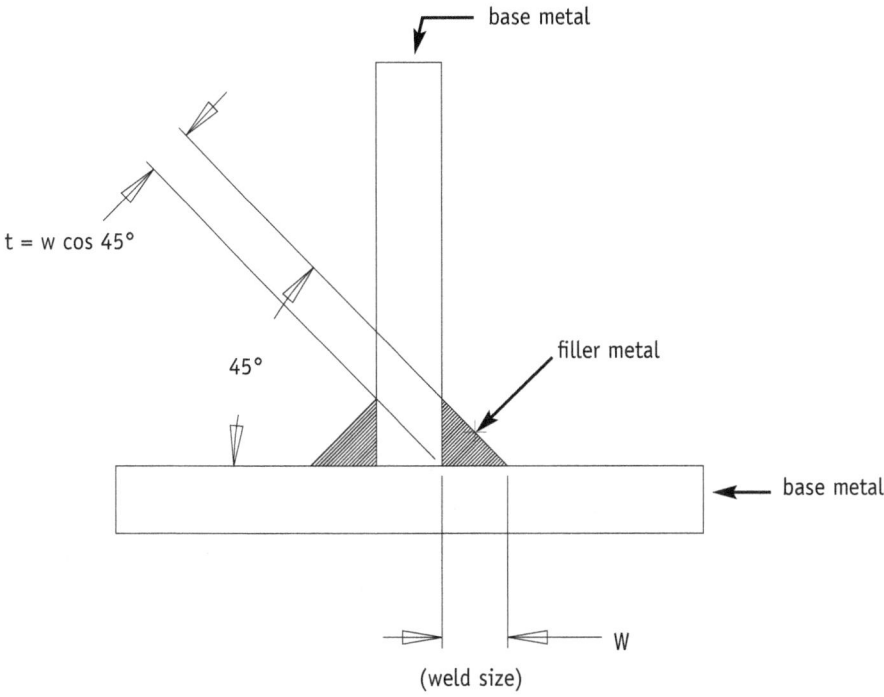

Figure 5-18. Typical double fillet weld cross section.

- Continuous fillet weld—runs the full length of the weld joint.
- Double continuous fillet weld—a continuous weld on both sides of the welded member; considered the strongest fillet weld and best able to resist impact loading and fatigue.
- Intermittent staggered fillet weld—short segments of weld, with spacing in between; weld deposits alternate from one side to the other side, as shown in Figure 5-19A.
- Intermittent chain welding—symmetrical weld deposits on both sides of the structural member, as shown in Figure 5-19B.

Fillet welds are used extensively in joining structural members, such as longitudinals to shell plate, and flanges to the webs of built-up frames. The strength of continuous fillet welds is generally not needed in most areas of small boat and yacht construction. Although continuous fillet welding is preferable in areas of high stress, repetitive loading, and vibration, avoid using it in other areas to reduce distortion and annealing. Unnecessary continuous welding, or welds larger than necessary, can cause full annealing of the base metal and excessive shrinkage.

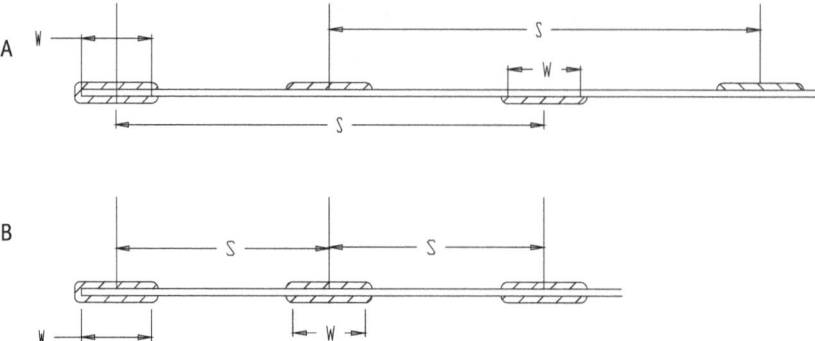

Figure 5-19. Intermittent welding: intermittent staggered fillet weld (A); intermittent chain fillet weld (B).

Shrinkage on the opposite side of the plate from the weld, commonly called "print-through," can result in an unsightly ridge on an otherwise smooth plate.

Use intermittent fillet welds in areas other than high-stress areas to reduce both production costs and distortion.

Minimum Size of Double Continuous Fillet Welds

As a rule, fillet welds are sized only sufficiently strong so that the thinner member of the base metal will fail in the heat-affected zone before either the throat of the weld or the boundary between the weld and the base metal fails. Welds larger than required do not offer additional strength to the finished weldment.

Classification societies specify 100 percent continuous welding for all butt welds and fillet welds subject to high stress. In areas subject to other than high stress, intermittent fillet welds are used. The optimum size of the fillet weld itself is controlled by the thickness of the thinner base metal and the alloys of the base metals and filler metal. The calculation of the optimum fillet weld size is based upon a symmetrical double continuous fillet weld. Table 5-2 shows results of weld size calculations I've prepared based on data from Kaiser Aluminum for commonly used marine alloys. This optimum size of a fillet weld is the same for both continuous and intermittent welds.

Weld size and the spacing of intermittent fillet welds are the major areas of concern for a boatbuilder, since this type of weld constitutes a large percentage of hull structural welding and represents a good percentage of weld failures. Historically, most fillet weld failures have occurred in slamming impact areas in the forward 50 percent of the waterline length between bottom longitudinal stiffeners

TABLE 5-2	Minimum size of double continuous fillet welds.					
Base material thickness (inches)	Base metal alloy/filler metal alloy					
	5052/5356	5052/5183	5083/5183	5086/5356	6061/5183	6061/5356
	Size of fillet weld (inches) (see "W" in Fig. 5-18)					
0.125	0.10	0.10	0.14	0.14	0.09	0.10
0.160	0.13	0.12	0.18	0.17	0.11	0.12
0.190	0.16	0.14	0.22	0.21	0.13	0.15
0.250	0.21	0.19	0.29	0.27	0.18	0.20
0.313	0.26	0.24	0.36	0.34	0.22	0.24
0.375	0.31	0.29	0.43	0.41	0.27	0.29
0.500	0.42	0.38	0.57	0.55	0.36	0.39
0.750	0.66	0.57	0.86	0.82	0.53	0.59
1.000	0.83	0.45	1.14	1.09	0.71	0.78

and shell plate on planing boats. In the after 50 percent of the bottom shell, where there is less slamming pressure, chain intermittent fillet welds are considered acceptable. Stitch, staggered, chain, or skip welding all refer to a short length of fillet weld, an interval, then another short length of weld.

On smaller craft not subject to any specific classification society standard, it is common to use empirical methods or rules of thumb to select weld sizes. This has proven quite acceptable in most cases. Some basic rules of thumb are as shown in Table 5-3.

With no known exceptions, utilization of the above rules of thumb to determine the size and spacing of intermittent fillet welds has not resulted in structural failures on small craft. The weld failures that have occurred are usually a result of poor welding technique, not size and spacing of welds. A few critical area checks for proper weld size and configuration as provided by the boat designer, along with the use of the above rules of thumb, should be adequate for most small craft.

CONTROLLING WELD-INDUCED DISTORTION

Some distortion of the weldment is common to all welding processes. This is caused by stresses from weld heat and expansion being locked into the metal: the more heat buildup, the more severe the distortion. Aluminum expands approximately twice as much as steel, which can cause problems if your welding experience is primarily

| TABLE 5-3 | Fillet weld rules of thumb. |

1. Use double continuous fillet welds:
    a. In areas of high stress, impact, repeated loads, or vibration:
        1) The forward 50 percent of the bottom of planing boats.
            (On small boats, approximately 35 feet LOA and less, intermittent chain welding is commonly used in this area with no apparent ill effects.)
        2) Engine beds, machinery foundations, bilge keels.
        3) In close proximity to the propeller, shaft struts, rudder.
    b. In other areas of high stress:
        1) End connections of primary and secondary members.
        2) Brackets connecting longitudinals to bulkhead stiffeners.
        3) Ends of all intermittently welded members for a length at least equal to the depth of the member, and around the end.
        4) Intermittently welded members that pass through slotted bulkheads, for a distance of 3 inches on each side of the intersection.
        5) Unbracketed stiffeners of shell plate, watertight bulkheads, and house fronts that do not end on a crossing member, for at least 10 percent of the length of the stiffener at each end and around the ends.
    c. Areas subject to moisture entrapment, such as the lower bilge.
2. Use intermittent fillet welding where continuous welding is not required.
    a. Use chain intermittent fillet welds in the aft 50 percent of the bottoms of planing boats, except as noted above. Center-to-center spacing of chain weld segments is three times the length of the segments.
    b. Use staggered intermittent fillet welds in other areas. Spacing of staggered weld segments to be 10 inches.
        1) Shell stiffeners in the topsides of planing boats.
        2) All shell stiffeners in the hulls of displacement boats.
        3) Bulkhead stiffeners.
3. The length of intermittent weld segments is to be 10 times the thickness of the thinner base metal, but not less than $1^1/_2$ inches nor more than 3 inches.
4. Provide water-stops where stiffeners pass through fuel-tight or watertight bulkheads.

with steel. You must be aware of aluminum's rapid rate of expansion with the application of heat. And be careful not to overweld. First-time aluminum-boat welders often make welds oversize, not realizing that this can result in substantial distortion. It is usually better to underweld than overweld. As a rule of thumb, make the fillet weld size approximately 1/6 inch less than the thinnest base metal, or to be more precise, use Table 5-2 for minimum fillet weld size.

Skilled welding-machine operators have learned how to control distortion by the use of various welding techniques. Other than heat control, restraining the welded joint and following a specific weld sequence are the most effective methods. Minimize warping by lightly tacking the seams of the structure being assembled until all weld restraints are in place. Weld restraints include structural members located near weld seams (or vice-versa) so they can help reduce distortion (Figure 5-20). You can also reduce weld-induced distortion by (1) a careful fit-up—seam gaps of 1/16 inch or less—which reduces heat buildup, and (2) welding the seams in a symmetrical sequence (a little on the port side, followed by a little on the starboard side). The latter tends to cause the individual distortions to cancel rather than accumulate.

To butt weld two flat, unrestrained plates so that the welded plates remain in a flat plane requires following a procedure that minimizes the effects of weld-related distortion. You accomplished this by holding the metal in the desired position during the welding process and the cooling period after welding.

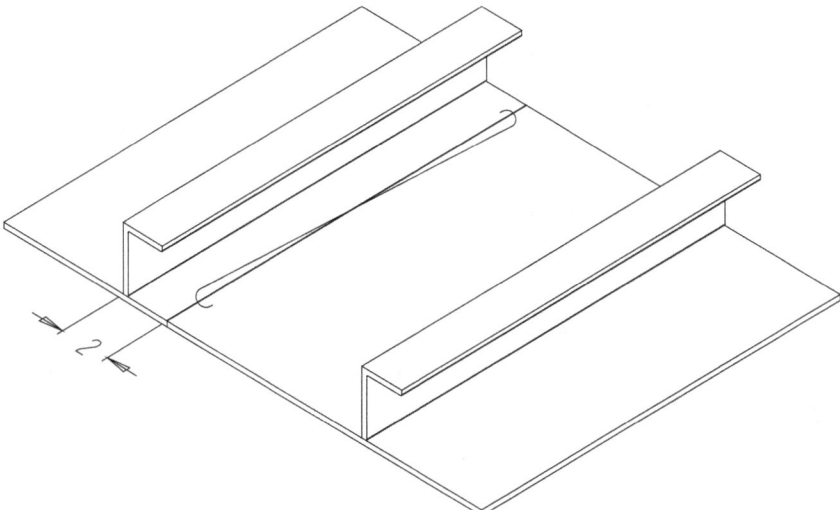

Figure 5-20. Placing a weld seam near a structural member that will also function as a weld restraint.

Prepare suitable stongbacks to span the weld joint. Strongbacks may be any straight, stiff material but are usually cut from scrap aluminum. They must be straight on the edge that will butt to the plates to be welded. In addition, make a notch cutout, called a *rat hole*, where the strongback will cross a weld seam to allow access for the tip of the welding gun. The notch may be any shape, but it must be large enough to allow the tip of a welding gun to pass.

Once you have the strongbacks, follow these steps to control distortion:

1. Clean the plate edges to be welded.
2. Lay the two plates on a flat surface and butt them together at the edges to be welded.
3. Place the strongbacks across the seams at about 12-inch intervals (see Figure 5-15). Be sure the plate edges are aligned and the strongbacks are firmly pressed down to ensure contact with both plate surfaces.

    While placing strongbacks, carefully align the plate edges between the strongbacks using some or all of the techniques shown in Figures 5-11, 5-12, and 5-13.
4. When you are satisfied with alignment, temporarily weld the strongbacks in place to both of the plates with 1-inch-long tack-welds. Place welds on only one side of the strongbacks to make them easier to remove.
5. After the strongbacks are welded in place, hand wire-brush the abutting plates.
6. Butt weld the seam, working around the strongbacks, following the back-stepping sequence shown in Figure 5-5.
7. Turn the joined plates over. Using a circular saw, back-chip the weld seam by sawing a kerf, which straddles the weld seam and is sufficiently deep to remove all contaminated weld metal (Figure 5-8).
8. Weld the seam using the back-stepping sequence, power wire-brush it clean, and repair any defects. Power wire-brush the seam after welding to remove any soot and inspect the weld.
9. Repair any obvious defects.
10. Turn the welded plate back over and break the strongbacks loose by bending them toward their tack-welds.
11. Grind flush any tack-weld remnants on the plate surface. Power wire-brush the weld seam to clean it, then inspect it and repair any defects.

The above procedure controls weld distortion in an axis that crosses the weld seam but does not control distortion that is parallel to the seam. An additional

Welding Aluminum

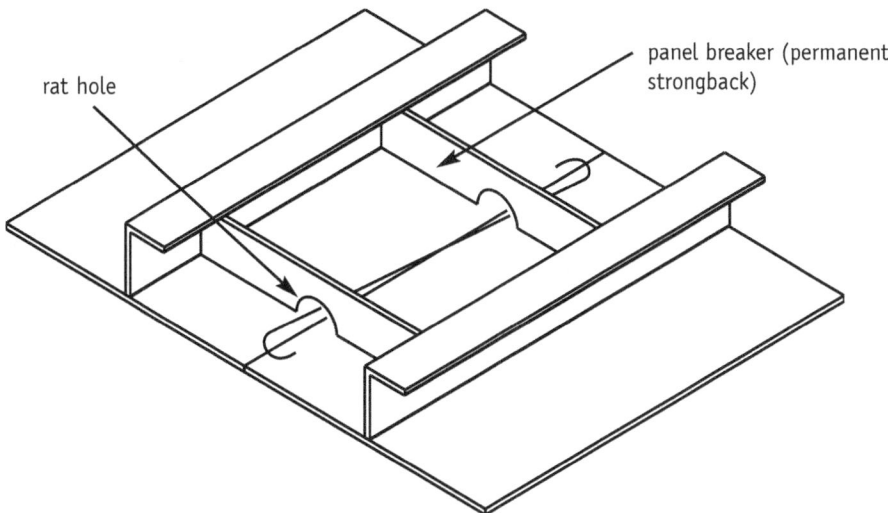

Figure 5-21. Permanent strongbacks.

strongback placed parallel to the weld seam and 2 to 3 inches away will provide adequate restraint to control this longitudinal distortion.

When butt welding in place on the boat, use the boat's structural members for strongbacks where possible, adding temporary strongbacks as needed. Make your first full weld pass on the inside of the shell plate. Apply the outside weld after the seam is back-chipped to sound metal.

Permanent strongbacks may sometimes be incorporated to hold a structure fair, similar to that shown in Figure 5-21. If they are later covered or otherwise out of sight, they usually don't cause a problem.

It's important to note the direction the plate edges move in relation to the final weld pass. The most movement is away from the final (after back-chipping) pass, as illustrated by Figure 5-22. The hot weld metal shrinks when cooling, forcing the slight depression in the joint when viewed from the cover-pass side of the

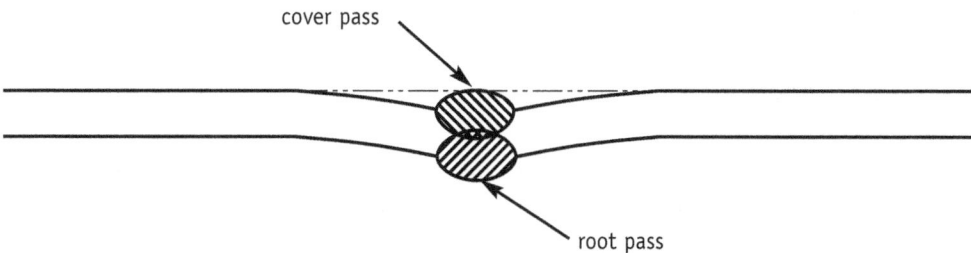

Figure 5-22. Direction of weld seam movement.

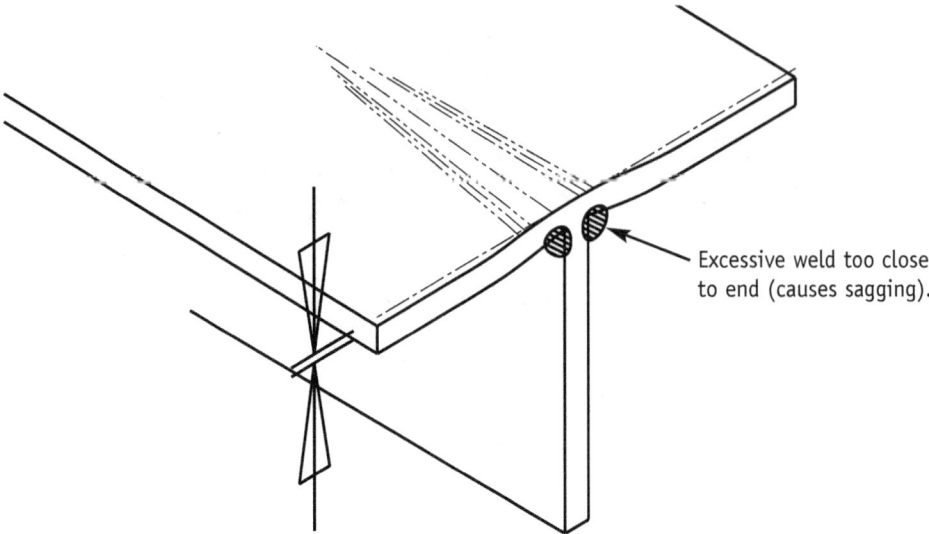

Figure 5-23. Excessive distortion at a plate-to-frame weld caused by welding too close to the plate edge.

plates. This shrinkage is usually the outside of the hull and can be advantageous in shaping a compound curve shell plate.

When positioning shell plates on the framework, secure the plates to the frame with very small tack-welds to hold down weld-induced distortion. Do not put any plate-to-frame tack-welds within 6 inches of the chine, gunwale, or other sight edge. Too large a weld between a frame member and a plate can cause unacceptable distortion (Figure 5-23). The badly deformed plate sketched in Figure 5-24 is the result of heavily welding the plate to the structure without the use of strongbacks or abutting plating for proper restraint. Alleviate this problem the same way: keep the tack-welds small and hold them back at least 6 inches from the plate edge.

To maintain a fair line at distinct sight edges where two plates meet, such as at the chine, follow a careful sequence of fit-up and tacking:

1. Use longitudinal strongbacks, set parallel to the weld seam (about 2 to 3 inches from the joint), to both fair the seam and to hold the fair line for tack-welding.
2. Stitch the seam on the outside using ¼-inch tack-welds at about 6-inch intervals, with the strongbacks holding the plate edges in a fair line. This step is essential to prevent any unfairness in the sight edge, which will be very offensive to the eye.
3. After securely tacking the plates, complete the inside fillet weld.

4. Back-chip the outside (including removal of the original small tack-welds) and complete the weld from the outside.

When the surface finish of the aluminum must be maintained, it is not acceptable to use welded-in-place strongbacks on the finished surface. You can minimize or eliminate the use of longitudinal strongbacks along sight edges by carefully fairing and dressing the plate edges:

1. Use a straightedge or a flexible batten to draw fair lines to aid in dressing the plate edges.
2. Dress them with a power hand plane or by careful grinding. Often the dressed plate edges can be pulled together by hand.
3. Align the plate edges by eye and tack-weld them to hold the fair line without the use of strongbacks. Alignment of the edges must be consistent, with one plate edge lapping the other a uniform distance. An example of improper alignment is shown in Figure 5-25.

The cumulative effect of weld-induced shrinkage can alter the final lines of a boat. On a sailboat, for example, the deck at the bow and stern will be slightly closer to the waterline than desired. This is caused by the large amount of welding and the associated stresses being greatest along the stem, which effectively arches the back of the boat. Since this arching is partially offset by the high stresses of a sailboat's rigging, it's normally disregarded.

Once weld-induced shrinkage is determined from a prototype boat, adjustments can be made on future

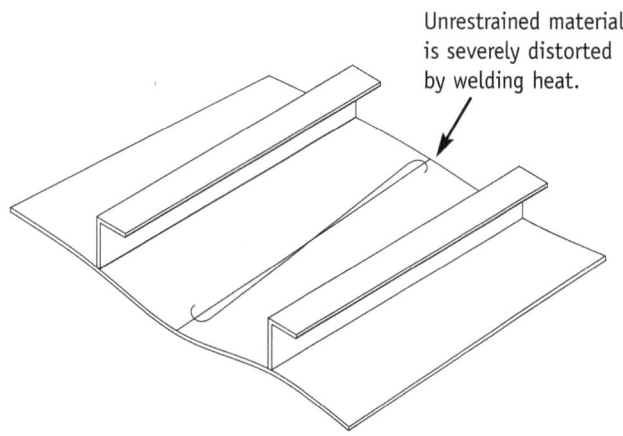

Figure 5-24. Distortion caused by welding to an unrestrained plate.

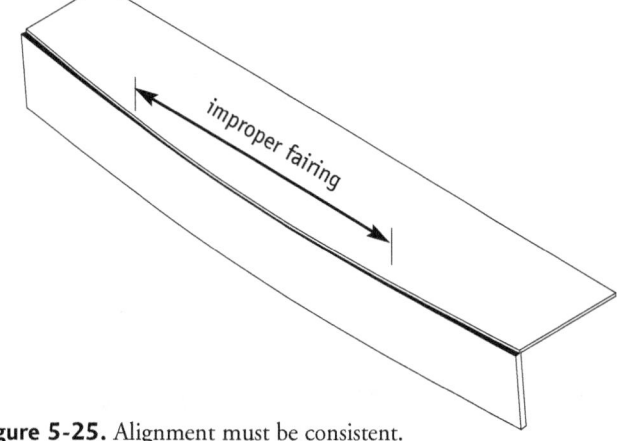

Figure 5-25. Alignment must be consistent.

identical boats to compensate for shrinkage. These adjustments can include changing the welding sequence, or actually changing the boat's layout dimensions slightly to allow for weld-induced shrinkage.

On large ships, a shrinkage allowance, or trim, is included on the plate to compensate for anticipated weld induced shrinkage. This is typically 1 or 2 inches of extra material at the base and ends of large flat panels—to be trimmed off during fit-up on the boat. On small boats, this trim allowance is eliminated or reduced.

A rule of thumb you can use regarding weld shrinkage is to estimate about 1/32 inch per panel stiffener. A large flat panel that will have, for example, six stiffeners (Figure 5-26) will shrink in length about 6/32 (or 3/16) inch. It doesn't seem to matter if the welds are continuous or intermittent.

Welding should always proceed in as symmetrical a manner as practical. If a boat hull is not welded symmetrically—that is, a little welding on the port side followed by a little welding on the starboard side—then the hull can be out of true. When a boat starts to lose its true lines, tack-welds start breaking, and bulges and kinks develop in the internal structure.

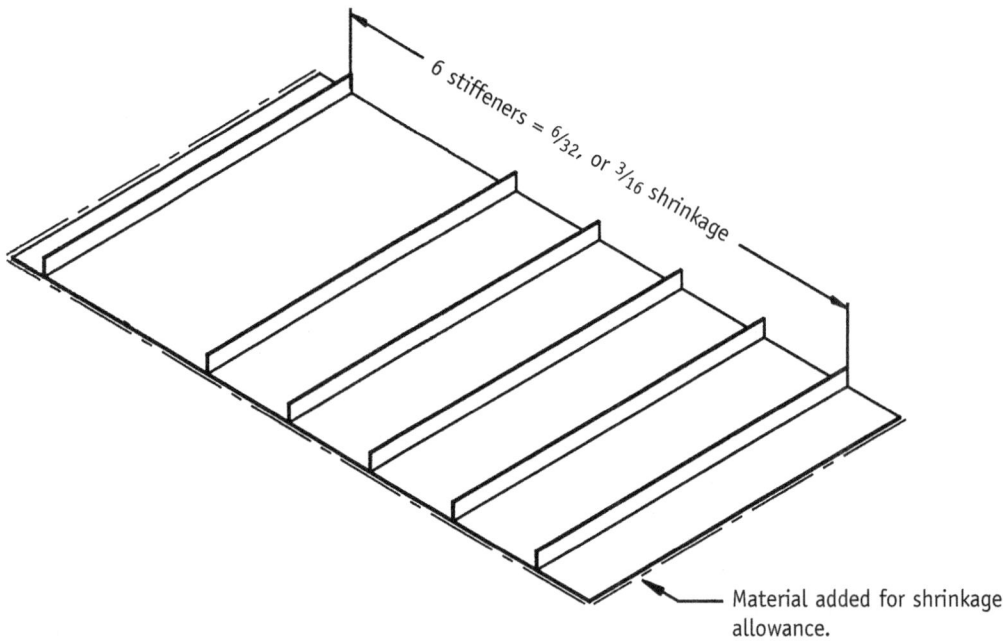

Figure 5-26. A flat panel with stiffeners.

POST-WELD CLEANUP

Cleaning up welds usually involves at least the removal of soot and unsightly excess metal. Welds may be ground down for a better appearance, and they're sometimes actually ground flush with the adjacent parent metal. The degree of post-welding cleanup often depends on the visibility of the weld. For example, don't worry about cleaning welds on the inside of a boat that you'll never see under normal circumstances. At the most, give them a quick hand brushing with a stainless steel wire brush or a wash-off with a cleaning solution. Use a cloth and wipe off the smoke on the surface of the parent metal alongside a weld.

Dirty or sooty-looking welds may require a cleaning solution, such as one of the aluminum brighteners sold in automotive stores. These chemically attack the aluminum and will change the surface texture to a uniform but somewhat duller finish than the mill-furnished bright finish. Streaking may occur if the cleaning solution runs down the surface. If this happens, apply the cleaning solution to the entire surface for a uniform finish. And you may need to do repeated applications and rinses to remove streaking. Dip small parts into a cleaning solution to remove dirt and soot.

GRINDING WELDS

When a weld needs to be ground flush with the parent metal, the common tendency is to dig into the weld joint with the grinding disc and remove more metal than necessary. As mentioned earlier, the reason for this is the slight inset of the parent metal at the joint, caused by the shrinkage of the larger mass of molten weld metal on the cover-pass side of the weld joint (see Figure 5-22).

For a truly flat weld joint, fill this depression entirely with weld metal, then grind flush.

It's almost impossible to do a quality job of grinding with a guard installed on the angle grinder because the grinding disc needs to be nearly parallel with the work to give a good flush surface. If you remove the guard, work carefully and use a full-face protective shield and safety glasses.

Grinding discs designed for aluminum all cut rapidly but leave behind a rough surface with deep scratches. The discs also wear down quickly and require frequent replacement if there is much grinding to be done.

To finish a weld bead after grinding, use a circular sander with an 80-grit sanding disc to remove most of the deep grinder scratches, then follow this with a 120-grit disc. (The 120-grit disc will load up fairly quickly and require frequent renewal.) Another fine finishing tool is a surface-conditioning and deburring disc. Standard Abrasives combines these discs with a Velcro holder pad to fit a 7-inch angle grinder. A similar product is manufactured by 3M under the Scotch-Brite brand name.

For a large weld requiring a lot of metal removal, careful use of a circular saw can greatly speed the removal of the bulk of the weld bead:

1. Place the front of the frame of the circular saw on the parent metal with just the tip of the blade over the weld bead.
2. Retract the guard with your thumb and start the saw.
3. Hold the saw securely, with the front of its frame on the parent metal, and slowly lower the blade onto the weld to be removed.
4. Hold the front of the saw on the work and gently rotate the saw from side to side over the weld bead.

Planing Welds

In some cases, you can use a handheld power plane to smooth a weld bead, but only for edge welds—such as along the chine. Do not use a power plane on flat surfaces—the edges of the cutter will gouge the parent metal if you don't hold the plane perfectly flat.

References

The Aluminum Association. *Aluminum Welder's Training Manual and Exercises.* Washington, D.C.: The Aluminum Association, 1986.
American Welding Society, Inc. *Guide for Aluminum Hull Welding.* Miami, Fla.: American Welding Society, Inc., 1983.
Kaiser Aluminum and Chemical Sales, Inc. *Welding Kaiser Aluminum.* Oakland, Calif.: Kaiser Aluminum and Chemical Sales, Inc., 1978.

CHAPTER 6

Aluminum Boat Lofting

Lofting is the term used to describe the laying out of a boat's geometry in full size by enlarging the lines drawing. This has traditionally been accomplished on a large floor area, called the *loft floor*. Once the lines are drawn full size, bulkheads, frames, girders, and miscellaneous parts are drawn within the parameters of the enlarged lines. Part templates are then constructed from the lines on the loft floor.

Over the past few years, lofting has been shifted from manual methods to the computer, eliminating the loft floor entirely and the need to construct wood templates in most commercial boatbuilding operations. However, a boatbuilder should clearly understand the principles of manual lofting prior to attempting computer lofting, and amateurs may still find manual methods practical. For these reasons, the chapter covers manual lofting in detail before launching into computer lofting.

All fabrication projects require layout work—measuring and drawing lines on the material to ensure it is cut to the correct size and shape. Projects with straight sides and square corners are laid out directly from the construction drawings, or blueprints, without any intermediate steps, but the long, sweeping curved lines of most boat designs are almost certain to complicate the layout process. A construction drawing could be drawn showing a boat's layout dimensions, but such a drawing would be so cluttered with dimensions that it would be nearly unreadable. For this reason, layout dimensions for curved lines are almost always omitted from construction drawings, requiring the actual shape of curved lines to be developed during the lofting process.

Because boatbuilding materials have some thickness, it is necessary to lay out the location of structural members to a specific side of the member. For instance, on a transverse frame, either the forward or aft side of the frame is used for laying out. The layout side for longitudinal members and flats also must be established. The layout side of the material is referred to as the *molded side*. A layout line showing the molded side is called the *molded line* (see sidebar later in this chapter). In the case of transverse frames, the molded side is usually the forward face of the frame in the forward portion of the boat, but it often shifts to the aft side of the frame in the after portion of the hull, depending upon the hull form. The assembly drawing, showing dimensions used to locate a part within the boat's structure, is always with reference to the molded line, and parts are located with the molded side of a part on the molded line. This topic will be expanded on later in this chapter.

Lofting goals, the terms used, and the techniques for laying down lines and fabricating templates are covered in this chapter in sufficient detail to construct a welded-aluminum boat. I would like to stress that your time spent lofting the boat, when approached in a logical manner, will be more than offset by the savings of time and improvement in quality of fit. Boatbuilders who utilize computer lofting greatly accelerate the construction time by use of parts cut out on computer-guided equipment.

A boat should be designed so that the construction will follow a logical, systematic sequence that minimizes the potential for error. Although the boat designer bears the primary responsibility for the design, the boatbuilder is responsible for the construction sequence (see Chapter 7).

In professional boatbuilding shops, the sequence is usually determined by the boat *loftsman*, who is intimately familiar with the boatbuilder's capabilities, including tooling and facilities. The loftsman is usually the most senior and experienced member of the boatbuilding crew. The loftsman's planned method of construction greatly influences the production costs and quality of the finished product.

It is important to stress at this point that aluminum-boat construction usually involves large developable shell plate panels that can be formed out of large sheets. These sheets will touch all internal framing, without gaps, if the shell plate is fully developable. Making sure that the hull surfaces are developable is of critical importance. Some boat designers will indicate that the hull form is a developable surface, when in fact some minor adjustments to the lines must be made by the builder (or loftsman) to properly define the surface as developable. For this reason, special attention must be paid to the techniques used to ensure that a surface is developable (see Chapter 3). Check the lines drawing to ensure surfaces are developable prior to starting full-size lofting. A manual method for checking for developable surfaces, using a scale model, is shown in Appendix C. An analytical method for designing a developable surface is found in *SNAME, Principles of Naval Architecture,* Vol. 1, *Stability and Strength,* page 13. The use of ship-design computer software is by far the fastest and simplest method to check for a developable surface. (See Chapter 3 for a complete description of developable surfaces.)

MANUAL LOFTING

Since boats are usually larger than a drawing board, several plywood sheets are laid on a floor to make a large drawing surface. The boat is drawn full size using the designer's lines drawings and table of offsets. Full-size plan, profile, and body plan views are drawn identical to the lines drawing, except for the scale factor. From these two-dimensional (2-D) views (and often some required auxiliary views), a 3-D description can be developed, allowing development of true shapes and sizes of the boat's components. Structural members are drawn, then cutting templates for parts are constructed to match these lines.

PREPARING THE LOFT FLOOR

The area where you will do your lofting should be well lighted and dry, and sufficiently spacious to allow full-size lofting of the boat's lines drawing without the interference of columns or posts. The floor should be reasonably flat, so that a string pulled taut across the floor can define a straight line. Ideally a band saw and a table saw should be located adjacent to the loft floor for cutting the wood templates and patterns.

The loft floor can be a layer of ¼-inch AC plywood (with side A face up) or other suitable drawing surface, tightly abutted, and well nailed down to provide a smooth surface. A coat of white latex paint is helpful for better line contrast.

A loftsman should always wear knee pads. It's no coincidence that the condition of very sore knees caused by kneeling for long periods is known as "loftsman's knees." Knee pads should be nonmarking (not black rubber) and soft. An ideal knee pad is a 12-inch-square pillow of soft 1-inch foam rubber secured by Velcro straps both above and below the knee. Since the profusion of lines and data on the loft floor may require weeks to develop, loft-floor etiquette also requires shoe removal prior to walking on the floor to avoid dirt and scuff marks that might obliterate markings.

When you lay down a new loft floor, allow at least 1 to 2 feet between the loft area and the wall at the baseline side of the loft floor. This provides you with a narrow walking lane and an area for the loose end of a flexible batten to extend during fairing of long lines. Since this lane is along the baseline, it allows you to see the loft floor from the same viewpoint as the lines drawing.

The length and width of the loft floor area should be large enough to draw the full-size boat lines. Minimum length and width of the loft floor is the boat's overall length and its *half-breadth*, plus about 1 foot additional around the perimeter. Additional room at the stern for development of a flat pattern for the transom and sufficient height for a superstructure, radar mast, or other items high above the DWL (design waterline) needing layout is a plus if the area is available.

If the available area is not large enough to loft the boat you're building full size, the lofted lines may be drawn to a smaller scale, or the longitudinal axis may be drawn to some scale other than full size. Another technique for a large boat is to loft half the boat length, then double back and loft the other half. However, these techniques are for limited loft-floor space and shouldn't be used unless absolutely necessary.

LAYING DOWN THE LINES

After you've sized the loft floor and nailed down and painted the plywood, you can begin the process of laying down the lines from the boat's lines drawing. Start with the basic *reference lines*, such as *waterlines* and *station lines*. These lines are called the *grid*, and since the grid lines are permanent, lay them out in black ballpoint. There will be numerous occasions to erase lines that cross the grid as lofting progresses, but if the basic grid reference lines are drawn on the floor with a ballpoint, they should remain intact.

The first line down is the *baseline*. Pull a taut chalk line near the edge of the loft floor and "snap" a line. Follow up with a straightedge and a ballpoint pen to harden the line. Next, select a point on the baseline about halfway down the loft floor (not on a plywood seam) and lay out a vertical line 90 degrees to the baseline to represent a *midships station*. Double check the initial loft-floor layout very carefully, since all reference lines will be laid out from these two lines. Waterlines will be drawn parallel to the baseline, and station lines will be drawn parallel to the midships station line.

The spacing between station lines will be shown on the lines drawing. Calculate the cumulative measurements from the lines drawing, and starting at the midships station, work both forward and aft to lay out and draw the station lines. Identify each line with its station number at both top and bottom, using a wide felt-tip marker, making the labels about 2 inches high.

Measuring up from the baseline, lay out and draw in the required waterlines parallel to the baseline. Identify each waterline with 2-inch-high figures at each end of the loft floor. This completes the basic grid.

LOFTING A DRIFT BOAT

A simple, flat-bottom, McKenzie River drift boat will serve as our example for an introduction to lofting. Figure 3-10 (see Chapter 3) is a reproduction of the lines drawing for this drift boat. Most boats will require considerably more detail on the loft floor than the drift boat, but the basic techniques are similar for all boats. Unique to the McKenzie River drift boat is that both the bottom and sides are parts of cylinders, or a cylindrical surface (see Chapter 3). The bottom is flat in the transverse axis, and the sides and transom slope at 30 degrees, as shown in Figure 3-3. This greatly simplifies checking for developable surfaces.

Laying Out the Basic Grid

The first step to loft any boat full size is, as described above, to draw the basic grid. The floor area needed to loft the drift boat is 4 feet by 16 feet, which will allow the boat's lines to be drawn full size. Lay down the loft floor as described above.

The lines drawing for the drift boat shows the station lines spaced 3 feet apart. One waterline located 16½ inches ABL (above baseline) and one buttock line located 16½ inches off CL (centerline) are also shown.

To transfer these lines to the loft floor:

- Start with the baseline (labeled baseline/centerline on the lines drawing) and draw it on the floor, locating it about 6 inches in from one edge.
- Lay out station 3 near the midpoint of the loft floor; all the other vertical stations will be laid out from this line. Position this station line at least 2 inches away from any loft-floor seam.
- Draw all the waterlines and buttock lines onto the floor. In this case, there is only one waterline and one buttock line given.

- Draw vertical lines parallel with station 3 for all station lines. Double check all layout lines for accuracy and correct any errors. Note: any error at this point will affect the shape of the boat.

This completes the basic grid for the drift boat.

Lofting the Profile and Plan Views

To loft the profile and plan views, use the *table of offsets* (TOE) found on the lines drawing (Figure 3-10). The table of offsets is actually two tables, one labeled "heights" and the other one "half-breadths." "Heights" is a measurement in the profile view above the baseline. "Half-breadths" is a measure in the plan view of the distance from the centerline to some point port or starboard. The letter "T" represents the transom station. Using the offsets from the tables, locate the positions of the chine and sheer at each station. These dimensions are measured up from the baseline and marked on the loft floor. Locate and mark the terminal ends of the chine and sheer line on the profile view. Connect these points with a smooth curve.

The procedure is as follows:

- Starting at station 1, the chine height is given in the heights table (Figure 3-10) as 0-7-2, or 0 feet $7\frac{2}{8}$ ($7\frac{1}{4}$) inches above the baseline (ABL). Mark this point on station line 1. Locate and mark the sheer height (2-6-6+) on station 1 at 2 feet $6\frac{13}{16}$ inches ABL.
- Continue the layout for both chine and sheer until all station line heights, represented by a point, show the location of the chine and sheer line in the profile view. Remember that a "+" at the end of a dimension adds $\frac{1}{16}$ inch; e.g., the 0-0-6+ station 2 offset for the chine designates 0 feet $\frac{13}{16}$ inches.
- In the profile view, draw in the points defining the line of the bow and rake of the stern. The chine offsets for these points are shown as dimensions and only on the lines plan, while the sheer offsets are shown in the table of offsets as well the lines drawing. Connect the chine and sheer points at each end with a straight line.
- Use a flexible batten to connect the points defining the chine and sheer, fairing the lines into smooth continuous curves. (Fairing a line with a flexible batten is described in Appendix D.)
- Follow a similar procedure, but this time using the offsets from the

half-breadths table, draw the plan view of the chine, sheer, and waterline on the loft floor. The profile and plan view should look like Figure 3-10 when completed.

Lofting the Body Plan

The *body plan* is a view from the front (or rear) of the boat showing one half of the stations, all stacked one on top of the other. This is the view that's used to develop the outline of the boat's frames, and it's the last primary view drawn on the loft floor. Only half of each station is drawn because the stations are symmetrical around the centerline. All needed information can be obtained from these half-breadth views, and they save both time and loft-floor space. Half-breadth templates will later be constructed over the body plan, and these will be flopped around the centerline during the layout process to lay out both sides of the part.

Locate the points for the half-breadth views by taking the dimensions from the loft-floor profile and plan views, and draw the half-side body plan full size on the loft floor. Determine the measurements by using a tape measure or, for better accuracy, a pickup stick. A *pickup stick* is a flat, straight strip of 1/8-inch wood about 1 inch wide and of some convenient length that is squared at one end. To use the stick to pick up a chine half-breadth dimension at station 1, select the loft floor plan view, place the squared end of the stick on the centerline at station 1, and place a mark on the stick where station 1 crosses the chine line. Use the distance between the end of the stick and the mark to transfer the chine half-breadth to the body plan view; place the squared end of the pickup stick at the centerline of the body plan view and mark the loft floor adjacent to the mark on the stick.

Calculator paper tape can be used for the same purpose, with one end carefully folded over square, and the tape rolled out and marked in a similar manner as the pickup stick, as shown in Figure 6-1.

The earlier step of fairing the lines of the profile and plan views (originally laid out using the table of offsets) with a batten removed any minor high or low spots from the curved lines and corrected any minor misalignments. Consequently the dimensions you pick up from the faired lines on the loft-floor plan and profile views are more accurate than those provided in the table of offsets.

After locating the points representing the chine, sheer, 16½-inch waterline, and 16½-inch buttock line locations at each station in the body plan, connect them with a smooth curve. If a continuous fair curve can be drawn through these points (fairing the sheer and chine curves in the body plan will require a selection

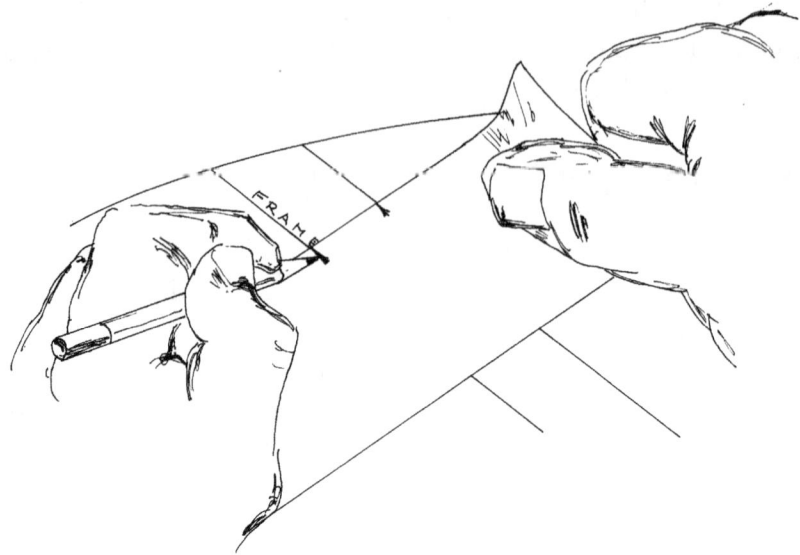

Figure 6-1. Using paper calculator tape to pick up dimensions from the loft floor.

of battens, from very stiff to very limber), the lines are fair in all three views. This checks the accuracy of the lofting.

This completes the lofting of the basic lines. You can put the lines drawings aside.

Lofting Structure

After you have the lines drawn on the loft floor, it's time to determine the actual location of each part shown on the construction drawing and to draw them in their proper locations on the loft floor so you can construct the patterns.

Frames

As the frames are not located at stations, you have to locate them on the loft floor. First study the construction drawing to find each frame's location in reference to a station line. Draw a single line—the molded line—for each frame in the profile and plan views. The molded line is simply one side—the layout side—of the frame (see sidebar Molded Line). The centerline of the frame (if you need it) is determined by the thickness of the material. (Figure 6-2 and Figure 6-3 show the commonly used molded line side of parts.)

MOLDED LINE

Aluminum materials have a thickness that must be taken into consideration during the lofting process. To compensate for material thickness, the term "molded line" or "molded face" is used to define the layout side of the material. The line that defines the molded side is the molded line, which is the line drawn on the loft floor.

To minimize errors, it is important that you use a consistent method of determining the molded line. Figure 6-2 shows the molded side of a frame in the forward portion of a hull. Note the bow is to the right in this drawing, so that the material thickness is aft of the molded line, resulting in a slight gap between the aft face of the frame and the bottom shell. In this manner, the frame can be cut to the exact size of the drawn line. If the molded side is on the aft face, then an adjustment for the frame thickness must be considered. If the hull bottom is rising in relation to the baseline aft of midships, then often the frame molded line is changed to the aft face of the frame.

Other molded lines are shown in Figure 6-3. All shell plate molded surfaces are on the inboard side of the shell. The molded side of decks and horizontal flat surfaces are to the underside of the plating. The molded line on longitudinal members is to the outboard side of the member.

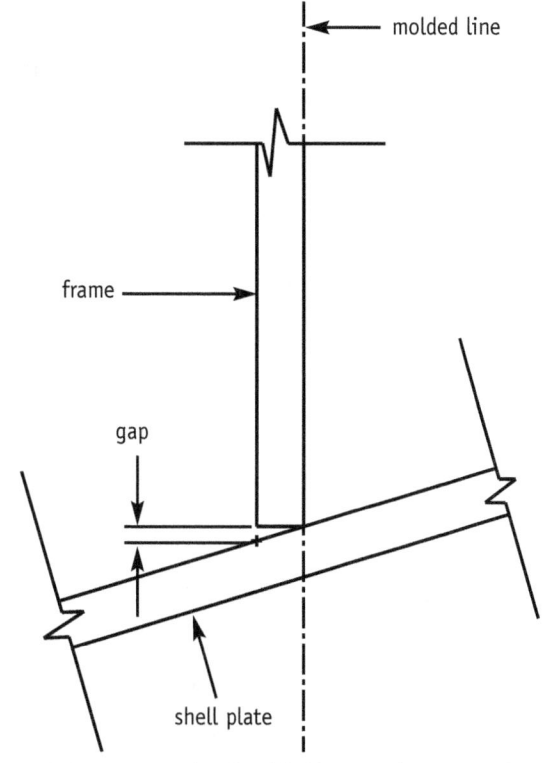

Figure 6-2. Correct side of molded line to place material on metal boats.

MOLDED LINE *(continued next page)*

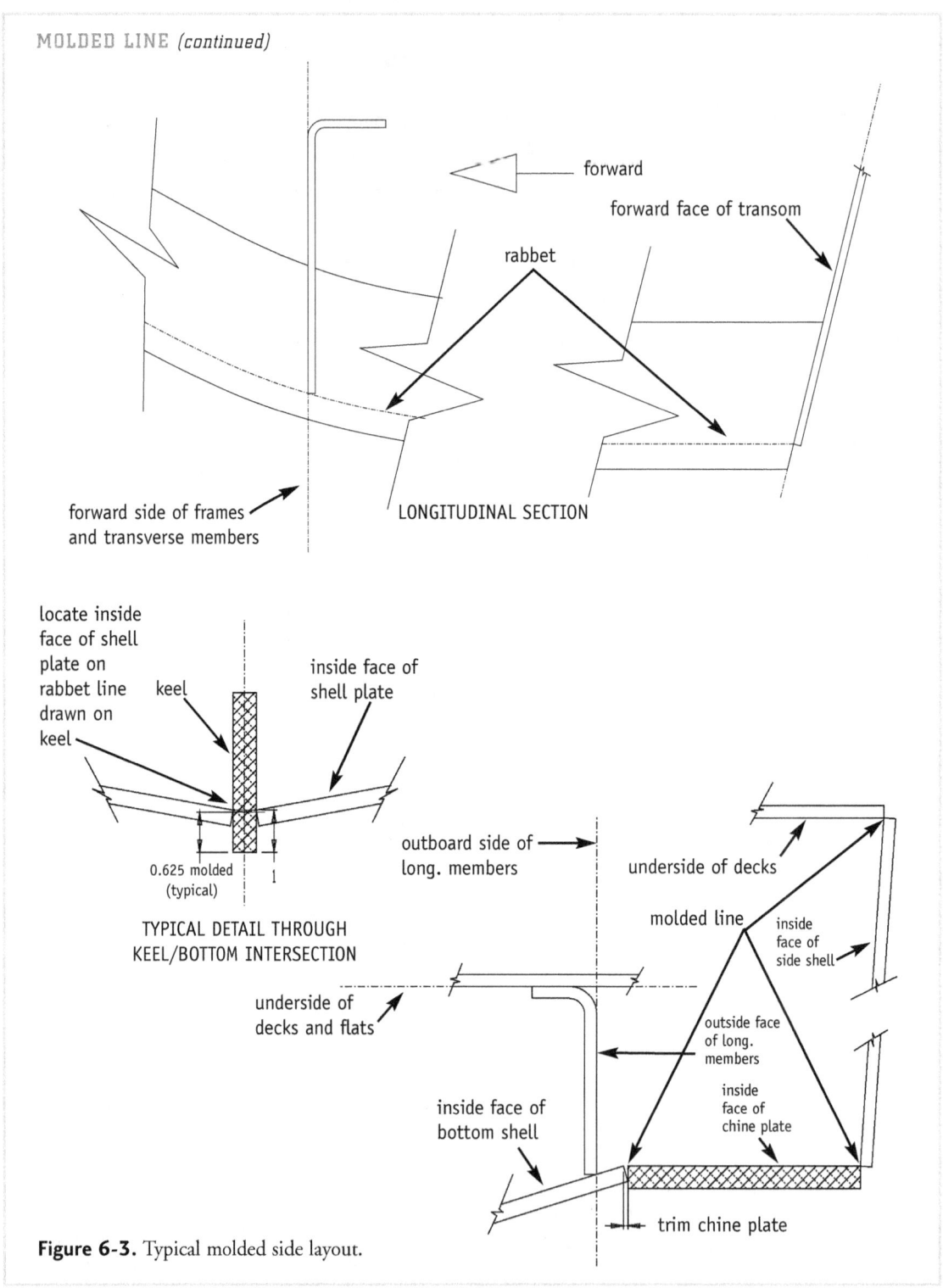

Figure 6-3. Typical molded side layout.

Aluminum Boat Lofting

After the frame lines are drawn on the loft floor in the profile and plan views, determine the location of the chine and sheer for each frame in the body plan by using the intersection of the frame lines with the sheer and chine lines. Transfer these points to the body plan and draw in the half-breadth frames. Determining the actual location of layout points for frames in the body plan from the plan and profile views involves (1) drawing a light, temporary line parallel to the centerline in the body plan view at the chine half-breadth distance, then (2) drawing another temporary line parallel to the baseline at the chine height. Where these lines cross is the actual defining point of the chine in the body plan view. Use the same procedure—picking dimensions and locating defining points—to locate the sheer. (The chine and sheer points of each frame should land on the fair lines that represent the chine and sheer in the body plan.) These half-breadth frames in the body plan are full size, so you can make a construction template directly from them.

Transom

Unlike the frames, the transom isn't vertical. The slope of the transom means it isn't shown in its true size in the body plan. To draw the transom ready for template making, it's first necessary to draw it in its true size, or flat pattern.

Develop the flat-pattern layout around the transom line in the profile view. Figure 6-4 shows a portion

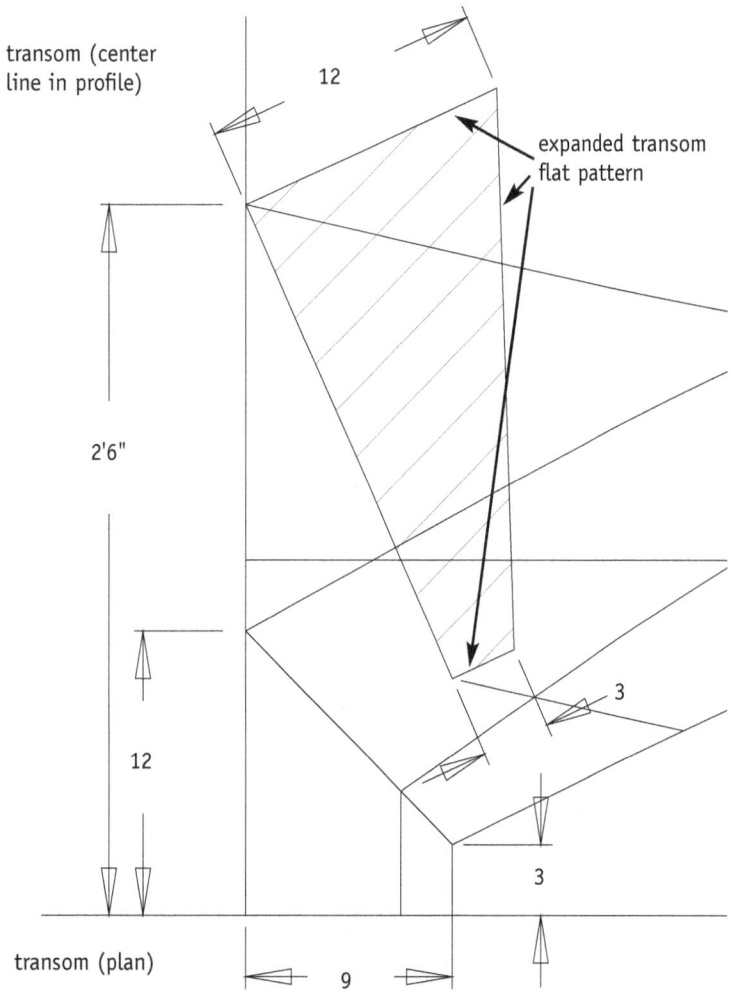

Figure 6-4. Developing the flat pattern for a transom.

of the loft floor at the transom. The line that represents the transom in the profile view on the loft floor is the true length of the transom at the centerline. Pick the transom half-breadth at the top and bottom directly from the plan view. Lay out the lines representing the top and bottom of the transom at 90 degrees to the transom centerline. Connect the end points of these two lines to complete the transom flat pattern.

Shelf at 16½-inch Waterline

The side shelf is located on the 16½-inch waterline, with the outer edge of the shelf against the shell plate, and the inboard, flanged face 21⅛ inches from centerline, as shown in the midships section view of Figure 3-11. The 16½-inch waterline already drawn on the loft floor defines the curved outer edge of the shelf, and a line drawn 1 foot, 9⅛ inches from and parallel to the centerline in the plan view defines the inboard edge. The shelf ends are located as dimensioned from station lines as shown on Figure 6-5.

This defines the side shelf in true size in the plan view (Figure 3-9). However, note the formed inboard edge of the shelf. To include material needed to form the edge, simply add material to the inboard face.

DEVELOPING TRUE-SIZE VIEWS

The bottom and sides of the drift boat are curved, developable surfaces and must be unwrapped. Other parts of the boat, including the small foredeck and the bottom and side plates, cannot be templated directly from the loft floor as drawn since none of these parts are shown in their true flat pattern size in any existing view. Each must have an *auxiliary view* developed before they are shown in true size.

Sometimes it is unclear if the view is a *true-size view*. One test for a true-size view of a flat object is to view the object when rotated 90 degrees to the existing view. If the object appears to be a straight line (edge on), the flat object is shown in true size. A good example of this is a station shown in the body plan view. When a station is viewed in either the profile or plan view, both of which are 90 degrees to the body plan, it will always appear as a straight line. Only objects located on a plane that is parallel with a waterline plane, buttock-line plane, or station-line plane can be picked directly from the loft floor without development of an auxiliary view.

The various methods of developing a true-size auxiliary view include the following: using folding lines, measuring girths to assist with layout of curved surfaces, calculating true size dimensions, and using triangulation. One of these, or a combination of methods, will allow development of an auxiliary view that meets the test for true size. Selection of the simplest method requires a little thought.

Folding Lines

The true-size view of the transom for the drift boat example was developed using the *folding-line method* (Figure 6-4). In this case, the true-size transom was laid out by placing an imaginary folding line on the centerline of the transom in the profile view. The new auxiliary view of the transom was then drawn 90 degrees to the profile view. This meets the test for true size. The formed edge for the shelf at the 16½-inch waterline was also a folding-line development, in that the vertical and horizontal portions of the formed edges were folded at 90 degrees in relation to each other, as shown in Figure 3-9.

The small foredeck on the drift boat is not in any plane shown in the basic three loft-floor views; it slopes aft and down when viewed in the profile view. To develop the outline of the foredeck for a flat pattern, it is first necessary to draw it on the loft floor in all three views, then to project from these views to draw an auxiliary view showing the deck in true size. Draw the foredeck in the profile view since it can be easily drawn with straight lines, using dimensions given in Figure 3-9. However, it cannot be drawn in the plan or body plan view until the slightly curved foredeck/hull intersection line is located. This is accomplished by locating a series of points along this line, then with the assistance of a flexible drawing batten, connecting them with a smooth curve.

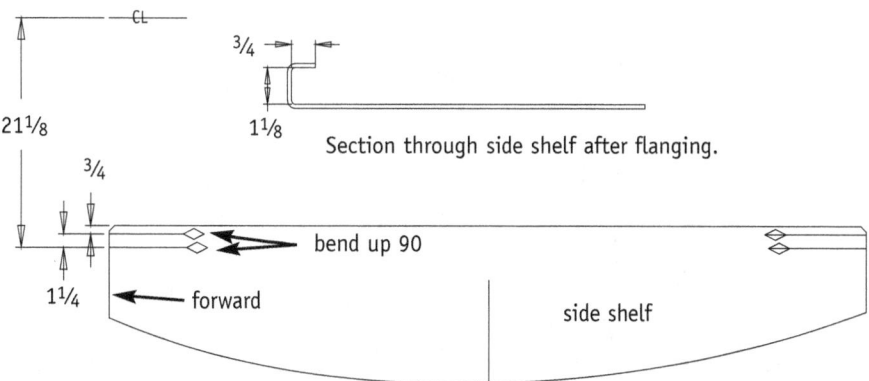

Figure 6-5. Shelf at the waterline.

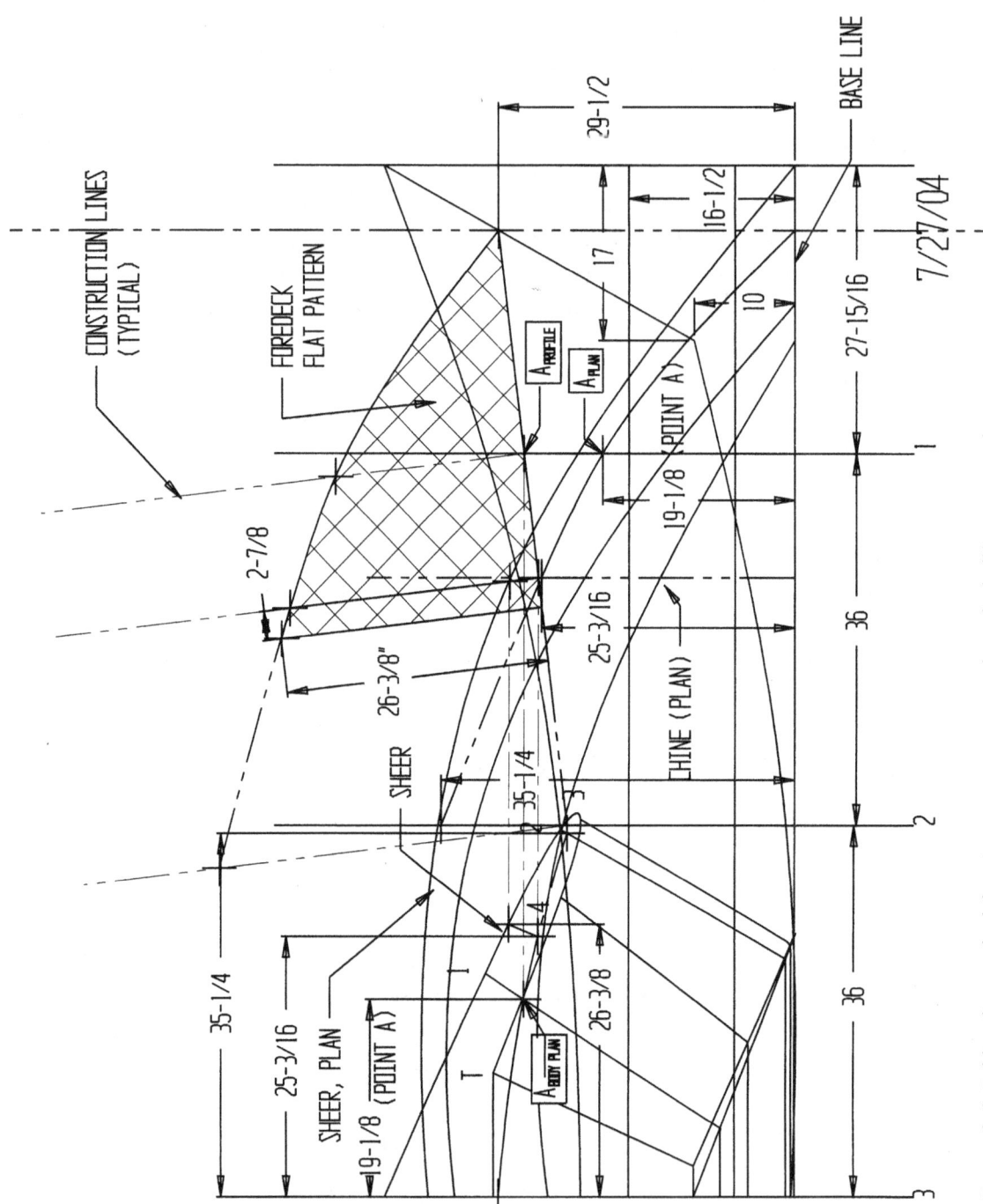

Figure 6-6. Folding line method: locating a common point along the hull/intersection lines.

Using Figure 6-6 as a guide, follow these steps to develop the foredeck:

1. Project the height on the loft floor from the baseline to the intersection of station 1 and the foredeck in the profile view (point $A_{profile}$).
2. Transfer this height to station 1 in the body plan view (point $A_{body\ plan}$) and make a small mark on station 1 to show the point.
3. After locating the point on the body plan view, pick the half-breadth of the point (which is 19⅛ inches) and transfer it to the plan view at station 1; make a small mark (point A_{plan}.) This will locate one point on the foredeck/hull side intersection in the plan view.
4. Project the aft end of the foredeck height in the profile view to intersect the sheer line in the body plan view and measure the half-breadth of the aft end of the foredeck (25³⁄₁₆ inches).
5. Project this dimension to the plan view to locate another point on the plan view of the foredeck.
6. Locate an additional point on station 2 by extending the foredeck line in the profile view to station 2.
7. Project points in a similar manner to obtain a half-breadth at station 2 of 35¼ inches.
8. Draw additional station lines that cross the foredeck line at convenient locations, and use the points on these additional stations to locate additional points.
9. When you've located sufficient points, use a batten to draw a smooth curve through all points that define the foredeck/hull intersection line in both the plan and body plan views.
10. The foredeck has a 2⅞-inch formed lip that turns up on the aft end, 90 degrees to the foredeck surface. To establish the extreme half-breadth of the lip, draw the lip as a straight line in the profile view, 90 degrees to the deck centerline.
11. Project a body plan view from the profile view with its top edge 26⅜ inches off the centerline, then draw the plan view by picking up offsets from the body plan view. This will complete the half-side drawing of the foredeck and its lip in the three basic loft-floor views.

The foredeck is not shown in true size in any existing view. However, an auxiliary view can now be projected from existing views to show the foredeck in true size. To draw it in true size, proceed in the same manner you used to draw the true-size transom. The centerline length of the foredeck is in true length in the profile view and is a convenient starting reference line. Steps are:

1. Use the foredeck line in the profile view as a folding line and project station lines at 90 degrees to assist with development of the true-size view.
2. Pick half-breadth dimensions for the defining points of the foredeck/hull side line from the plan view, and plot the half-breadth of each station on the new true-size view.
3. Connect the points with a smooth curve to complete development of the foredeck/hull curve in the true size view, as shown in the cross-hatched portion of Figure 6-6.
4. Add the lip to the flat pattern by drawing a line 2⅞ inches from and parallel to the aft edge of the foredeck.
5. Pick up the extreme half-breadth of the lip from the body plan. Later bend this lip up to 90 degrees.

Girths

Curved surfaces can often be developed into flat patterns by measuring along the perimeter, or *girthing* the curve, a simple method of developing a flat pattern for a curved surface free of twist, such as the drift-boat bottom. To confirm that the bottom is free of twist, look at the body plan view, and you'll see that the station lines on the boat bottom are parallel. This proves that the bottom is cylindrical, as opposed to being conical or a nondevelopable surface. As discussed previously, a cylindrical or conical surface can be developed from a flat pattern (see Chapter 3).

Girthing is accomplished by placing a flexible batten along a curved line that is shown in its true length and marking the batten where it crosses reference marks. When the batten is straightened out, the distances between the reference marks reflect the true distances along the girth of the arc.

You can expand the drift-boat bottom plate into a flat pattern with the steps below. A convenient place to do this is over the loft-floor plan view of the bottom.

1. Girth the true-length line representing the bottom centerline of the boat in the profile view—place marks on the girthing batten for each location where the batten crosses a station line, and at the bow and the stern ends of the bottom.

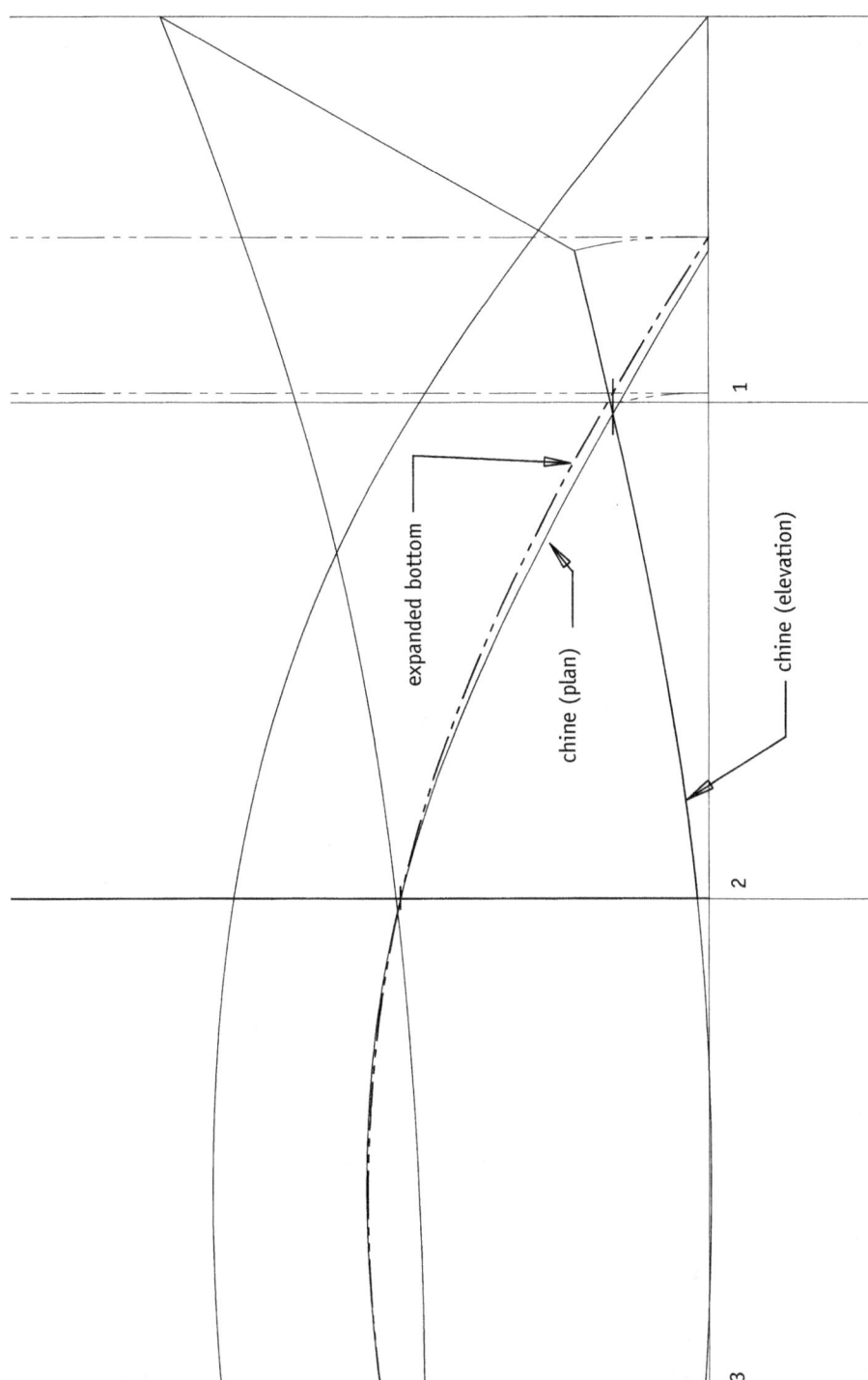

Figure 6-7. Marking girth using a batten.

2. Place the station 3 mark on the girthing batten on station 3 on the loft floor at the boat centerline as a starting point.
3. Mark the girths representing station locations on the loft floor from the batten (Figure 6-7), expanding the longitudinal axis of the bottom to compensate for its curvature.
4. Draw new station lines on the loft floor representing the true-size view station lines.

Since the boat bottom is flat in the transverse axis, station lines are shown in true length in the plan view. Therefore, the half-breadth dimensions do not change at each station in the true-size view. Project half-breadths to the true-size station lines, locating reference points to draw a true-size, or expanded, bottom half-breadth view.

Calculation

True-size patterns can often be laid out using *calculated distances*. Cylinders can be developed into flat patterns by calculating the circumference. Various geometric shapes can often be developed by mathematical methods. Flat patterns for forming are often developed by calculating material stretch-out, as described in Appendix B.

Mathematical methods for calculating true lengths are often faster and more accurate than other methods. Using mathematical methods to determine distances and angles is usually combined with other methods to develop true-size views.

Triangulation

If a surface is determined to be developable, true-size patterns are often laid out by *triangulation*. This technique can be used to develop a very close approximation of a true-size developed surface that is difficult or impossible to develop by other methods. The side shell plate of the drift boat is a developable surface in that it is a portion of a cylinder, as is evident by the station lines being parallel in the body plan view of the lines drawing.

The triangulation procedure follows:

1. Break the developable surface into workable-size segments, break these segments into triangles, and then determine true lengths of each line segment that define the triangles.

2. Swing an arc of radius equal to the true length of a line segment from a starting reference point on a straight line to intersect with the line at some point.
3. From the original starting point and this new point, draw other similar arcs.
4. Locate the third point to define a triangle where these arcs intersect.
5. On the loft floor, lightly draw in the lines representing the triangle through these points.
6. Use the same technique with swinging arcs to develop adjoining triangles, drawing them on the loft floor. Be sure to locate the center of each arc at the corners of the initial defined triangle.
7. Continue this process until the entire network of interconnecting triangles forms one large surface.
8. Later develop the true-size flat pattern by joining the points of each triangle located on each edge of the large surface by either straight or curved lines.

When a curved surface is laid out using triangulation, there is some error. This is because the method of determining the length of curved lines (which will be used as the radii for drawing arcs for triangulation) actually reflects the lengths of the chords of the arcs, not the distance around the arcs. The chords represent the straight line distance between the two ends of an arc. It's obvious that in an area of extreme curvature, the difference between the chord length and the perimeter length around the arc can be significant. To minimize error, divide curves with a lot of curvature into many short segments.

Another method to reduce error in areas of extreme curvature is to actually measure arc lengths by girthing. However, for all practical purposes, chord lengths are adequate to approximate the length of segments of a curve when expanding shell plate as long as the intervals between segments approximate station line spacing. This should result in about 9 or 10 segments for a typical small-boat shell plate expansion.

To develop side shell plate for the drift boat, draw approximately 8 stations in the boat length to allow accurate triangulation of the side shell. On our example drift boat, station spacing was much too far apart to allow accurate side shell plate development into a flat pattern. I shortened the interval by adding an additional station between each existing station, resulting in nine segments. Each of these segments was then divided into triangles, as shown in Figure 6-9.

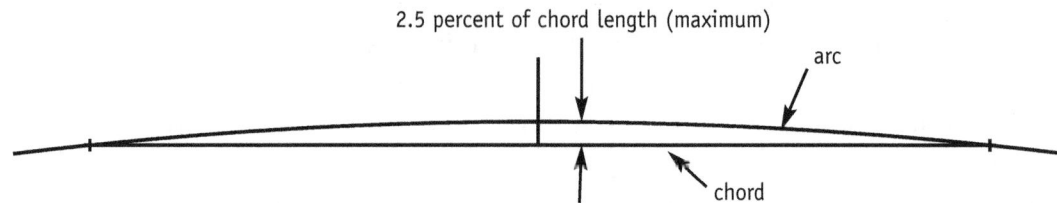

Figure 6-8. Allowance between an arc and its chord should not exceed 2.5 percent.

Before starting the actual process of drawing arcs, you must first determine the true lengths of the triangle sides you're using as arc radii. A careful analysis of the loft floor will reveal which lines are shown in their true length and which aren't. It's more common than not that the true length of a line is not shown in any existing view on the loft floor. When a true length is not shown, determine it by drawing an auxiliary view of the line showing it in its true length.

The length of the station sides, as shown in the body plan view (Figure 3-8), are in true length and can be picked directly from the loft floor for arc radii. The only other side shell line shown in true length is the bow of the boat at centerline, shown in the profile view. All other line segments must be developed into their true length.

A rapid method of drawing an auxiliary view of a line in true length is by measuring the length of the line in the plan view and the change in elevation of the same line's end points in the profile view. Then use these two distances as the base and altitude of a triangle, with the resulting hypotenuse of the triangle being the true length of the line (Figure 6-9). Use this true length as the arc radius for triangulation. You can calculate true lengths based on the two sides of a right triangle picked from the loft floor, or simply draw them on the loft floor and measure. Either method is rather tedious and time-consuming but it is required if you want an accurate flat pattern.

Side Shell Development

Select a point at some convenient location on the profile view, about midships as a starting point. The profile view is a convenient starting point to triangulate the side shell into a true-size view, or as more commonly called in shipbuilding, the shell plate expansion. Figure 6-10, line DN, corresponds to station 3 of the elevation view shown in Figure 6-9. This starting point is labeled point D in Figure 6-10 and corresponds to where station 3 intersects the chine in the profile view.

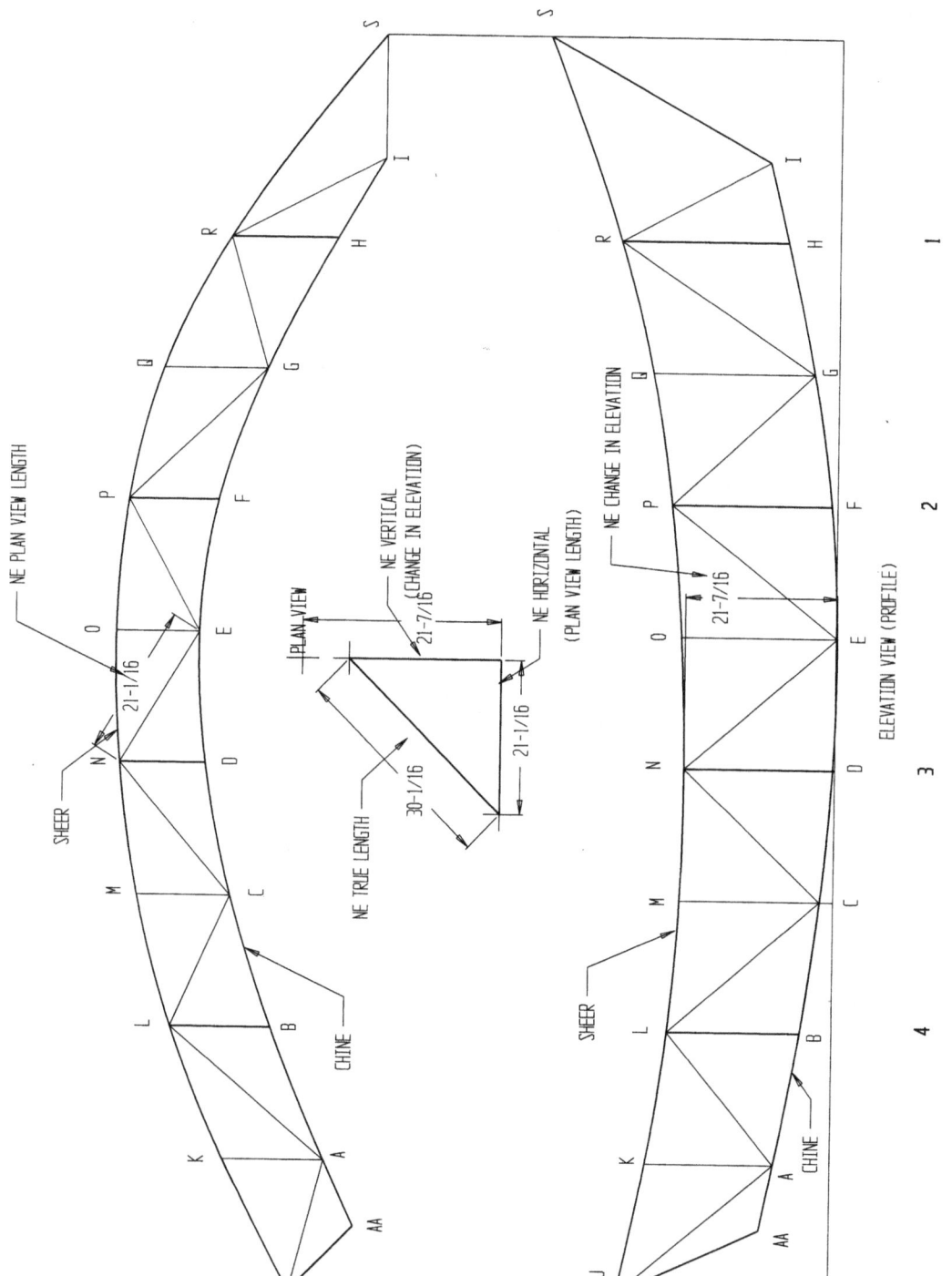

Figure 6-9. Adding stations allows for more accurate triangulation.

A line superimposed over station 3 in the profile view now can be considered station 3 in the expansion view. The shell plate expansion will expand both forward and aft, up and down, from station 3 and point D, as shown in Figure 6-9.

To locate the point on the plate expansion representing the side shell at the sheer at station 3 (point N):

1. Measure the true length of station 3 between chine and sheer from the body plan (Figure 3-8).
2. Measure vertically up from the baseline from point D on the shell plate expansion (Figure 6-9) and make a mark; label this mark point N. This new point N locates the point where the sheer line intersects station 3 in the expanded flat pattern.
3. From point N, swing an arc with a radius equal to the true length of segment NE. (Since the chord of the curve NE is not shown in its true length in any existing view, its true length must be developed by using the plan view length and change in elevation as the base and altitude of a triangle; the hypotenuse of the triangle will be the true length of the straight line chord NE, determined as shown in Figure 6-9.)
4. From point D, draw an arc with radius equal to the true length of chine segment DE. (The true length of DE must also be determined.)
5. These two arcs intersect at point E. (Trammel points on a stick of some convenient length work well for swinging arcs, as shown in Figure 6-11.)

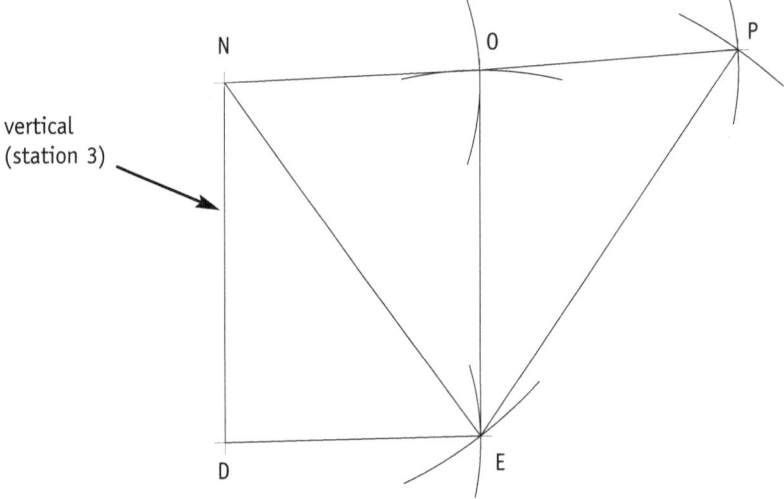

Figure 6-10. Shell plate expansion using true lengths.

6. From point E, draw an arc with true length radius EO, and from N, draw an arc with true length radius NO, intersecting at point O. Repeat this process, using true lengths for segments of the chine, sheer, stations, and diagonal lines between stations until all points defining the perimeter of the flat pattern are located.
7. Connect the points located by this triangulation with smooth curves for the chine and sheer, and by straight lines for the stem and transom. This will result in a pattern for the expanded shell plate.

Manual shell plate expansion is a time-consuming and tedious task. Since the introduction of the computer and programs designed to develop surfaces into flat patterns, manual shell plate expansion is seldom used. A discussion on unwrapping surfaces using the computer is found later in this chapter.

TEMPLATES

The development of flat patterns, or templates, is the end result of the lofting process. The body-plan view gives a clear exterior outline for transverse frames. As

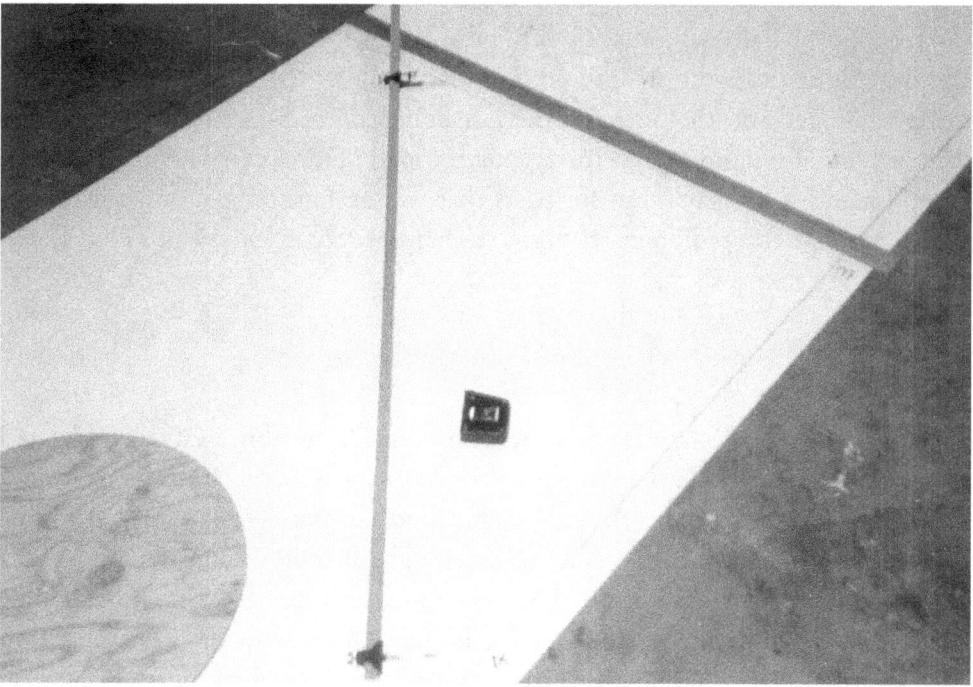

Figure 6-11. Trammel points used to draw large arcs.

Figure 6-12. Frame half-breadth templates and corresponding component templates for the individual frame parts.

you draw additional parts of the structure on the loft floor, you can determine the location of frame cutouts for through-passing longitudinal members, decks and other lofted structures. With one eye on the construction drawing of the part to be templated and the other on the loft floor, you can develop templates that will include all required data to lay out the part. Developing templates is not complicated for flat parts, but for parts that will be formed, you must take into consideration bend radii and resulting stretch-out. Some typical plywood frame templates are shown in Figure 6-12.

Flanges

Often aluminum boat frames and other components are fabricated out of sheared or sawed plate with a flat-bar face plate, or *flange*, welded to one edge to form a T or an L section. This results in a strong composite section but is subject to distortion caused by the heat of welding, and straight or uniform lines are not always simple to maintain. Forming the metal plate into an L section with a press brake in place of welding can speed up production and improve quality. The L section bent from flat plate is commonly called flanged plate. It's often more economical to bend a lot of material into flanged plate in some standard length at one time.

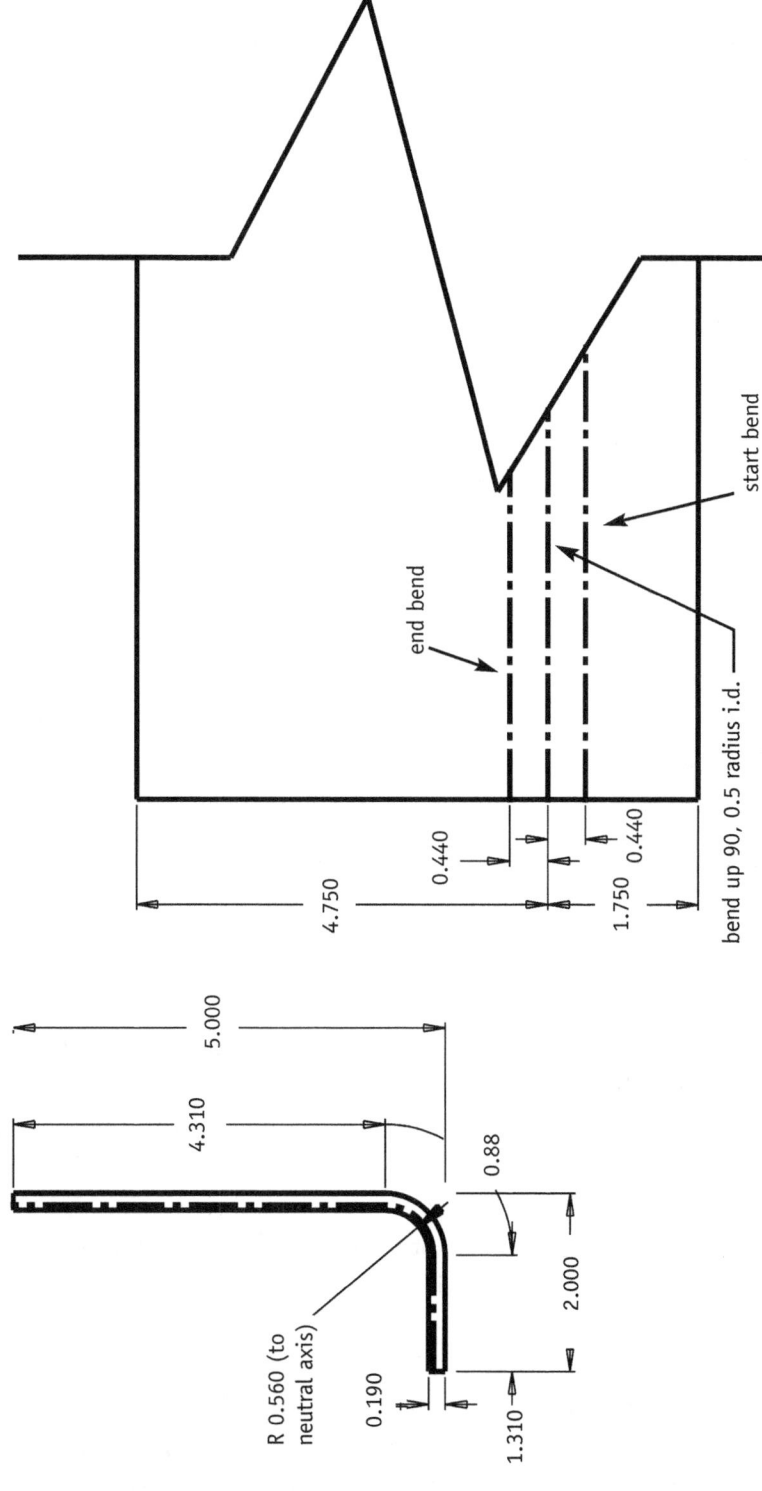

Figure 6-13. Flanged plate layout for 5-by-2-by-3/16-inch angle (alloy 5086-H32).

If a simple flanged plate is formed from a flat sheet of 3/16-inch aluminum into an angle shape with outside dimension of 5 inches by 2 inches, it will not be 7 inches wide but some lesser dimension. The reduction in material width is because of the required bend radius. (Aluminum material requires some minimum bend radius or it will fracture.)

In the case of 3/16-inch aluminum in alloy 5086-H32, this bend radius is 1.5 to 2.5 thicknesses (Appendix B), or 0.28 inch to 0.47 inch, depending on the grain of the material. (The grain usually runs the long dimension of the plate, with bends in this axis requiring the larger bend radius.) Therefore, in this case, a 0.47-inch (rounded up to 0.5) inside bend radius was selected (Figure 6-13). The neutral axis of formed aluminum plate is about one-third the thickness of the material, measured from the I.D. face. To determine the proper stretch-out width of the part, the length along the arc with a radius of 0.56 inch is used, giving a stretch-out of 0.88 inch.

The dimensions, as viewed in the cross section of the flanged plate and measured along the neutral axis, are the true length, or flat-pattern dimensions, to be used for layout. (See Appendix B for laying out press brake bends.)

The true-size flat pattern to form 5-by-2-by-3/16-inch flanged plate out of aluminum alloy 5086-H32 is 6½ inches wide, with the centerline of the bend 1¾ inches in from one side, as shown in Figure 6-13.

Template Construction

You can construct templates from any available flat material, including cardboard, plywood, nailed together strips of wood, Masonite, or metal. A good all-around template material for aluminum construction is thin plywood, preferably with one A-grade face. Plywood is easily cut with a jigsaw, or other hand or power tools commonly found in a home workshop.

Templates must be constructed and marked consistent with shop fabrication capabilities. Otherwise they will be of little use if the process required to fabricate the part with the template is beyond the capability of the shop that will build the boat. If you are like most individuals or small boat builders and do not have a press brake on premises, you will need to know the capability of the press brake at the shop that will do the forming for your boat. An example is the length of the brake: if the bed can only brake a piece of metal 6 feet long, it doesn't make much sense to develop a template for a piece of metal that requires a formed flange 20 feet long. If no press brake will be available for the project, you will need to modify the templates to allow for fabricated instead of formed items.

The shape of each template and the markings on it will determine the characteristics of the part. Therefore, be sure you clearly mark each template with such critical information as the part identification, the quantity of finished parts required per hull, the material type and thickness, and references to the boat centerline and at least one waterline. If forming is necessary, the template will need a notation of the centerline of the bend, as well as the radius, angle, and direction. Notes such as "bend up 90 degrees" or "bend down per template" are essential. On bends of larger radius than the press-brake male die, include "start bend" and "end bend" references, as well as the radius of bend.

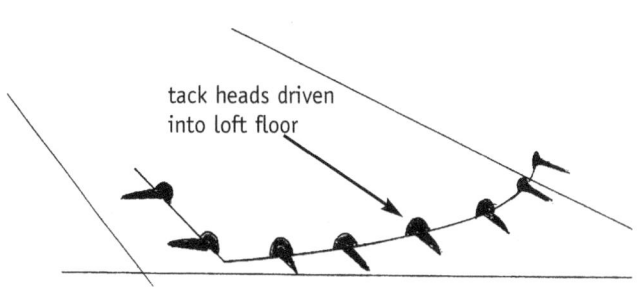

Figure 6-14. Carpet tacks used to pick up lines from the loft floor.

It's not uncommon to have a template for the outline of the entire half-breadth of a frame plus individual component templates for the parts required to assemble the frame. Figure 6-12 shows a frame half-breadth template along with templates for the individual frame parts for a 23-foot sportfishing boat.

All templates should be carefully cut out, dressed, and marked as to specifics required to complete the part. It's a good idea to bundle templates in a logical manner to maintain accountability for each template.

Notches and Slots

When you must fit a through-passing member into a slot, you'll need a suitable clearance since aluminum tends to be very sticky in a tight fit. For this reason, do not make a notch the same width as the material that will fit in the notch. Allow 0.04 inch (1 mm) clearance between parts and all around notches and slots. This clearance also compensates for a small amount of slag that may be present when using plasma arc cutting. A 0.04-inch clearance makes a snug fit (suitable for boatbuilding) that is easily weldable.

Picking Up Lines

A number of methods are commonly used to *pick up the lines* from the loft floor and transfer them to template material. To minimize the time required for this

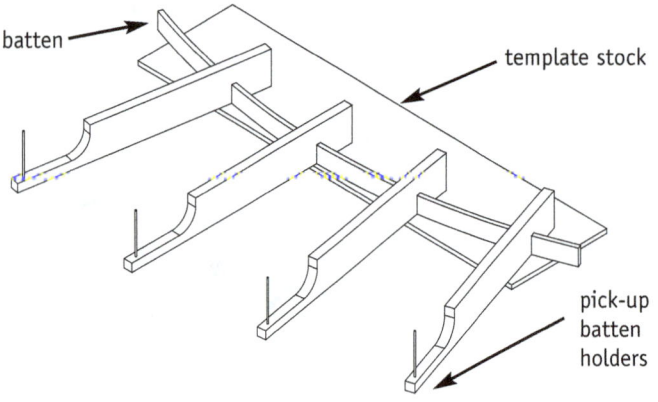

Figure 6-15. Picking up a line using a batten and holders.

job, you are likely to use a combination of two or more of the following techniques:

Tracing. You can trace the shape to be templated from the loft floor onto paper. Place the tracing on the template material, and make a series of punch marks on the traced lines to transfer them to the template material.

Carpet tacks. Place the heads of carpet tacks or small box nails on the lines to be picked up, and drive one edge of the tack heads into the loft floor (Figure 6-14). Put the template material on top of the embedded tack heads, and apply sufficient pressure to impress the marks of the tack heads into the back side of the template material. Connect the marks with a drawn line.

Pick-up batten. Secure a batten in position on the loft floor by driving finish nails alongside the batten. Fabricate several batten holders and place them over the pick-up batten as shown in Figure 6-15. Drive a finish nail through the small end of each batten holder and into the loft floor to hold the holder in position. The slots in the batten holders will grasp the batten and hold it sufficiently firm to retain its shape. After all batten holders are in place, remove the nails from alongside the batten, letting the batten holders hold the batten in the required position. Lift the batten and the free end of the batten holders slightly, and slip a piece of template material under the batten. Trace the batten line onto the template material.

Straightedge. Use a straightedge to transfer straight lines to template stock by laying the straightedge along the line to be picked up. Place the template material over the straightedge so the ends of the straightedge extend from beneath the template material on both sides, and draw a straight line on the template material, aligned with the extended ends of the straightedge.

LOFTING MISCELLANEOUS COMPONENTS

Lofting of a boat does not stop with the development of the basic hull framing and shell plate. Other components that must be fabricated and attached to the hull in some manner often require additional lofting in special areas. On the drift boat, additional lofting was needed to lay out the seat-locker box, and lofted lines were consulted to lay out the oarlock installation. On boats more complex than the drift boat, special lofting projects can continue during the entire construction process. Access to the loft floor is needed for layout of engine beds, cabins, propeller struts, fuel tanks, and any number of special add-ons.

Engine Bed

To properly install the main propulsion engine and gear, the engine bed and centerline of the propeller shaft must first be laid out. Factors to consider are location of the engine to best suit the vessel arrangements, shaft angle and location, engine gear angle (if any), adequate clearance of the engine from boat structure (2-inch minimum is a good rule of thumb for small boats), and access to the engine for oil change and service. To accurately locate the engine mounts at the desired location within the hull, you need a trip back to the loft floor.

1. Look at the engine and gear drawings—furnished by the engine dealer—for the dimensions to accurately locate the engine mounts within the boat. Locate them on the loft floor at the desired engine location.
2. Draw the centerline of the shaft on the loft floor in the profile view, and locate the engine and gear centerlines on the floor.
3. Draw the location of the engine mounts on the engine and gear on the loft floor. If you plan to use adjustable flexible engine mounts, consider their height when setting engine bed elevations.
4. Draw a level line on the body plan view representing the base of the engine flexible mount.
5. Draw a vertical line in the body plan view representing the half-breadth distance to the center of the engine mount.
6. The intersection of these two lines is the location of the engine mount.
7. Check the engine body plan to ensure adequate structural clearance.

Once you've located the bases of the engine mounts on the loft floor, you can confirm adequate clearance, determine engine accessibility, and complete the actual design of the engine bed. For structural strength, the engine bed girder will usually have a stout top flange welded in place. In order to increase the depth of the engine girder, and for ease of access to the engine-mount bolts, the flange atop the engine girder is toed outboard. (This requires moving the engine girders toward the centerline about 1 inch so the engine mount bolts can penetrate the flange.) Access, or "lightening" holes are often cut into the sides of the engine girder for access to the bottom of the engine.

Transverse structures in the way of the engine and engine bed often require modification to suit the engine installation. Perform any modifications on the loft floor, then incorporate them in the affected part.

The development of shell plate into a flat pattern by triangulation was described above. You can use this technique with any developable surface in the boat's structure, including twisted chine bars, longitudinal frames, hull stiffeners that curve in space to remain normal to the shell plate, and other applications that previously were developed by mocking up. The techniques needed to accomplish this type of lofting can usually be figured out by studying the problem and applying principles discussed up to this point.

Additional lofting information is included in several appendices at the back of this book. Appendix B, Calculating Material Stretch-Out for Brake Bending, has already been mentioned. Appendix C details lofting techniques required to ensure a surface is developable from flat material. You can find manual lofting techniques needed to develop larger and more complicated boats in the references at the end of this chapter.

COMPUTER LOFTING

Computer-assisted design, better known by the acronym CAD, has proven to be a very effective tool for lofting boats. CAD lofting is a natural continuation of manual lofting, except the medium used is a computer instead of a full-size loft floor. Some boatyards, using a two-dimensional (2D) CAD program, loft by following the same 2D procedures; that is, using three views similar to a lines drawing. This requires cross-checking between views to obtain a 3D perspective, similar to manual lofting. Since a number of CAD programs have the capability of working in three dimensions (3D), a single master isometric drawing of the boat can replace the three-view concept. This view can be rotated to view the loft from any angle, which provides a much clearer picture. Once the full benefit of computer lofting is realized, rarely does a boatyard return to full-fledged manual lofting. Increased lofting speed and accuracy are only a part of the benefit. When combined with computer-guided automatic cutting, part cutting and the assembly time of the boat are greatly accelerated.

There are a number of computer programs and lofting techniques employed to do CAD lofting, layout, and nesting for automatic cutting. You will need ship design software, such as ProSurf 3 from New Wave Systems (www.newwavesys.com), to develop the long, curved lines required for a boat hull design. This type of program usually includes a provision to determine hydrostatic characteristics of the hull. You will also need a professional 3D CAD drawing program, with surface modeling capability. (Key Creator is a good 3D program that also has a surface and solid modeling capability. See www.kubotekusa.com.) Data from the ship design software that has defined the basic hull parameters is imported into the CAD program for detail design. Additional programs may prove very useful, including unfolding programs that will expedite layout of flanged parts.

When drawing a boat using CAD, the bow should point to the left. Since a computer will determine the distance to the right of station 0 on the x-axis as a positive number, it is preferable to orient the boat drawing with the bow to the left. Station 0 is set at the intersection of the baseline and station 1 in the profile view. In this manner, distances aft of station 0 are always positive numbers.

Lofting in 3D

Since 2D CAD lofting is basically similar to manual lofting, only 3D computer lofting will be discussed in this book.

The first step is to determine the basic hull parameters; that is, the long lines that define the ship's hull geometry. The simplest method is to draw the lines using ship design software. Enter data from the lines drawing and table of offsets into the ship design software using control points defined by 3D coordinates (x,y,z). Prosurf produces a surface model showing all hull exterior surfaces. You can manipulate these surfaces to become developable surfaces by locating a good spread of ruling lines. Once you are satisfied with the hull surfaces in the ship design program, export the surface model to a 3D CAD program for the final lofting.

Figure 6-16 is a 3D surface model that has been imported into

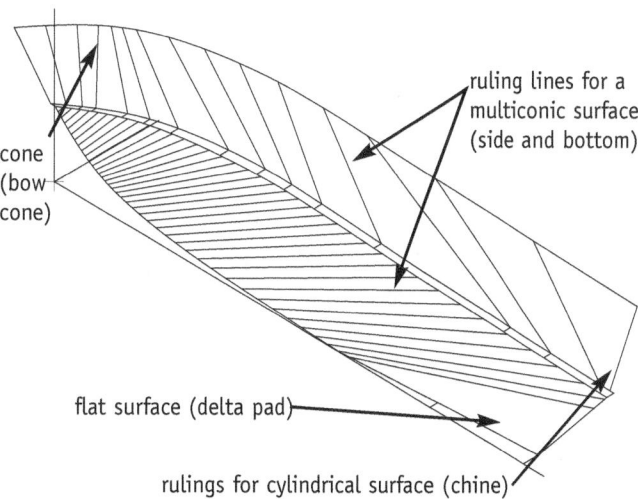

Figure 6-16. Typical computer-generated surfaces of a planing boat, showing types of developable surfaces (conical and cylindrical) and ruling lines.

a 3D CAD program from a ship design program, showing developable hull surfaces with ruling lines. (The model is shown as a half-side model since it is symmetrical about the centerline, eliminating the necessity to draw both port and starboard sides.) This surface model has been modified slightly in the CAD program to fit the boat design parameters by adding a delta pad and a slight stern overhang of the bottom plate. Details were added to the model, including framing, and are shown in Figure 6-17. (Text has been added to this model for illustrative purposes, but text will not normally be included in the loft.) This 3D model can be rotated and inverted to show the model in almost any orientation. Figure 6-17 shows a 24-foot-by-8-foot-6-inch sportfisher hull half-side surface model that was printed from the Key Creator 3D CAD program.

When entities consisting of lines, arcs, and splines are used to define the boat's geometry, the result is called a *wire frame* model. A wire frame model can only display a surface at its edges. For surfaces that are two-dimensional, such as a flat

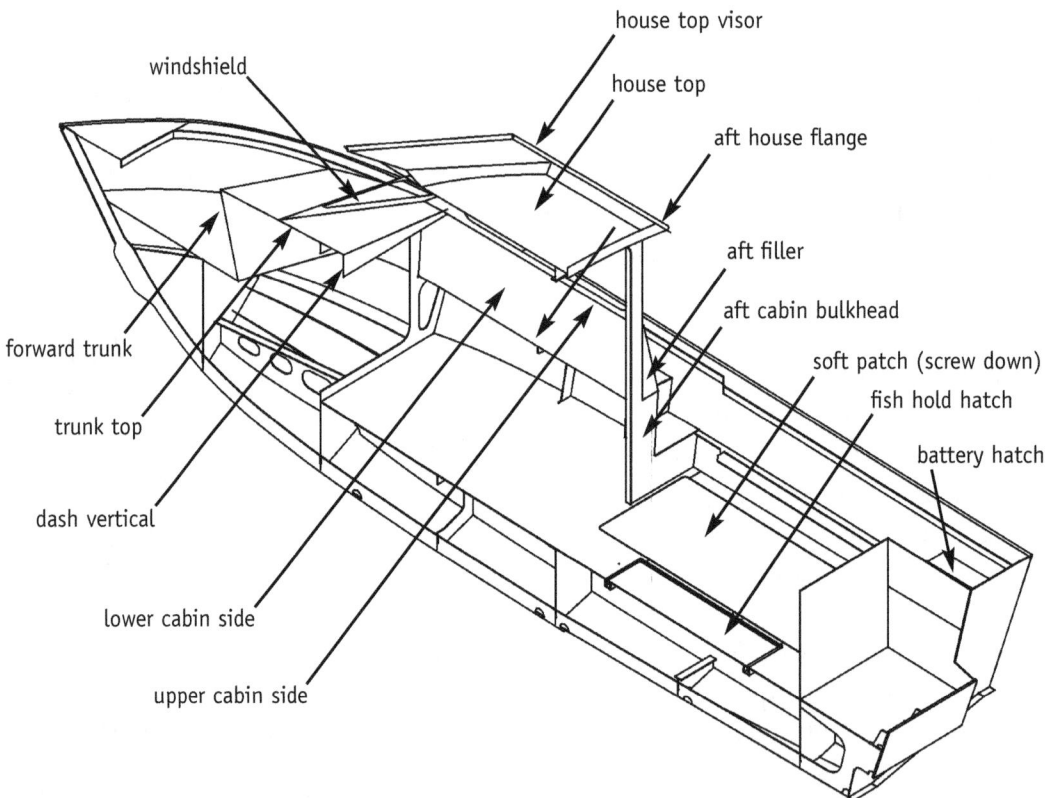

Figure 6-17. CAD-generated isometric half-side rendering of a 24-foot sportfishing boat.

panel, this is usually sufficient. However, when a surface twists through 3D space, as commonly found on boats, a better definition of the surface is needed to define the region between the edges. In conventional manual layout, the method for approximating the surface between surface edges is by using waterlines, buttock lines, diagonals, and station lines. In (3D) computer lofting, this region is called a surface and is defined mathematically by a grid of crossing splines, which represent the surface. By cutting this surface using cutting planes, the geometric shape of the hull parts can be obtained.

A further refinement to the model is to alter the surface model to become a solid model of the surface, showing the thickness of the surface material. A solid is in actuality a series of surfaces, bonded at the edges, that define an object in space. All of these bonded surfaces are combined to become one single solid. A solid model can be worked similar to a surface, but in addition, surface mass properties can be obtained, which is very helpful when doing weight calculations.

One particularly time-consuming and often difficult procedure in manual lofting is flat plate development of shell plate. Using CAD, surfaces can be unwrapped rapidly to include layout lines for framing.

Designing a Developable Surface

To design a developable surface (see Chapter 3), you must first draw a preliminary surface by establishing the edge curves that closely define the desired surface. In defining these edge curves, use as few control points (nodes) as possible: preferably a start and end node, and not more than two nodes along the curve, for a total of four nodes. Once you've established a preliminary surface between two edge curves, locate the ruling lines on the surface that will adequately define the surface.

Ruling lines on a developable surface are commonly located using ship design software. Usually some adjustments to the original edge curves are required to obtain a fully developable surface. By moving the nodes on the perimeter edge curves even a very small distance, the ruling line pattern can change dramatically. Ruling lines should cover the entire surface with a consistent pattern of lines, as shown in Figure 6-16. Once you've located a good spread of ruling lines by manipulating control points on either one or both defining edge curves, you can assume the surface to be developable from flat sheet material.

Fairing of edge curve lines is done in a manner similar to using a flexible batten on a manual loft floor. By limiting the number of node points on an edge curve, you will greatly simplify the fairing. However, when you need numerous nodes to properly define the edge curve, use an overlay curve. This computer routine, which magnifies the curvature of the underlying curve, can be found in ship design software. In the Prosurf 3 program, for example, it is called a "K-curve." Fair the edge curve by manipulating nodes of the edge curve until the K-curve closely matches the edge curve.

To finalize the surface model, repeat, as needed, the process of fairing edge curves to obtain the desired surface shape with a good spread of rulings lines. By making minor adjustments to the locations of nodes on the edge curves, you should be able to obtain a fair developable surface model. The finished surface model then has faired edge curves and properly displayed ruling lines drawn between edge curves, and it is within an acceptable tolerance to comply with the design lines. This is your computer-generated lines drawing, ready for lofting. In Figure 6-16, sides and bottom surfaces are multiconic, the chine is cylindrical (parallel rulings), and the delta pad is a flat surface.

Layout of Framing

Frames and girders must conform to the surfaces of the hull. Traditionally this would be done by connecting points—located by using the intersections of buttock lines, waterlines, stations, and diagonals—with a spline. But all these lines are one step removed from the developable-ruled surface. It is better if the cuts made to define the shape of these members are taken from the ruling lines, which accurately define the shape of the hull. This is done quickly and accurately by CAD software, using a surface modeling program that creates the outlines of frames and girders by defining the intersections of cutting planes with the hull surface. These intersections (or points) are shown as a smooth curve that runs through these points.

Scaling

One of the benefits of 3D computer lofting is the ability to scale a design, either fully or unidirectional by axis (x, y, or z). In other words, being able to increase the length of the boat, but maintain the width and height, or scale by different values on different axis. This is a very powerful design tool that will save many hours of effort when doing dimensional changes. Experience has shown that once a surface is determined to be developable, then scaling that surface, either fully or unidirectionally, will result in a new developable surface.

Aluminum Boat Lofting

Molded Line

Maintaining a consistency when determining the molded surface (or line) will make things much simpler in a computer-generated drawing. By always using the same location for the molded line, progressing beyond the lines drawing and detailing of parts will be much simpler. Figures 6-2 and 6-3 show typical methods of determining the molded line for an aluminum boat.

Burn Sheets

After parts are lofted and detailed, 3D parts are unfolded or unwrapped onto a single flat plane. The parts are then assembled into batches by material and thickness. Selection of stock plate size is usually based upon economics. (Normally the larger the size of the plate, the higher the cost.) *Nested parts* must maintain some edge clearance from each other to allow the cutting machine to operate properly (½ inch is a suggested minimum). Cutting to an edge causes the machine to run off the plate, creating problems. About ¾-inch clearance between parts is common. (Closer clearance is possible after consulting with your cutting service, or "burn center.") The parts are arranged to minimize waste. These sheets are called *burn sheets*. (See Figure 6-18.)

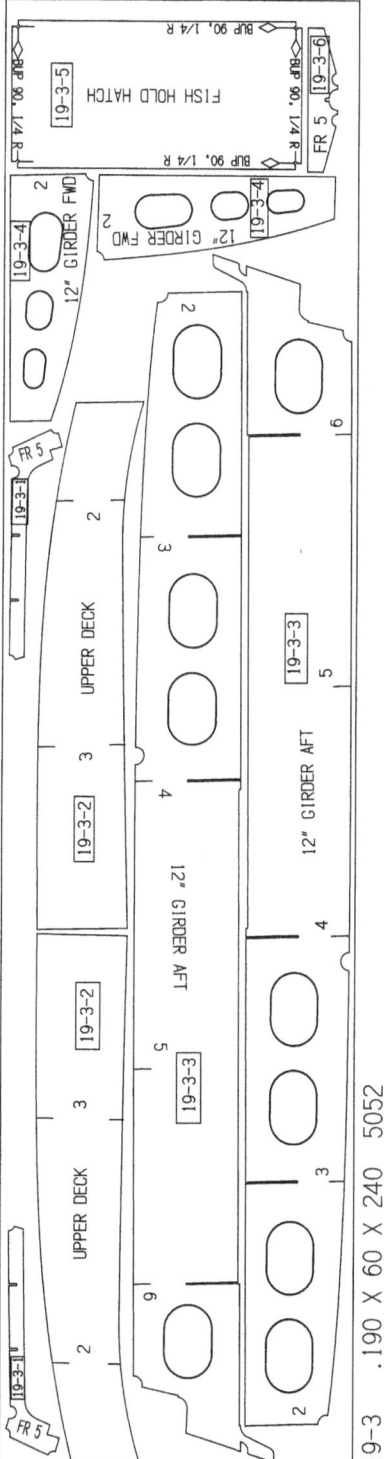

Figure 6-18. Nested cutting drawings (also called burn sheets) for computer-guided plasma or water-jet cutter. (Specmar, Inc., Scappoose, Oregon)

Checking the Burn Sheets

Since a burning machine works in 2D, drawings developed with 3D CAD must be carefully checked to ensure that the parts to be cut are in a 2D plane, and that the projection is perpendicular to that plane of the parts, so that they are all shown in their true size. This can be accomplished by projecting the drawing onto a single plane. The drawing must also be checked to ensure that there are no double burn lines (one on top of another) and that lines do not have any breaks.

Not all cutting programs can work with splines. For this reason, it is common to convert all splines to a series of short straight line segments called polylines.

Submit burn sheets to a burn center in Autocad DWG or DXF format. It is usually prudent to submit burn sheets in DWG format so that the burn center can correct minor errors before processing the parts.

References

Kilgore, Ulman. "Developable Hull Surfaces." Fishing News Ltd., 1967.

Lewis, Edward V. *Principles of Naval Architecture.* Vol. 1, Stability and Strength, p. 13. Jersey City, N.J.: SNAME, 1988.

Vaitses, Allan H. *Lofting.* Camden, Me.: International Marine Publishing Company, 1980.

White, Gerald T. *Problems in Small Boat Design: Multiconic Development of Hull Surfaces.* Dobbs Ferry, N.Y.: Sheridan House, 1959.

CHAPTER 7

Aluminum Boat Construction Sequence

Fabricating components and assembling them into a complete boat will progress rapidly and accurately, as long as you exercise some forethought. Before the detail lofting of the components, you must first determine how you will assemble the boat. Then you can loft, template, and fabricate the boat's component parts to conform with your assembly plan. Your templates should incorporate proper assembly references, such as clearly defined waterlines and buttock lines. You will transfer these reference lines to the component part that you fabricate from the template, and use them later when assembling the boat.

As with any assembly project, an adequately rigid, level, and square assembly platform will greatly expedite construction. *Assembly platforms*, or *jigs*, vary widely; yours will depend upon the size of your boat and the assembly sequence you'll use. Except for production boats constructed with extrusions, aluminum boats have been traditionally constructed inverted on some type of assembly jig to make positioning and welding the bottom and side plates easier. A boat with a lot of internal framing will usually require a simpler jig than a boat with few frames.

Precut boats, whose bottoms and sides are cut using automatic cutting equipment, will often be constructed right side up, starting with the bottom plate, then adding the frames.

Small production-built planing boats using chine and keel extrusions are usually assembled right side up in a cradle-type jig. The hull bottom material is forced down into the jig, where it's welded to the keel extrusion to form a "V" bottom.

Figure 7-1. Starting the assembly of a computer-cut 32-foot landing craft. The craft was assembled on the floor and without a jig, due to the accuracy of the computer-cut parts. (Aliboats, Botswana)

Larger boats and boats constructed without the use of keel and chine extrusions usually have both transverse and longitudinal framing. Since this frame structure develops the hull form, it doesn't need a jig. Such boats are called *self-jigging* designs and are usually assembled inverted.

Precut boats, or "kit boats," that are usually cut by computer-guided equipment are often assembled right side up and follow a different assembly sequence than conventionally cut boats, regardless of size. Because of the accuracy of the cut parts, including shell plate, the boat bottom plate is set into a very simple cradle, or simply set on the floor over wood *dunnage*. Then the framework is placed on the bottom plate, following the layout marks on the plate. Figure 7-1 is a 32-foot landing craft assembled on the floor without a jig. Alignment is maintained by ensuring that the boat goes together symmetrically, and that layout marks and precut notches all align.

DESIGNING AN ASSEMBLY JIG

An *assembly jig* can be as simple as a flat plate on the floor with uprights tack-welded to it at frame locations, or as complicated as those found on the assembly lines in production shops. For most single-boat projects (one-offs), a simple rigid framework with some provision to hold the components in position during assembly will do. The jig should also provide for the rapid and accurate alignment of the various parts to a reference waterline and to the boat's centerline. A well-thought-out jig is usually simple and greatly speeds the boatbuilding process; however, you will need to keep a few things in mind as you design your jig.

Moving the Jig and Boat

Often during the assembly stage, it becomes necessary to move the boat about in the shop. With this in mind, construct the jig in such a way that you can move the entire structure about on the shop floor without damage to the jig or boat. Pipe rollers or a heavy dolly under a sturdy jig are two options for repositioning the boat or even moving it outside temporarily. On larger boats, you can use the assembly jig base as a moving dolly. Construct the jig with two parallel main beams about 8 feet apart. Then the jig, with the boat sitting on it, can be skidded to a crane for turning right side up. The base spacing of 8 feet allows the jig to be skidded onto a flatbed trailer without additional framework. The 50-foot sailboat shown in Figure 4-21 was erected over twin I-beams.

Figure 7-2. A 25-foot workboat inverted on an elevated fabrication base.

Accessing the Inside

The ability to access the boat's interior while the boat is on the jig is another factor to incorporate into your jig design. Allow adequate height for crawling between the gunwale and the shop floor while the boat is inverted on the jig, as shown in Figure 7-2.

Establishing the Waterline

The *assembly reference waterline* is a common height reference you will use while assembling the boat. Select the location of this waterline early in the project and locate it so it's at a convenient height from the floor. As a general rule, it should be about chest-high from the shop floor. Then ensure that every component of the boat, that must be located for height, shows the assembly reference waterline. If the component is located in such a position that the assembly reference waterline can not be located on it, then some other waterline must be used to determine the part's proper elevation.

Design and mark the jig so the centerline and the assembly reference waterline can be quickly and easily seen from any position.

SELF-JIGGING BOATS

Most home boatbuilders do not feel comfortable developing shell plate flat patterns using the manual process. If the required flat patterns are not available, an aluminum boat constructed as a one-off project—such as a home-built boat—should be designed with internal framing, which then becomes a rigid skeleton for the boat. With a rigid skeleton, you can pattern the shell plate directly from the boat's framework. And the framework often is stiff enough to allow the bottom and side plates to be attached without the need for additional jigging to develop the boat's shape.

A boat framework with husky transverse and longitudinal members is most likely strong enough to prevent any frame twisting during the installation of shell plate. This type of hull only requires an assembly jig that is rigid enough to hold the frames in position until the longitudinal members are in place. Once framing members are in place, the jig need only hold the boat in a level and untwisted position for plating.

The assembly of an aluminum boat with self-jigging framing usually involves erecting prefabricated frames, a stem/keel, the transom, and any other members necessary to complete the framework. Clearly mark each part with reference lines for the centerline and some common waterline. During assembly, place these reference lines in alignment to ensure the proper alignment of the framework.

Even with a self-jigging framework, you need some type of assembly platform to hold the parts in position until they can be welded. The boat shown in Figure 7-3 was assembled over a floor area covered with ⅜-inch surplus aluminum plate. The assembly jig consisted of vertical posts tack-welded to the aluminum covered floor. The plan-view locations of the frames were drawn on the aluminum plate.

Figure 7-3. Turning over a 45-foot sailboat hull.

Vertical aluminum members, similar to posts, were erected at each frame location and tack-welded to the aluminum-plate floor. Then the boat's frames were simply clamped to the posts to start the assembly sequence. Although very simple, this assembly fixture was also very cost effective.

Parts that are cut and marked using automatic computer-guided equipment often do not need an assembly jig, since notches in both transverse and longitudinal members provide adequate rigidity and self-align.

Production Boat Jig

A number of small, professionally built, welded-aluminum boats have minimal interior framing. Such boats require some type of jig to hold the bottom and side plates in position during assembly. The jig must be strong enough to provide accurate alignment for assembly and adequate restraint for welding.

Assembly Jig Material

You can construct an assembly jig from any available material. If it's economically feasible, use aluminum for the jig so you can tack-weld temporary boat-to-jig braces to it.

Aluminum Boat Construction Sequence

The cost of jig material for a large boat can be significant. For boats larger than 30 feet that are to be constructed inverted, consider a rigid structural-steel I-beam base. You can bolt aluminum upright members to this base to support framing during assembly.

FABRICATING BOAT FRAMES

Each transverse frame usually consists of a number of pieces, each one templated from the loft floor with sufficient detail to fully define it. If the part is to be formed or flanged, the template should be for the flat pattern so that all the pieces can be laid out on the aluminum sheet and cut at one time. Figure 6-12 shows a typical set of frame templates consisting of a half-breadth exterior outline template and the individual parts templates needed to construct frame two of a 23-foot sportfishing boat.

Figure 7-4 shows a typical welded frame with welded-on flanges. The web of the frame was assembled first, and then the flange was added. Figure 7-5 shows a frame constructed using flanges that were formed on a press brake. Additional cutouts that were cut into the frame during fabrication are shown in Figure 7-6.

To assemble frames accurately, you will need a layout slab, which is nothing more than a piece of aluminum plate large enough to lay out the entire frame. A

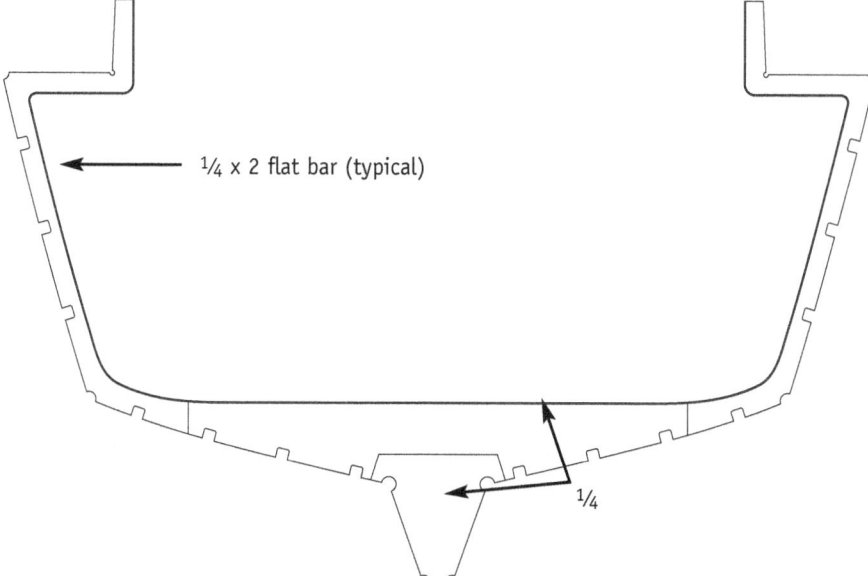

Figure 7-4. Fabricated frame with welded-on flanges.

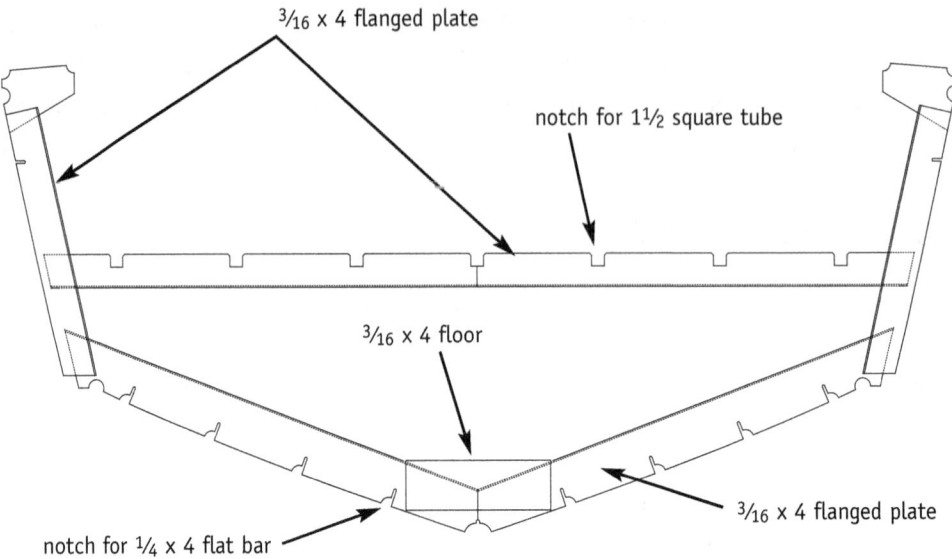

Figure 7-5. Fabricated frame with formed flanged parts.

large section of the bottom shell plate is commonly used for this purpose. The working side of the slab will be marred by grinding and welding, so you'll most likely want to turn that side inward when you later install the plate on the boat.

With the layout slab in place, you're ready to assemble a frame:

1. Lay out a centerline and the reference waterline on the slab at right angles to each other. Use these to accurately position the half-breadth exterior outline template for the frame to be assembled.
2. Lay the template on the slab. Trace the perimeter of the template on the slab to create the frame outline—both port and starboard sides.
3. Place the cut-out individual parts on the outline.
4. Align the waterlines and buttock lines on the parts with the slab reference lines. Check for discrepancies in alignment.

Important note: Often parts do not fit exactly and may require trimming to fit both the frame outline and the reference centerline and waterlines. The cumulative effect of small inaccuracies in lofting, templating, and cutting causes these discrepancies. Correct them at this time, and ensure that the reference layout lines all line up accurately.

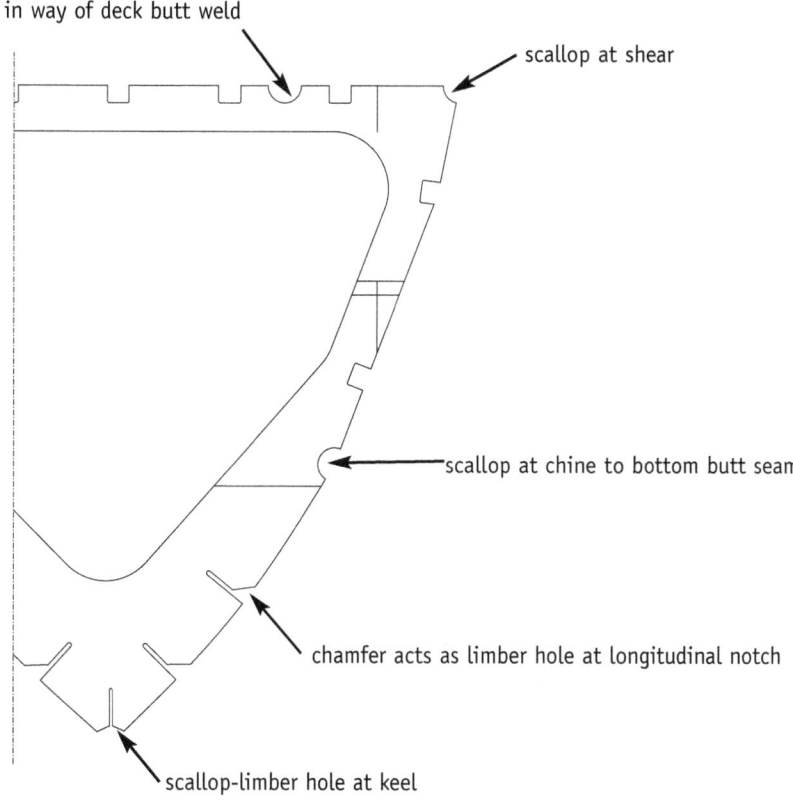

Figure 7-6. Typical transverse frame showing scallops and limber holes.

5. Tack-weld small angle clips to the slab around the perimeter of the frame half-breadth template. Holding the individual frame parts in contact with the clips assures the correct exterior shape.
6. Once you've positioned the frame parts, tack-weld them to the slab in preparation for assembly welding.
7. After welding all the joints, break the tack-welds loose by grinding, and turn the assembled frame over.
8. Back-chip the welds, and weld the back side.
9. Attach any required welded-on flanges after the frame is assembled.
10. Once the frame is completed, check the reference waterlines and centerline, and correct their locations on the finished frame, if necessary.
11. Remove any temporary alignment clips from the slab, grind the weld beads flush, and proceed to the next frame.

12. When all frames are fabricated, clean the slab of all welds and return it to your stock for later use as the boat's bottom plate.

Aluminum to aluminum has a very high *coefficient of friction* when compared to other boatbuilding materials. Consequently, aluminum does not slide on aluminum well, requiring some thought on clearance between pieces when fitting parts together. A substantial amount of pressure is required to force-fit an aluminum flat-bar into a notch on an aluminum part that has no clearance between the part and the flat bar. Check all notches and cutouts for proper fit with a sample piece of material before calling the prefabricated frames complete. This is especially important for the interlocking egg-crate type of transverse and longitudinal structure.

ERECTING THE BOAT FRAMEWORK

Some small aluminum boats are assembled by simply pulling the parts together and tack-welding them in place, as is the case with the McKenzie River drift boat shown in Figure 7-7. Two pieces of ½-inch plywood to assist in positioning the bottom and side plates are the extent of the simple jig. But as a boat's design becomes more complex, so does the assembly jig.

Most aluminum boats built in limited quantities have interior framing that is assembled prior to the placement of shell plate. Follow the steps below when using a simple assembly jig consisting of vertical upright posts located at intervals corresponding to the boat's transverse frame spacing.

1. Pre-clean the abutting edges of frames, keel, and any other critical parts that will define the boat's hull form.
2. Clearly mark the reference waterlines and centerline on these parts before erecting them (usually inverted on the assembly jig).
3. Use a level to mark the reference waterline on the assembly-jig uprights. A laser level is an excellent choice. If you must work around a structure and cannot maintain a consistent line of sight, use a water level, as described in Appendix F.
4. Establish the boat's centerline on the jig and string a taut line to represent it.
5. Align the frames with the reference waterline and the centerline, and temporarily secure them to the assembly jig.

Aluminum Boat Construction Sequence 169

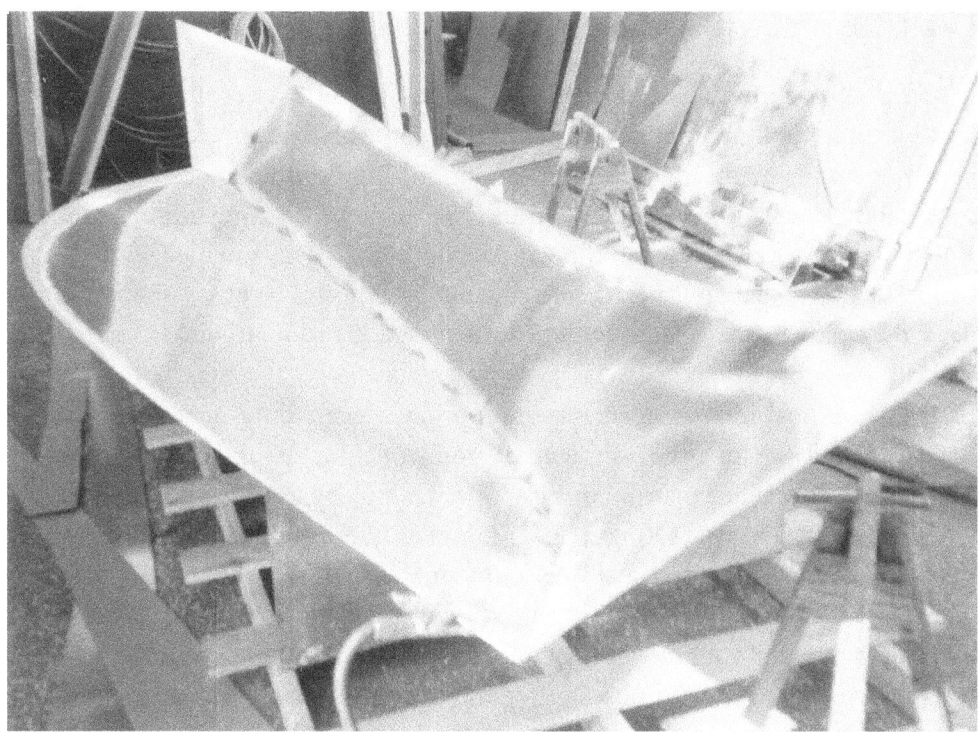

Figure 7-7. Assembling a small aluminum boat such as a McKenzie River drift boat requires only a simple jig.

6. Locate the stem bar, keel, transom, longitudinal members, and sometimes the chine bars on the erected framework and lightly tack-weld them in position; be careful to observe the distortion precautions detailed in Chapter 5.
7. Determine if you need temporary additional strongbacks and restraints to maintain alignment and a fair structure. Pay particular attention to the chine bars and stem bar since these items are normally sight edges.
8. Tack-weld additional flat-bar strongbacks down the full length of the chine bars and stem bar before tacking the adjoining shell plate. This will reduce any tendency for the chine or stem bar to go out of alignment.
9. Install any additional items that require careful fit-up, such as formed gunwale parts, engine-bed girders, cockpit wells, etc. (It is easier to install these now before attaching the shell plate because of better accessibility for welding.)
10. Securely tack the adjoining shell plate into position.

FAIRING THE BOAT STRUCTURE

When all boat framing has been erected, place a slender strip of thin wood at various locations along the framework, using it as a flexible *batten* to ensure that the boat is fair and the framing has no pronounced high spots. If you find any high spots, check the position of the offending frame member to be sure it's properly aligned with the reference waterline and centerline. Fair in any high spots with a batten, mark the part for metal removal, and either grind or plane it down to the desired height. Pay particular attention to the ends of longitudinals for fairness with the stem bar.

If longitudinal framing members are too low, there will be a gap between the shell plate and the longitudinal member. You can eliminate the majority of these low areas, after the shell plate is positioned on the hull, by using a saddle and wedge, as explained in Chapter 5 (Figure 5-13). Since the positioned shell plate is very rigid, the framework will usually bend to fit the shell plate, not the other way around. If the framing member is so rigid that the shell plate is actually pulled in, then relieve the framing member by making a few temporary cuts in the member to facilitate pulling it into place. After the member is pulled into position and tack-welded in place, reweld the temporary cuts in the framing member.

During the fairing process of a hull that is being developed from flat plates, use a straightedge to make sure the framing is consistent with a developable surface. If the shell plate is developable, the orientation of the straightedge should be easy to locate by moving it about the hull surface. In the forward third of a planing hull bottom, a straightedge oriented at—as a general rule—about 45 degrees to the centerline will touch both the keel and the chine, with all framing members in contact with the straightedge. If the framing is in contact with a straightedge oriented in the correct direction, the hull should develop out of a flat sheet of material. A line drawn on the structure where the straightedge lies will be the location of a ruling. If there are local high spots on the ruling, grind them down until the straightedge touches all members along the ruling. Use a flexible batten to fair in adjacent areas.

If you cannot orient a straightedge to lie flat on the hull surface in at least one direction, then the shell plate will not develop. Appendix C provides one method of modifying the boat's lines to conform to a developable surface.

LIMBER HOLES AND RAT HOLES (SCALLOPS)

It will be far easier to make all cutouts in framing members adjacent to the shell plate before the shell plate goes on. Structural members in contact with the shell plate should have *limber holes* where entrapped moisture would tend to collect when the boat is right side up. Rain, spray, and condensation should be able to pass through framing members to the bilge.

Before the shell plate is installed, analyze the structure to determine the need for limber holes and their locations. Cut half circles with a radius of about 1½ inch (or one-third the depth of the member, whichever is smaller) in the structural member at the desired locations. Be sure insulation or other parts won't plug limber holes and restrict the free passage of water. You may want to enlarge limber holes located along the keel in the bilge area to provide a less-restricted flow to the bilge pump.

Rat holes, sometimes referred to as *scallops*, are similar to limber holes but are cut into structural members in the way of shell-plate butt-welded seams. Their purpose is to allow 100 percent access to the inside of the seam to ensure proper welding (Figure 7-8). After testing and repairing all the weld seams, you can plug the rat holes.

Water stops prevent liquid in a fuel tank from traveling between the surface of the shell plate and a longitudinal between *fillet* welds. Weld a continuous fillet weld between the structural member and the shell plate, as shown in Figure 7-9.

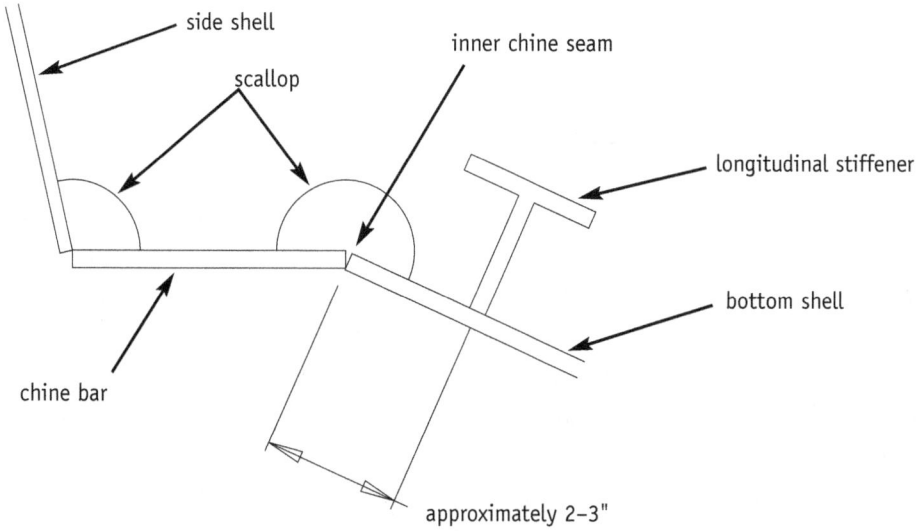

Figure 7-8. Locating scallops (rat holes) in the way of weld seams.

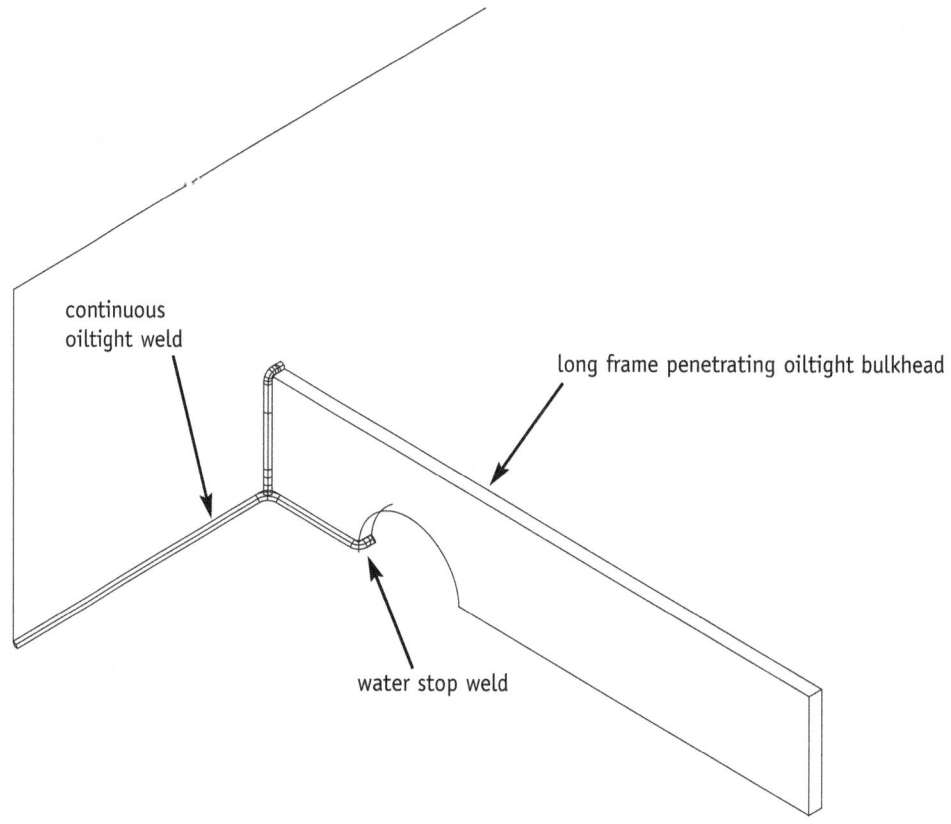

Figure 7-9. Longitudinal frame member penetrating oiltight bulkhead.

Framing End Connections

When a longitudinal member passes through a notch in a transverse frame or bulkhead, a very small portion of the frame carries the load, which can result in *tripping*, or crushing the frame web. A common solution is to add a vertical stiffener (as shown in Figure 7-10) to bulkheads, which acts as both bulkhead stiffener and a load-carrying member. For longitudinal members that terminate at a frame, add a chock at every other longitudinal (as a minimum), as shown in Figure 7-11.

A common detail for stopping a longitudinal member a short distance from a watertight or fuel-tight bulkhead is shown in Figure 7-12. A small gusset tripping bracket, added on both sides of the bulkhead, carries the load from the longitudinal to the transverse bulkhead. If it is necessary to terminate a longitudinal member on shell plate, then taper the end of the longitudinal at least 1:3 to reduce the stresses at the end of the longitudinal, as shown in Figure 7-13.

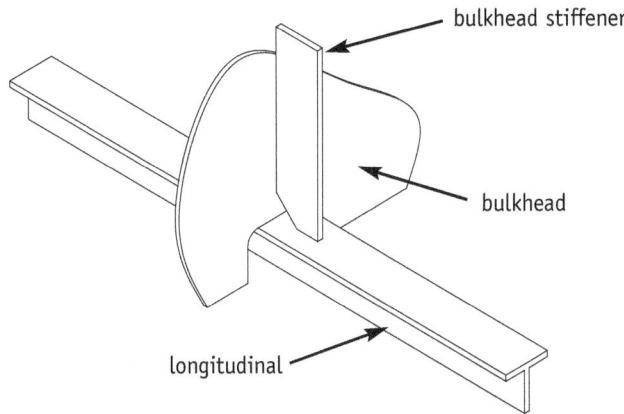

Figure 7-10. Bulkhead stiffeners should land on crossing members to prevent crushing the bulkhead in the event of a grounding.

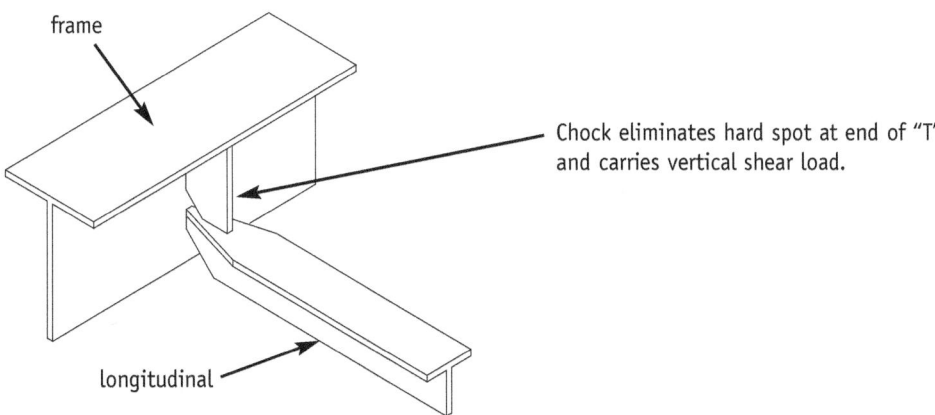

Figure 7-11. A chock prevents hard spot and carries vertical shear forces from longitudinal to frame.

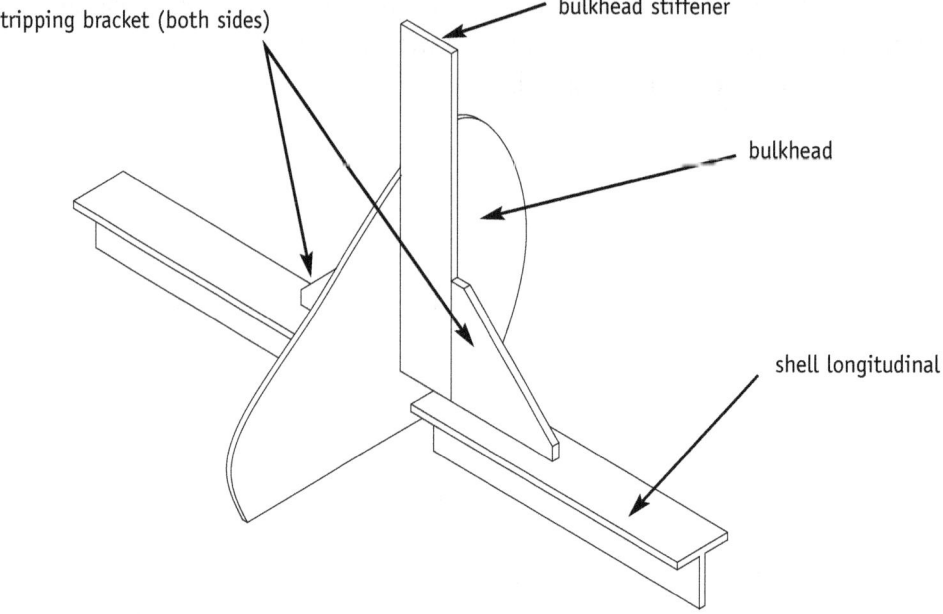

Figure 7-12. Tripping bracket carries load from bottom longitudinal to vertical bulkhead.

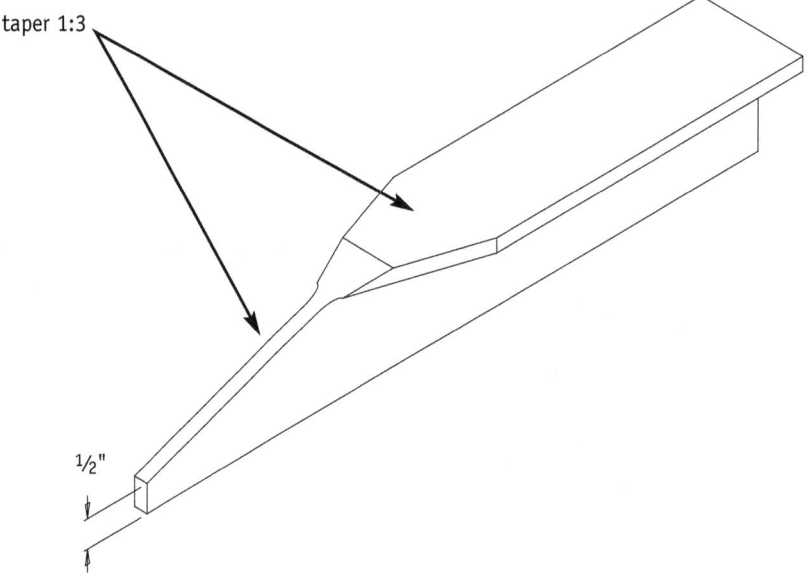

Figure 7-13. Taper ends of members to avoid hard spots.

FIT-UP OF SHELL PLATE

The manner in which you install the shell plate can cause warping of the boat framework if done incorrectly. On larger boats that require more than one plate to cover the hull bottom, install the larger, flatter portions of shell plate first, securely tacking them in place. They cause minimal movement of the framework during installation and, once installed, impart considerable stiffness to the structure. This added stiffness will help hold the framework in place, thus minimizing distortion, when you install shell plate that requires twisting.

Because the bottom plate of a chine boat is usually flat and relatively large in the after portion, install it before the side plates. Accessibility to the inside surface of the bottom is also much easier before the side plates are on (assuming that you built the hull inverted). The curvature forward in the bottom plates of modern planing boats is gradual enough so that you can usually pull the plate material into position manually without the need to pre-roll the plate.

The sequence of installing shell plate on smaller boats differs because the bottom plate often is one piece. Experience has shown that it's easier to fit the pointed forward end of the bottom plate first. If the wider portion of the bottom shell plate is clamped to the boat framework first, then the bow end is pushed down to contact the boat framework; the shell plate will develop a greater curvature as it moves forward. This normally results in only the tip of the bow end of the shell plate touching the framework, with a gap between the bow end and the clamped-down portion. It can be difficult to force the shell plate down to meet the framing to eliminate this gap and often requires some preformed curvature in the shell plate. On the other hand, if the pointed bow end of the shell plate is clamped to the frame first, the plate will usually wrap around the structure with considerably less gap when pushed down into position, and preforming won't be required.

Steps to fit up the bottom plate follow:

1. Starting at the bow end, align the pointed end to the proper location on the framework, and either clamp it in place or wedge it, using a saddle or dog welded to the framework (see Figure 5-13). Don't tack-weld it yet; some side-to-side movement of the plate may still be necessary during fit-up.
2. Apply gentle downward pressure—assisted by gravity—to the shell plate suspended aft of the bow, until it comes in contact with the framework. Slight side-to-side movement may be required to maintain the correct alignment with the stem bar.

3. As fitting progresses toward the stern, clamp the plate to the framework to hold it in position.
4. When the entire length of the bottom plate is in proper alignment, tack it securely to the framework and remove the clamps.

Shell panels on small planing boats can often be cut from a single large piece of material, needing no seams other than on the perimeter. However, this requires that the hull framing be designed and constructed to comply with the requirements of a developable surface (see Chapter 3).

Where a hull is not fully developable, the hull panels can be broken up into smaller panels, using butt-welded seams between them to complete the plating. As a rule of thumb, use the largest hull panels that are practical to minimize welding. The hulls shown in Figures 3-2 and 7-3 are not fully developable and have a number of shell-plate butt seams.

Shell plate can be cut to the approximate size by first making a pattern of the area to be plated. This is easily done on small boats by draping a large piece of corrugated cardboard over the structure and marking it around the panel perimeter with a pencil. (Suppliers often pad aluminum shipments with corrugated cardboard; save this material for templates.) Cut out the cardboard pattern with a knife. Typically you can use the same pattern to lay out the shell plate for both sides of the hull, but it's not uncommon for boats to be slightly out of symmetry, so fit the pattern carefully to the opposite side and note any adjustments before you cut the material.

For large surfaces, construct a shell-plate pattern from strips of plywood placed over the framework. Mark the strips from the framework, trim them to fit, clamp them in place over the boat framing, and nail them securely together. Add diagonal braces to ensure the pattern retains the correct shape. When the pattern is complete, lay it on the floor. If it lies flat, it's a developable surface; if it has a bulge or won't lie flat, the panel isn't developable, and you must reduce its size.

After the shell plate is cut out to fit the pattern, clean the inside surfaces for welding to the framing, and clean around the perimeter for welding to adjacent plating. Check the boat framing for adequate limber holes and welding rat holes in the area to be plated (Figure 7-6), and if needed, cut them out before proceeding. Position the panel on the boat's pre-cleaned framework and temporarily secure it in place with clamps.

After the piece is clamped in position, it must be worked into contact with framing and adjoining shell plate while maintaining an overall fairness (techniques to align plates are detailed in Chapter 5). Each piece of shell plate may require a different sequence of fit-up and tacking, depending upon the judgment of the boatbuilder. Special clamps, such as woodworker's furniture clamps that fit on long lengths of pipe, can be used to clamp difficult areas. Portable come-along pullers, pry bars, mallets, and plain old-fashioned muscle power are commonly employed to obtain the desired fit-up. Don't overlook the assistance of a helper to briefly hold two plates together while they are tack-welded. Remember to make the tack-welds only large enough to hold the plate in position and to place them in order to minimize distortion.

On larger boats, place saddles on the inside surface of the shell plate straddling internal framing, and use wedges to force the shell plate into contact with the plating. Use the flat bar/lever technique shown in Figure 5-11 and the strongback techniques shown in Figure 5-13 to fair abutting plate edges together. Keep in mind that these techniques will damage the plate surface finish.

Once one shell plate has been fitted and tack-welded in place, fit adjacent plates. The gap between the adjoining plates should not exceed 1/16 inch.

HULL WELD-OUT

After the fit-up, start welding the shell plate on the seams inside the boat. Following the prescribed welding sequence outlined in Chapter 5, weld all watertight hull seams inside. After the inside hull seams are 100 percent welded, back-chip the welds from the outside and weld the outside of the seams (Figure 5-8). Make the final weld of the shell plate to the framework only after all hull-plate butt welds are completed. This welding sequence reduces weld-heat-induced distortion.

On an aluminum hull, perform the final shell plate weld-out as follows:

1. Weld the transverse butt seam closest to midships, starting at the keel and welding outboard on both the port and starboard sides. This allows the unrestrained shell plate to be drawn toward the welded transverse seam.
2. Move to the transverse seam immediately forward of the one just welded and weld it out in the same manner, alternating with short lengths of weld on the port and starboard hull sides.
3. Move to the transverse seam immediately aft of the midships transverse seam and weld it out in a similar manner.
4. Repeat this process until all transverse shell plate butt seams are welded.

5. After the transverse seams are welded, begin the longitudinal seams. Weld midships on the keel seam, progressing both forward and aft. This lets the bottom plate slide sideways toward the keel when the plate-edge-to-keel weld cools and shrinks.
6. After the keel weld is complete, weld the next longitudinal seam outboard from the keel, both port and starboard, starting midships and working both ways.
7. Weld the bottom plate to the chine bar or to the side plate at the chine, depending on the chine design. This allows the bottom plate to pull the side plate toward the keel slightly instead of locking in high stresses.

By following this sequence, weld-heat-induced stresses are not allowed to accumulate.

Visualize the hull plate as a sheet that can slide over the framework to compensate for shrinkage at the weld seams and not cause the framework to buckle because of locked-in stress. It should be obvious that a lot of welding along one side of a plate will warp it. It should also be obvious that if both sides of the plate are welded in some symmetrical sequence, distortion should be considerably reduced.

WELDING THE FRAMEWORK TO THE SHELL PLATE

After all the watertight hull-plate seams are welded, weld the frames and longitudinals to the shell plate. These welds will show a definite shrink mark through the hull side, but the marks can be greatly reduced by intermittent-welding and keeping the individual welds small. For a watertight bulkhead that must be continuous-welded to the shell plate, put a 100 percent fillet on one side only and skip-weld the other side. A double continuous fillet weld to the shell plate will be very distinct on the outside hull surface and should only be used if absolutely required.

The weld between longitudinal members and the hull bottom can, in most cases, be intermittent. Use a welding sequence that includes reversing the direction of weld-bead travel at the end of each stitch weld, traveling back over the just-welded bead for about 1 inch to prevent crater cracks (see Chapter 5 and Figure 5-5). Continuous-weld at least one side of the forward third of the longitudinals on the bottom shell plate of a planing hull. Slamming-induced stress will often cause a zipper-effect weld failure on stitch welds in this area. Be sure to weld around the ends of all framing to discourage the start of weld cracks.

TURNING THE BOAT OVER

On a small boat, you can carefully turn over the hull after the shell plate is tacked in position so the inside hull-seam welding can be done with the boat right side up. This allows better ventilation of the smoke from the welding, eliminating a lot of welder discomfort. The easier access, better lighting, and flat welding position will speed weld-out. When the inside welding is complete, turn the hull over once again to complete the outside welds. Resituating the hull lets you do most of the welding in the flat position.

On larger boats that can be difficult to turn over, it's desirable to complete the bulk of the hull-bottom interior welding prior to turning the boat over as dirt and debris will fall into the bilge area when the boat is upright and complicate the weld-out of the interior framing. This is contrary to the procedure used for small boats that can be easily turned repeatedly. Once the larger boat is turned upright, it will not be turned upside down again. This is another reason to complete the interior welding while the boat is inverted, so that the exterior welding, particularly on the bottom, can be accomplished in the flat position.

Turning a boat over that's less than 40 feet can usually be accomplished without a crane if the task is carefully thought out. If the shop ceiling is high enough, the boat can often be rolled over inside, using automobile tires as padding between the hull and the shop floor, and overhead beams and rafters as attachment points for come-alongs and small hoists (Figure 7-3). Larger boats are usually moved outside and turned over with a mobile crane. Mobile cranes with two hooks can be rigged so the boat can be rolled over in the air without touching the ground.

WATERTIGHT TESTING OF WELDS

A soapy-water bubble test is the most common method of checking for pinholes in watertight welds. Brush soapy water over the weld to be tested. Direct an air hose (from a compressor) to the opposite side of the plate from the soapy water and blow air directly on the weld. This is called an air-wand test. An air wand is simply an on/off valve between the air hose and a short piece of pipe of some convenient diameter and length used as the wand.

Proper use of the air wand results in a small increase in air pressure at the weld. If air can pass through the welded area, bubbles will appear in the soapy solution on the opposite side of the plate. Test all weld seams that are required to be watertight in this manner, and mark any detected leaks for repair. Conduct a final air-wand test after all repairs have been made.

FINAL METAL WORK

After all watertight hull welds have been tested and repaired as necessary, the boat is ready for the additional metal work needed to complete the project. Some items that make up the boat can be more economically prefabricated independent of the hull. Since a boat hull or deck will have some distortion caused by welding, prefabricated items, such as a center console or a cabin, may not fit exactly to the desired surface. Compensate for this distortion by incorporating a small amount of additional metal, called trim, in the prefabricated item (see Chapter 5). Cut this additional material to fit during the scribing-in of the part to the boat structure (Figure 7-14). If you add 1 inch of trim to the base of the item being joined to the deck, then place the scribe line 1 inch above the deck line so that when the console is trimmed in, it will be at the correct height, and there won't be any welding gaps.

To complete the boat hull, finish the gunwales and install the decks. Attach all trim, including rubrails, pad eyes, and other miscellaneous weldments. If an aluminum cabin or console is required, install it at this time.

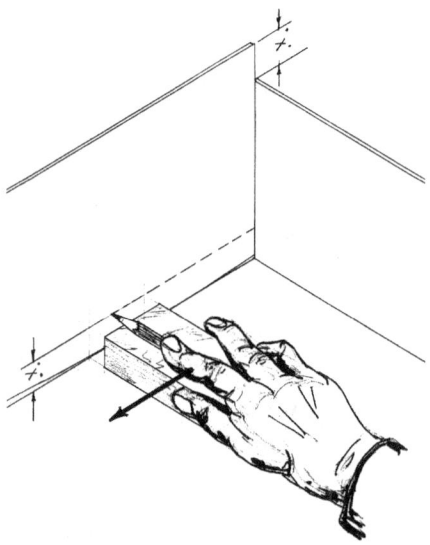

Figure 7-14. Scribing in a panel for fit-up using a pencil and a wood spacer block.

CHAPTER 8

Sailboats

Most aspects of sailboat and powerboat construction are identical, but in some areas, sailboats demand more skill and time. This is particularly evident in the shape of the hull. Most sailboat designs call for round bilges, so a nondevelopable shell is common—in contrast to the conically developed plating on most planing powerboats. Some sailboat hulls are designed with multiple chines to simulate a true round bilge. The sailboat hull shown in Figure 4-21 is actually a multiple-chine boat, with such narrow *strakes* that it approaches a round bilge hull form.

Nondevelopable sailboat hulls are almost always constructed by welding the shell plates over a skeleton of transverse and longitudinal members. (The methods for constructing a hull with developable shell are found in Chapters 5 through 8.) The only additional tooling needed to form a nondevelopable hull is a bending roll (Figure 4-19) to preform shell plate into gentle curves.

ALUMINUM MASTS

Sailboat masts have traditionally been made of wood. A number of boats still have wood masts, and there are still some wood-mast builders around. Carbon fiber masts are growing in popularity, but the vast majority of sailboat masts manufactured today are made of extruded aluminum. Cost and efficiency of an aluminum mast are its primary advantages; while a wood mast takes time and effort to maintain and carbon fiber masts are very expensive, an aluminum mast is relatively inexpensive and almost maintenance free.

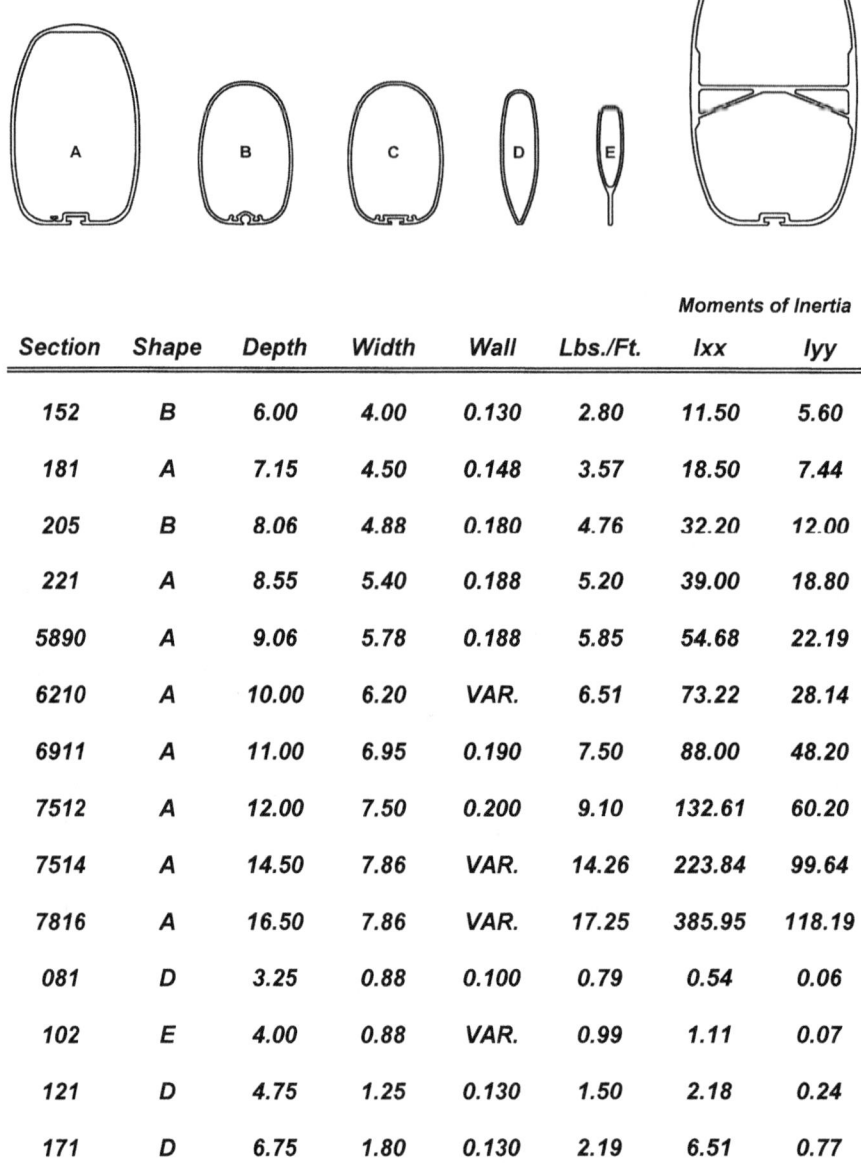

Section	Shape	Depth	Width	Wall	Lbs./Ft.	Moments of Inertia Ixx	Iyy
152	B	6.00	4.00	0.130	2.80	11.50	5.60
181	A	7.15	4.50	0.148	3.57	18.50	7.44
205	B	8.06	4.88	0.180	4.76	32.20	12.00
221	A	8.55	5.40	0.188	5.20	39.00	18.80
5890	A	9.06	5.78	0.188	5.85	54.68	22.19
6210	A	10.00	6.20	VAR.	6.51	73.22	28.14
6911	A	11.00	6.95	0.190	7.50	88.00	48.20
7512	A	12.00	7.50	0.200	9.10	132.61	60.20
7514	A	14.50	7.86	VAR.	14.26	223.84	99.64
7816	A	16.50	7.86	VAR.	17.25	385.95	118.19
081	D	3.25	0.88	0.100	0.79	0.54	0.06
102	E	4.00	0.88	VAR.	0.99	1.11	0.07
121	D	4.75	1.25	0.130	1.50	2.18	0.24
171	D	6.75	1.80	0.130	2.19	6.51	0.77

Figure 8-1. Typical mast cross sections. (Courtesy Forespar)

The aluminum spar has evolved from the rather large cross section and relatively thin-walled extrusions of 50 years ago to the smaller, thicker extrusions of today. The larger, thin-walled masts were slightly lighter but had more wind resistance, and the thin walls presented some difficulties when drilling and tapping for threaded fasteners. The smaller and thicker modern mast section offers less wind resistance and more readily holds a tapped-in threaded fastener. Welding is also easier on the thicker mast.

Various mast manufacturers have aluminum extrusion dies designed for their products. Typical mast cross sections are shown in Figure 8-1. Mast sections can be round, oval, or some special shape, and they often include a slot for the boltrope or slugs on the luff of the sail. The aluminum alloy used is usually 6061-T6 or 6061-T651. The T6 temper gives the alloy its high strength; any temper lower than T6 will not be as strong (see Chapter 2). To protect the T6 temper, welding on the mast is limited in scope and location to areas not subject to high stress.

Aluminum masts may also be constructed of preformed and butt-welded sheets, but this is typically limited to masts too large to practically fabricate with a standard extrusion, or those with long tapering sections.

MAST LOADS

Masts are subject to high compressive loads and, as with any long, slender column, failure from buckling can occur. Intermediate spreaders and shrouds (guy wires) reduce the tendency of a mast to buckle. The spreader locations are support points that resist buckling. Masts are most subject to failure by buckling in the center of the span between support points, with the longest span between support points normally being between the main deck and the lowest set of spreaders. If you construct a mast from two or more lengths, locate the splice at other than this critical section to reduce the possibility of the joint, stiffened by the use of a sleeve, contributing to a load failure.

MAST MODIFICATIONS

A mast extrusion may require cutting, welding, drilling, and installation of fasteners before it's ready for installation. Modifications to the basic extrusion can be fairly simple or quite extensive, depending on the size and complexity of the boat.

Splicing

Mast extrusions can be manufactured to any length by special order, but as a practical matter, the upper limit is usually about 40 feet—the longest extrusion that

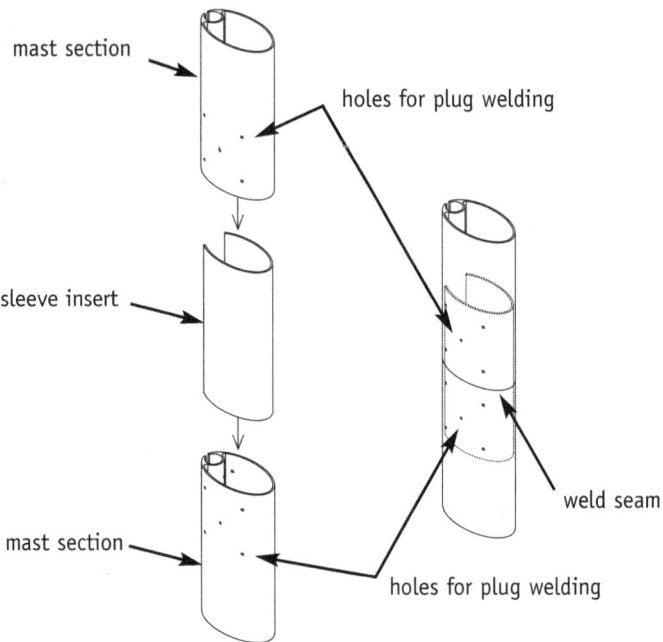

Figure 8-2. Using a sleeve as a mast splice.

can be economically handled and shipped. Any mast more than 40 feet long usually requires a *splice*.

Splicing is usually accomplished by welding, but because of the annealing effect of weld heat, 6061-T6 loses considerable strength in the weld zone. To minimize the loss of mast strength, fit an internal sleeve inside the mast centered on the weld seam (Figure 8-2). Ensure the length of a splice sleeve is at least eight times the maximum mast width.

In a pattern similar to that shown in Figure 8-2, drill the ends of the mast with holes about 1 inch in diameter to be used for plug welding. Slide the sleeve inside the mast sections and butt-weld the stub ends of the mast together. Plug-weld the mast to the sleeve through the drilled holes.

Taper

Tapering a mast at the top is aesthetically pleasing and improves efficiency by reducing weight aloft and decreasing windage. The common practice is to taper

Sailboats

the upper 20 percent of the mast. Always locate the taper on the forward side of the mast, leaving the aft side as a straight surface upon which to mount the sail track.

Tapering can be either straight or cambered. For a straight taper, remove a slender triangle from each side of the mast and force the forward face of the mast back to abut the aft edges of the cutout. Butt weld the abutting edges of the cutouts together. A small triangular section at the bottom of the taper may have to be removed from each side of the mast to allow the forward portion to hinge back, as illustrated in Figure 8-3.

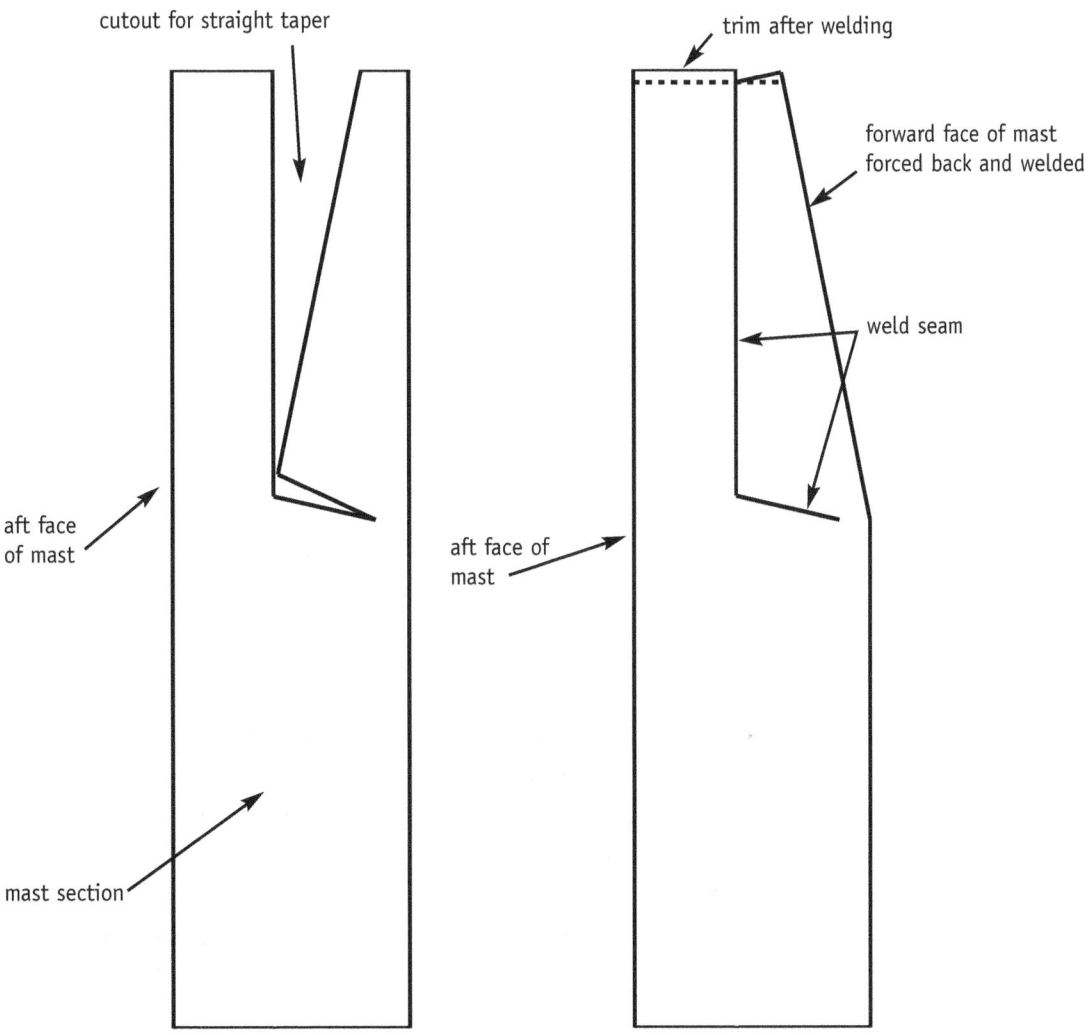

Figure 8-3. Straight mast taper.

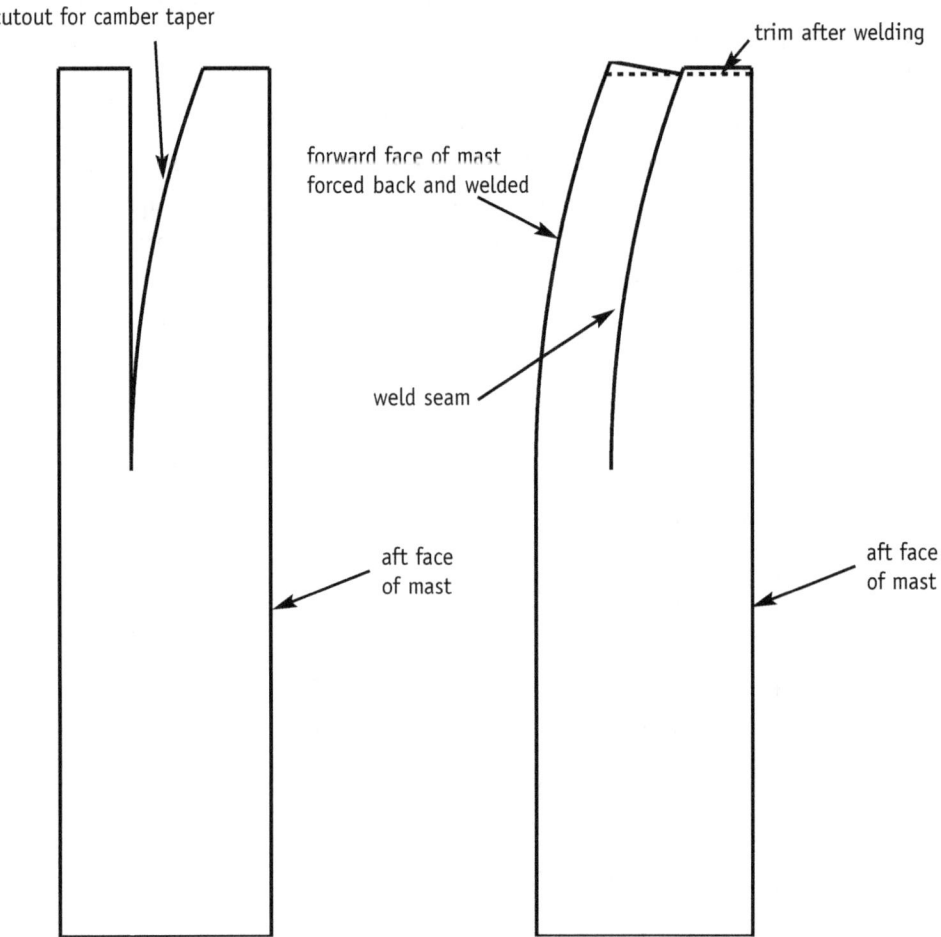

Figure 8-4. Cambered mast taper.

For a cambered taper, again remove triangle sections from the mast, but in this case give the aft leg of the cutout a gentle camber (Figure 8-4). This technique eliminates the need for the additional triangular cutout required for a straight taper. When you force the forward side of the mast back for welding, it will take a gentle camber.

Other more-complex tapers are used on racing-boat masts, depending upon design criteria.

Sailboats

Cutouts

All holes, slots, and cutouts in a mast must be made properly, or they can be the start of a crack. There must be no sharp corners. The corners of all cutouts for spreaders, sheaves, shrouds, etc., must have a smooth and uniform radius. Gently make a small radius at all sharp edges as well by sanding or other means. Figure 8-5 shows a cutout for a spreader compression member and a hole for a tang through-bolt. The cutout in Figure 8-6 is for an internal halyard exit. Note the buffing marks on the mast. The buffing not only removes all sharp corners, but it also removes dirt and oxides in areas that may later require welding.

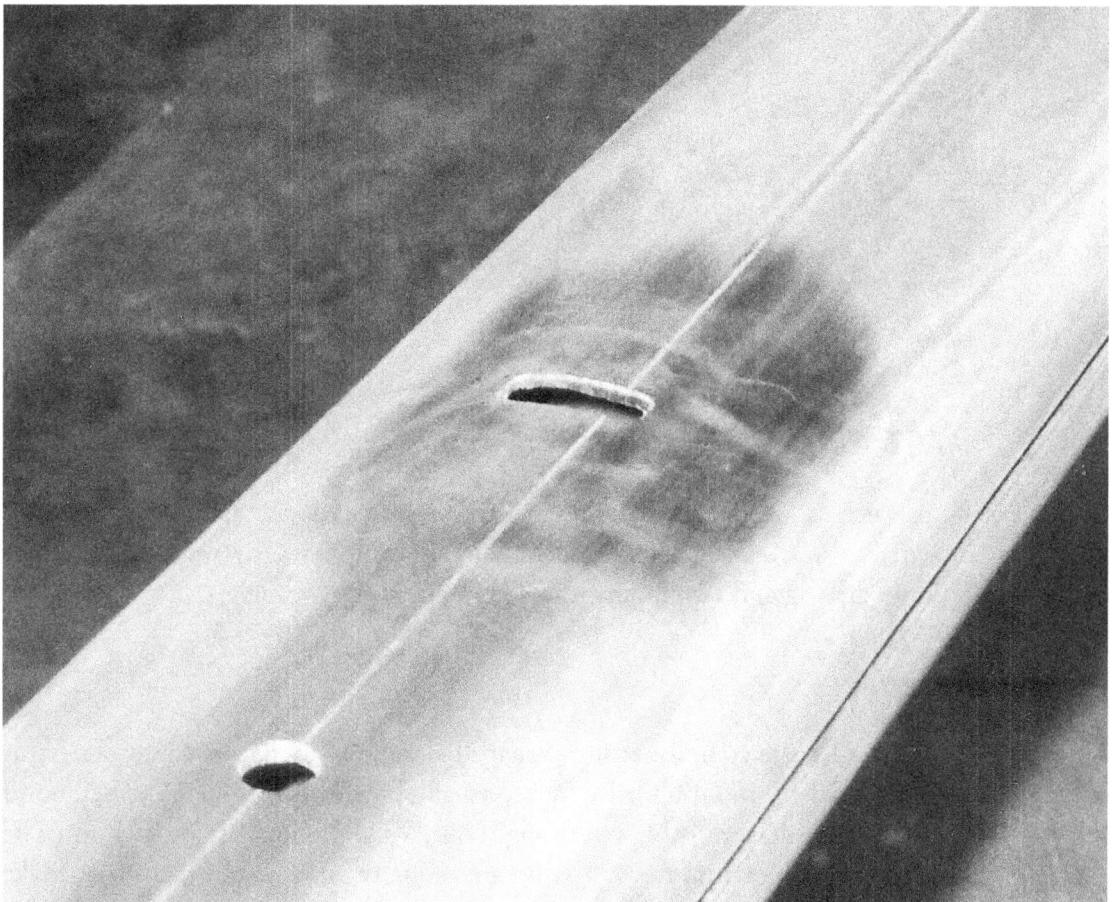

Figure 8-5. Cutout for spreader compression member (note hole for tang through-bolt).

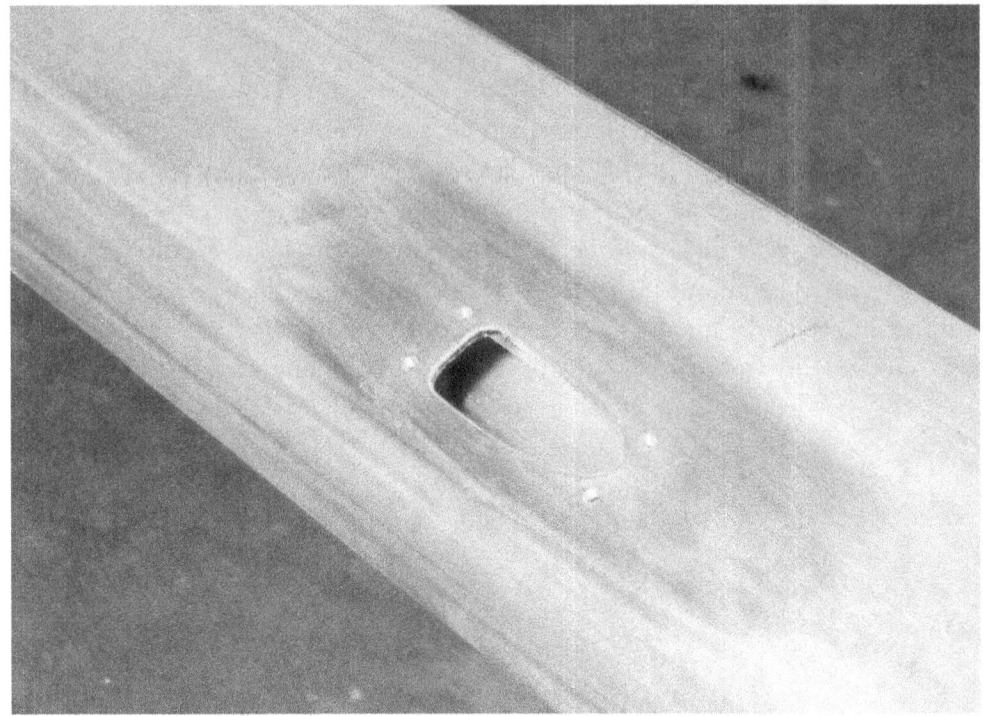

Figure 8-6. Cutout for internal halyard exit.

MAST ATTACHMENTS

Items such as spreaders, masthead fittings, winch bases, and tangs must be attached to a mast to make it functional. They are made by welding, through-bolting, drilling and tapping for threaded inserts, or riveting.

Spreaders

Mast spreaders are commonly airfoil-shaped aluminum extrusions. Spreader extrusions are available in a number of sizes, usually in alloy 6061-T6. The method of attaching spreaders must be well thought out. Welding to the mast itself must be kept to an absolute minimum to avoid annealing the metal with weld heat. Make any weakening cutouts or attachment holes in areas subject to the least stress—usually along the sides (port and starboard) of the mast.

Rigging tension puts high compression loads on the mast section at the spreaders, and the working of the mast results in minor movement between it and

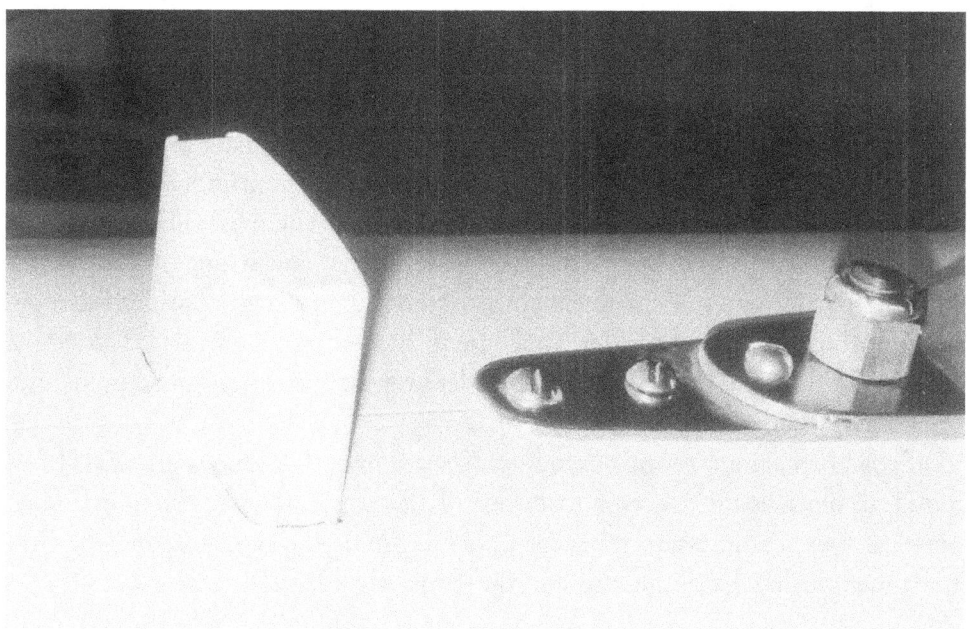

Figure 8-7. Special extrusion for spreader attachment on left.

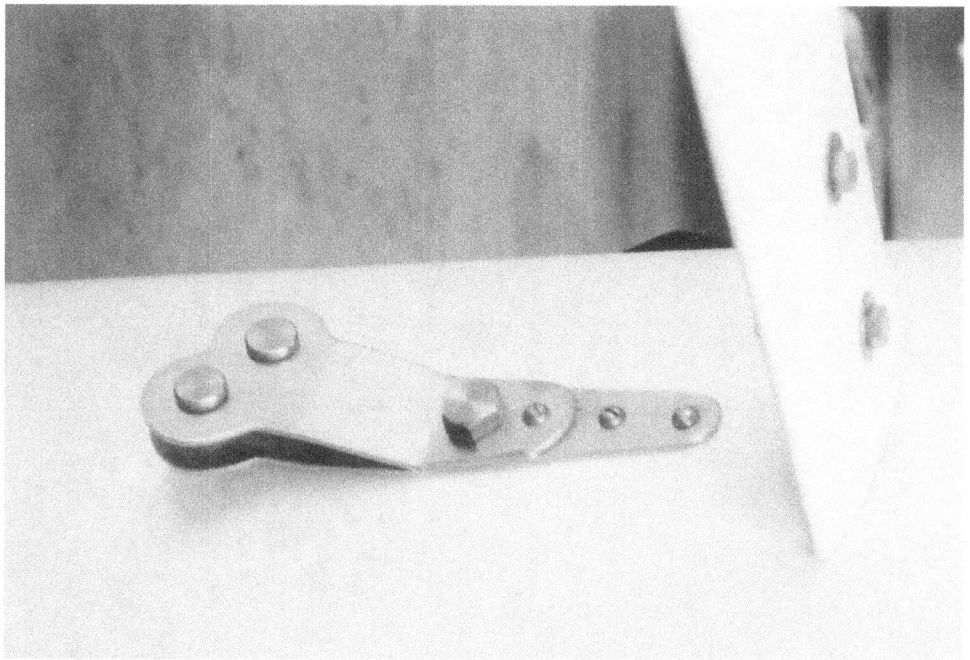

Figure 8-8. Spreader attachment over internal compression member on right.

the spreaders. It's a common practice to insert a stout piece of aluminum through the sides of the mast at the spreaders to relieve the compression load and to reinforce the spreader-to-mast joint. Special extrusions available for this use (Figure 8-7) are inserted through carefully cut slots in the mast (Figure 8-5) and lightly tack welded in place. The spreader extrusions slip over the compression member and are through-bolted to it to attach the spreaders to the mast (Figure 8-8).

While this method of spreader attachment is clean and strong, it is also difficult to repair. If you anticipate extended blue-water cruising, consider the more traditional method of spreader attachment shown in Figure 8-9. Fasten the attachment fitting to the mast at the spreader location by drilling and tapping into the mast section.

If you are making a repair or modification to a mast with thin walls, as are often found on older boats, it is wise to through-bolt the spreaders to the mast attachments and use compression tubes to prevent crushing the mast section. The rigid attachment fitting distributes the spreader loads over a larger area of the mast.

Figure 8-9. Spreader attachment using traditional pad and clevis.

Figure 8-10. Conventional spreader mast end fitting.

Attach the spreader to the mast by fitting a rectangular-shaped piece into the inboard end of the spreader extrusion (Figure 8-10) and bolting it into the mast attachment (Figure 8-9).

At the outboard end of the spreader, insert a piece of solid aluminum—slotted to receive the shrouds—and weld it to the extrusion (Figure 8-11). Drill small holes through the insert block allow the shrouds to be lashed to the ends of the spreaders with a number of wraps of seizing wire pulled tight with pliers.

When designing any through-mast spreader member, keep in mind that normally electrical wiring (and often halyards) are routed inside the mast. Not only is a wire route necessary, but moving wire-rope internal halyards can cause extensive

Figure 8-11. Outboard end of spreader.

damage to an internal aluminum member. One method of minimizing damage to this member is to place a wear strip on it. Look carefully at the member shown in Figure 8-7. It is designed for a small stainless steel wear bar to fit into the fore and aft edge of the member to act as a chafing strip.

Tangs

Mast tangs are usually through-bolted. A typical tang installation is shown in Figure 8-12. In order to adequately tighten the tang attachment bolt and not collapse the mast section, insert a pipe sleeve through the mast—a ½-inch ID by ⅝-inch OD tube for a typical ½-inch attachment bolt—to act as a compression member for the through-bolt. Drill a ⅝-inch-diameter hole through both sides of the mast (Figure 8-5) and fit the sleeve into the mast, making it flush with the outside faces. When you bolt the tang in place, the bolt will tighten against the sleeve instead of crushing the mast section. An additional benefit is that the sleeve provides a slightly larger bearing area to support the tang. Add screws to prevent the tang from rotating and increase the joint strength. Screw them into drilled and tapped holes in the mast, paying careful attention to prevent possible damage to halyards.

Figure 8-12. Typical aluminum mast tang installation.

Internal Wiring

Secure the internal wiring to the mast to prevent it from moving around and chafing on the internal surfaces and halyards. Accomplish this by enclosing the internal wiring in a piece of plastic (PVC) pipe conduit riveted at about 3-foot intervals to the inside surface of the mast (Figure 8-13).

Use only marine-quality electrical wiring, such as marine-grade wire and cable from Ancor Marine. Use a tinned type 3 conductor that has heavy and durable insulation. Install soft grommets at the entry and egress points for the wire to

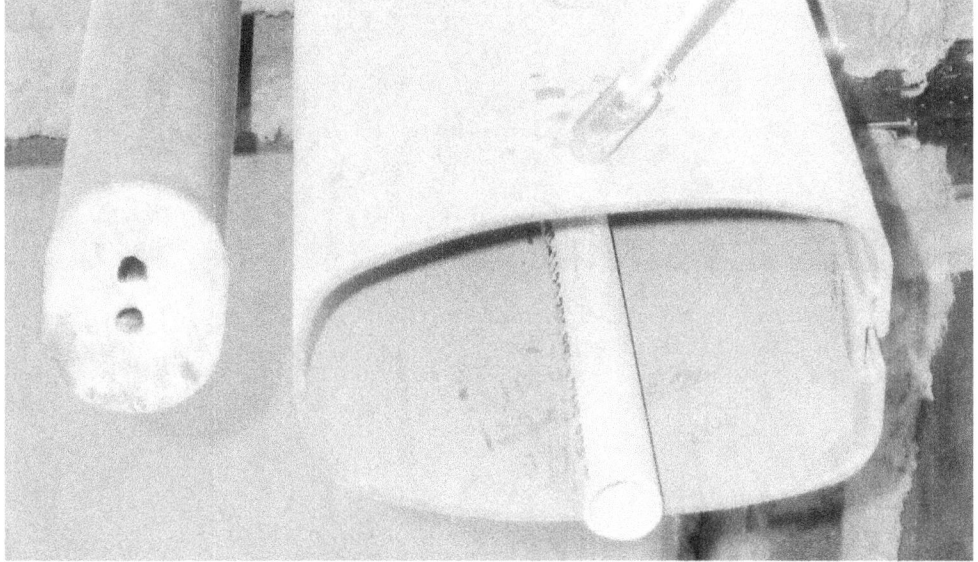

Figure 8-13. PVC conduit for internal wiring.

prevent chafing of the insulation. With keel-stepped masts, exit the wires just below the main deck level. Wiring that exits from the lower portion of the mast is more subject to damage from chafing, dampness, or sea water.

Masthead Fitting

Most masthead fittings are fabricated of aluminum and welded to the top of the mast. Notch the masthead fitting into the mast as well as butt weld it to the top (Figure 8-14 and Figure 8-15).

Figure 8-14. Welded aluminum masthead fitting.

Other Attachments

Weld flat plates to the mast to provide winch bases (Figure 8-16). Pop-rivet small items like mast lights (a popular alternative to spreader lights—see Figure 8-17),

Sailboats

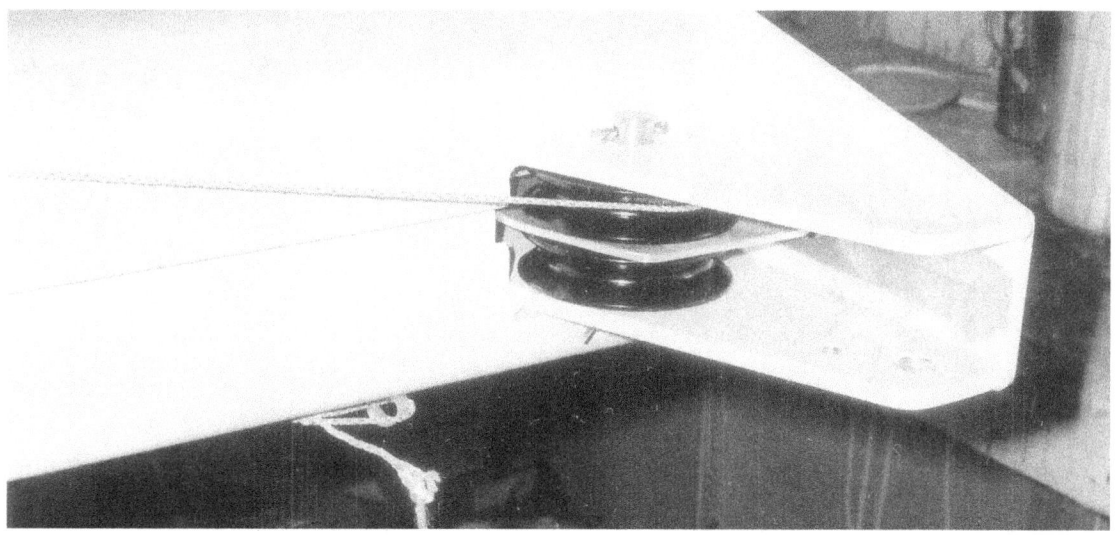

Figure 8-15. Aluminum masthead fitting with sheaves installed.

or attach them with screws into drilled and tapped holes. Use only stainless steel or aluminum fasteners in the mast, and coat threaded fasteners with an antiseize compound. For threaded fasteners you expect to repeatedly remove and replace, use stainless steel Heli-Coil inserts, which are available at automotive suppliers.

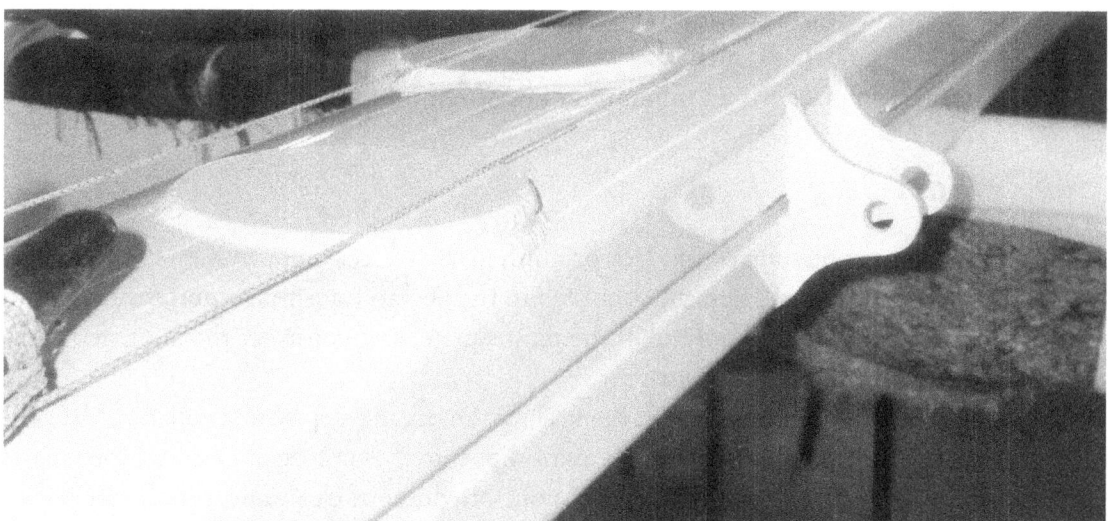

Figure 8-16. Mast-mounted winch base.

Figure 8-17. Mast light installation.

MAST PERIPHERALS

A number of additional related items are needed to both support the mast and to complete the rig of a sailboat. Many of these can be fabricated out of aluminum, either as an integral part of the boat or as a separate, independent piece. Because of the inherent strength of an aluminum deck, hardware can often be bolted directly to it without additional under-deck reinforcement. When a special equipment foundation, such as a winch base, is required, it can be fabricated and welded in place with a minimum of deck reinforcement.

Mast Step

Masts may be stepped on deck or on the keel. A deck-stepped mast needs a compression member from the deck step to the keel to transmit compressive forces to the keel. Trim the butt end of the mast square, and construct the mast step compatible with a square mast butt.

If the mast is stepped on the keel, construct the step with a collar on the outside of the mast; i.e., so that the mast slips into the mast step. Deck-stepped masts usually fit over a male step extension, providing a clean and protuberance-free joint. This requires drilling and countersinking the mast, and drilling and tapping the step for the flathead screws that will fasten the mast to the step. Whatever the design of the step, it should provide for proper venting and drainage of the mast.

For masts that pass through the weather deck, a boot is required to maintain watertight integrity. Use a neoprene rubber boot (a section of inner tube can make an excellent mast boot) and protect it from sunlight by a canvas cover (which also presents a neat and finished appearance).

Chainplates

Rigging on a welded-aluminum hull is normally attached to fabricated chainplates approximately abeam the mast (for the shrouds), an extension of the stem bar at the bow for the forestay, and an extension of a stout centerline stiffener at the stern for the aft stay. Construct chainplates of aluminum alloy 5086 and weld them to the boat's framework. Tremendous forces are transmitted through the chainplates and stay fittings, requiring material that is considerably thicker than the shell plating. The holes through aluminum chainplates are subject to egging out, so it is advisable to swage in stainless steel hole bushings.

Toerail

A slotted deck-edge rail is often used for securing rigging. Such rails can simply be flat bar that is drilled or punched then welded in place. This also makes a good toerail, a sturdy attachment point for stanchion sockets, and a natural outside edge of a deck-edge gutter.

Winch Foundations

A short length of pipe slightly larger in diameter than the winch base makes one of the simplest and most professional-looking winch foundations. But since large-diameter aluminum pipe is quite expensive, circular winch bases are usually rolled out of plate. Cap the base with a circle of aluminum plate of adequate thickness to hold the mounting bolts for the winch. Scribe the circular winch base to fit the contour of the deck and to obtain the desired orientation of the winch in relation to the deck. Once the winch base fits, but prior to welding it in place, cut a large hand-access hole through the side of the base, and then weld the base into position on the boat.

Miscellaneous Deck Items

Boom traveler supports, boom crutches, dorade boxes, foundations for deck hardware, and other miscellaneous items can be rapidly constructed from aluminum and welded to an aluminum deck. Such items look very professional and are relatively easy to construct.

BALLAST KEEL

The ballast keel of a welded-aluminum sailboat is often constructed hollow with ballast carried internally. If the ballast keel is fabricated of aluminum separate from the hull, installing the ballast is greatly simplified. If it isn't practical to have a separate keel section, consider leaving a small section of the boat's shell plate off until the ballast is placed. It's much easier to place ballast through a hole in the

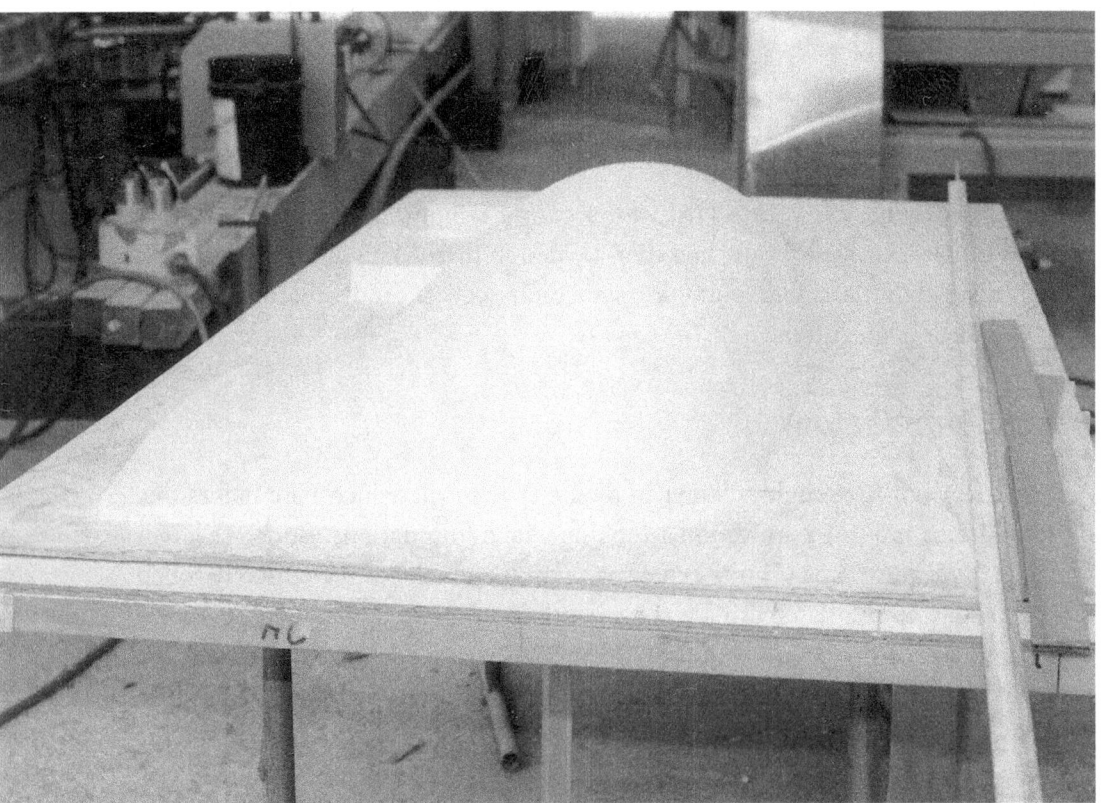

Figure 8-18. Half-side pattern being prepared for a cast lead keel for a 51-foot racer.

shell than to carry it down through a hatch. After the ballast is placed and sealed, weld the omitted plate in place over the opening.

The ballast can be made of lead, iron, or any other heavy material, and it is either solid or, as with molten lead, liquid and thus poured into the keel. Internal ballast is placed into a hollow keel in predetermined amounts and locations. The location is commonly by compartment, which is the space between framing members. The location of the ballast and the amount to be placed in each compartment is usually determined by the naval architect. It is important to carefully weigh the ballast and record its location as you place it in the boat.

The ballast must be isolated to prevent *galvanic corrosion* (see Chapter 11) of the aluminum hull. When using solid ballast, a heavy asphaltic mat is a good solution. Locate it at the bottom of the keel and up the keel sides between the aluminum and the ballast. Pour hot tar around the ballast to remove air pockets and to lock it firmly in place, then seal the ballast chamber. In the case of molten lead ballast, seal the ballast chamber by welding cover plates over the ballast to prevent moisture from entering the cavity.

Position external cast lead ballast on the bottom of a deep fin keel. Figure 8-18 shows the construction of a pattern for a cast lead keel for a 51-foot racer.

Ballast Materials

Lead is the most desirable ballast material because of its *density*—708 pounds per cubic foot. The melting point of lead—621 degrees Fahrenheit—is well below marine aluminum (1,200 degrees), allowing molten lead ballast to be poured into a hollow aluminum keel. Lead ballast is the highest-density ballast that is economically practical.

Interestingly, since 100 percent pure lead is very hard to find, some avid racing sailors determine the difference between pure lead and the actual specific gravity of their particular lead ballast, and then make up the difference by inserting a small amount of tungsten (which weighs 1,205 pounds per cubic foot) or exotic and even heavier by-products of nuclear reaction.

Older cruising boats have commonly been fitted with cast iron or steel ballast (491 pounds per cubic foot) bolted to the exterior of the keel. Some cruising boats use internal steel ballast—*steel punchings*, small pieces of scrap steel or iron, or small cast pigs placed cold inside the keel cavity.

Concrete does not make a good ballast when compared with other available materials. The weight of concrete is only 144 pounds per cubic foot, as compared to aluminum, which is 169 pounds per cubic foot. However, concrete can be used if sufficient volume within the keel area is available. Melted-down zinc anodes are a poor choice, in that zinc, at 446 pounds per cubic foot, weighs less than the much cheaper steel.

Lead Ballast

Lead can be purchased from salvage metal dealers. Be advised that salvage lead can contain a high percentage of other elements, which in most cases will result in an alloy with a specific gravity less than pure lead. Because of the high cost of pure lead, most boatbuilders use salvage lead for ballast. Take some specific gravity tests during the pouring of the lead to satisfy yourself that the lead is nearly 708 pounds per cubic foot.

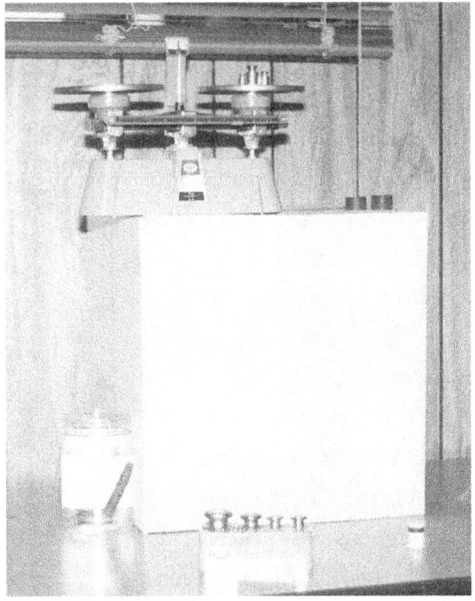

Figure 8-19. Apparatus to determine specific gravity of a lead sample.

For a fee, a lab can test your lead to determine its *specific gravity*, or you can do it yourself if you have access to a chemist's balance-beam scales and some weights calibrated in grams. The process follows:

1. Weigh a lead sample suspended in the air by a thin thread.
2. Weigh the suspended lead sample submerged in a beaker of water (located below the scale, as shown in Figure 8-19).
3. Calculate the difference between the two weights. Because 1 cubic centimeter of water weighs 1 gram, this difference equals the amount of water displaced, which equals the volume of the lead sample in cubic centimeters.
4. Divide the weight of the lead sample weight (in grams) by the volume (in cubic centimeters) to obtain the specific gravity of the sample. (The specific gravity of pure lead is 11.3423 grams per cubic centimeter.)

Molten Lead

In using lead as the ballast, you can pour molten lead directly into a hollow aluminum keel, pack it in cold pieces, or use a combination of molten lead and cold pieces.

When you work with molten lead, safety precautions are absolutely essential. Lead emits toxic (poisonous) fumes in the molten state that can cause lead poisoning if inhaled. In addition, alloying elements and contaminants often found in lead can add to the toxic fumes. Specific respirators are available for filtering out the lead particles. Ordinary paint respirators will not suffice! And ample ventilation is a must.

Lead in the molten state can also cause severe burns. Protect the molten lead from all water or liquids—water splashed into molten lead will cause an explosion that will throw the molten lead into the adjacent area! Never work with molten lead without safety goggles, a full-face shield, heat-resistant gloves, full-length coveralls or work clothing—no exposed skin–and a respirator. Contact your local safety-supply outlet for the appropriate respirator and other protective gear. To find the applicable OSHA (Occupational Safety and Health Administration) safety standards for working with molten lead, search the Internet for "OSHA lead standard 1910.1025."

Working with molten lead is very hot work. Be careful of overheating, and be sure you have good ventilation and plenty of fresh air and drinking water.

Cutting Lead

If you purchase lead in the form of large cast sows, you must cut them down in size to fit into your melting pot. Unfortunately cutting lead can be very frustrating. It clogs up saws, and it doesn't burn like steel. The simplest method of cutting it is to use a rosebud type of oxyacetylene torch and melt off chunks, although some boatyards use chain saws.

Melting Pot

To melt lead, you need a melting pot. A steel chamber about 2 feet in diameter and 3 feet high, mounted on legs so the bottom of the pot is about 30 inches above the shop floor, makes an excellent melting pot. A trip to a salvage yard will usually locate a suitable container that you can modify with a steel-cutting torch. If the pot has fairly thick walls, ¼ inch or heavier, it will better retain heat and simplify the job of melting lead. (A standard 55-gallon steel drum is too light.)

Install a valve in the bottom of the pot for tapping off the molten lead—an ordinary household faucet can be used for this even though the packing will burn out. Since most impurities will rise to the top, the molten lead drawn from the valve should be relatively pure.

Use a large rosebud torch, fueled by either oxygen-acetylene or propane, to play the heat directly on a small amount of lead in the melting pot until the lead melts. Continue to hold the torch flame in contact with the lead in the pot and add additional solid lead to the molten lead until the pot is about half full of molten lead. To maintain the lead in a molten state, keep the flame in near proximity to the molten lead, either holding the torch or carefully placing it on top of the pot. (Again, keep in mind lead fumes are toxic. Be sure you are wearing the correct protective clothing, gear, and respirator and the space is properly ventilated.)

Pouring Bucket

You will need a pouring bucket strong enough to handle molten lead. It should be constructed of ¼ inch or heavier steel to retain heat. Fit it with a pouring lip and a handle to tilt it for pouring. The lifting bail should be similar to a pail handle, allowing the bucket to be held up and dumped at the same time. A pouring bucket about 18 inches in diameter and 18 inches high will contain 1,300 pounds of lead when 70 percent full! Use an overhead hoist attached to the lifting bail to move the bucket to the pouring area. A sketch of a lead-pouring bucket is shown in Figure 8-20.

Pouring Molten Lead

When you determine that a sufficient amount of molten lead is in the melting pot, open the pot valve and fill the pouring bucket to the desired level. Weigh the bucket and molten lead. Move the pouring bucket over the keel cavity and dump the lead into the keel. Now weigh the empty bucket to determine the net weight of the lead you just poured into the keel. Repeat this process until you have poured in the required amount of ballast.

It is not important that the layers of lead solidify between pours (effectively forming a cold seam). It's more important not to overheat the keel aluminum, so numerous small pours are better than a few large pours.

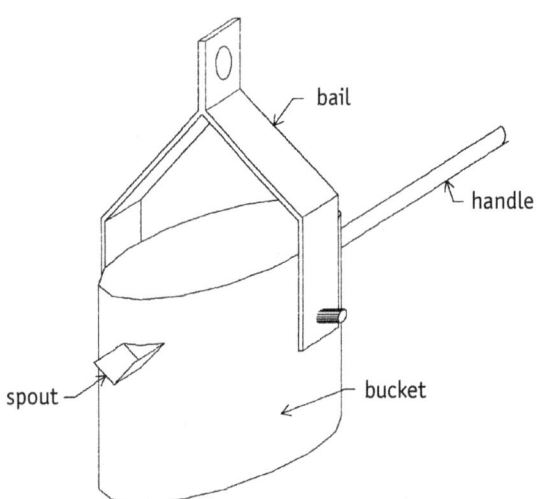

Figure 8-20. Lead-pouring bucket.

Molten lead solidifies quickly once it's poured into the keel, so it's a bad idea to place a large amount of solid, cold lead into the keel cavity and pour molten lead over it to fill the voids. The rapid solidification of the lead may result in air gaps between solids. On the other hand, careful placement of some solid lead to ensure that no voids will be formed when the molten lead is poured is a satisfactory method of filling the cavity and reduces the amount of melting required.

Preparing the Keel for Molten Lead

Hot, molten lead will cause the aluminum keel to expand rapidly. To hold the keel sides in the desired position until the lead cools, weld exterior strongbacks to the keel, locating them no more than 6 inches apart. After the lead has cooled, remove the strongbacks, and grind and sand all welds flush.

Sealing the Lead

Before you place the lead ballast in the keel, ensure that the cavity is watertight. If water enters the keel near the lead, it will provide the necessary *electrolyte* (see Chapter 11) to foster corrosion between the lead and the aluminum keel. To prevent this from happening, prior to placing the lead ballast, seal the keel cavities that will contain ballast with temporary aluminum plates and air-test the structure to about 3 psi. Repair any leaks that are found. Remove the temporary cover plates and pour the lead. Be sure to leave adequate room between the lead and the cover plate to allow the plate to be rewelded—lead that melts and flows into the area of the seal weld will contaminate the weld area and make seal-welding impossible. After pouring the lead, weld the cover plates in place and air-test the seams, repairing them if necessary.

Solid Ballast

Lead or steel ballast can be placed into a hollow keel in solid form. Pack the ballast as densely as possible, then restrain it. A common method of restraining solid ballast is to pour molten tar over it.

To isolate the solid ballast from the aluminum keel:

1. Line the bottom and sides of the cavity with a layer of heavy roofing felt.

2. Place a layer of ballast over the felt, making sure the ballast doesn't touch the aluminum keel sides.
3. Pour hot tar over the ballast until it is firmly held in position.
4. Pack additional ballast into the cavity, and again pour hot tar over it to lock it in place.
5. Repeat this process until all the ballast is installed.
6. Weld cover plates over the ballast area to seal it from bilge water.

To minimize air gaps between ballast solids, triangular bars can be cast that allow very close packing. This works particularly well with lead since it's easily cast into triangular ingots. You can fabricate a simple casting mold from either steel or aluminum angle, as shown in Figure 8-21.

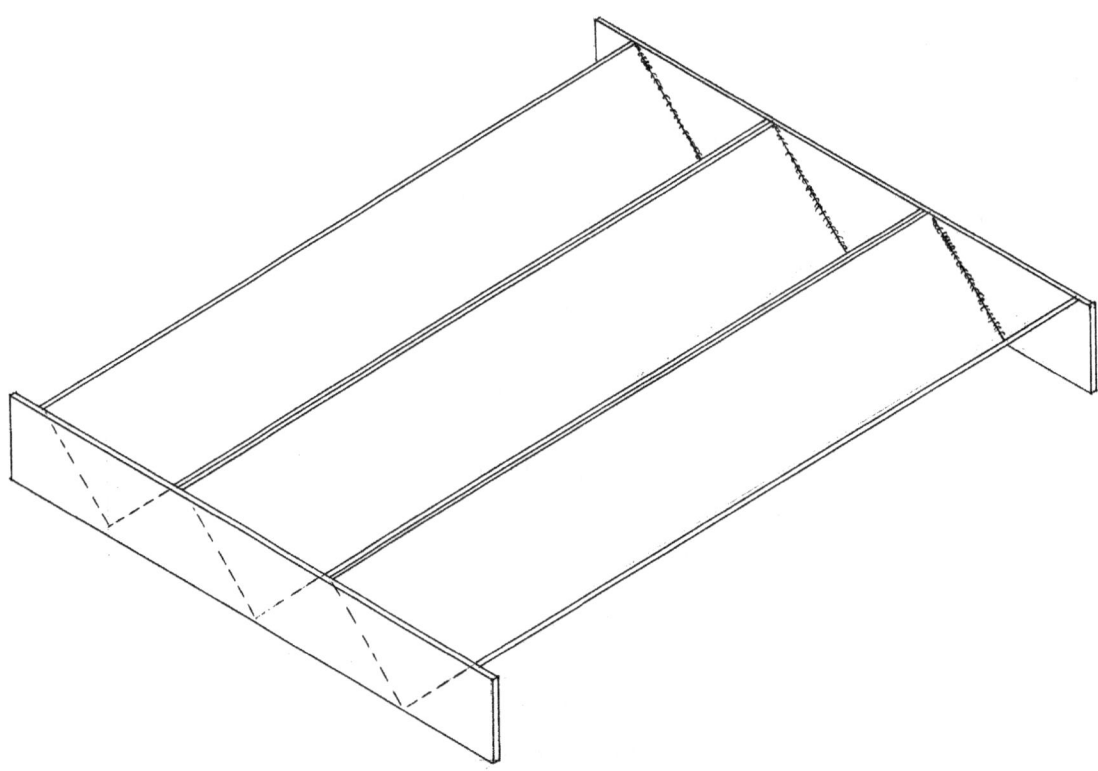

Figure 8-21. Mold for casting triangular lead ingots, made from aluminum or steel angle.

CHAPTER 9

Propulsion Systems and Controls

Modern propulsion systems can be reciprocating or turbine engines, gasoline or diesel fueled, and inboard or outboard mounted. Power can be delivered through conventional propellers, stern-drive (inboard-outboard) units, or water jets. And the wide range of horsepower ratings and suggested applications for each system requires some difficult choices. First determine the performance you'll need, then work backward to arrive at the best system for the application.

ENGINE SELECTION

If you select a propulsion system primarily for speed, you'll also usually get reduced reliability and fuel economy. If you select a system for power, you'll sacrifice speed and fuel economy. If your primary consideration is fuel efficiency, you'll lose speed and power. Work with your designer to identify the propulsion system that will provide the best compromise between performance and efficiency for your specific boat.

Another consideration is the intended uses of the boat. A boat operating in shallow water and rivers and subject to grounding may be best served by a water-jet unit. For offshore operations requiring a high level of reliability, good fuel economy, and minimum fire hazard, a diesel engine is indicated. If a large, clear area in the stern of the vessel is needed, a mid-ship engine installation may be required. And if the boat is to be constructed by a novice, ease of installation may be a major consideration, suggesting outboards or inboard-outboard power.

The initial out-of-pocket cost of a propulsion system is also a big factor. For example, although diesel engines have a number of advantages over gasoline engines, the initial cost of a diesel engine can easily more than double the cost of an equivalent gasoline-fueled engine.

Only after performance objectives, operating parameters, and budget implications have all been examined can the right propulsion system be selected.

Diesel Engines

Boatowners almost always select diesel for reliability and operating economy, as well as the much lower fire hazard of diesel fuel when operating offshore. Diesel engines are more reliable and usually more fuel efficient than gasoline engines.

Diesel engines are of three types: *naturally aspirated*, *turbocharged*, or *turbocharged with after-cooling*. By altering the amount of fuel an engine can efficiently burn, these various configurations provide a range of horsepower ratings.

Naturally aspirated. In a naturally aspirated (i.e., not turbocharged) engine, the volume of air drawn into each cylinder on the downward stroke of the piston determines the amount of fuel that can be efficiently burned. Therefore, engine horsepower rating is limited by the amount of air available.

Turbocharged. A turbocharger delivers increased air volume into the cylinders, but compression of the air by the turbocharger also increases the air temperature. The horsepower rating of a turbocharged engine is limited by the turbocharger speed and the internal temperatures.

Turbocharged with after-cooling. The addition of a water-cooled after-cooler between the turbocharger and the engine's intake manifold provides cooling for the hot compressed air from the turbocharger. Cooling the air increases its density and allows more fuel to be burned. Horsepower rating is limited by internal temperature limits, turbocharger speed, and the structural limits of the engine. Figure 9-1 shows a typical after-cooled turbocharged diesel engine in the form of a Volvo Penta inboard-outboard.

Diesel engines are commonly given horsepower ratings at specified rpm settings. It's important to compare definitions for each manufacturer's ratings to obtain a true comparison. Technical data furnished by diesel engine manufacturers is usually much more complete than that provided by gasoline engine manufacturers. Supporting data for the Volvo D6-310 (the engine in Figure 9-1) is shown in Figure 9-2.

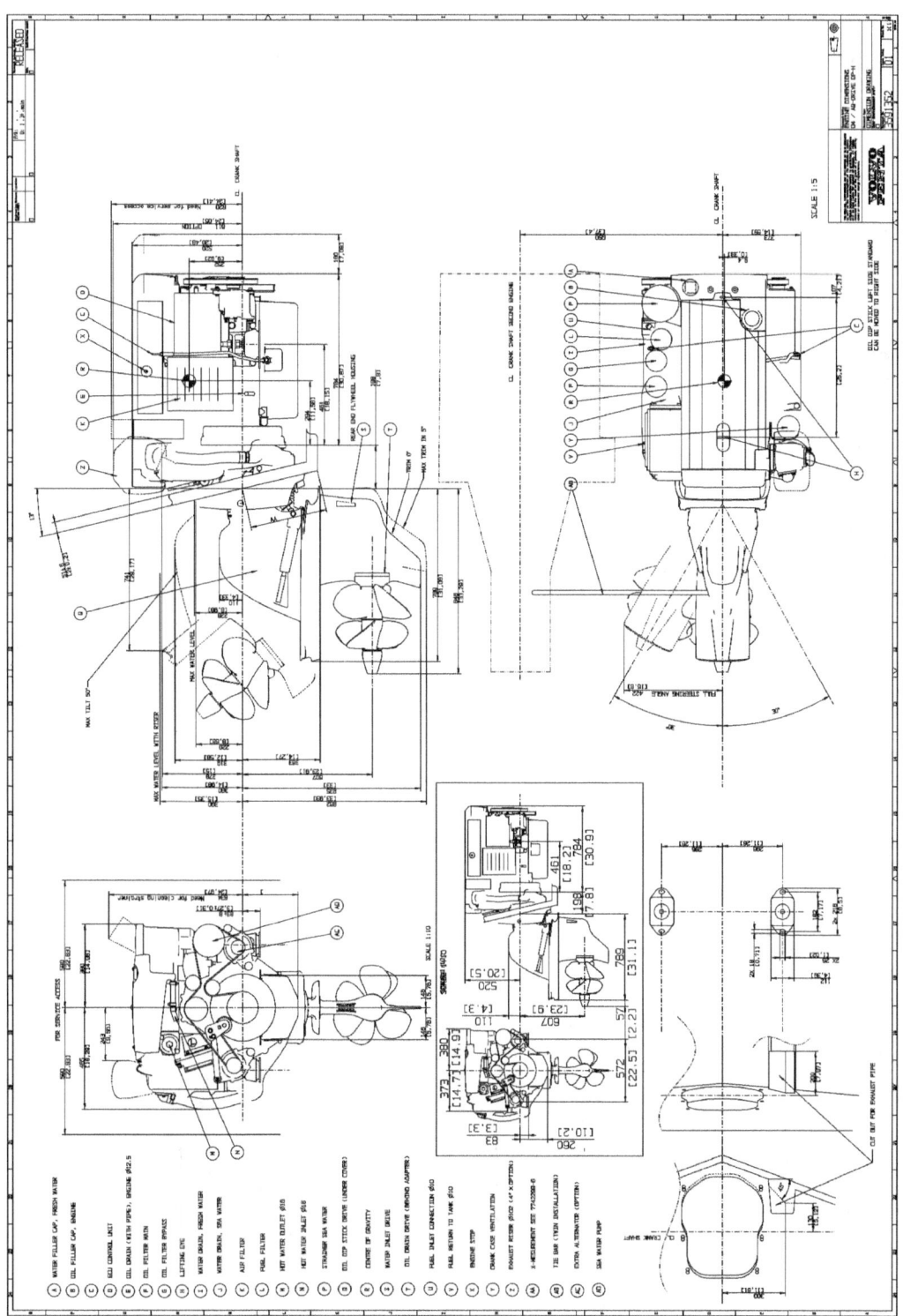

Figure 9-1. Installation drawing for a Volvo Penta diesel inboard-outboard. Such figures are often available from the manufacturer in DXF format for use in CAD. (Courtesy Volvo)

D6-310/DP

Technical description:

Engine block and head
- Cylinder block and cylinder head made of cast-iron
- Ladder frame fitted to engine block
- 4-valve technology with hydraulic lash adjusters
- Double overhead camshafts
- Oil-cooled pistons with two compression rings and one oil scraper ring
- Integrated cylinder liners
- Replaceable valve seats
- Seven-bearing crankshaft
- Rear-end transmission

Engine mounting
- Flexible engine mounting

Lubrication system
- Easily replaceable separate full-flow and by-pass oil filter
- Seawater-cooled tubular oil cooler

Fuel system
- Common rail fuel injection system
- Control unit for processing the injection
- Fine filter with water separator

Air inlet and exhaust system
- Air filter with replaceable insert
- Crankcase gases vented into the air inlet
- Exhaust elbow or exhaust riser
- Freshwater-cooled turbocharger

Cooling system
- Thermostatically regulated freshwater cooling
- Tubular heat exchanger with separate large volume expansion tank
- Coolant system prepared for hot water outlet
- Seawater strainer and easily accessible impeller pump

Electrical system
- 12V two-pole electrical system
- 115A marine alternator with Zener-diodes to protect the system from peak voltage, and integrated charging regulator with battery sensor cable for maximum use of alternator
- Fuses with automatic reset
- Auxiliary stop button

Instruments/control
- Complete instrumentation including key switch and interlocked alarm
- Digital Power Trim instrument with analog or digital reading
- EVC monitoring panels for single or twin installations
- Electronic remote control for throttle and shift
- Plug-in connectors

Drive
- Complete with transom shield, and installation components
- Max tilt angle 50° (adjustable)
- Protective zinc anodes to prevent corrosion
- Built-in kick-up function to reduce possible damage, in the event the drive strikes an underwater object
- Electrical shifting performed by electronic actuator
- Power Trim with one-button operation in twin installation
- Fully integrated water inlet and exhaust system
- Fully hydraulic power-assisted steering system
- Isolated propellers to prevent corrosion

Accessories
An extensive range of accessories are available. For detailed information, please see the Accessories & Maintenance Parts catalog (www.volvopenta.com).

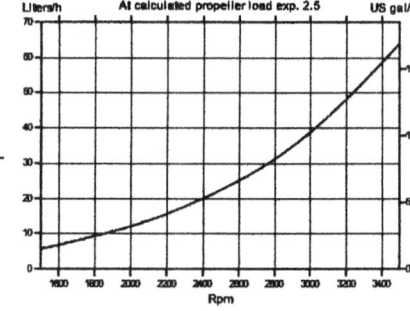

Technical Data

Engine designation	D6-310 A
Crankshaft power, kW (hp)	228 (310)
Propeller shaft power, kW (hp)	219 (298)
Engine speed, rpm	3500
Displacement, l (in³)	5.5 (336)
Number of cylinders	6
Bore/stroke, mm (in.)	103/110 (4.05/4.33)
Compression ratio	17.5:1
Volvo Penta Duoprop drive	DPH
Ratio	1.76:1
Dry weight with DP, incl. prop. & PS, kg (lb)	750 (1653)

Duty rating: R4 & R5
Technical data according to ISO 8665. With fuel having an LHV of 42,700 kJ/kg and density of 840 g/liter at 15°C (60°F). Merchant fuel may differ from this specification which will influence engine power output and fuel consumption.
The engine will meet future comprehensive emission requirements to be introduced in Europe and the US in 2006.

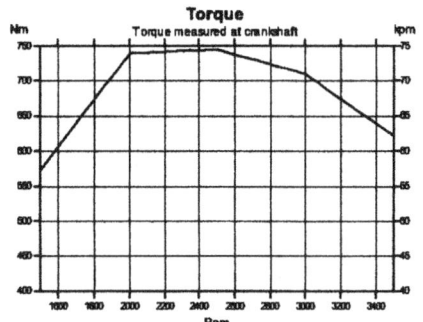
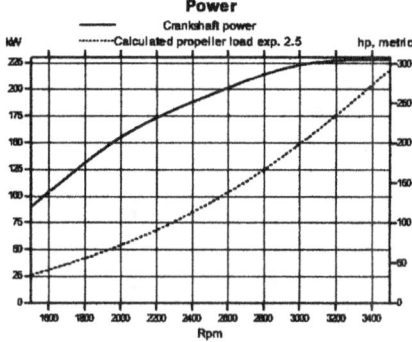

Figure 9-2. Manufacturer's performance data for a Volvo D6-310 DP engine. (Courtesy Volvo)

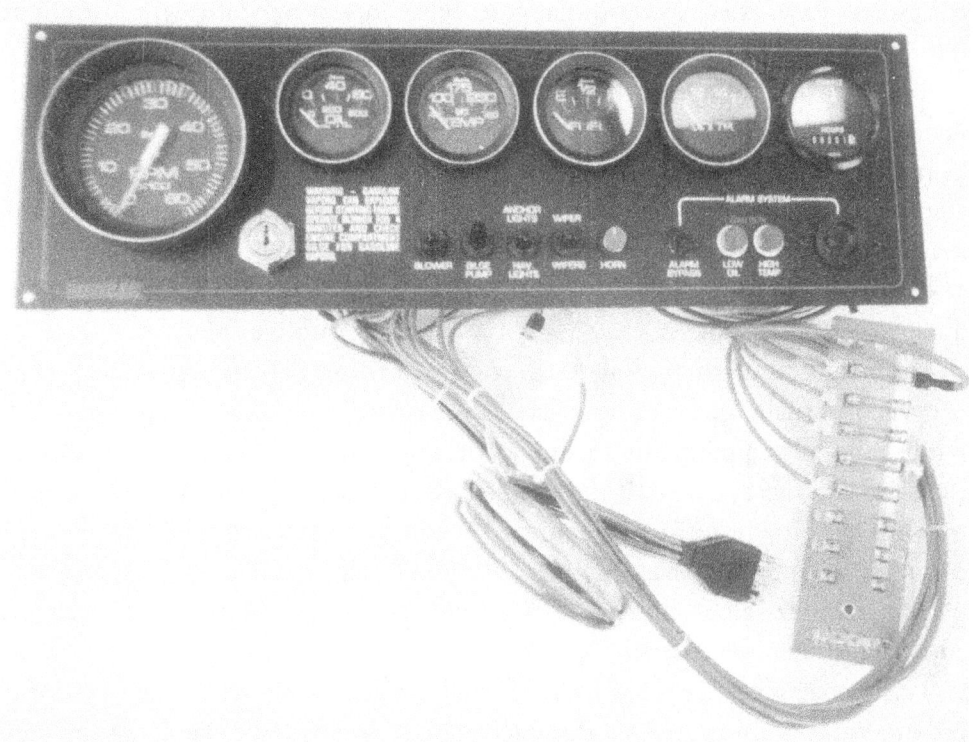

Figure 9-3. Prefabricated instrument panel and wiring harness.

When comparing diesel engines, contact engine dealers in your area for information on specific brands. Ask the dealers for product information that includes rated horsepower, weight, fuel consumption, gear ratios, duty cycle, availability, and any other pertinent data.

If you plan to operate the vessel in salt water, you'll need to make sure the engine you select is freshwater cooled and equipped with the required heat exchanger and seawater circulating pump.

For the first-time builder, it's very nice to have a pre-wired instrument panel and a pre-bundled wiring harness (Figure 9-3).

Gasoline Engines

Most small powerboats (less than 30 feet) are powered by gasoline engines, either inboard, inboard-outboard, or outboard. Gasoline engines are both safe and reliable when installed, operated, and maintained correctly. The principal advantages of gasoline engines are lower initial cost, high horsepower-to-weight ratios, and the ready availability of maintenance facilities.

Factory-available options on inboard and inboard-outboard engines usually include freshwater cooling, pre-bundled instrument harnesses, and pre-wired instrument panels. Larger alternators or dual alternators may be mounted to the engines for increased electrical capacity. Power take-offs for various applications may also be available.

Gasoline engines generally turn at much higher rpm than diesel engines to obtain their rated horsepower. Most U.S. marine gasoline inboard engines are based on successful automobile engines converted for marine applications. This conversion usually includes water-cooled exhaust risers, a raw-water circulation pump, and all requirements to meet federal regulations concerning small-craft electrical and fuel systems. (If the engine has a carburetor, than a marine carburetor with backfire protection is required.) Freshwater-cooled heat exchangers are a common option when operation in seawater is anticipated. Figure 9-4 is an example of a marine engine manufacturer's gasoline engine fitted with a heat exchanger and exhaust manifold risers.

Gasoline engines are rated by cubic inch or liter displacement and by horsepower at maximum rpm. As with diesel engines, compare the standards and conditions used to determine horsepower and engine efficiency when evaluating relative engine performance. Marine engine manufacturers are very reluctant to

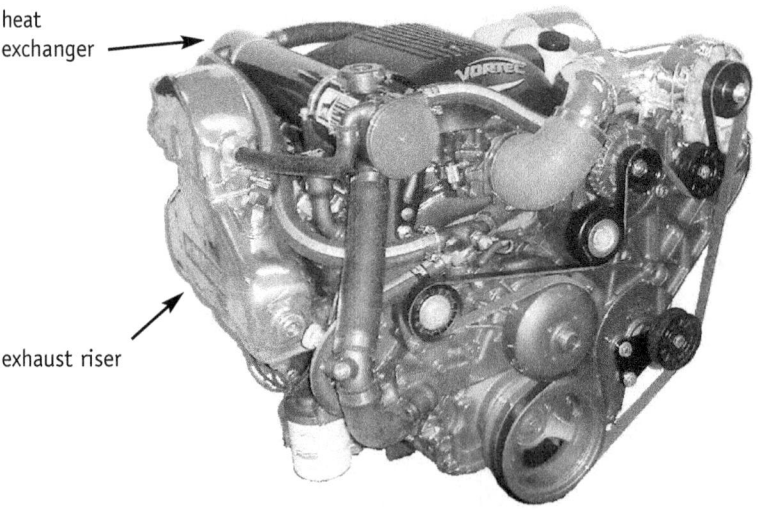

Figure 9-4. Vortec 6.0 L supercharged engine with heat exchanger and exhaust risers.

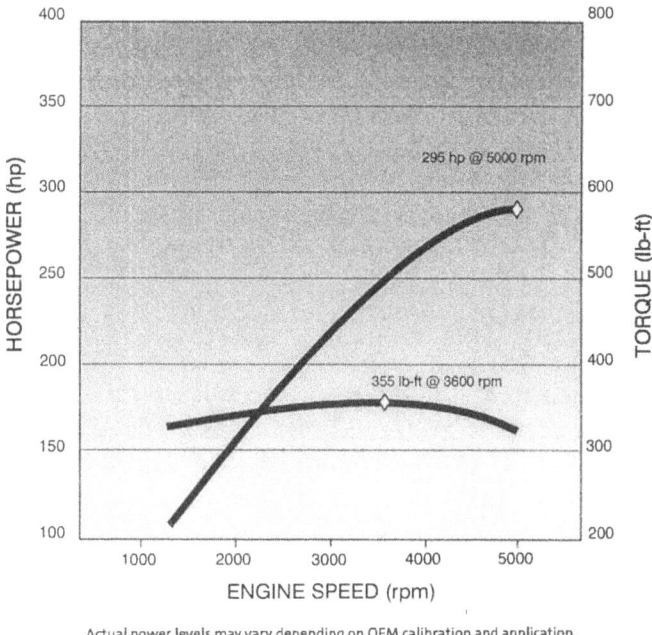

Figure 9-5. Performance data for Vortec 5.7 L V-8 gasoline engine. (Courtesy GM)

provide fuel consumption information because of variables associated with boat design. A manufacturer's representatives may be able to provide some fuel consumption data based on specific boat designs. An example of manufacturer's performance information for the Vortex 5.7 L V-8 is shown in Figure 9-5.

Turbines

Turbine engines using jet fuel have been successfully used for special marine applications. The turbine is used in place of a reciprocating engine and drives a propeller or a water jet through a reduction gear. Jet turbines have been used primarily on larger boats, usually military, and have little application to smaller boats. Because of high fuel consumption, the turbine is used for sprint speed only; conventional diesel engines are used for fuel economy when cruising. Due to their high fuel consumption, jet turbines have fallen out of favor and been replaced by lightweight high-speed reciprocating diesel engines in the larger size ranges.

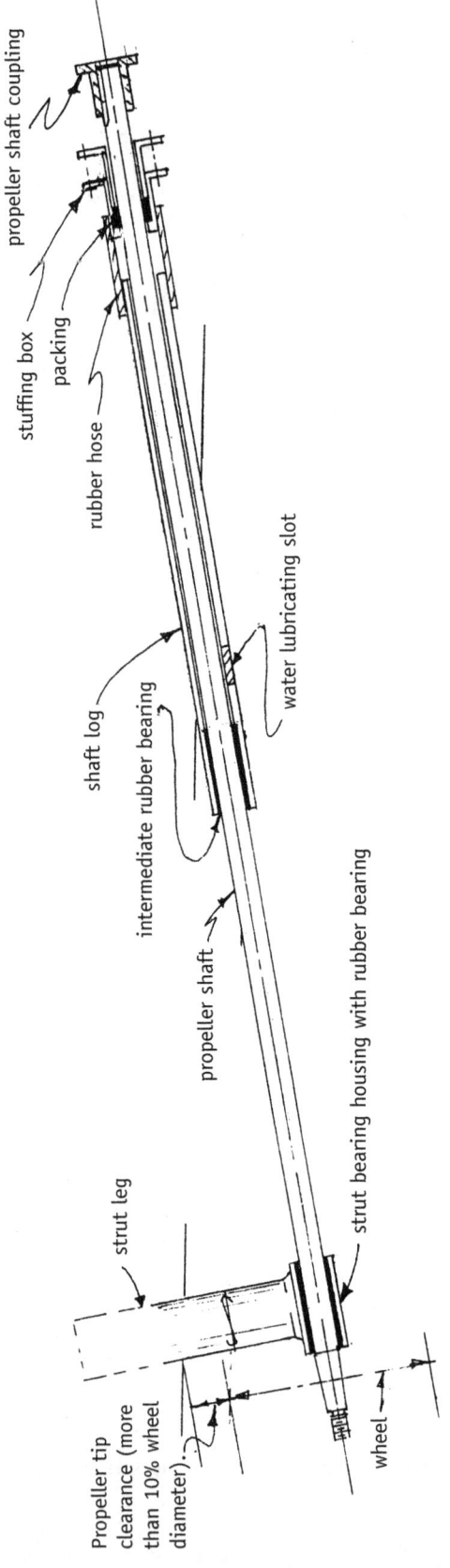

Figure 9-6. Inboard engine propeller shaft assembly.

DRIVETRAIN SYSTEMS

A propulsion system includes the propulsion engine, transmission, propeller shaft and bearings, strut, and propeller or water-jet unit. Drivetrain system refers to all the components of the propulsion system except the engine and transmission. The most common drivetrain systems for aluminum boats are conventional shaft and propeller, inboard-outboard (I/O), outboard, and water jet, and each one has specific advantages. The intended use of the boat will greatly influence the selection of the drivetrain. Other considerations are cost, ease of installation, and reliability.

Conventional Shaft and Propeller

A conventional propulsion system is an inboard engine delivering its power through a transmission with reverse capability and a preset reduction gear. The components of the drivetrain system are a propeller shaft with a through-hull stuffing box, a shaft log, shaft bearings, and a propeller. The drivetrain also commonly includes a strut with a bearing for additional shaft support (Figure 9-6).

A conventional drivetrain system affords the designer more freedom to customize the installation than do other drive systems. The system is simple; consequently, it's very reliable. The cost of materials is low when compared with other drive systems. However, the conventional shaft-and-propeller system is also the most labor intensive to install because it requires a separate rudder, which isn't required for outboard, I/O, or water-jet systems.

Mounting the engine. The Mercruiser MIE 5.7 L inboard gasoline engine with a Borg-Warner in-line gear, as shown in Figure 9-7, is a good example of a readily available inboard gasoline engine. The forward engine mounts are on the engine block, and the aft mounts are on the gear housing—a typical configuration.

In aluminum boats, use flexible engine mounts for electrical isolation and for vibration and noise abatement. Purchased separately from the engine, isolation mounts consist of a cast housing with a rubber interior. Install them between the boat's engine bed and the mounting brackets on the engine. When installed properly, they effectively "rubber mount" the engine.

Any inboard engine installation should take into account the accessibility of the engine for service. Consider provisions for changing the engine and gear oil. Provide ready access to belts, spark plugs, and other items that will need periodic servicing.

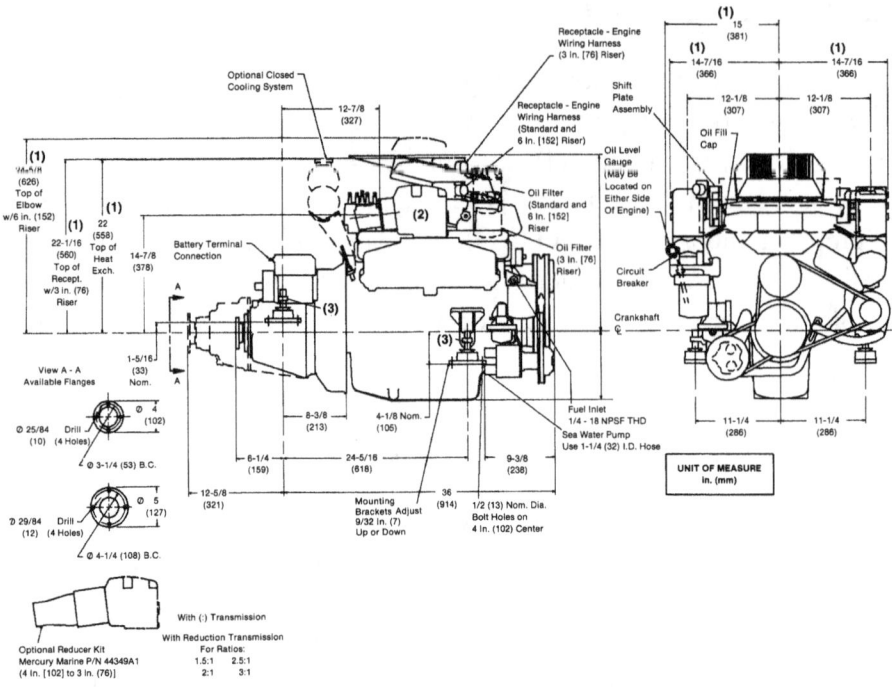

Figure 9-7. Mercrusier 5.7 L inboard engine with Borg-Warner gear. (Courtesy Mercury Marine)

Marine transmission. Again, your choice of transmission will depend on how you will use your boat. High-speed boats—ski boats, for example—require high propeller rpm for maximum acceleration. Workboats are more likely to require pulling power and will generally use lower rpm to maximize torque to large propellers.

Another transmission selection consideration is shaft angle. A large deviation from horizontal by the propeller shaft will cause a loss of thrust. Also, if the crankshaft is out of level more than 15 degrees, engine oil will run to the low portion of the oil pan, possibly causing oil scavenging problems that can result in engine damage. When excessive shaft angle is evident, consider an alternate transmission configuration, such as a down-angle gear or a V-drive (Figure 9-8), to reduce the engine inclination.

Choose the best gear configuration for your application based on the relative importance of speed, pulling power, and fuel economy. Consider propeller size and pitch prior to finalizing the gear ratio, since the propeller acts as an additional gear in the drivetrain.

Propeller shaft. When determining propeller-shaft diameter for light pleasure-boat service with the prop protected by a skeg, a *design strength safety factor* of 2:1 is acceptable, that is, the strength of the shaft is twice as strong as needed to handle the maximum anticipated load. Methods for calculating shaft sizes can be found in ABYC Section P-6, "Propeller Shafting Systems." For race boats, workboats, and diesel-powered boats, higher safety factors of 5:1 to 10:1 are recommended by ABYC guidelines.

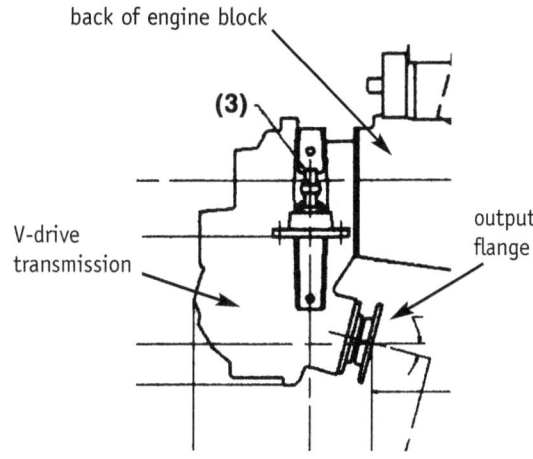

Figure 9-8. Borg-Warner V-drive.

Another factor in the design of a propeller shaft is the diameter of the propeller. The propeller diameter should be not more than fifteen times the diameter of the propeller shaft.

Propeller shafts on aluminum boats are usually stainless steel in alloy 17-4PH. Other special alloys developed by manufacturers specifically for aluminum boats can be obtained from shafting suppliers. For example, Aquamet 19 and 22 are common stainless steel alloys used for shafting (www.aquamet.com). Other shafting materials, including commercially available alloys of stainless steel (other than 17-4PH) and copper-bearing alloys (bronze, for instance), should not be used.

When the material type, boat use, safety factor, and propeller size are all considered, the process of propeller-shaft design can get complicated. For this reason, let the engine manufacturer's representative, the propeller shop, or the naval architect select your prop and design your prop shaft.

Shafting needs to be straight, but since absolute straightness is almost impossible, acceptable amounts of variance have been established over the years by experience. Permissible variances are well specified in applicable published standards. (For additional information on straightness, and on shaft diameter, see ABYC Section P-6.)

Aside from inherent straightness variances, unsupported lengths of a shaft will deflect under their own weight and so require intermediate bearing support. Boats up to about 40 feet LOA seldom have shaft lengths long enough to require supports other than at the rigid shaft coupling at the reduction gear and a bearing at the propeller strut. This is called a two rigid bearing arrangement.

The propeller-shaft shop will do the actual calculations to determine the length of the propeller shaft; however, you will need to give them some measurements. Here's how:

1. Weld the strut in place.
2. Locate the main engine with the gear attached in the hull and visually align.
3. Measure the distance from the face of the gearbox output flange to the aft end of the propeller strut.
4. Provide this information to the propeller-shaft shop, and they will determine the shaft length from this measurement.

The propeller shaft should be prepared by an experienced propeller shop familiar with the standards and calculations required. And by having the same shop provide the prop as well as prepare the shaft, it will reduce the potential for error.

The prop shop will add to the measured distance the additional shaft length for the propeller hub, threads for the nut, and clearance between the strut and the propeller hub, in accordance with established standards. The shop will machine the coupling provided with the engine gear to suit the shaft diameter. A keyway will be cut into the propeller shaft and in the gear coupling for the installation of a key to prevent the shaft from rotating within the coupling. A standard taper with a key and threads for a propeller nut will be machined on the aft end of the shaft. Specifications and tolerances for propeller-shaft ends, propeller hubs, and shaft couplings should be in accordance with applicable standards (SA Standard J755 Marine Propeller-Shaft Ends and Hubs and J756 Marine Propeller-Shaft Couplings, and ABYC P-6-4.1).

Propeller shaft bearings. On small aluminum craft, a nonmetallic water-lubricated rubber bearing is the simplest and least expensive shaft bearing. The bearing consists of a nonmetallic outer sleeve with a rubber lining bonded inside it. The rubber portion has molded grooves for water lubrication.

Install the shaft bearing into the shaft strut with a light press-fit. Shaft bearings are normally secured by two stainless steel setscrews, and the bearing sleeve will be slightly drilled to promote a good mechanical grip by the retainer setscrews.

Ample water must be available to lubricate rubber bearings. Strut bearings exposed on both ends to free-flowing water are adequately cooled. Bearings located within or at the end of the shaft log must have provision for free-flowing water to lubricate and cool them. Water entering only from the aft end of the bearing is not sufficient: a raw-water inlet and scoop forward of the bearing is often used to establish the necessary flow. For bearing installations entirely within the shaft log, lubricating water may be supplied by the discharge flow from the main engine raw-water pump to ensure bearing lubrication during engine operation.

Intermediate bearings. Water-lubricated rubber bearings are not used for intermediate bearings that support the shaft inside the hull; for this function, choose either a ball-bearing pillow block or a flange-type bearing rated for marine service.

Bearing strut and housing. Since aluminum shrinks considerably more than steel when welded, welded-aluminum boats require special attention to the alignment of the strut. The best way to ensure an accurate alignment between the strut and the reduction gear output coupling is to line-bore the assembly after all welding is finished. Line-boring requires a special setup with a long boring bar that machines the inside of the strut-bearing housing in perfect alignment with the engine. The strut is machined only after all welding in the vicinity of the engine and strut that could cause distortion has been completed. This method is regularly used on large ships but, because of the expense, is seldom used in modern small-boat building.

A suitable alternative to line-boring is fitting the strut-bearing housing to a dummy shaft installed in the required position in the hull. Slide the strut-bearing housing over the dummy shaft, place the prefabricated strut legs into position on the hull, and weld them in place. (Strut legs usually pass through the shell plate and are welded to internal framing. The step-by-step procedure to align the strut with a dummy shaft is detailed in Appendix E.) Adjustments during final engine alignment, after the boat is in the water, will compensate for any minor misalignment that may exist.

Shaft log. The propeller-shaft log is usually a section of heavy-wall aluminum pipe sufficiently long enough to pass completely through the hull. The alloy of the shaft log should match the adjacent hull material, but the pipe's wall thickness should be thicker than the adjacent shell plate to allow for possible machining during final alignment of the propeller shaft. Enough of the shaft log must protrude into the hull through the bottom plate to allow attachment of the rubber hose that connects the log to the stuffing box (Figure 9-6).

Locate the shaft log with the same dummy shaft used to locate and install the strut. Cut away sufficient hull material to slide the shaft log through, use temporary bushings or shims to center it around the dummy propeller shaft, and tack-weld the log in place. Complete the final weld-out of the shaft log at the same time as the final weld of the propeller-shaft strut—after all other welding in the vicinity is finished.

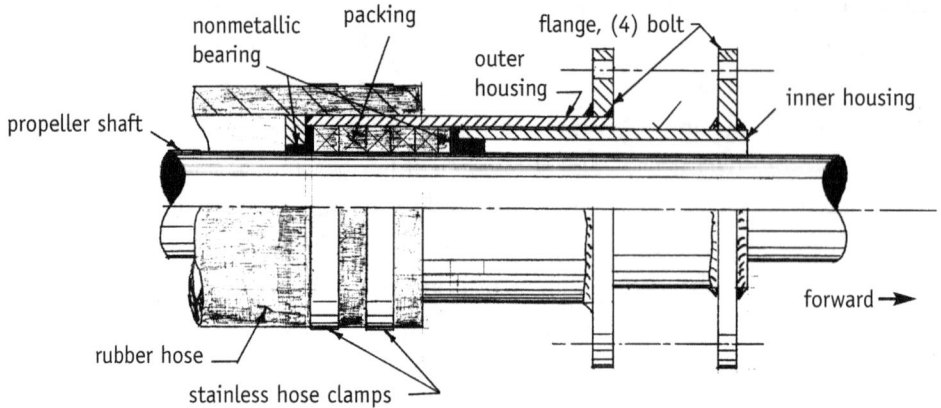

Figure 9-9. Aluminum stuffing box assembly.

Alignment of the shaft log isn't critical unless it includes a bearing. The propeller shaft should have at least 1/8-inch clearance all around inside the shaft log.

Stuffing box (packing gland). Most stuffing boxes are made of bronze and are not compatible with aluminum hull construction. However, there are several options. You can obtain an economical aluminum stuffing box from Baywood Inc., in Sedro Woolley, Washington. Or you can fabricate a stuffing box from aluminum (Figure 9-9) and use wax-impregnated flax packing for a sealant. Or forgo the conventional stuffing box entirely for a commercially available shaft seal (Figure 9-10), constructed of rubber and stainless steel and using O-rings to maintain watertight integrity, such as the units offered by Lasdrop (www.lasdrop.com).

Engine installation. After the engine bed has been installed in the hull and all the work that would otherwise be difficult to accomplish after the engine is installed is complete, the installation of the propulsion system can start.

To install an inboard engine:

1. Rig a sling to suspend the engine and attached gear at approximately the angle it will assume after installation.
2. Position the nuts on the flexible engine mount's adjustment screws for equal up and down travel; this is to ensure adequate adjustment in either direction during engine alignment.
3. Bolt the mounts to the engine and gear.
4. Carefully position the engine mounts over the engine bed and lower the engine until there is no weight on the hoist.

Now perform the following alignment steps:

1. Set the main propulsion engine and gear onto the engine bed.
2. Position the propeller strut and shaft in the hull and temporarily align the shaft with the engine.
3. Mark the engine bed girders for drilling of engine-mounting bolt holes. Remove the shaft and the engine.
4. Drill engine-mounting holes and relocate the engine on the bed.
5. Weld the propeller strut in place, reinstall the shaft, and realign the engine to the shaft.
6. Install and tighten engine-mounting bolts.
   This completes the alignment of the main engine while the boat is in the shop. (For more detailed engine installation and alignment instructions, see Appendix E.)

Figure 9-10. Shaft seal. (Courtesy Nautical Specialties)

Perform the final alignment with the boat in the water—after its temperature has stabilized, its fuel tanks are full, and a normal load is aboard.

INBOARD-OUTBOARD

The stern drive, also known as the inboard-outboard or simply I/O, is the most popular small-boat inboard gasoline propulsion system available today. This popularity is based on low price, ease of installation, and the capability of raising the propeller (lower unit) for trailer transport. Most I/O units have a built-in exhaust system that discharges through a hollow propeller hub, eliminating the need to fabricate and install an exhaust system. The outboard portion of the I/O unit swivels for steering, eliminating the need for a separate rudder assembly, and it's installed in the very stern of the boat, which is where you want it for most planing boats.

The complete I/O package from the dealer will normally include an inboard engine, the I/O unit equipped with power tilt, and options such as a pre-wired instrument panel with a harness, freshwater cooling, a larger alternator, and power steering.

I/O units are available for gasoline and diesel engines in a broad range of horsepower ratings. They are available with a single propeller, with dual contra-rotating propellers, and as heavy-duty units intended for commercial work and diesel power.

I/O Installation

Installation of a standard I/O unit is one of the simpler propulsion-system installations. Check the installation drawing provided with the I/O unit for proper layout of the engine beds and transom.

Design for I/O. To fit the geometry of the I/O unit, the transom of the boat must rake aft at about 12 degrees where the unit will be installed. Most I/O units require a transom of 2-inch minimum to 2¼-inch maximum thickness. When installing, don't use the aft engine mounts normally found on the gearbox; instead, bolt the engine securely to the portion of the installed I/O unit that is inside the hull.

Installation of the transom-mounted unit. Since the transom material on an aluminum boat is likely to be considerably less than 2 inches thick, you will need to build up the transom with some type of spacer to achieve the 2- to 2¼-inch thickness I/O units require for a proper watertight seal. The watertight seal is between the I/O unit and the transom exterior face. Place the spacer material on the inside of the boat—it does not have to be watertight. Some boatbuilders fill this space with scrap aluminum. Others use aluminum channel, sculpted to fit the cutout contour. Some even use wood—an especially poor choice since the wood rots and can contribute to corrosion of the aluminum.

The best spacer is an aluminum casting (Figure 9-11) made specifically for this application. (Such castings are available from Baywood Inc, PMP 476, 826 Metcalf Street, Sedro Woolley, Washington 98284; phone [360] 855-0818.) Simply place the casting against the back side of the transom plate and weld it in place. A cast spacer makes for a very neat and simple installation and has much to recommend it.

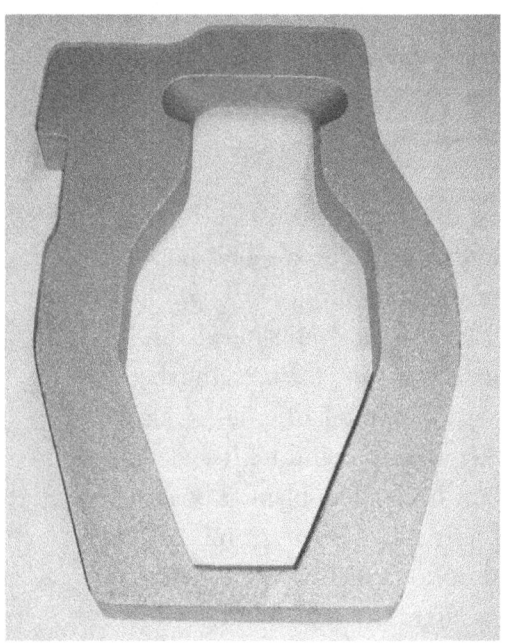

Figure 9-11. A cast-aluminum spacer is used to provide adequate transom thickness for an I/O installation.

Use the mounting template supplied with the I/O to mark the transom for the cutout and the location of the mounting-bolt holes. Make the cutout and install the transom filler, then drill the mounting holes through both the transom and the filler. Assemble the I/O transom-mounted unit to the transom by following the manufacturer's instructions.

I/O Engine Installation

Prepare the engine for installation by following the detailed engine-preparation data provided by the engine supplier. Ask your I/O dealer for the use of the special alignment tool required to align the engine and the transom-mounted I/O unit. This tool is a rod about 2 feet long designed to pass through the I/O unit and into the engine coupler spline.

Install the I/O engine as follows:

- Mount the I/O unit on the transom.
- Set the engine on the engine bed in approximate alignment with the I/O unit and mark the girders for drilling of the isolation-mount bolts.
- Temporarily remove the engine, drill the mount holes, and reset the engine.
- Pass the special alignment tool through the I/O unit into the engine coupler spline for final alignment.
- Tighten down engine-mount bolts.

The balance of the engine installation is done by following the manufacturer's instructions.

Because the I/O dealer has the expertise, not to mention special drill templates and alignment tools, you may consider having him install the unit in your boat, but if you're mechanically inclined, you can do it yourself with few problems.

WATER-JET PROPULSION

The water jet is one of the simplest and most reliable of propulsion systems. The principle is simply to squirt water out of a nozzle, causing the boat to move in the opposite direction to the water flow. Contrary to popular belief, the water-jet outlet does not have to be underwater. Water-jet propulsion operates on the principle that force = mass × acceleration and does not need "something to push against." Loosely defined, force in this case is the thrust pushing the boat, mass is the weight of the water pumped, and acceleration is the change of velocity of the water between entering and leaving the pump.

One very simple water-jet system uses a gasoline-driven water pump set in the boat, with its suction hose overboard, and the discharge water squirting out over the stern. The force of the discharging water propels the boat forward. Some small drift boats used for steelhead fishing on the Northwest rivers have actually been powered this way.

Principal advantages of a water jet are its ease of operation in shallow water and its ability to survive an impact with the bottom and continue operation. Because water jets can ingest small rocks without any apparent damage, they are ideal whitewater boats. Boats with rugged and lightweight aluminum hull construction and water-jet propulsion systems have proved to be the most popular on Pacific Northwest rivers over the past 30 years.

Water-jet boats have the additional advantages of a clean bottom with no prop to foul and minimum danger to swimmers. Because of the water jet's simple construction—basically a water pump—it has proved very rugged and maintenance free. The water-jet unit doesn't require a gear box in the drivetrain since the reverse function is accomplished by deflecting the water stream exiting the jet unit. This reversing deflector, often referred to as the bucket, is integral to the jet unit. In spe-

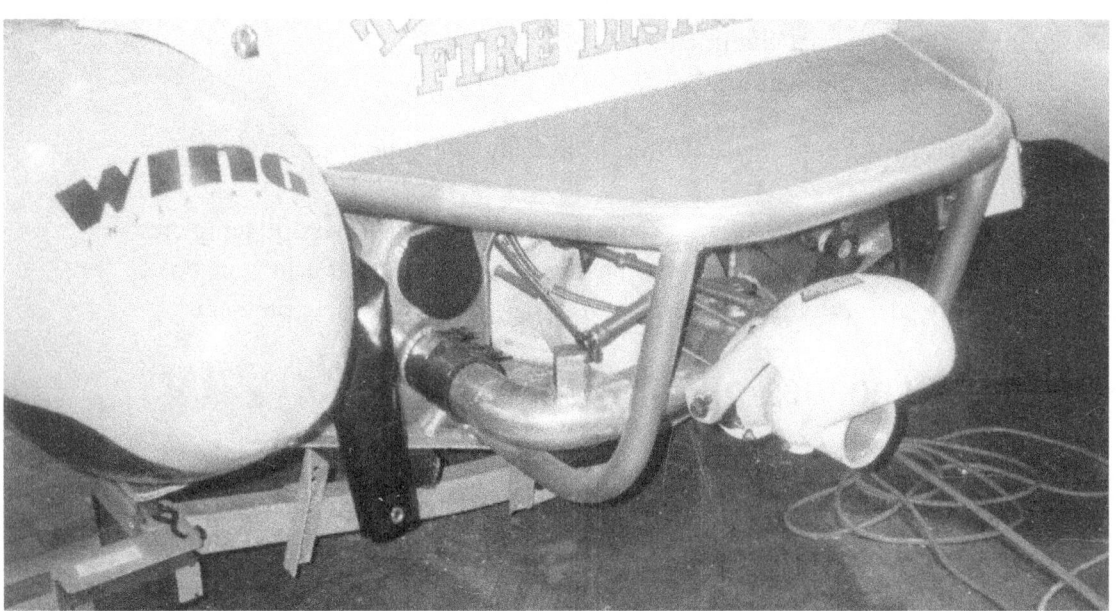

Figure 9-12. Fire pump attachment on water jet.

cial applications where a power take-off is used (such as a high-velocity fire-fighting pump), a gear may be included to disconnect the jet unit from the engine. Northwind Marine (www.northwindmarine.com) has developed a method to take water for firefighting directly from the water-jet unit, as shown in Figure 9-12.

Since water-jet boats are often used in rough whitewater, it's not uncommon to fit them with a foot throttle to allow quick rpm reduction when the boat is airborne.

Water-Jet Hull Design

C. W. F. Hamilton of New Zealand, one of the leading manufacturers of water-jet propulsion systems, recommends the following boat specifications:

- Planing hull with a nearly constant deadrise angle—i.e., keel and chine lines parallel—in the after third of the hull
- Deadrise angle of more than 10 degrees at the stern
- Keel that rises gradually from a point about one-third of the boat's waterline length back from the stem
- At least one horsepower for every 22 pounds of boat weight for best performance (see reference listing at the end of the chapter)

The hull bottom should have a flat area in the stern for mounting the flat intake screen. It should also be clean—free of a keel or strakes that will disturb the water flow to the intake—for a minimum of 6 feet forward of the intake.

Water-Jet Installation

A $1^{1}/_{16}$-inch hull thickness in the area of the jet intake is standard for axial-flow jet units like Hamilton and Kodiak. (Hamilton was a pioneer in water-jet units, and its designs have become somewhat of a standard for axial flow units.) Since aluminum boats used for whitewater work rarely have bottoms thicker than $3/16$ inch, you must install a bottom plate spacer. You can purchase one from the water-jet manufacturer or construct one yourself, as follows:

1. Begin with $7/8$- or 1-inch-thick by 2-inch-wide aluminum flat-bar and fabricate a "picture frame" to suit the jet intake opening.
2. Drill and tap this frame and install stainless steel Heli-Coil inserts to match the bolt size and pattern for the jet intake.

3. Cut the boat bottom away to suit the jet unit inlet, and weld the picture-frame mounting base around the cutout.

This installation avoids any leakage around the intake mounting bolts since they do not pass through the hull's bottom plate.

Mounting bases are also made of cast rubber (available from Kodiak Marine, Portland, Oregon). This type of base is simply placed on the hull plate in the area of the water-jet intake and through-bolted to the hull. Use the data supplied by the propulsion-unit manufacturer to locate the intake and transom cutouts.

Install the inboard engine by setting it on the engine bed in close alignment with the water jet. A short driveshaft with universal joints, commonly called a spicer shaft, is normally used to connect the engine to the water-jet unit.

OUTBOARD PROPULSION

The outboard is the most popular method of powering a small boat. The outboard's principal advantages are the ability to trim, no requirement for a separate rudder, and minimal installation labor. The additional interior room provided by mounting the engine outside the hull and the ability to raise the propeller for ease of trailering are also nice features. Because of the outboard's self-contained and portable nature, the engine can be removed for repair with minimal effort.

Over the past few years, four-cycle, or four-stroke, outboards have been very well received by boatowners, for both their quiet operation and fuel economy. Large outboards, up to 250 hp, in both single- and twin-engine installations, are now commonly used on both pleasure and commercial boats, often preempting the use of inboard-outboard units.

Outboards can be fitted with water-jet lower units.

Designing for an Outboard

Like an I/O, the outboard requires a minimum and maximum transom thickness for mounting. Consult your dealer for recommended transom thickness, cutout location, and clearances for your particular outboard. (ABYC Outboard Engine, Transom, and Engine Well Dimensions, Section S-12, establishes recommended standards.) The height of the transom is measured from the deepest point of the hull bottom to the sill of the outboard motor cutout. Below are specific transom heights based on horsepower:

- For up to 30 hp: 15 inches for a short-shaft outboard; 20 inches for a long-shaft
- For more than 30 hp: 20 inches for long shaft; 24 inches for extra-long shaft
- For more than 140 hp: 30 inches for a double extra-long shaft

The standard transom slope is 14 degrees plus or minus 2 degrees, but many experienced boaters and builders prefer a transom angle of about 17–19 degrees, which allows the boat to be trimmed bow-down.

Installing the Outboard

Small-horsepower outboards are installed by simply clamping them securely in position. Larger-horsepower units are through-bolted to the transom to ensure proper attachment. Because of the weight of a large outboard, you may need mechanical assistance to lift it onto or off the transom, necessitating a special eyebolt screwed into the top of the motor as the lifting attachment point. You can get these from the dealer.

Outboard motors are commonly mounted on stern brackets to increase the boat's interior room. Brackets are also popular for mounting small trolling motors. Hydraulically adjustable brackets are available for use in large outboard installations, and manually adjustable units are available for use with smaller motors. Fixed (nonadjustable) brackets are usually custom made by the boatbuilder. For optimal performance, design the bracket so that the propeller is raised about 1 inch for every 12 inches of distance it is moved aft of the transom. One disadvantage of brackets is that the boat's center of gravity can be shifted too far aft, which can result in a tendency for the boat to "porpoise."

Routing the various controls to an outboard motor may require cutting some holes. Use the installation information provided with the outboard to locate and size these openings.

The correct height of the propeller in relationship to the bottom of the boat is a factor of boat speed and propeller selection. Select the optimum height, in relation to the *antiventilation* (or *cavitation*) plate located on the lower unit above the propeller, as follows:

- Work application (heavy load, slow speed): 1 to 2 inches below the bottom of the boat

- Normal duty (average load, average speed): flush with the bottom of the boat
- Sport application (waterskiing, etc.): 1 to 3 inches above the bottom of the boat
- High performance (maximum-speed application): 4 inches or more above the boat bottom

CONTROLS

A single-level control, in which both the throttle and the forward/reverse gear are operated by the same control lever, is the most commonly installed control system on small boats. A number of manufacturers supply both control heads and control cables. Control heads and the surface they're mounted on should be able to withstand a force of 75 pounds in any direction, and the throttle and gear lever (or levers) should not be closer than 2½ inches from the steering wheel for proper hand clearance.

Controls operate in the natural direction; that is, the lever moves forward to engage the engine gear in forward and back to engage reverse. When the throttle is advanced, engine rpm advances, and when it's pulled back, rpm declines. The same concept applies to trim-tab installations: raising the trim switch to the up position raises the bow, and lowering the switch lowers the bow.

On single-engine boats with twin-lever, single-function controls, the starboard (right) lever is the throttle, and the port (left) lever the gear. For dual-engine control stations with two single-lever controls, the port-engine control is on the port side of the dual control head, and the starboard control on the starboard side. For dual-engine installations with separate throttle and gear levers, the throttle levers are alongside each other so they may be operated together with one hand. This will put the shift levers outboard of the throttles, port and starboard.

The ABYC recommends that the throttle be identified by a red knob or some other means (surface texture, shape, etc.) to distinguish between throttle and gear. Shift controls include a neutral position indication, usually a detent. Start-in-gear protection should be included to prevent starting an engine with the prop engaged.

Control cables are normally commercially available push/pull types designed for marine applications and sized to suit the specific controls. The control cable for the throttle is usually color-coded red. You can do your own color coding with red tape wrapped around the control end of the cable to minimize the possibility of accidentally crossing the throttle and gear cables during maintenance work. Install control cables with a minimum number of bends—none with a tighter radius than specified by the cable manufacturer—and securely fasten them in place. Be sure to keep cables away from the engine's exhaust system.

Pay particular attention to electrically isolating engine controls; stray voltage can flow through the controls (and the metal console) to the hull. Electrically isolate the controls from the hull to ensure engine isolation from the hull. This is required to maintain a single-point negative ground of the boat's electrical system, as detailed in Chapter 11. Be sure to isolate metal controls from a metal hull. The simplest method is to mount the control head on a nonconductive surface, such as wood or plastic. If you mount the control head to a metal console that is in electrical contact with the hull, use isolation gaskets and bushings around the mounting bolts. Be sure you also electrically isolate the control cables, including any attachment clips, from the hull.

STEERING

The helm unit may be a reel type, a rack-and-pinion, or a rotary hydraulic pump. Steering systems may be motor mounted or hull mounted. A motor-mounted steering system is rigidly mounted to the propulsion unit, transmitting most of the steering stress to the engine mounts. An example of this is an outboard-motor steering unit that threads into the framework of the outboard; only the steering cable or hydraulic lines are attached to the hull.

Conversely, a hydraulic cylinder attached to the rudder and the hull is an example of a hull-mounted steering system, transmitting steering stresses directly to hull structure. A hull-mounted steering system must be capable of sustaining a considerable load in either direction along the axis of the steering output mechanism, requiring you to give appropriate consideration to the hull structure supporting the steering gear.

Helm units and the steering wheel itself must be capable of withstanding a considerable force, such as a 200-pound operator thrown against them during a rough ride. Slamming forces on a pleasure boat can reach 4 g's at the bow and 2 g's at the center of gravity, so it's not unreasonable to expect 3 g's at the steering station during a fast run in rough water. The helm and the structure supporting it must be capable of withstanding these high potential forces.

Pay particular attention to the mounting of freestanding steering consoles. The loads at the helm are compounded at the base of the console because of the lever effect of the height of the console. Freestanding consoles have a bad habit of breaking loose during a rough ride and causing operator injury. Steering consoles must not be simply bolted to the floorboards; weld or through-bolt them securely to the boat's framing.

ABYC P-17 specifies tests to insure the acceptability of installed steering systems.

Selection of a Steering System

Steering systems for small powerboats can consist of the tiller of a small outboard, a steering wheel controlling a rudder, a stern drive, a water jet, or a (typically larger) outboard. Remote steering is commonly a hardware item purchased separately from the propulsion system. For small boats, steering control is affected by means of a reel-type helm unit with push/pull cable, a rack-and-pinion helm unit with push/pull cable, or a hydraulic steering system with a rotary hydraulic helm pump and a hydraulic cylinder. However, ultimately, all three push and pull at the steering attachment point for the rudder, outboard, stern-drive unit, or water-jet outlet. Cable-over-pulley steering, once common, is very seldom used on newer boats and isn't recommended for boats of more than 50 hp. (Recommended guidelines for cable-over-pulley steering are found in ABYC P-18.)

Whether a steering system will be motor- or hull-mounted depends on the steering configuration provided with the propulsion system. Outboard motors, I/O units, and water jets usually have provisions for engine-mounted (propulsion unit) steering systems. Conventional inboard installations require a rudder, which is a hull-mounted steering system. Whether you choose cable-and-reel, cable-and-rack-and-pinion, or hydraulic steering is a matter of the boat's intended use, personal preference, and your budget. High-horsepower installations require heavy-duty steering systems, such as rack-and-pinion units with heavy-duty cables or hydraulic steering systems. As a general rule, a reel-type steering system with a push/pull cable is least expensive, followed by a rack-and-pinion helm with a push/pull cable. The most expensive is hydraulic, but if multiple steering stations or considerable change of direction of steering cables is required to avoid interferences, hydraulic steering may be the most economical selection. Steering systems and cables come with detailed assembly and installation instructions, and they're sized to suit the boat size and horsepower.

PROPELLERS

Propellers used on aluminum boats should not be constructed of copper-bearing materials, such as bronze, because the sacrificial nature of aluminum to copper

Propulsion Systems and Controls

will result in hull corrosion. Stainless steel or aluminum propellers are required for aluminum boats.

There are many considerations in selecting a propeller, or in boating vernacular, the "wheel," and there is no known formula to automatically calculate the ideal propeller size for a given boat. Most major marine-engine manufacturers can provide excellent propeller selection data upon request, but your best selection data will come only from actual tests with various propellers. Most prop shops have loaner propellers just for this purpose.

You need to be familiar with a few terms to discuss wheel selection with your prop shop:

- Diameter: the diameter of the circle scribed by the propeller blade tips.
- Pitch: the distance the propeller would travel in one revolution if it were rotating in a solid—like a screw through wood. The theoretical distance traveled (in inches) in 1 minute is calculated by rpm × pitch.
- Slip: since the propeller is rotating not through a solid, but a liquid, the loss of forward motion through the water is known as slip. Slip is the difference between the theoretical distance a propeller of a given pitch would travel in one revolution and the actual distance it travels, usually expressed as a percentage.
- Pitch ratio: the pitch of a propeller divided by its diameter.

As a general rule, select the largest-diameter propeller—within practical limits—that you can turn at its most appropriate turning speed.

These limits are:

- Size of the propeller aperture
- Type of operation (workboat, planing boat, etc.)
- Shaft angle required for a larger propeller—a large propeller may require an increased shaft angle to provide adequate clearance between the hull and the blade tips
- Weight of the propeller, shaft, and gear relative to boat size
- Minimum boat draft requirements

Outboard and I/O propellers are usually configured with a hollow center for the engine exhaust outlet.

An excellent publication on propeller selection, *Everything You Need to Know about Propellers,* is available from Mercury Marine, Fond du Lac, Wisconsin. It is no longer in print, but it can be viewed or printed from the Internet at http://www.mercurymarine.com; click 'Propellers,' then "Fundamentals."

EXHAUST SYSTEMS

Exhaust systems for outboards and I/Os are included with the machinery and require no additional fabrication; engine exhaust exits through the hollow center of the propeller. Commercially available marinized automotive engines, as typically used with water-jet units, are commonly equipped with water-cooled exhaust risers. The risers are raw-water cooled and mix the water with the exhaust at the outlet, allowing the use of a rubber exhaust hose downstream of the cooling-water inlet. Complete the exhaust installation for engines mounted above the waterline and equipped with water-cooled exhaust risers by simply installing a muffler in the nonmetallic section of the wet exhaust line and routing the exhaust overboard—preferably through the transom.

Conventional engines not equipped with wet exhaust risers, and engines mounted below the waterline require some special provisions to get the exhaust

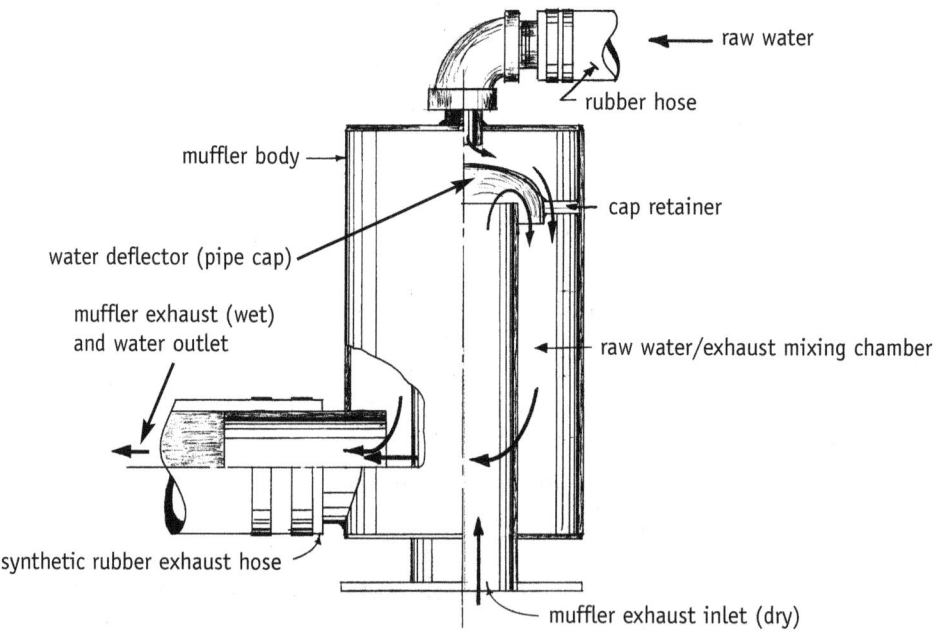

Figure 9-13. Fabricated exhaust muffler with cooling water inlet.

safely out of the boat. Either a wet or a dry exhaust system may be installed. (ABYC, Section P-1, "Installation of Exhaust Systems for Propulsion and Auxiliary Engines" covers exhaust systems in detail.)

A wet exhaust system cools, or partially cools, the exhaust gases and exhaust line with water entering into the exhaust stream. Flexible wet-exhaust hose available from marine hardware suppliers that complies with ABYC P-1, Section 1-7, may be used for exhaust pipe in the water-cooled section of the exhaust line. Dry sections of the exhaust system are constructed of high-temperature- and corrosion-resistant materials.

A fabricated muffler for a typical wet exhaust system for mounting below the waterline is shown in Figure 9-13. Fabricate the muffler and other hot sections of the exhaust system from stainless steel, preferably alloy 316. Use nonmetallic materials, such as an approved wet-exhaust hose, in areas that are located after the cooling water enters the exhaust system, usually just after the muffler. On maximum-performance boats, where weight savings are more important than cost, titanium has been used with excellent results for both the wet and dry sections.

Install a section of flexible metal pipe, called flex or wrinkle belly, between the exhaust manifold outlet and the start of the dry section of the exhaust pipe. This flexible pipe keeps strain from developing on the exhaust manifold from the movement of the engine. A custom shop can make up the flex with a flange on each end to attach it to the exhaust system.

Insulate hot sections of the exhaust system in areas subject to fire hazard and, to prevent burns, in all exposed areas that exceed 200°F. Hot-pipe insulation is usually fiberglass and may be obtained for this application, preformed to suit the pipe, from a refractories supplier or through your engine dealer.

A considerable amount of heat will be generated by a dry exhaust pipe, and you'll need to incorporate some provision to carry this heat overboard. One option is to build suitable air vents from the outside to the engine exhaust area to assist with flushing the hot air out of the compartment. Adding a forced-air blower will supplement the air vent method. Movement of the hot air overboard can be by natural convection if the hot pipe is encased in a sheet metal shroud that is provided with a way to vent overboard at a location higher than the exhaust pipe.

As with the engine controls, the exhaust system needs to be electrically isolated from the hull to protect the single-point negative ground. High-temperature insulation, in addition to the thermal protection it affords, can also provide excellent electrical isolation between the metal exhaust pipe and the exhaust system supports. Rubber exhaust hose doesn't require further electrical isolation.

When attaching rubber exhaust hose with hose clamps, be careful not to over-tighten the clamps. Exhaust hose has a steel wire wound into the hose to prevent collapsing, and an over-tight hose clamp can cut through the rubber of the hose and make electrical contact with the hose clamp, potentially breaking the electrical isolation of the system.

References

American Boat and Yacht Council, Inc. *Standards and Recommended Practices for Small Craft.* Millersville, Md.: American Boat and Yacht Council, Inc., 2005.

C. W. F. Hamilton & Company, Ltd. *Product Range and Application Guide.* Christchurch, New Zealand: C. W. F. Hamilton & Company, Ltd.

Gerr, Dave. *Propeller Handbook.* Camden, Me.: International Marine, 1989.

U.S. Coast Guard Boating Safety. "Boatbuilder's Handbook." U.S. Coast Guard. http://www.uscgboating.org/safety/boatbuilder/index.htm.

CHAPTER 10

Fuel Systems

Of the two standard marine engine fuels—gasoline and diesel—gasoline is by far the more regulated due to its more explosive nature. The proper design and installation of a fuel system is well documented in ABYC's publication *Standards and Recommended Practices for Small Craft*. These standards incorporate USCG regulations and offer additional nonmandatory specifications to provide a safe and reliable fuel system. The USCG regulations are intended to prevent the most serious fuel-related hazards in boats carrying gasoline: fire and explosion. The fuel system, along with ventilation and electrical requirements associated with it, is one of the few areas for which the Coast Guard has firm regulations concerning small craft. They maintain a website showing all applicable small-boat building regulations at http://www.uscgboating.org/safety/boatbuilder/. Applicable gasoline fuel tank regulations are found in 33 CFR 183, Subpart J.

GASOLINE FUEL SYSTEMS

Basically, the engine compartment and any other area that might contain gasoline fumes must have positive ventilation (i.e., a blower) to remove explosive vapors, and it must be protected from electrical sparks.

The fuel system comprises the tank (or tanks), fill, vent, and supply lines. The supply line should have a shut-off valve near the tank, and the system should include an antisiphon valve to prevent fuel from draining into the bilge in the event of a broken fuel line. A separate fuel filter is required between the fuel tank and the engine-mounted fuel filter. A length of flexible fuel hose is installed between the end of the rigid supply line and the engine to isolate the fuel line from engine vibrations.

Fuel Tanks

Gasoline fuel tanks are subject to USCG inspection. Although you can fabricate a gasoline fuel tank, the testing requirements to achieve compliance with the regulations make it uneconomical for the occasional tank builder. A professional fuel-tank builder can provide fuel tanks at a reasonable cost that will meet all required standards.

Fuel tanks constructed from marine-alloy aluminum are the best choice for aluminum boats. The tanks must be a minimum of 0.090-inch-thick material per ABYC H-24 and should use fittings manufactured of aluminum alloys 5052,

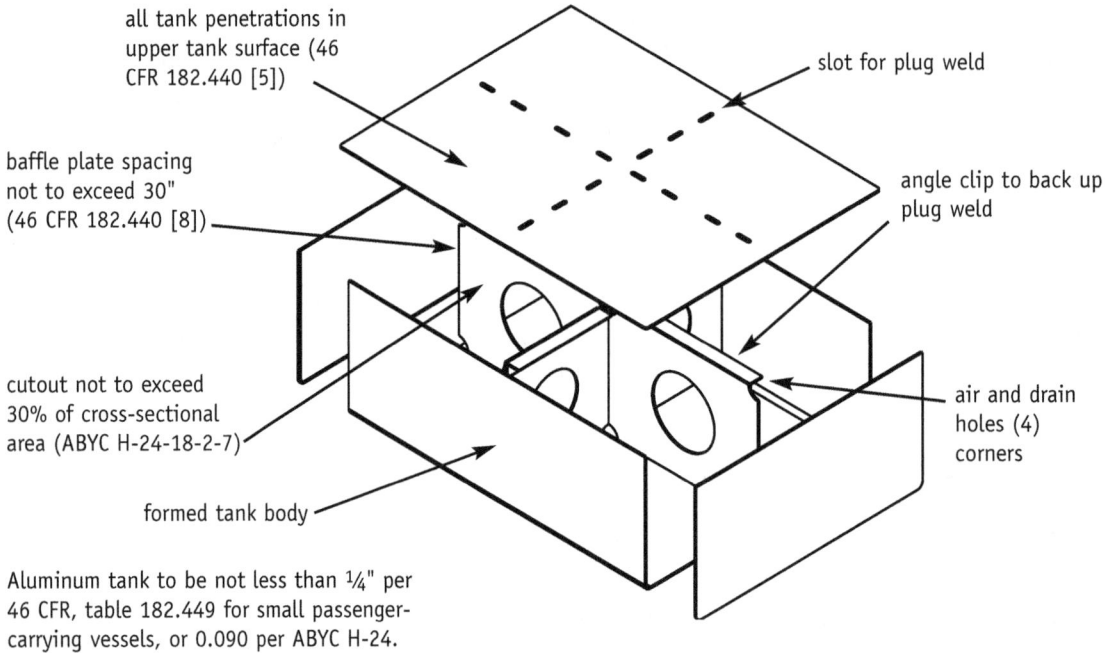

Figure 10-1. A typical aluminum fuel tank body.

5083, 5086, 6061, or 6063, or 300-series stainless steel. Never use copper-bearing alloys, such as brass, in direct contact with aluminum. Fuel tanks installed on small passenger-carrying vessels must be a minimum of ¼-inch thick per 46 CFR 182.440, Table 182.440(a)(1). A typical fuel-tank body is shown in Figure 10-1.

Except for the fuel supply fitting, gasoline fuel tanks must not be fitted with an outlet such as a drain valve for withdrawing fuel, and all openings in a fuel tank must be at the top. Fuel tanks must be designed to prohibit standing water from accumulating on them. Adequate provisions for secure mounting—such as bolt-down clips or straps—must be included. Fuel tanks are to be *electrically bonded* (see Chapter 11) to the hull. Suitable access to fuel tanks is required for inspection and repair. Tanks that will contain gasoline cannot be integral with the hull (i.e., where at least one side of the tank is the actual hull shell plate) or be used to support any boat structure or deck.

Fuel tanks require slosh baffles at least every 30 inches with suitable openings at the top for air passage and at the bottom for fuel. These baffles prevent liquid fuel from sloshing from side to side or fore and aft (called free surface effect), a situation that can seriously affect vessel stability. Openings in baffles are not to exceed 30 percent of the cross-sectional area. All threaded tank fittings must be tapered pipe thread (NPT). A label bearing the manufacturer's name and address and the statement "This tank has been tested under 33 CFR 183.514" is required. The tank should also be labeled with the date of manufacture, the maximum test pressure, the material specifications, and the type of fuel to be placed in the tank (per ABYC [H-24] recommendations).

Because of the high g-forces experienced at the bow of a planing boat, the Coast Guard has placed restrictions on locating fuel tanks in the bow unless the tank has met certain rigid test standards. Fuel tanks labeled "Must be installed in the aft portion of the boat" may not be used in the bow area.

Gasoline Fuel Lines

Fuel lines may be either hose or metal pipe and must comply with USCG requirements. Hose used for the fill pipe, vent line, or supply line to the engine must be USCG type A or USCG type B. Metallic fuel lines may be seamless annealed copper, copper-nickel, or nickel-copper. Unfortunately, copper-bearing alloys must be carefully isolated from the aluminum hull and tanks to minimize galvanic corrosion problems (see Chapter 11). Stainless steel, which does not cause galvanic corrosion of aluminum, is an excellent choice for fuel lines for an aluminum boat even though it isn't one of the approved fuel line materials listed by ABYC or the USCG. Contact your local USCG inspection office for approval prior to using stainless steel for fuel lines.

On small boats, nonmetallic hose is often used for the entire fuel and vent lines, eliminating all potential for galvanic corrosion.

Metallic fuel lines must be secured to the hull structure with nonabrading and galvanic-isolating clips, such as electrical line support clips with synthetic rubber cushioning. Secure flexible fuel lines to hull structure similar to electrical conductors, using snap-ties or some other type of nonabrading attachment.

Fuel Tank Vent

The fuel vent originates at the highest point of the fuel tank. Run it to the outside of the hull—well above the waterline to prevent water intrusion—and fit it with a suitable flame arrestor screen that you can clean. The minimum inside diameter (ID) for a vent line is 7/16 inch. Separation between compartment ventilation openings and fuel tank vent line termination shall be at least 15 inches to comply with ABYC H24.13.6.

Fuel Fill

The fuel fill must be located so that any fuel that may be spilled during fueling does not run into the bilge area and create an explosive hazard. The tank fill must be grounded to the hull. In practice, the metallic fill neck is usually mounted to the aluminum hull structure in such a manner that it is electrically bonded to the hull and does not require a separate bonding conductor. The minimum ID of fuel fill hose is 1 1/8 inches.

Fuel Valves

Manually operated fuel-system valves must be of a design suitable for the marine environment. They must have positive stops in both the open and closed position and be easily recognized as open or closed. Electrical fuel-selector valves of the automotive type may not be used (see USCG Boating Safety Circular 71, dated April 1991).

Fittings

Most readily available fuel-line fittings are of copper-bearing alloys, which should not be used in direct contact with the aluminum fuel tank. The available selection of fittings and valves manufactured of suitable stainless steel is limited. You can use copper-bearing fittings as long as you provide a galvanic barrier, such as a 300-series stainless steel nipple, to isolate the fitting from the aluminum, as illustrated in Figure 10-2. Other methods of isolating copper-bearing fittings from the fuel tank include the use of a stainless steel bushing or the installation of a short piece of stainless steel pipe between the aluminum and the brass or copper. These prevent direct contact between the aluminum and the copper-bearing alloy, reducing corrosion potential.

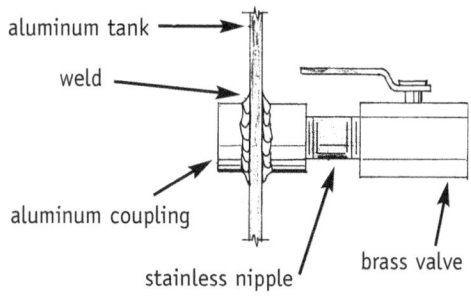

Figure 10-2. Method to attach brass fuel valve to aluminum tank.

Use flare-type tube fittings for fuel systems. Do not use compression-type fittings.

Gasoline Fuel System Installation and Test

Never use the fuel tank as part of the hull's structural support. Mount it securely to the boat's structure and electrically bond it to the hull. On an aluminum boat, separate electrical bonding of the fill neck and vent fittings normally is not required since the hull acts as a conductor to ground.

You will need a method of determining the quantity of fuel in the tank. Automotive-type electrical fuel-gauge units are not recommended because they are commonly single-wire installations, using the auto frame as the other conductor. Always use two-wire marine units on an aluminum boat.

Secure all hose connections in the fuel system (for example, where the fill hose attaches to the fill neck) with two stainless steel hose clamps that tighten with a screw. USCG regulations do not allow the use of spring clamps.

After installation, pressure test the entire fuel system to a minimum of 3 psi or to a head of fuel equal to one and a half times the maximum distance from the lowest point to the highest point (the top of the fill neck or vent, whichever is greater), making sure there are no leaks.

To perform a head test to one and a half times the maximum head, follow the steps below:

1. Plug all but one fuel system opening.
2. Add a standpipe to the remaining opening. The standpipe must have a minimum vertical rise equal to one and a half times the vertical distance from the bottom of the tank to the top of the fill neck or vent. (For example, if the distance from the bottom of the tank to the top of the vent or fill is 10 feet, then you'll need a total head of 15 feet [1.5 × 10].)
3. Using this figure, locate the standpipe anywhere on the fuel system, but be sure the top is at least 15 feet above the lowest point of the fuel system.
4. Fill the system with fresh water; calculate 0.432 psi per foot of standpipe height. For this example, 15 × 0.432 = 6.48 psi. Since this is more than 3 psi, this test will suffice. (The minimum standpipe height that will allow a test to 3 psi is 6.94 feet.)

Ventilation for Gasoline-Powered Boats

Both powered and natural ventilation systems are required in gasoline-powered boats with enclosed engine compartments. The USCG ventilation-system standard is somewhat unique in that it requires the boat operator to keep the powered and natural ventilation systems in working order (33 CFR 183, Subpart K, "Ventilation").

Power ventilation system. A forced-air, explosion-proof ventilation blower is required in an enclosed engine compartment. This must be activated prior to starting the engine to extract any explosive fumes from the boat. The intake duct must extend to the lower third of the compartment but be above the normal level of bilgewater. The size of the blower depends on the size of the compartment. You can determine the size you need by referencing ABYC H-2 for gasoline engines and Figure 10-3.

Regulations also require the posting of a warning label in plain view of the operator and near the engine ignition switch to remind the boat operator to run the blower for four minutes prior to starting the engine. The warning label must also direct the operator to check that the bilge is free of gas fumes before starting

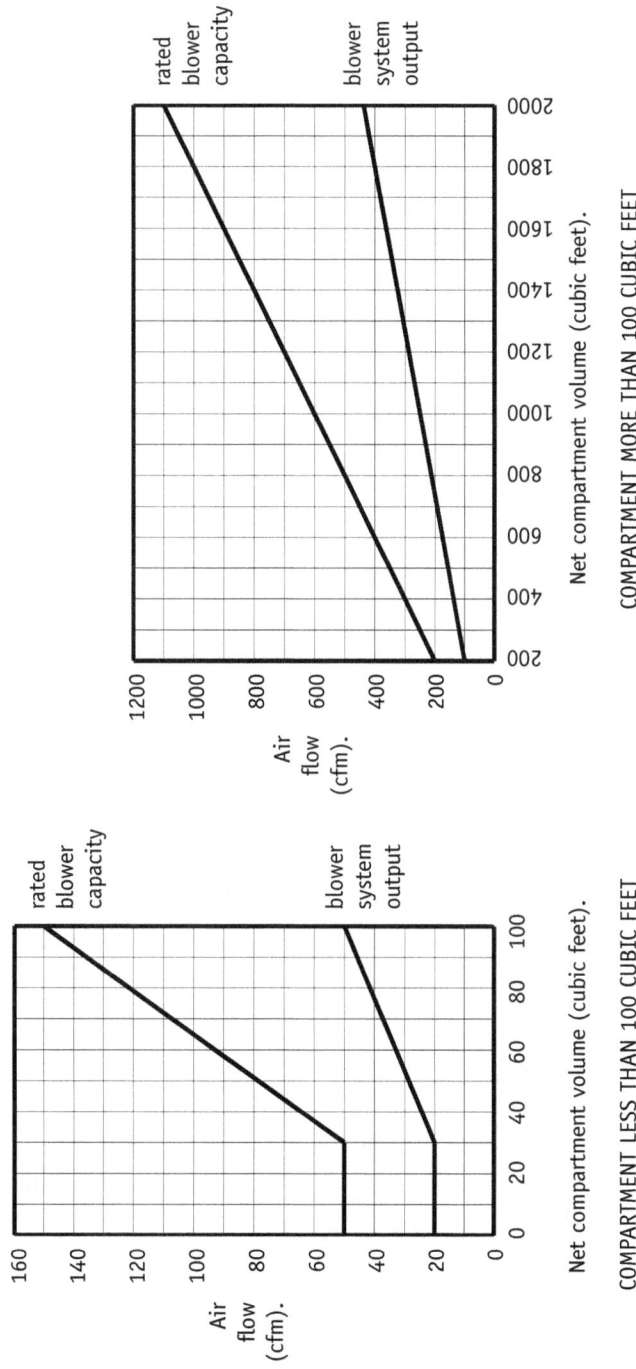

Figure 10-3. Compartment blower cubic feet per minute (cfm) requirements by compartment size in cubic feet.

> **WARNING**
>
> Gasoline vapors can explode, resulting in injury or death. Before starting engine:
>
> - Check engine compartment bilge for gasoline or vapors
> - Operate blower for four minutes
> - Verify blower operation
>
> Run blower when boat is operating below cruising speed.

Figure 10-4. Engine-compartment ventilation warning label.

the engine. An appropriate warning label (Figure 10-4) is often included in the package with a new marine bilge blower.

Natural ventilation system. The intake opening on the exterior of the boat must face forward. A duct must extend from the exterior exhaust opening to the lower third of the engine compartment but be above the normal level of bilgewater. The orientation of the exhaust opening is usually aft but must be such that a natural flow of air will enter and exit the engine compartment when the boat is under way. The required sizes of natural ventilation openings are shown in Figure 10-5.

DIESEL FUEL SYSTEM

Since diesel fuel is considered nonexplosive, standards that pertain to fire hazard are considerably relaxed. The fuel system for diesel fuel is similar to the one used for gasoline—with the following exceptions.

Diesel-Fuel Tank

Diesel-fuel tanks are constructed like gasoline tanks, except that a drain valve is permitted at the bottom of the tank, and an additional fuel inlet to the tank, often

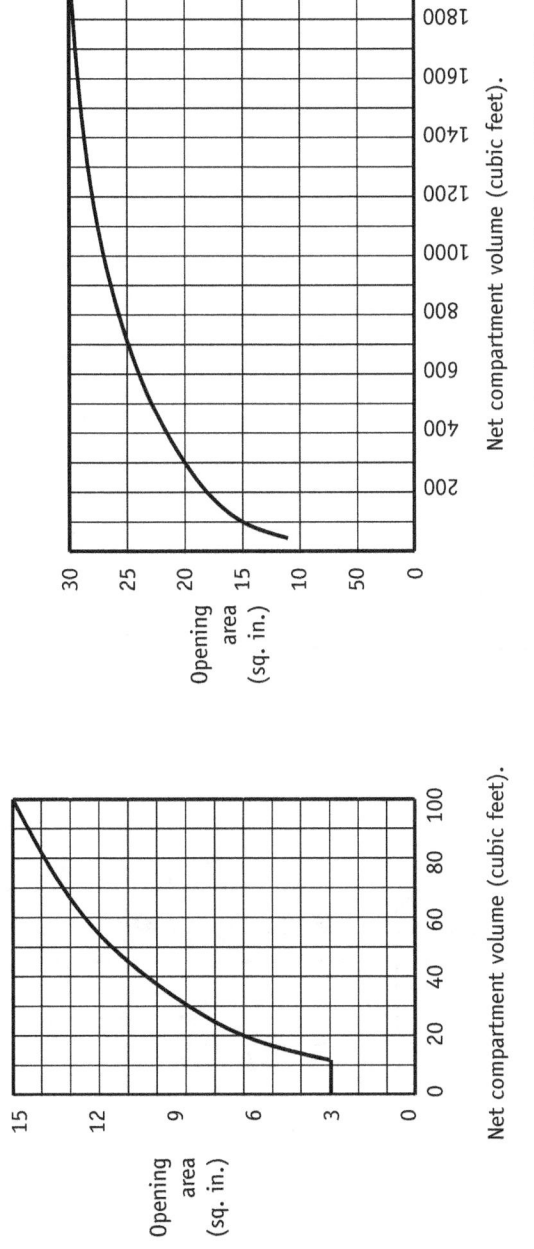

Figure 10-5. Cross-section requirements for engine-room ventilation openings.

located alongside the fuel outlet port, is required for the fuel return line. Although diesel tanks may be constructed integral with the hull, it isn't a good idea for aluminum boats. Because of the nature of the fuel, diesel tanks are very difficult to keep fuel tight: diesel fuels will penetrate where water will not. For a diesel tank to be fuel tight, it must be welded under ideal conditions, which because of limited access, out-of-position welding, and cleanliness problems—are much more difficult to achieve when building integral tanks. Minor weeping from integral

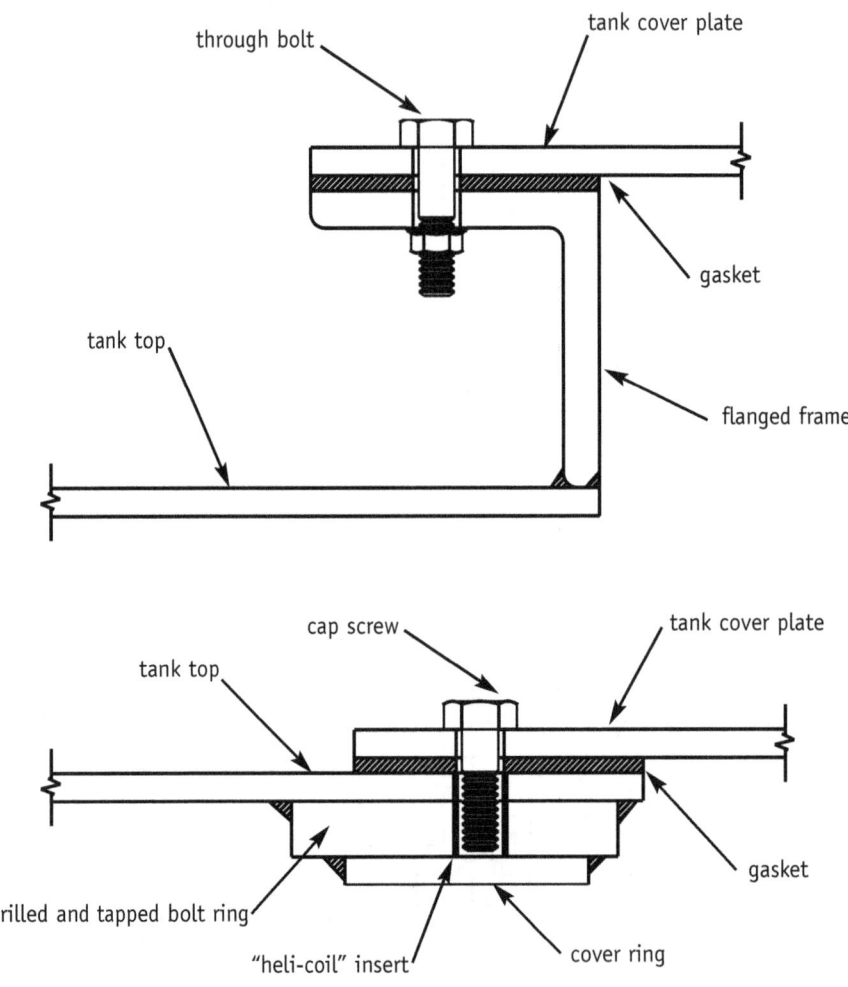

Figure 10-6. Fuel-tank cover-attachment details.

tanks is almost impossible to repair and can be very annoying and potentially hazardous. The best option for the amateur builder is to install diesel-fuel tanks purchased from an established boat fuel-tank manufacturer to insure the required weld quality and conformance to slosh baffle requirements.

On larger diesel fuel tanks found on large boats, it is wise to incorporate clean-out ports in the tops of the fuel tanks for periodic inspection and tank cleaning. Normally circular in shape, clean-out ports should be at least 16 inches in diameter to allow full arm and shoulder access. Cover plates should be attached by welded studs or some other method that doesn't allow fuel to escape around attachment bolts. (Fuel can stand in the fill neck, causing a head on the tank at the clean-out opening.) A neoprene gasket under the lid should ensure a tight seal. Figure 10-6 shows two methods for obtaining a fuel-tight inspection cover.

Diesel-Fuel Lines

Black steel pipe, at least schedule 40, may be used for diesel-fuel lines in place of copper or copper-bearing alloys. Do not use galvanized pipe. (The USCG authorizes the use of seamless steel pipe or tubing providing equivalent safety to copper, nickel-copper, or copper-nickel tubing with 0.035-inch-minimum wall thickness for use in small passenger-carrying vessels. This is per 46 CFR 182.455, "Fuel Piping.")

Ventilation

There are no ABYC or USCG requirements for natural or forced-air engine-compartment ventilation for small boats pertaining to the explosion hazard of diesel-fuel fumes (ABYC H-32.5.3).

References

American Boat and Yacht Council, Inc. *Standards and Technical Information for Small Craft.* Millersville, Md.: American Boat and Yacht Council, Inc., 2005.
U.S. Coast Guard Boating Safety. "Boatbuilder's Handbook." U.S. Coast Guard. http://www.uscgboating.org/safety/boatbuilder/index.htm.
U.S. Department of Transportation. *Code of Federal Regulation.* Title 33, Part 183, Subpart J, "Fuel Systems." Washington, D.C.: U.S. Department of Transportation (U.S. Coast Guard), 2003.

———. *Code of Federal Regulation.* Title 33, Part 183, Subpart K, "Ventilation." Washington, D.C.: U.S. Department of Transportation (U.S. Coast Guard), 2003.

———. *Code of Federal Regulation.* Title 46, Parts 166–199, "Shipping," Subchapter T. Washington, D.C.: U.S. Department of Transportation (U.S. Coast Guard), 2000.

CHAPTER 11

The Electrical System

Since stray electrical currents can cause extensive damage to an aluminum hull, aluminum boats are particularly sensitive to poor wiring practices. It is imperative that the hull never be used as an electrical conductor for the boat's electrical system. All electrical equipment must be connected to both terminals of the battery by a full two-wire system, and the hull must never be used as a common ground. Consult ABYC standards prior to installing the boat's electrical systems.

Most automotive equipment—windshield wipers and fuel-gauge sending units, for example—are constructed with a single-wire arrangement. The metal frame of the automobile is expected to serve as the second conductor. Such items may be used on an aluminum boat only if they are carefully electrically isolated from the hull and provided with an electrical ground wire back to the battery's negative terminal.

To minimize stray-voltage problems and ensure a *single-point ground*, electrically isolate (from the hull) all of the boat equipment that uses electrical power, including the controls and exhaust system.

Only the boat's *bonding system* can use the hull as a conductor. Connect a single-point negative ground from the main-engine negative terminal to one of the engine girders to ground the electrical-power distribution system to the aluminum hull. This ground is a means of maintaining the negative side of the circuit at ground potential and is not to carry current under normal conditions.

DC ELECTRICAL SYSTEM

On small boats, 12-volt DC electrical systems are the norm, while 24-volt systems are becoming common on larger boats. We will address only 12-volt systems here, but all information is applicable to 24-volt systems, which in any case use DC-DC converters to step down the voltage for use with 12-volt equipment. (Twenty-four-volt systems have the advantage of smaller equipment and cabling size.) USCG regulations that pertain to the electrical systems of small pleasure boats

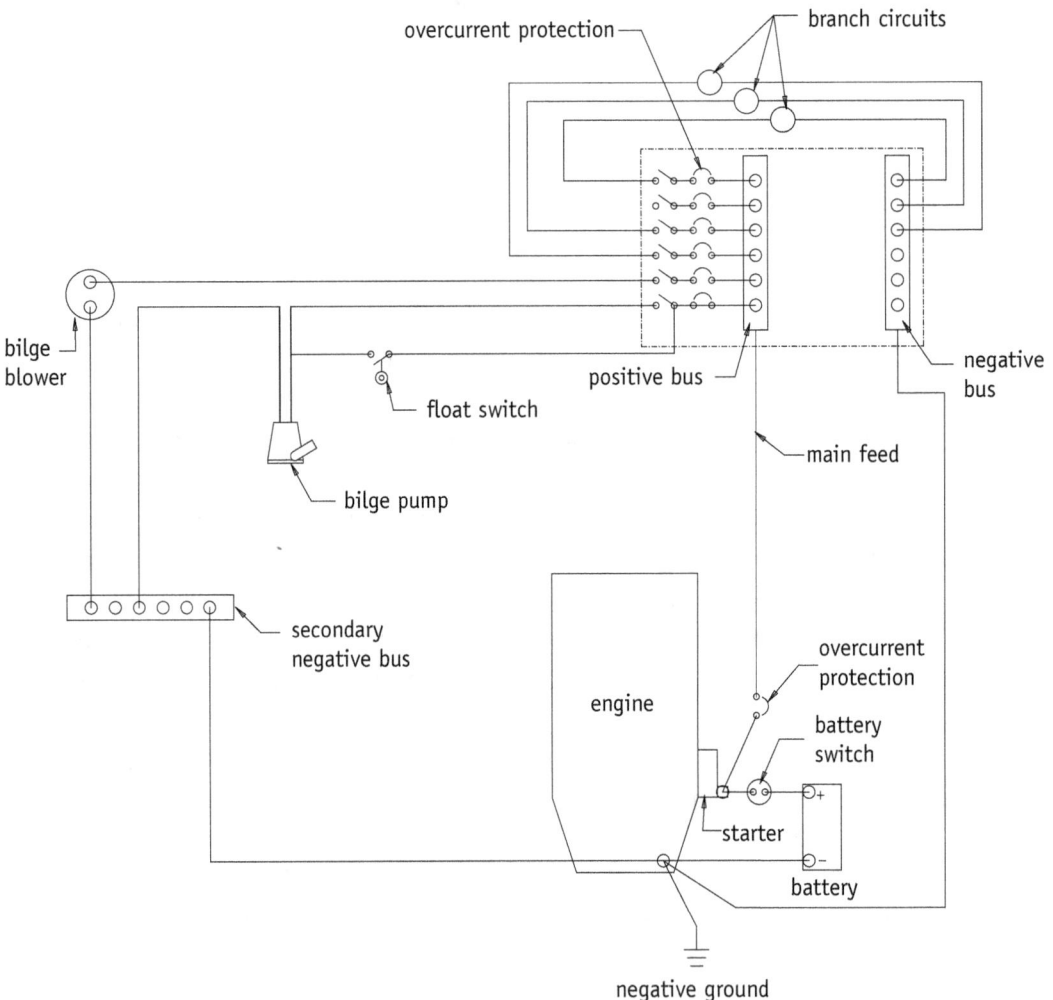

Figure 11-1. Twelve-volt DC electrical distribution system schematic.

only apply to boats that are powered by inboard gasoline engines. The primary emphasis is the risk of igniting gasoline vapor. Consult the USCG website at http://www.uscgboating.org/safety/boatbuilder/electrical/183-401-a.htm for current USCG requirements. Other industry standards and practices are strictly voluntary. Recommended guidelines are provided by the ABYC.

A representative 12-volt DC electrical distribution system for an aluminum boat, with a single-point negative ground, is provided in Figure 11-1. Note that this is a two-wire insulated return system with no part of the circuit, in particular the negative, connected to any ground, making it a totally isolated system. A short jumper cable from the engine negative ground to the aluminum hull engine girder provides the single-point negative ground connection.

The electrical power to energize the DC distribution system is taken from the positive terminal of the starter solenoid. A circuit breaker, sized to protect the DC system, is placed in the main positive feeder cable near the selector switch (per ABYC E-11.12.1), and the cable is connected to the positive bus bar of the main power distribution panel. From the distribution panel, branch circuits, which are individually protected by circuit breakers (or fuses), lead to the boat's various electrical items.

Circuits for electrical equipment mounted in the boat forward of the distribution panel are completed by a connection to the negative bus of the power distribution panel, which in turn is connected to the engine negative terminal. For equipment mounted aft—closer to the engine than to the distribution panel—wire runs may be shortened by using a secondary negative bus bar located aft and connected to the engine negative terminal.

DC Electrical Load Calculations

To determine the size of the main power-distribution panel, the main-circuit-breaker capacity, and main-cable size, you'll need to calculate the anticipated electrical load. One method is to develop two lists—let's call them list A and list B—similar to those shown in Table 11-1. List A will include those items that must be available on a continuous basis and are considered necessary for safety at sea. List B will include those items that get intermittent use and aren't normally required for safety at sea. A 3 percent voltage drop is acceptable for list A, 10 percent drop for list B.

To properly calculate the *total amperage* (amps) required for lists A and B, you'll need the *actual operating amperage* of each item. While some items will be

TABLE 11-1	**Electrical load worksheet.**		
List A (3 percent)		**List B (10 percent)**	
Navigation lights	_____	Cigarette lighter	_____
Bilge blower	_____	Cabin lighting	_____
Bilge pump	_____	Horn	_____
Windshield wiper	_____	Additional electronics	_____
Radio (transmitter)	_____	Trim tabs	_____
Depth sounder	_____	Power trim	_____
Radar	_____	Toilet	_____
Search light	_____	Anchor windlass	_____
Instruments	_____	Winches	_____
Alarm system (standby)	_____	Freshwater pump	_____
	_____	Wash-down pump	_____
	_____		_____
			_____
		Total list B	_____
		a. 10 percent list B	_____
		b. Largest item list B	_____
		Total estimated list B load*	_____
		*Larger of a. or b., above	
Total list A	_____	Total estimated list B load	_____
		Total load required	_____

rated in amps, many will indicate only wattage. Convert watts to amps using the following formula:

$$\text{AMPS} = \text{WATTS}/\text{VOLTS} \text{ or } \text{WATTS} = \text{AMPS} \times \text{VOLTS}$$

Table 11-2 provides a representative list of amperage for some marine items, but you should get actual amperage draw for your equipment from the equipment label plate or manufacturer's data.

Draw a table similar to Table 11-1. Enter the actual or estimated amperage draw for all required equipment under list A and total list A. Enter the actual or estimated amperage draw for all equipment shown in list B, and total this list. Calculate 10 percent of list B. Enter the total estimated list B load as the larger of 10 percent of list B or the single largest amperage draw item in list B.

To determine total amperage load, add the total of list A plus the total estimated list B load.

Circuit Protection and Conductors

Install fuses or trip-free, manual-reset circuit breakers in all the DC circuits to provide overload protection. Fuses are now seldom used because the fuse element melts when providing *overcurrent protection* and are destroyed when a load (amperage) exceeding their limit passes through them. Circuit breakers are load-sensitive switches that open a circuit, if a threshold-exceeding current flows through it. The current-carrying requirements of each application will determine the conductor (wire) size (measured in circular mils) and type. Bundle conductors when possible and route them where they will be safe from damage and clear of bilgewater. Plastic snap ties work well for both bundling wires and securing the bundles to structure attachment points. Where wiring passes through metal bulkheads or other structure, install rubber grommets to protect the wires from damage.

TABLE 11-2	Typical amperage ratings.
Item	Amperage
Navigation lights (each)	2.0
Bilge pump	12.0
Bilge blower	4.0
Windshield wiper (each)	5.0
Radio (VHF)	5.0
Radar	3.3
Fish finder	17.0
Cabin lights (each)	1.0
Horn	5.0
Trim tabs	18.0
Wash-down pump	6.3
Heater (engine hot water)	11.0

TABLE 11-3	Required and recommended marine wiring color codes.
Required Marine Wiring Color Codes	
Green	Bonding
White (W) or Black (B)	Return, negative main
Red (R)	Positive main, particularly unfused
Recommended Marine Wiring Color Codes	
Yellow with red stripe (YR)	Starting circuit
Brown/yellow stripe (BY) or yellow (Y)*	Bilge blower
Dark gray (Gy)	Navigation lights, tachometer
Brown (Br)	Generator armature, alternator charge light, pumps
Orange (O)	Accessory feed
Purple (Pu)	Ignition, instrument feed
Dark blue	Cabin and instrument lights
Light blue (Lt Bl)	Oil pressure
Tan	Water temperature
Pink (Pk)	Fuel gauge
Green/stripe (G/x) or (G/Y)	Tilt down or trim in
Blue stripe (Bl/x)	Tilt up or trim out

* If yellow is used for DC negative, blower must be brown with yellow stripe.

Color codes specified by ABYC for DC electrical systems under 50 volts are provided in Table 11-3, and adherence to these color codes is highly recommended. Color coding may be accomplished on systems wired from a single spool of wire (i.e., with one color of wire) by using colored sleeves or tape at the ends. If tape is used for color coding, use at least two full turns of tape at least 3/16 inch wide.

Determining Conductor Wire Size

Select wire large enough to ensure that adequate voltage reaches your equipment. Knowing the length of the conductor and the amperage requirement of the device being serviced will allow you to determine the required cross-sectional wire size in *circular mils* (1 circular mil [CM] = 0.0005067 mm^2). This is accomplished by plugging these values into the following formula for calculating voltage drop.

$$E = \frac{(10.75)(L)(I)}{CM}$$

Where: 10.75 is a constant and:

E = voltage drop in volts

L = length of the conductor in feet (to and from the device)

I = current in amps (from the device rating)

CM = conductor size circular mils

Rewrite this equation as:

$$CM = \frac{(10.75)(L)(I)}{E}$$

Now you can easily calculate conductor size in circular mils. Convert this into gauge size by consulting Table 11-4.

TABLE 11-4	Wire sizes.
Gauge	Circular Mils
18	1,600
16	2,400
14	3,800
12	6,000
10	10,000
8	15,000
6	26,000
4	38,000
2	63,000
1	78,000
0	100,000
00	126,000
000	160,000

Example: The total length of the wire run from the positive power source to a bilge pump and back to the negative terminal (the nearest negative busbar) is 20 feet. The pump is rated at 12.0 amps.

Determine the voltage drop (E) by multiplying 12 volts times the allowable 3 percent drop (list A, Table 11-1): 12 × 0.03 = 0.36 volts. Plug this number and the two values above into the formula to determine the minimum wire size in circular mils:

$$CM = \frac{(10.75)(20)(12)}{0.36} = 7166.7$$

Consult the wire-size table (Table 11-4). Since 7,166.7 circular mils is the minimum wire size, look up the next larger standard size, which is 10,000 circular mils. This corresponds to a gauge size of 10, so use 10-gauge wire to connect the bilge pump.

A much faster method of determining the needed wire gauge is to consult standard wire-gauge tables (Table 11-5) for either a 3 percent or 10 percent voltage drop. From the length of conductor and the amperage requirement of the device, the tables will provide you with the correct wire gauge. To look up the wire size in the table for the previous example, find the 20-feet column in the table designated "12 volt DC, 3 percent voltage drop" and follow it down to where it

TABLE 11-5	12 VDC conductor size for 3% and 10% voltage drop.						
	Length of conductor in feet						
	10	15	20	25	30	40	50
amps	Wire gauge (12 V DC, 3 percent voltage drop)						
5	18	16	14	12	12	10	10
10	14	12	10	10	10	8	6
15	12	10	10	8	8	6	6
20	10	10	8	6	6	6	4
25	10	8	6	6	6	4	4
30	10	8	6	6	4	4	2
40	8	6	6	4	4	2	2
50	6	6	4	4	2	2	1
60	6	4	4	2	2	1	0
amps	Wire gauge (12 V DC, 10 percent voltage drop)						
5	18	18	18	18	18	16	16
10	18	18	16	16	14	14	12
15	18	16	14	14	12	12	10
20	16	14	14	12	12	10	10
25	16	14	12	12	10	10	8
30	14	12	12	10	10	8	8
40	14	12	10	10	8	8	6
50	12	10	10	8	8	6	6
60	12	10	8	8	6	6	4

intersects the 15 amp row—the closest value exceeding the 12-amp pump rating. This gives you a wire size of 10 gauge. (Note: ABYC recommends that no boat wiring be less than 16 gauge.)

Battery Capacity

Most small boats have a single 12-volt battery, but on boats requiring more electrical capacity to run such things as refrigeration and winches, it's a better practice to have two or more 12-volt batteries connected in parallel. The cranking battery(s) must have at least the cold-cranking amperage required by the engine manufacturer. In addition, the battery's rated reserve capacity should be sufficient to power the load in list A of Table 11-1 for a minimum of one and a half hours. (See ABYC E-11.7.1.1.1.2.2.)

Battery Charging

If the propulsion-engine alternator is the only battery-charging device aboard, then its rated output must be at least equal to the total calculated load (Table 11-1). On most small boats, the standard 50- to 60-amp alternator will suffice. If engine running time is minimal and batteries are deeply discharged, then the alternator must be large enough to quickly recharge the batteries. The primary factor in sizing an alternator is determining the maximum current capacity the batteries can absorb. This is best left to a professional, but a good description of the procedure to size an alternator can be found in *Boatowner's Mechanical and Electrical Manual* by Nigel Calder.

BONDING DC SYSTEMS

Boats should be fitted with an electrical bonding system that provides a low-resistance electrical path between otherwise isolated metallic items. The bonding conductor fulfills several functions:

- Provides protection against electrolytic (galvanic) corrosion caused by stray voltage.
- Prevents possible electrical shock from metallic enclosures of electrical equipment.
- Provides a path to ground in the event of a lightning strike.
- Minimizes radio interference.

A common bonding conductor on boats with nonconducting hulls—such as fiberglass—usually runs fore and aft and is connected to the negative ground of the DC electrical system. Individual bonding conductors connect the items being grounded to the common bonding conductor. Bonding conductors are color-coded green.

On a boat with an aluminum hull, the hull itself can act as the bonding conductor. For items that are electrically isolated from the hull, bond them by running a separate conductor between each item and the hull. Be sure these bonding conductors are of the same size as the DC negative of the bonded equipment and attach them between the metallic framework of electrical items and the metal hull. Under no circumstances use the bonding conductor as a part of a current-carrying electrical circuit. The bonding conductor should only be active in the event of a short circuit.

In the event of a short circuit, the hull will act as the bonding conductor from the short-circuited item back to the single-point negative ground.

CATHODIC PROTECTION

Cathodic protection is the reduction or prevention of corrosion of a metal by making it cathodic by the use of sacrificial anodes or impressed currents.

Corrosion of the hull and underwater components can be caused by dissimilar metals, such as copper, in electrical contact with the aluminum hull and in a current-conducting solution such as seawater. To reduce this potential for corrosion, do not use dissimilar metals below the waterline or in wet spaces. Aluminum is very reactive with most common marine metals and requires electrical isolation from dissimilar metals by the use of insulators. Use sacrificial zinc anodes below the water to protect an aluminum hull from electrolysis. Attach anodes by through-bolting, using 300-series stainless steel fasteners, or welding metal straps embedded in the anode to the hull.

Aluminum is *anodic* (less noble), or high on the galvanic scale, as shown in Table 11-6; therefore, it is sacrificial to *cathodic*, or more noble, materials lower on the scale. When aluminum is electrically connected to a more noble material, for example copper, *galvanic corrosion* occurs, causing the aluminum to corrode. If you cannot avoid using metals located lower on the galvanic scale (more noble or cathodic) than aluminum, install sacrificial anodes made of a material that is higher on the scale than aluminum, such as zinc. The anodes (made of zinc) will corrode instead of the more noble metal (aluminum), protecting the aluminum hull. (You have, in effect, sacrificed the zinc anodes.) A good barrier coat of paint will provide additional protection to an aluminum hull.

Sacrificial hull anodes are unnecessary on small boats that spend the vast majority of their life out of the water. If an aluminum boat without permanently installed sacrificial anodes is to spend a prolonged period in salt water, temporary sacrificial anodes can be attached to the metallic hull structure with a conductor and lowered over the side to provide some protection at the moorage.

LIGHTNING PROTECTION

An aluminum hull is an electrical conductor. If external components such as a mast are all electrically connected to the hull through direct metal-to-metal contact or proper bonding procedures, ABYC E-4.10 suggests that no further protection is necessary for lightning, since current will flow through the hull to ground without resistance. This should provide adequate assurance that passengers are protected from lightning strikes.

AC ELECTRICAL SYSTEM

Alternating current (AC)—50 to 60 Hertz (Hz)—isn't normally found aboard small boats. When it is used, it's normally supplied by a shore-power connection. If you plan to have 60 Hz AC power on your aluminum boat, you should hire a professional electrician who is familiar with marine installations. AC power can be extremely dangerous if not installed correctly. ABYC E-11, "AC and DC

The Electrical System

TABLE 11-6 Galvanic series of metals in sea water.

Anodic or least noble	Corrosion potential range (in millivolts)
Magnesium and magnesium alloys	−1,600 to −1,630
Zinc	−980 to −1,030
Aluminum alloys*	−760 to −1,000
Cadmium	−700 to −730
Mild steel	−600 to −710
Wrought iron	−600 to −710
Cast iron	−600 to −710
13% chromium stainless steel, type 410 (active in still water)	−460 to −580
18-8 stainless steel, type 304 (active in still water)	−460 to −580
Ni-Resist	−460 to −580
18-3, 3% Mo stainless steel, type 316 (active in still water)	−430 to −540
Inconel (78% Ni, 13.5% Cr, 6% Fe) (active in still water)	−350 to −460
Aluminum bronze (92% Cu, 8% Al)	−310 to −420
Nibral (81.2% Cu, 4% Fe, 4.5% Ni, 9% Al, 1.3% Mg)	−310 to −420
Naval brass (60% Cu, 39% Zn)	−300 to −400
Yellow brass (65% Cu, 35% Zn)	−300 to −400
Red brass (85% Cu, 15% Zn)	−300 to −400
Muntz metal (60% Cu, 40% Zn)	−300 to −400
Tin	−310 to −330
Copper	−300 to −570
50-50 Lead-tin solder	−280 to −370
Admiralty brass (71% Cu, 28% Zn, 1% Sn)	−280 to −360
Aluminum brass (76% Cu, 22% Zn, 2% Al)	−280 to −360
Manganese bronze (58.8%Cu, 39% Zn, 1% Sn, 1% Fe, 0.3% Mn)	−270 to −340
Silicone bronze (96% Cu Max, 0.80% Fe, 1.5% Zn, 2% Si, 75% Mn, 1.6% Sn)	−260 to −290
Bronze-composition G (88% Cu, 2% Zn, 10% Sn)	−240 to −310
Bronze ASTM B62 (thru-hull) (85% Cu, 5% Pb, 5% Sn, 5% Zn)	−240-to −310
Bronze-composition M (88% Cu, 3% Zn, 6.5% Sn, 1.5% Pb)	−240 to −310
13% Chromium stainless steel, type 410 (passive)	−260 to −350
Copper-nickel (90% Cu, 10% Ni)	−210 to −280
Copper-nickel (75% Cu, 20% Ni, 5% Zn)	−190 to −250
Lead	−190 to −250
Copper-nickel (70% Cu, 30% Ni)	−180 to −230
Inconel (78% Ni, 13.5% Cr, 6% Fe) (passive)	−140 to −170
Nickel 200	−100 to −200
18-8 stainless steel, type 304 (passive)	−50 to −100
Monel 400, K-500 (70% Ni, 30% Cu)	−40 to −140
Stainless steel propeller shaft (ASTM 630:#17 & ASTM 564:#19)	−39 to +130
18-8 stainless steel, type 316 (passive) (3% Mo)	0.0 to −100
Titanium	−50 to +60
Hastelloy C	−30 to +80
Stainless steel shafting (bar) (UNS 20910)	−250 to +60
Platinum	+190 to +250
Graphite	+200 to +300
Cathodic or most noble	

* The range shown does not include sacrificial aluminum anodes. Aluminum alloy sacrificial anodes are available that have a maximum corrosion potential of −1100 mV.

Electrical Systems on Boats," is an excellent guideline to use when designing marine electrical systems to insure safe operation.

Corrosion caused by a faulty shore-power connection can cause extreme hull damage in a very short time. You must electrically isolate the shore-power system, including the ground wire, from the hull. Stray voltage in a marina often finds a circuit through the shore-power ground. Electrical isolation of the shore power is easily accomplished by installing a marine-type isolation transformer on board and running all shore electrical power through this transformer.

References

American Boat and Yacht Council, Inc. *Standards and Recommended Practices for Small Craft.* Millersville, Md.: American Boat and Yacht Council, Inc., 2005.

Calder, Nigel. *Boatowner's Mechanical and Electrical Manual*, 3rd ed. Camden, Maine: International Marine, 2005.

Kaiser Aluminum & Chemical Sales, Inc. *Aluminum Boats*, 2nd ed. Oakland, Calif.: Kaiser Aluminum & Chemical Sales, Inc., 1978.

Smead, David, and Ruth Ishihara. *Wiring 12 Volts for Ample Power.* Seattle, Wash.: Rides Publishing Company, 1990.

U.S. Coast Guard Boating Safety. "Boatbuilder's Handbook." U.S. Coast Guard. http://www.uscgboating.org/safety/boatbuilder/index.htm.

U.S. Department of Transportation. *Code of Federal Regulation.* Title 46, Subchapter T, "Small Passenger-Carrying Vessels." Washington, D.C.: U.S. Department of Transportation (U.S. Coast Guard), 2000.

CHAPTER 12

Woodwork and Insulation

Small production aluminum boats usually don't have wood aboard, with the exception of the floorboards, and even those are usually covered with some type of all-weather material. On boats up to about 20 feet, decks may also be wood—normally ¾-inch plywood over aluminum-angle subframing—secured with self-tapping stainless steel screws and well painted. Such decks are usually covered with some type of nonskid material, and they aren't watertight. Wood use on small production-built aluminum boats is strictly for reasons of economy and convenience—not for aesthetics or physical comfort.

For boats larger than 20 feet, wood decks, when used, are bolted to aluminum margin plates welded to the side shell at the gunwale. Subframing may be wood or aluminum, depending upon the type of deck and the structural requirements. Although wood decks have been used successfully on steel hulls, aluminum expands and contracts much more than steel, causing the attachment bolts to egg out the bolt holes, resulting in leaks. For an aluminum hull, the best building material for a watertight deck is aluminum.

Special-purpose boats and yachts requiring a very high quality interior often incorporate generous quantities of wood. Wood is used on the exterior as well, primarily for decorative purposes. The boat shown in Figures 12-1 and 12-2 was constructed as a showpiece to demonstrate special aluminum-coating systems and special equipment. Its decks are aluminum, covered with teak that was glued in place (held in position during the curing of the glue with a vacuum blanket). It

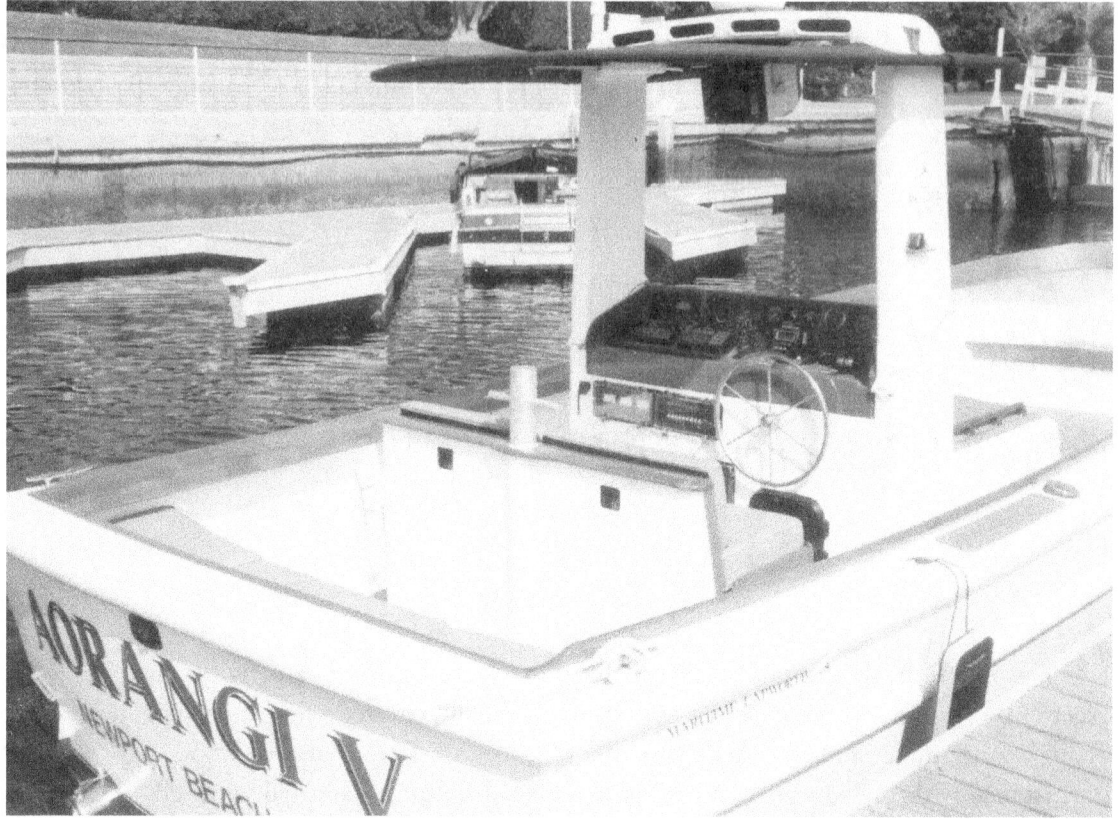

Figure 12-1. Wood-trimmed 28-foot aluminum workboat by Maritime Outfitters, Newport Beach, California.

also features a bright mahogany console top and is trimmed with a bright mahogany coaming around the perimeter of the working deck.

One advantage of wood is its light weight, even compared with aluminum. Wood is about 25 percent the weight of aluminum of equivalent thickness, a significant factor for interior decks. Wood interior decks are also easier to work with, water doesn't easily condense on them, and the wood has better thermal and acoustic insulating properties than aluminum.

FURRING OUT

The required preparation of the hull for the installation of wood components such as interior decks, finish bulkheads, and joiner work is known as *furring out*. By following an established sequence of tasks in furring out the inside of an

Woodwork and Insulation

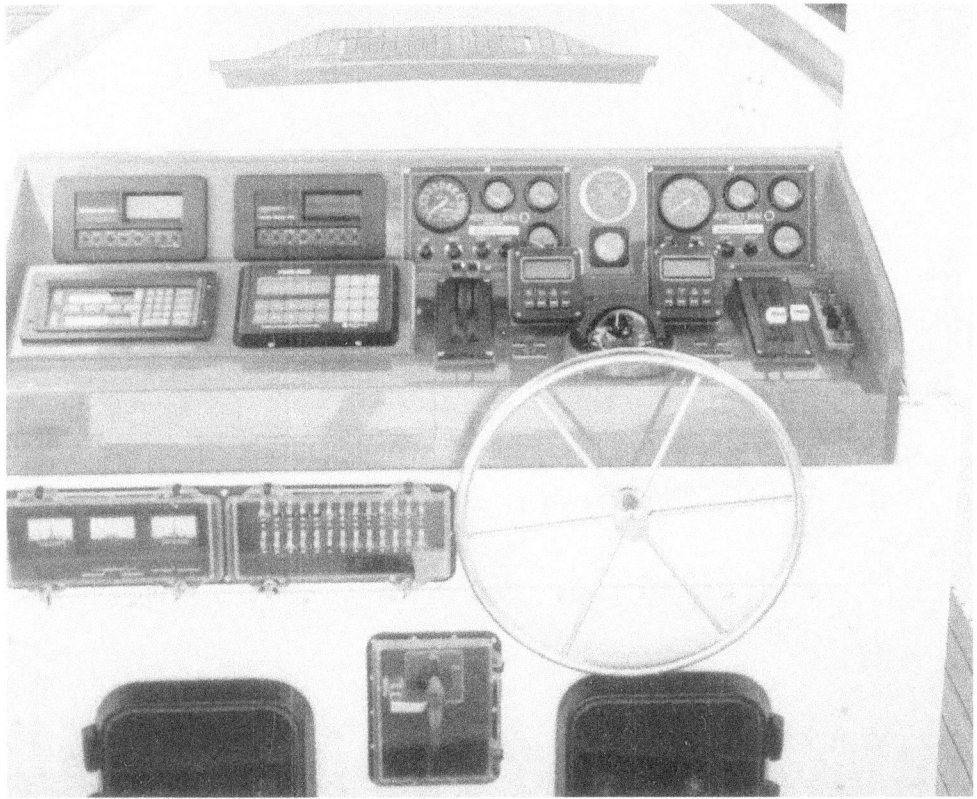

Figure 12-2. Mahogany-topped operator's console.

aluminum boat, you will save both time and labor. Because of the nature of this preparation, thermal and acoustic insulation are included in this section.

Attachments

Attach woodwork to an aluminum hull by first bolting or screwing pieces of wood—furring strips or furring blocks—to structural members (Figure 12-3). In some cases, you will have to weld small pieces of metal called furring clips to the boat's aluminum structure to provide attachment points for the furring.

Use 300 series stainless steel fasteners to attach the furring. Quarter-inch stainless steel hex-head bolts with flat washers are commonly used to attach wood to furring clips. For attachment to sheet metal, you can use self-tapping screws, provided the pilot holes are the right size, which may require a little experimenting. One word of caution about self-tapping screws in aluminum: because

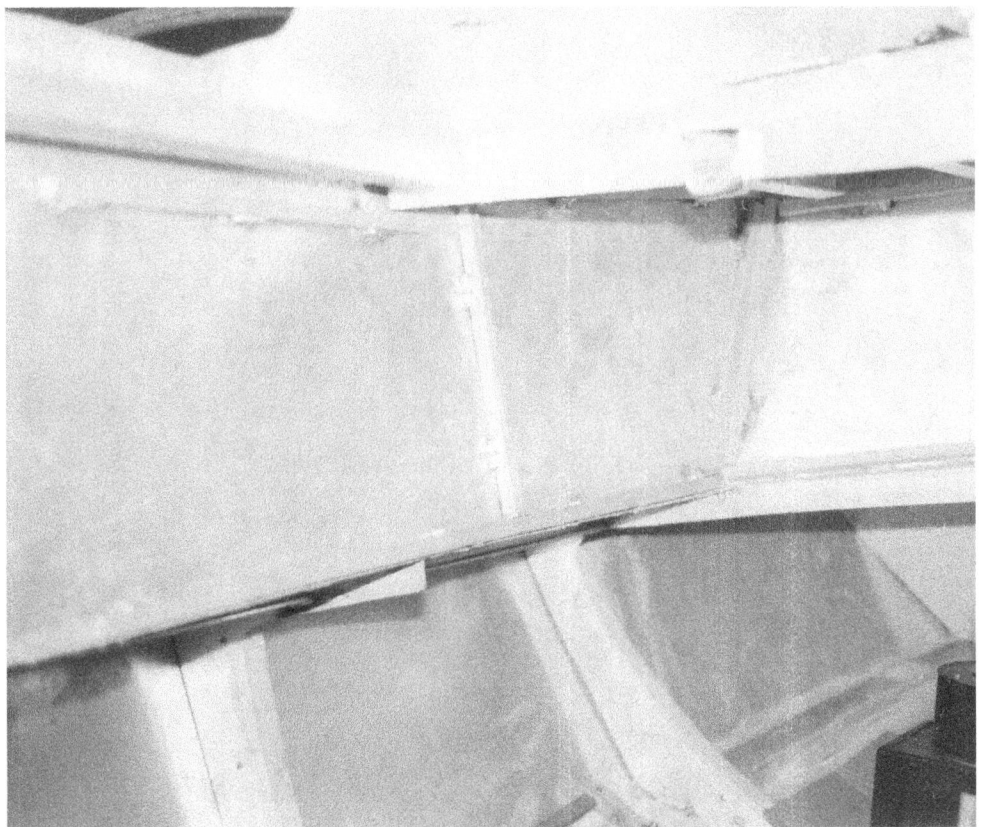

Figure 12-3. Furring strips attached to furring clips.

aluminum has a tendency to be very sticky, trying to install a self-tapping screw in an undersize hole will result in the head of the fastener twisting off 99 percent of the time. The same goes for trying to cut threads in aluminum with a stainless steel bolt.

Instead of welding, you can glue furring clips in place with a glue specifically designed for metal-to-metal joints. Gluing is especially useful on a light structure that will show objectionable weld shrink marks or in an area that might be subject to fire or explosion because of weld heat. One effective adhesive for this use is Versilok, an acrylic structural adhesive manufactured by the Lord Corporation, Industrial Adhesives Division, Erie, Pennsylvania (www.lord.com).

One major advantage aluminum construction has over steel is that no paint barrier coat is required over aluminum-to-aluminum joints to protect against corrosion. Unlike steel, you can tack-weld furring clips to an aluminum boat without regard to an interior coating system. But furring out an aluminum boat is not totally without hazards. Do not place aluminum in contact with woods treated with copper compounds (e.g., many forms of pressure-treated lumber), or wet or unseasoned woods of any kind, or the aluminum will corrode. If aluminum will be in contact with wood and therefore subject to moisture, protect the metal by coating it with zinc-chromate primer and painting the wood with zinc-chromate, aluminum pigmented, or bituminous paint. Where dry, untreated wood is used in areas that will normally remain dry, it is not necessary to coat aluminum-to-wood adjoining surfaces.

Furring Strips

Since you will be using furring strips or blocks to attach most interior woodwork, fashion them from dry wood of a type suitable for the intended purpose, such as pine or Douglas fir. Attach furring strips or blocks to the structure or to clips as needed to fully secure the interior (Figure 12-4).

Figure 12-4. Furring blocks for attaching teak ceiling.

POLYURETHANE INSULATION

The best hull insulation and flotation for an aluminum boat is polyurethane foam. It's available in a number of densities, but 2-pound (per cubic foot) is the best density for withstanding the minor scrapes and impacts associated with the marine environment. Polyurethane foam comes in precut 4-by-8 sheets (in almost any thickness), in a liquid two-part pour, or as a spray that can be shot directly onto the area requiring insulation or flotation. If used for floatation, a 2-pound-density foam is often used.

Polyurethane foam provides both acoustic and thermal insulation. Where it covers the aluminum, it prevents moist air from contacting the cold metal, eliminating condensation problems. It also provides excellent flotation in the event of swamping.

Polyurethane foam does emit hydrocarbons during the foaming process and is subject to environmental restrictions. Review applicable OSHA 1910.134 on the Internet for required respiratory protection measures.

Sprayed-In-Place Polyurethane Foam

Spraying is the most common method of installing polyurethane foam in boats. Foam can be purchased in units of 1, 15, or 50 cubic feet from RHH Foam Systems, Inc. (www.rhhfoamsystems.com). These are package items including a disposable spray gun. Or you can hire a contractor with the special equipment needed to apply the foam. Sprayed-in-place foam insulation is commonly applied to a thickness of about 2 inches or to the height of the hull structural members, whichever is less. The foam rises during the rapid curing cycle, and the surface of the foam takes on a shiny appearance. The uniformity of the foam's thickness and the smoothness of its surface are directly related to the skill of the spray-gun operator.

The shiny exterior skin is harder than the material lying just under the surface, and it acts as a seal against water entry. The foam below the surface exhibits very good water resistance as well, but if it's exposed, it will take on small amounts of water, so don't break the surface of the foam unless absolutely necessary.

In areas not subject to moisture, it may be desirable to smooth off the foamed-in-place insulation for a uniform surface. This can be done with a knife or saw, but surprisingly it is much more difficult than it appears. To facilitate rapid foam removal, some foaming contractors plane the surface using a special foam plane with eggbeater-like blades that provide a uniform foam surface.

Install insulation foam from about the first longitudinal stringer below the design waterline up, leaving all bilge areas clear. Mask areas that are to be left free of foam. Because sprayed-in-place foam is very sticky and extremely difficult to remove after it sets, complete selected installations before spraying the foam on the hull. These include all hull furring clips and furring strips as well as wiring raceways and below-deck piping (Figure 12-5). Install machinery and complete the finish work after the foam is in place.

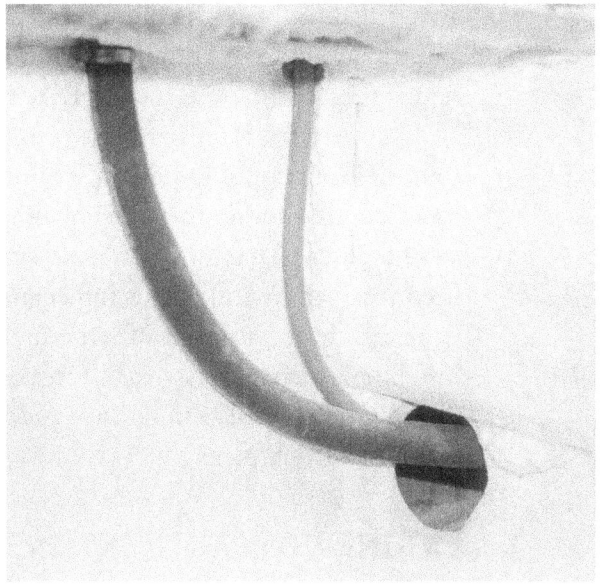

Figure 12-5. Sprayed-in-place polyurethane foam on the inside of the hull.

Pouring Polyurethane Foam

Polyurethane foam is also available from most marine hardware stores in a liquid two-part system that when mixed expands into foam with about a 2-pound density. It is used to fill voids and provide flotation in inaccessible areas. As it foams, the liquid expands to approximately 30 times its initial volume. This has been known to exert enough pressure to bulge out or even rupture bulkheads and other confining structures. Avoid this risk by paying very close attention to the amount of foam you pour into an enclosed cavity. Properly applied, a 1-quart unit will yield 1 to 1¼ cubic feet of foam. When applying polyurethane foam, a minimum temperature of 72 degrees is required.

The chemical reaction causing the liquid to expand into foam also emits gases that can be corrosive to aluminum as well as causing potential respiratory problems for the workman. Be sure workmen have the appropriate clothing and protective gear prior to start of work. Insure the area being insulated is well ventilated both before and after pouring the foam to allow these corrosive gases to escape.

Polyurethane Sheet

Sheet polyurethane foam is available in a number of densities, but 4-pound is the recommended density for boat insulation. Cut the foam to size with a knife and attach it directly to the aluminum plate with an insulation adhesive. Both the sheet foam and the adhesive should be available from any large insulation and refractories distributor (such as E. J. Bartells Co., www.ejbartells.com).

Use sheet foam on flat areas of the superstructure where a very uniform and smooth insulation is required. Eliminate any air gaps at the joints between panels by using yet another form of polyurethane foam—the aerosol cans of foam that can be purchased at any hardware store. Route any wiring after the panels have been installed by simply cutting channels into the surface of the foam.

A significant amount of structural strength can be added to a flat panel by installing a structurally strong interior panel over a foam core. Gluing plywood directly to the insulation on the inside face of the insulation board will result in a strong sandwich panel.

ENGINE-COMPARTMENT INSULATION

Engine-noise levels in a metal boat can be quite high. The metal hull and structural components are excellent sound conductors and tend to transmit the noise throughout the boat. To quiet an aluminum boat requires sound-deadening insulation that is in direct contact with the metal to reduce the vibration and break up the sound waves.

The insulation around an engine and in engine spaces is usually subject to rougher treatment than that in other areas, partly due to periodic engine maintenance. In addition, engine-compartment insulation can be subject to elevated temperatures and contact with oils, suggesting special insulation requirements.

Hot areas, such as dry exhaust stacks, are usually insulated with high-temperature fiberglass insulation (which has replaced the asbestos insulations used in the past). The insulation material is often covered with fiberglass cloth to protect the surface from damage. This type of insulation is available to fit over pipe and fittings and can also be obtained from insulation and refractories dealers, such as E. J. Bartells.

On small inboard-powered boats with the engine(s) covered by a box, you can insulate the engine box itself using a rubber-like material. This is an expanded closed-cell material that is flexible and has a low flame-spread rate. One such product is Armorflex, available in black in sheets with thicknesses ranging from ¼ inch to 2 inches (www.armacell.com). Glue it in place with Armstrong #520 adhesive. For a very quiet boat, a number of other effective sound-deadening fire-resistant special insulations are available, including lead-lined fiberglass.

CABIN SOLE (DECK)

Plywood decks are lighter than metal and provide for easier through-cutting of hatches and attachment of joiner work. Interior decks are usually ¾-inch plywood laid over aluminum structural supports. Attach the plywood to the structure either by direct bolting, drilling and tapping for screws, or driving screws into furring strips. This method is usually much faster and easier than installing wood support framing, since attaching wood framing to the hull will almost always take more effort than aluminum framing.

Cabin soles, or decks, can be finished in any manner desired. A very nice teak and holly plywood is available from marine hardwood dealers that looks like a real teak deck (see Figure 12-6), but since some of the teak veneer is very thin, you should be very selective in using it on decks that will bear a lot of foot traffic.

Figure 12-6. Teak and laminate interior of a 23-foot sportfishing boat.

HEADLINER AND BULKHEAD PANELING

The choice of headliner material depends upon your preference, but in all cases, headliners and paneling should be washable. One very nice headliner is a fiberglass, textured sheet used in commercial food-processing facilities. One source of specialty paneling is Specialty Products and Insulation Co. (ww.spi-co.com). Glue paneling over the insulation with insulation adhesive, or install it with thin wood battens screwed to pre-placed furring strips. For a professional look, use 300 series stainless steel oval-head screws with counter-sunk washers to hold the headliner-securing battens in place.

Areas that have compound curvature, such as the hull sides toward the bow, are most easily paneled with wood strips installed with a small gap between them (Figure 12-7). Finish the wood strips by oiling, varnishing bright, or painting. Attach them to pre-placed furring strips, and either plug the screw holes or use

Figure 12-7. Teak ceiling installed and ready for teak plugs.

oval-head stainless steel screws and counter-sunk washers. The strips shown in the photo have been installed with countersunk screws and are ready for wood plugs.

Bulkhead paneling can be any rugged material. Teak plywood is always popular. Other paneling options, including exterior medium-density fiberboard (MDF) with a polyester-impregnated paper overlay, are available from marine-wood suppliers. To prevent any fasteners from showing, join the panels with pieces of wood (preferably teak or mahogany) that have been shaped into special corner or edge moldings with recessed grooves to take the paneling (Figure 12-8 and Figure 12-9). One source of overlay fiberboard as well as teak and other marine woods is East Teak Trading Group, Inc. (www.eastteak.com). Special moldings, prefabricated wood handrails, louver doors, cabinet doors, and specialty marine wood items can be obtained from a number of sources. Browsing the internet should result in suitable sources.

Woodwork and Insulation

Figure 12-8. Teak corner moldings on boat interior.

Figure 12-9. Prefabricated galley unit.

Figure 12-10. Galley unit installed and trimmed. (Note hinged helmsman's seat.)

The various types of paneling and methods of installing and joining them mentioned above were used by Specialty Marine of Scappoose, Oregon, to construct the interior of the 23-foot sportfishing boat shown in Figure 12-8. Note the use of oval-head screws and counter-sunk washers on the trim strip between the windshield panes.

Construct built-in furniture—berths, galley units, etc.—from paneling and shaped wood moldings. Prefabricating these units in the shop (Figure 12-9) can improve quality and reduce production time. The panels shown in Figure 12-9 are medium-density panels with a plastic laminate. A fire-resistant panel similar to that shown can be obtained from Thermax Marine (www.thermaxmarine.com). Attach panels with screws or bolts. In the event you are using wood trim, glued joints are a must. Fit all cabinet doors and drawers with some suitable device to prevent accidental opening in a seaway. Drawers are often fitted with a lift-and-pull stop. Securely fasten the furniture units to the hull structure, and then install the final trim (Figure 12-10) to complete the interior woodwork. Be sure you provide some means of access to get behind all units for inspection.

WINDOWS

Rubber, snap-in-place, automotive window retainer moldings can be effectively used on metal boats. Where the superstructure or hull is thin, this type of window retainer is very economical.

Woodwork and Insulation

Figure 12-11. A 23-foot sportfisher fitted with a water-jet propulsion.

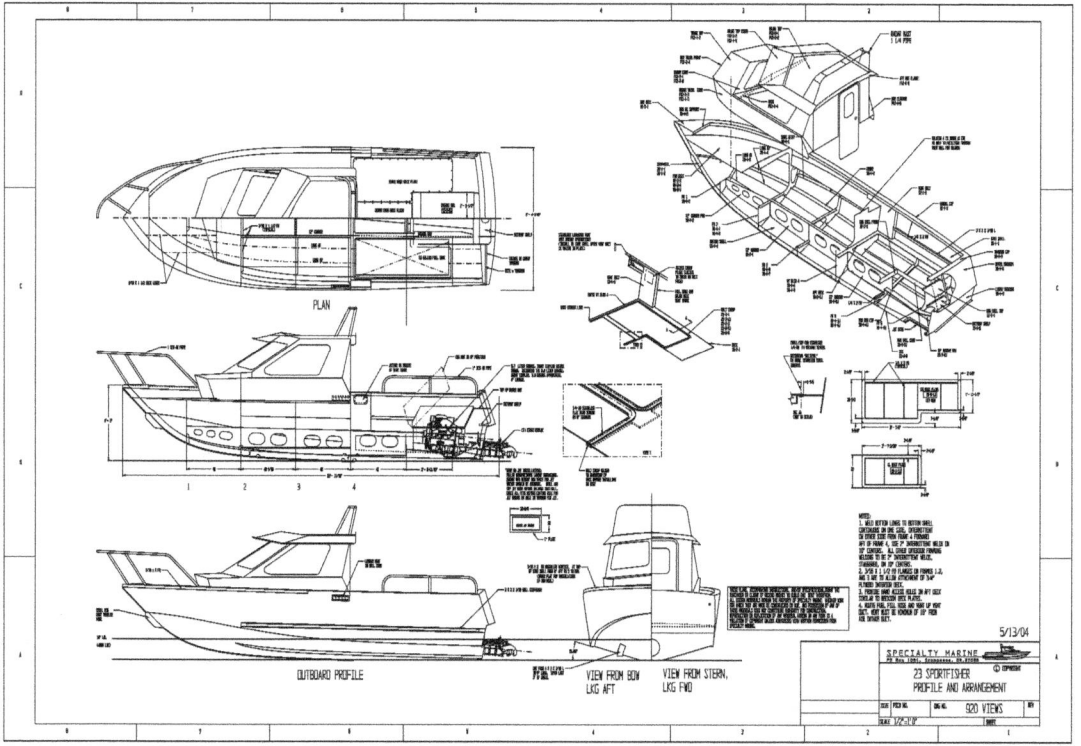

Figure 12-12. Assembly drawing for the 23-foot sportfisher in Figure 12-11. This boat was assembled from a precut metal kit, Specmar, Inc., Scappoose, Oregon.

Opening windows and high-quality marine windows require a rigid frame. Most marine-hardware stores can provide both off-the-shelf and custom windows with aluminum or plastic frames. You'll need to pay some attention to the thickness of the house side at the window opening to order the proper frame.

Superstructure side panels requiring windows are not always free of twist, and glass twists very little. If you need a window in a twisted panel, construct a special recess of aluminum to make a flat area for the window installation.

A finished 23-foot sportfisher, fitted with inboard-outboard propulsion, is shown in Figure 12-11. The assembly drawing for this boat with a water-jet propulsion system is shown in Figure 12-12. The precut metal kit can be purchased from Specmar, Inc., in a number of propulsion options, including water jet, outboard, and inboard/outboard. It can be found on Specialty Marine's website, www.specmar.com.

Aluminum Painting Systems

CHAPTER 13

A properly constructed and maintained aluminum boat doesn't need paint to protect the hull from corrosion. On boats that will spend prolonged periods in salt water, where marine growth on the hull can be a problem, antifouling paints may be used. In fact, other than antifouling bottom paint, the hull surfaces of most commercial aluminum boats are not painted at all. This is one of the biggest cost savings of an aluminum hull when compared with other hull materials.

Owners of yachts and small pleasure boats, however, often desire painted hulls for cosmetic purposes. The combination of a properly prepared aluminum surface and a properly applied paint system can assure a very satisfactory paint bond. The keys here are proper preparation of the surface and proper application of the paint system. All too often paint is applied to aluminum hulls that have not been properly prepared. And if the paint system isn't compatible with the marine environment, premature paint system failure—blistering and peeling—is a virtual certainty.

The labor required to fair an aluminum hull in preparation for a high-gloss finish can easily exceed the man-hours to construct the hull. This applies to both nondevelopable and developable surfaces. Welded-aluminum boats constructed with nondevelopable surfaces, such as round-bilge sailboats, are constructed of a series of small developable surfaces with abrupt surface changes at plate seams, while boats constructed of developable surfaces may not be as fair as desired due to distortion from weld heat. In both cases, the desired fair surface can only be obtained by the application of fairing compounds to fill depressions and by manual long-board sanding—both labor intensive.

In the early 1970s, during a time of intensive building of large aluminum sailboats, automotive polyester body putty was the standard hull-fairing compound. Filler was used extensively on those round-bilge boats—constructed of a number of small, rolled plates—to achieve the smooth, high-gloss finish required. The filler was applied to the hull surface, sanded flush, and then painted. Unfortunately, the polyester putties used were later discovered to slowly absorb water, resulting in premature paint system failure. Epoxies using inert fillers, such as microballoons, have replaced polyester body putty, and this seems to have a much better success rate.

There are various trade-name *paint systems* (which include fairing cements) available for use on aluminum boats. A typical paint system includes some type of surface preparation, such as a special primer, a barrier coat, and a finish coat. It also includes anti-fouling paints compatible with aluminum.

When looking for a paint system for a larger luxury yacht, keep in mind you not only need an excellent product, you also need excellent technical assistance from the manufacturer when you encounter problems. This lack has been a shortfall of at least one large paint manufacturer, to the chagrin of a number of yacht builders and owners. For this reason, not only should you carefully research the product itself before you select it, but you should find out what the manufacturer offers in the way of technical assistance. If the paint system fails, the paint manufacturer always blames the applicator, but having a technician from the paint manufacturer on-site during the painting of a large yacht should confirm proper adherence to established application procedures and techniques.

PAINTING SMALL WELDED PRODUCTION BOATS

Some small-aluminum-boat manufacturers in the Pacific Northwest commonly use automotive paints, which aren't formulated for underwater application. The rationalization here is that the boat will spend the vast majority of its life out of the water. In addition, most of the paint schemes are such that the painted surfaces are above the waterline.

For an excellent-looking exterior finish, manufacturers commonly apply automotive-type body putty to specific areas of the boat that show any type of surface irregularity. The process of filling, sanding, and painting is the same as that used on automobiles. As a matter of fact, a number of small-boat manufacturers sub-

Aluminum Painting Systems

Figure 13-1. 17-foot 6-inch Kenai with cosmetic exterior hull side paint. Decal strip on side masks the shrink marks caused by weld heat print-through at deck height.

contract out the hull painting to automotive body shops since they have the expertise and special equipment not normally available at the boatbuilder's facility. Automotive paints do provide a very attractive finish and will last for a reasonable period of time; however, it is interesting that the boat-manufacturer's warranty in most cases does not cover the paint system.

Figure 13-1 shows a welded-aluminum boat with minor automotive body fairing cements at weld seams. Note the bottom is not painted, and the use of an automotive decorative decal that effectively masks the weld shrink mark located where the watertight deck is welded to the hull. This boat was painted with automotive paint and has shown no adverse effect after five years. Most of its life has been out of the water, however.

The use of automotive body fillers and paints is not the proper way to finish an aluminum boat that will be left in the water. Boats normally left afloat must be painted in accordance with the marine-coatings manufacturer's recommended materials and procedures, or the paint system will prematurely fail. Figure 13-2 features a large welded-aluminum yacht with a high-gloss finish. Fairing compounds and paints were provided by Awlgrip Marine Coatings.

Figure 13-2. Power yacht *Shana* constructed by Sovereign Yachts, Seattle, Washington.

Marine Coatings

Increased awareness of the potential environmental impact of the chemicals in fairing and painting systems have resulted in a number of national and local restrictions. These can be a major problem for the occasional aluminum-hull painter. Paint systems that will do an excellent job on a hull aren't practical for the home builder, due to the extreme health hazards and the Environmental Protection Agency's (EPA's) regulations requiring the use of special equipment during application. Even hull preparation—the use of an etching solution that ultimately flows into a drain or storm sewer, for example—can violate EPA regulations. If the paint system you want to use poses a risk to the environment, let a professional boat shop, equipped to meet EPA requirements, do the work. Make sure the shop you select is familiar with fairing and painting aluminum.

If you want to do your own painting, you'll need a paint system you can practically apply. Keep in mind that the application of a marine paint system can be both time consuming and expensive compared with an automotive-type finish.

Some paint systems, rather than calling for the use of etching solutions, are designed to be applied over a surface that has been mechanically prepared. Sandblasting is not recommended as a method of mechanical surface preparation because of the need to carefully monitor both air quality (per EPA regulations) and because the abrasive may contain contaminants that will damage the aluminum.

Hull Preparation and Painting

Each manufacturer of an aluminum-hull painting system has its own hull-preparation and painting procedures, which should be followed for the best results, but as a general rule, the procedures all call for these steps:

1. Abrade the exterior of your aluminum hull—by sanding or by using abrasive pads—to roughen and clean the surface.
2. Etch the hull using a preparation primer (often phosphoric acid primer or wash system). This changes the chemical properties of the aluminum surface to ensure better paint adhesion.
3. Apply a fairing compound to areas showing general unfairness or dents. Sand the fairing compounds as necessary to blend into the surrounding surfaces.
4. Reapply the preparation primer to sanded areas along side of fairing compound applications.
5. Apply a primer coat.
6. Apply high-build barrier coats both above and below the waterline in accordance with manufacturer's recommendations.
7. Complete the job above the waterline by applying the hull finish paint.
8. Apply antifouling paint below the waterline for boats that will be in salt water.

A typical above-the-waterline aluminum-hull painting system can be reviewed on the Awlgrip Marine Coatings website, www.awlgrip.com.

Antifouling Paint

Antifouling paint below the waterline is required to finish the job for boats that will be based in salt water. In general, do not use copper-based paints on an aluminum hull because of galvanic corrosion problems, although some boatbuilders have had success applying conventional copper-based antifouling paints over a very high build-up of barrier coat of nonmetallic paint. Tin-based TBT (tri-butyltin) is no longer allowed for boat antifouling paints, but some of the major marine paint manufacturers, including International Marine Coatings and Pettit, have formulated new antifouling paints especially for aluminum boats.

Another option is an antifouling paint that does not contain toxic elements, but rather sloughs off, preventing marine growth from adhering to the surface. This is an ablative antifouling paint that works via the movement of the hull through the water gradually wearing away the coating. As a result, a fresh, fully potent layer of antifouling paint is always exposed to the water. The longevity of the antifouling paint is a function of the boat's velocity through the water. The faster the boat goes, the faster the antifouling paint will slough off. Additional information is available on the E-Paint Company website, www.epaint.net.

Another method to reduce or eliminate marine growth is to coat the bottom of the boat with Nyalic coating. This is a smooth, hard, slick coating that discourages marine growth, and barnacles do not seem to adhere to it. Commercial users haul out the boat on an annual basis and simply blast off the weeds and slime with water. For more information on Nyalic, check their website at www.nyalic.com.

References

Awlgrip. "Awlgrip Marine Application Guide." Awlgrip. http://www.awlgrip.com/awlgrip_pages/application_guide.htm.

E-Paint Company. http://www.epaint.net.

APPENDIX A

Laying Out a Camber Curve

Decks and house tops normally have a slight curvature athwartships to assist with drainage and impart stiffness. This curvature is called *camber*, or *crown*. Camber is always an arc of a circle unless specified otherwise. Decks can have a constant camber, meaning one camber curve will fit all areas of the deck, or they can have camber curves that vary from bow to stern.

The simplest deck camber is the *constant-camber curve.* When a boat designer specifies a 6-inch camber curve, he means that the crown of the camber at the deck centerline is 6 inches higher than the sheer (deck edge) at the maximum beam of the deck. This same camber curve is used for the entire deck area. This type of curve works well for decks that have a fairly uniform width, such as a house top or a section of deck midships.

In the area of the bow, where the beam of the deck will progress from near zero at the tip of the bow and grow progressively wider the farther aft you travel, a variation from a fixed radius camber curve is necessary to prevent a reverse curve in the sheer near the bow, as shown in Figure A-1. To prevent this reverse curve in the sheer, a constantly changing radius camber over the length of the deck must be developed.

The use of a variable camber in boat decks is not uncommon. Often a boat designer doesn't specify a camber curve. He indicates the amount of deck camber by drawing the boat's centerline and sheer heights in the profile view of the lines drawing. Then on the table of offsets, he calls out the heights (distance above

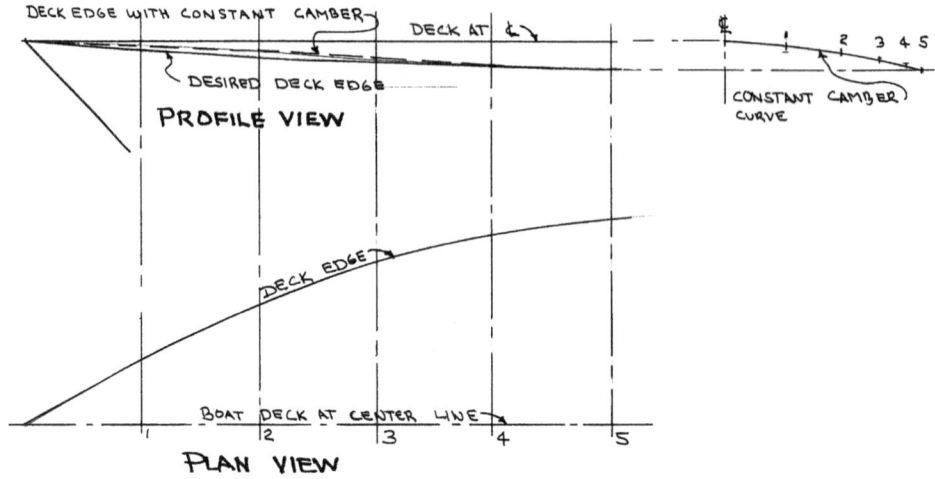

Figure A-1. The sheerline effect of a fixed- (or constant-) camber deck.

baseline) and half-breadths (distance from midship outward) for the sheer and the centerline heights for the deck at the station lines. From these offsets, you can develop the individual camber curves for each station.

It is often impractical to actually draw the arc of the camber curve—its radius is too large for loft-floor space. The usual practice is to drawn the camber curve in half-breadth. Then later, if needed, you can duplicate the camber for the other half of the curve to construct a full-size, full-width template.

One common method of camber-curve development is to draw a quarter-circle segment with a radius equal to the specified camber height, as shown on the left side of Figure A-2. You can obtain a close approximation of a camber arc by holding the camber height (ad) constant and stretching line ab and arc db like a rubber band to become line ac and arc dc, effectively stretching the circle segment into a long curve (dc). This new curve is a close approximation of the true camber curve.

The mechanics of doing this stretching starts by dividing the quarter-circle arc (db) and the baseline (ab) into four equal parts (Figure A-2). Join the segment division points, and use the lengths of each of these lines as heights when drawing the camber curve. These heights are shown as y1, y2, y3, and y4 in Figure A-2.

Lay out the half-breadth camber curve with the base (line ac in Figure A-2) equal in length to the maximum half-breadth of the boat's deck. Divide line ac

Laying Out a Camber Curve

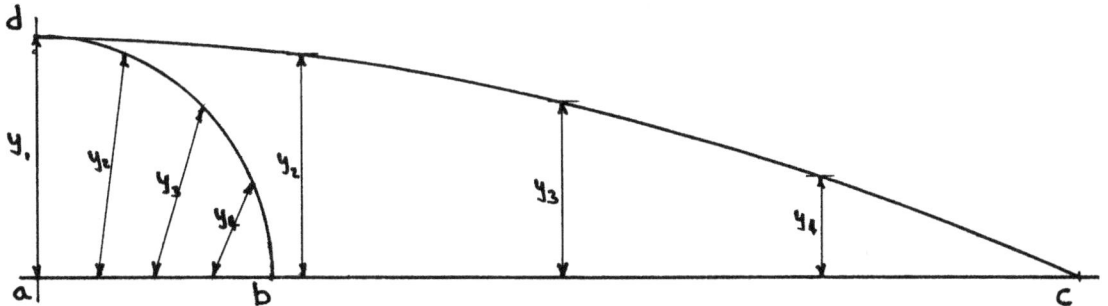

Figure A-2. Developing a camber from a quarter circle.

into four equal intervals and lay out the heights (y1, y2, etc.) to locate heights of the camber curve above line ac and draw in the curve (dc) using a flexible batten. Curve dc is not a true arc of a circle, but a very close approximation that has proven through experience to be sufficiently accurate for most boatbuilding circular cambers.

It's possible to have a camber with other than an arc of a circle—a parabolic arc, for instance—as the basis of the camber. Each special camber requirement must be developed individually.

FINDING THE RADIUS OF A CAMBER ARC

In some cases, it is possible to determine the actual radius of the camber arc when given only the camber height at the boat's center line and the half-breadth of the camber curve. This is easy to calculate.

Using Figure A-3 as a reference, x equals the half-breadth of the camber curve, y equals the camber curve height at center line, and R is the unknown radius. The formula for calculating the radius is derived from the Pythagorean theorem for a right triangle, $a^2 + b^2 = c^2$, as follows:

$$x^2 + (r-y)^2 = r^2$$

$$x^2 + r^2 = x^2 + 2yr + y^2 = r^2$$

$$x^2 - 2yr + y^2 = 0$$

$$x^2 + y^2 = 2yr$$

$$r = \frac{x^2 + y^2}{2y}$$

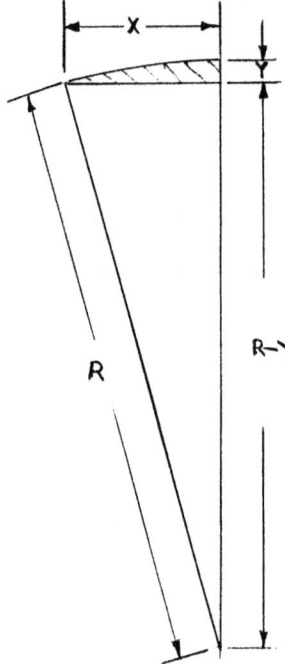

Figure A-3. Calculating the radius from the camber arc.

APPENDIX B

Calculating Material Stretch-Out for Brake Bending

Bending aluminum with a press brake is one of the most economical construction techniques in aluminum-boat building. Because aluminum stretches predictably when it is bent, you must establish the proper flat-pattern size of the sheet of aluminum prior to bending in order to achieve the desired finished dimensions of the bent part. It is also necessary to correctly locate the bends and mark them on the flat pattern.

Simple layout of a bent flange requires locating the centerline of the bend in relation to at least one side of the material to be formed. This centerline of bend is a straight line that will make contact with the male die of the press brake during the bending operation.

In addition to locating the center of bend, make sure the bend radius is sufficiently large to prevent fracturing during forming. Minimum bend radii for various aluminum alloys are shown in Table B-1. Before calculating the distance around the arc to be formed, or stretch-out, consult this table to make sure the bend radius selected will not fracture the alloy.

As a general rule, the thicker the material, the larger the bend radius required to prevent material fracture. The minimum bend radius is expressed as a direct relationship to the thickness of the material being formed, abbreviated as t. A minimum bend radius of ½ t for ¼-inch aluminum, for example, is ⅛ inch. Aluminum typically has a grain—usually parallel with the long dimension of the

TABLE B-1	Minimum bend radii for 90-degree cold bends in various aluminum alloys, shown as a multiple of material thickness, "t."				
Alloy/Temper	Material Thickness				
	1/8	3/16	1/4	3/8	1/2
5052-0	0–1 t	0–1 t	0–1 t	½–1½ t	1–2 t
5052-H32	½–1½ t	½–1½ t	½–1½ t	1–2 t	1½–2½ t
5086-0	0–1 t	0–1 t	½–1 t	1–1½ t	1–2 t
5086-H32	1–2 t	1½–2 t	1½–2½ t	2–2½ t	2½–3 t
5086-H34	1½–2½ t	2–3 t	2–3 t	2½–3½ t	2–4 t
6061-0	0–1 t	0–1 t	0–1 t	½–2 t	1–2½ t
6061-T6	1½–3 t	2–4 t	3–4 t	3½–5½ t	4–6 t

full sheet—and best resists fractures when formed at 90 degrees to the grain. Table B-1 indicates minimum bend radii both with and across the grain.

To calculate the *stretch-out* of a bend, you must consider the distance around the male forming die of the press brake. For example, for a 90-degree bend, this distance represents one-quarter of the circumference of the male die. Include this measurement in the layout of the material to be bent.

Experience has shown that aluminum will stretch more than it will compress when bending on a press brake. Since material being formed has a thickness, some plane within the material must be established as the layout plane. This plane is the neutral axis and is about one-third of the material thickness being formed, measured from the inside of the bend.

Use a radius equal to the inside radius of the bend plus one-third the material thickness to calculate the stretch-out for a flat pattern. To expedite determining stretch-out, refer to Table B-2, which shows the stretch-out for 90-degree bends, and use the following formula to calculate the circumference of a circle, as follows:

$$S = 1.57 \, (r + t/3)$$

Where:

S = Stretch-out (inches)

r = radius of bend (inches)

t = thickness of material (inches)

Calculating Material Stretch-Out for Brake Bending

TABLE B-2	Stretch-out for 90-degree cold bends.						
ID Bend Radii	Material Thickness (inches)						
	1/8	5/32	3/16	1/4	5/16	3/8	1/2
1/4	0.456						
3/8	0.655	0.672	0.688	0.719			
1/2	0.851	0.868	0.884	0.785			
5/8	1.047	1.064	1.080	1.112			
3/4	1.243	1.261	1.276	1.308	1.342	1.374	
1	1.636	1.653	1.669	1.700	1.735	1.766	
1 1/4	2.028	2.046	2.061	2.093	2.127	2.159	
1 1/2	2.421	2.438	2.454	2.485	2.520	2.551	2.617
2	3.206	3.223	3.239	3.270	3.305	3.336	3.402
3	4.776	4.793	4.809	4.840	4.875	4.906	4.972
4	6.346	6.363	6.379	6.410	6.445	6.476	6.542
5	7.916	7.933	7.949	7.980	8.015	8.046	8.112
6	9.486	9.503	9.519	9.550	9.584	9.616	9.682

PROBLEM 1: FUEL-TANK LAYOUT WITH 90-DEGREE BENDS

Lay out a fuel-tank bottom and side flat pattern for press-brake forming that will produce inside dimensions of 24 × 21 × 20 inches, as shown in Figure B-1. Use 3/16-inch (0.190) aluminum alloy 5052-H32 and a 3/4-inch bend radius.

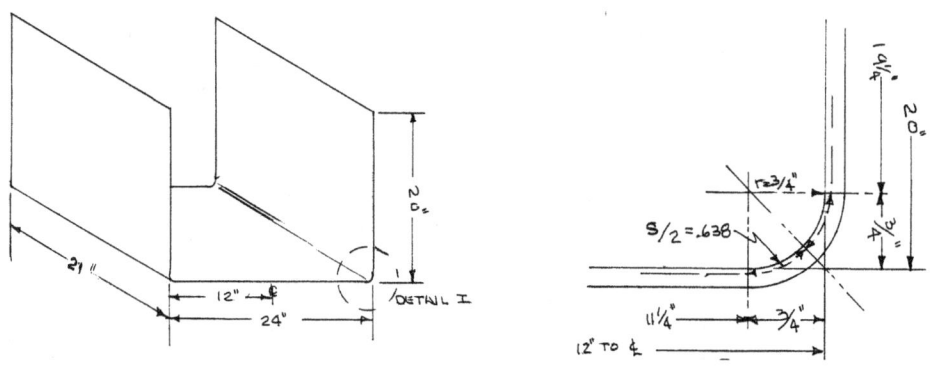

Figure B-1. Laying out a 90-degree bend for a fuel-tank bottom.

Solution

- First check the minimum safe bend radius. From Table B-1, the minimum safe bend radius is ½ to 1½ t for 3/16-inch 5052-H32 aluminum—½ t (0.093) if formed across the grain or 1½ t (0.281) if formed parallel to the grain. The selected ¾-inch (0.750) radius is safe.
- Make a sketch showing the detail of the corner (see Figure B-1) with a ¾-inch inside radius and layout dimensions to the inside of the plate. Consult Table B-2 to determine that the stretch-out for a ¾-inch-radius, 90-degree bend in 0.190 material is 1.276 inches. To find the center of the bend, divide 1.276 by 2 to obtain 0.638.
- Start the process of the flat-pattern layout at the upper right corner of the sketch in Figure B-1. Determine the location of the *start* of the first bend by subtracting the inside radius of the bend from the finished dimension—20 minus ¾ in this case—or 19¼ inches (see Detail I in Figure B-1). To find the *center* of the first bend, add 0.638 (as determined above) to 19¼ (19.25 + 0.638) to obtain 19.888—rounded off to 19⅞ inches. Draw a line 19⅞ inches from the far left side of a 21-inch-wide blank piece of material, as shown in Figure B-2. This will be the centerline of bend for the first bend.
- To lay out for the next bend, it's easier to work to the center of the symmetrical plate. Starting at the first bend centerline, add the stretch-out from centerline to the end of the bend plus half the distance of the center flat portion. This is 0.638 + (12 − ¾), or 11⅞ inches to center

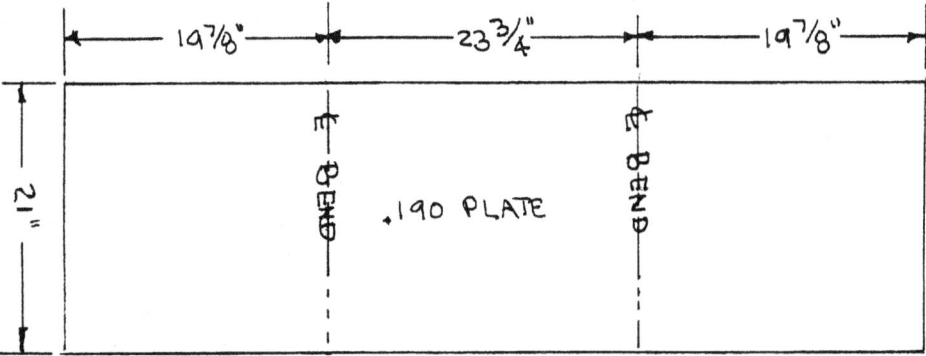

Figure B-2. Flat pattern with stretch-out.

of the plate. This puts the layout line for the second bend at 2 × 11⅞, or 23¾ inches from the first centerline (Figure B-2). The end of the plate is then another 19 ⅞ inches, for a total material length (stretch-out) of 63½ inches.

PROBLEM 2: LAYOUT FOR OTHER THAN 90-DEGREE BENDS

Lay out the flat pattern for a cockpit floor with the cross section shown in Figure B-3. Lay out for finished dimensions to the outside of the material using ¼-inch 5086-H32 formed with inside bend radii of ¾ inch.

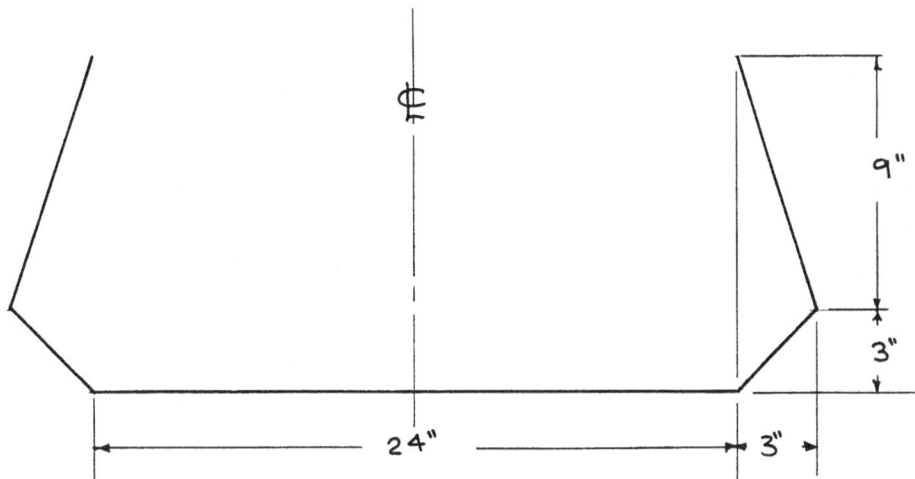

Figure B-3. Cross section of formed cockpit well.

Solution

- Sketch the shape to be developed (Figure B-3) on the loft floor. Draw in the rounded corners, as shown in Figure B-4. Scale the dimensions of the flat areas from the loft floor, and measure angles A and B. They are 45 and 71¼ degrees, respectively. Modify the formula S = 1.57 (r + t/3) by dividing by 1.57 by 90 to obtain stretch per degree of bend.

The new formula is:

$$S = A(0.01745)(r + t/3)$$

Where:

S — Stretch-out in inches

A = Angle of bend in degrees

r = radius of bend (inches)

t = thickness of material (inches)

From Figure B-4, angle A = 45 degrees, angle B = 71 1/4 degrees, r = 0.750, and t = 0.250.

$$SA = (45)(0.01745)(0.750 + 0.25/3) = 0.65$$
$$SB = (71.5)(0.01745)(0.750 + 0.25/3) = 1.04$$

- Now simply use these calculated stretch-outs for the arcs of angles A and B to complete the layout of the flat pattern in a manner similar to Problem 1.

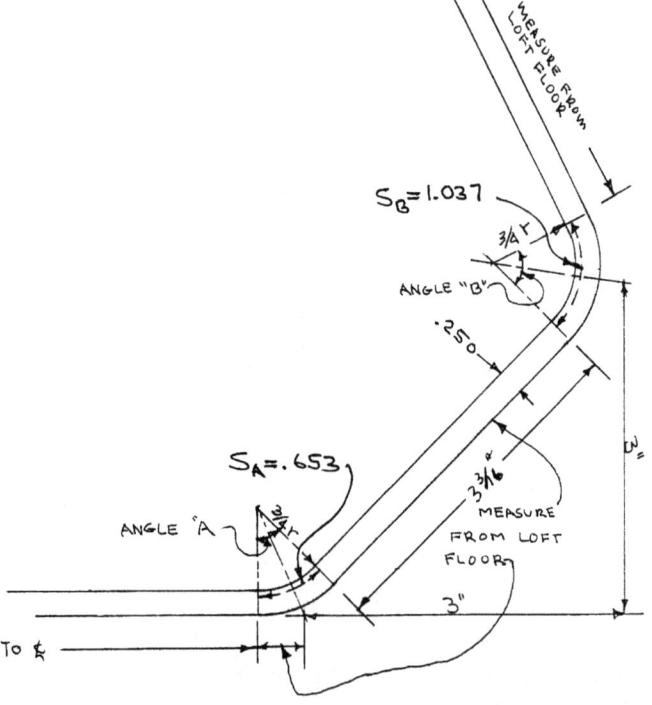

Figure B-4. Laying out bends other than 90 degrees.

APPENDIX C

Modifying the Lines for a Developable Surface

To easily form large, flat sheets of rigid material, such as aluminum, into a hull shape free of twists, the hull form must consist of *developable surfaces* (see also Chapter 3). A developable surface is made up of flat areas, sections of cylinders, and sections of cones. Each of these surfaces individually can be developed from a flat sheet of material. When they abut each other on a hull surface, a smooth transition from one form to another allows the *composite surface* consisting of cones, cylinders, and flats to be formed from a single flat sheet.

All developable surfaces consist of an infinite number of straight lines, called elements or rulings, which run normal to the direction of curvature. In addition, where each different developable surface abuts on a hull, there exists a common straight-line element to both surfaces. Figure C-1 is an example of one such surface with cones, cylinders, and flats sharing straight-line elements. The location of straight-line elements on a hull surface is the key to determining that the surface is developable.

The edges of a developable surface are defined by two lines in space. These lines can be straight or curved, and they're called *directrixes* of the developable surface. When a straight line, called a *generatrix*, lies on a flat plane that is touching and tangent to both directrix curves, it is an element of the surface, as illustrated in Figure C-2.

For a hard-chine hull bottom, the keel (or stem) at the centerline is one directrix and the chine can be the other directrix. Elements are located by finding the

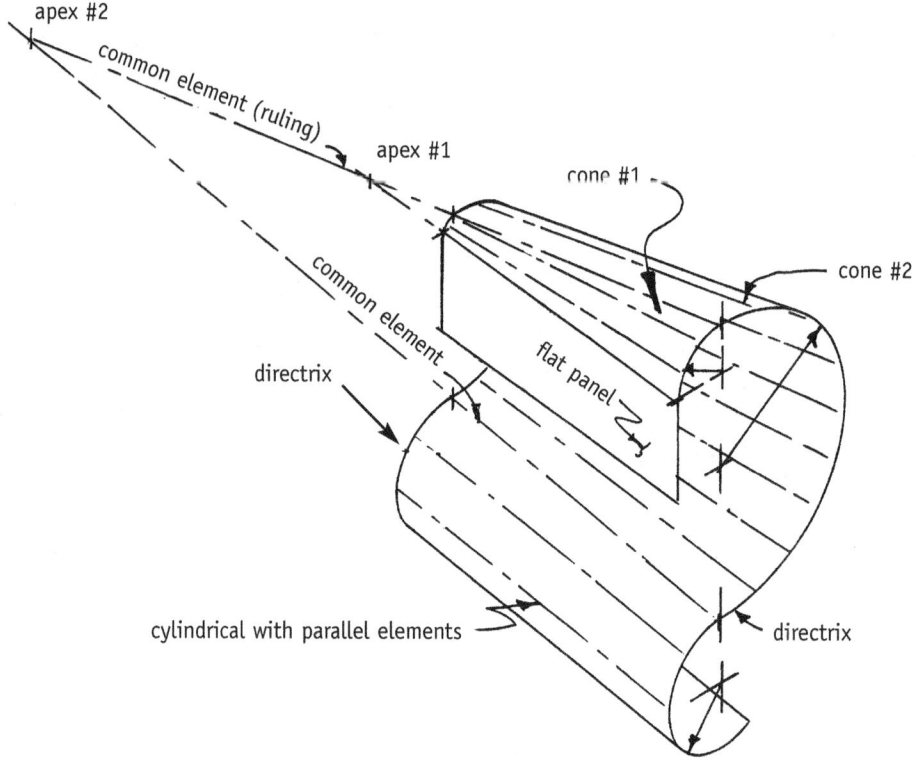

Figure C-1. Developable surface combining flat, cylindrical, and conical surfaces.

location of the straight lines that will be in continuous contact with the shell plate between the sheer and chine. These elements are called *rulings* in the boatbuilding industry. The rulings of a developable surface cannot be located at random, but must be located in a plane tangent to both directrix curves (Figure C-2).

DESIGNER'S METHOD OF CONICAL DEVELOPMENT

In order to understand the logic used to determine if a hull surface is developable, you should first understand the procedures the designer follows. One method to design a developable surface for the bottom plate is to hold either the directrix at the chine or stem fixed and pick some point as an apex of a cone, making the bottom contour a portion of a cone. A straight line from the apex point touching both directrix curves becomes one element on the cone's surface. Continuing this process will develop a sufficient number of elements to construct the bottom con-

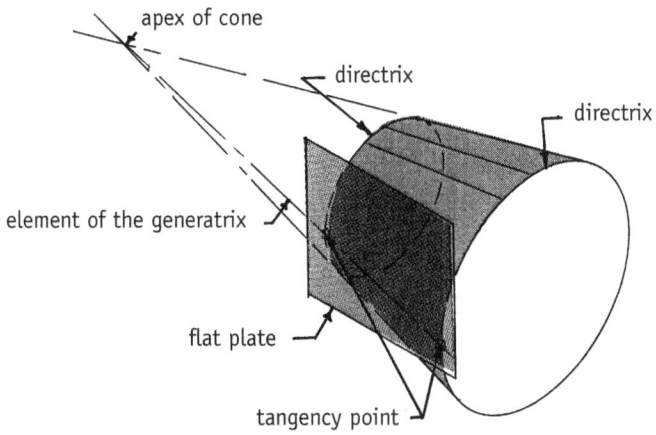

Figure C-2. Elements of the generatrix of a conical surface. Note the directrix and the extended apex of the cone.

tour. If one directrix location is known and an apex point is selected, the other directrix can be developed to fit the elements.

To design a hull bottom that will develop out of a flat plate, the designer first draws a line for the chine in both profile and plan views. The location of the chine line is based on the desired boat performance and designer's experience. This line becomes one directrix of the bottom developable surface. The stem bar, although curved in the profile view, is a straight line in the plan view and is the second directrix curve defining the bottom developable surface. The stem bar has yet to be defined in the profile view to conform with a developable surface.

To actually accomplish a design for developable bottom plate, the designer, after the chine line has been established, develops the shape of the stem in profile to conform to a developable surface, as follows:

- Based on the designer's experience (and some trial and error), an apex point is selected from which to draw rulings in both the plan and profile views.
- In the example (Figure C-3), the first rulings (in lowercase letters) were drawn from the apex point in profile—marked Apex of a cone, Elev.— to meet the chine line in the profile view at each station.

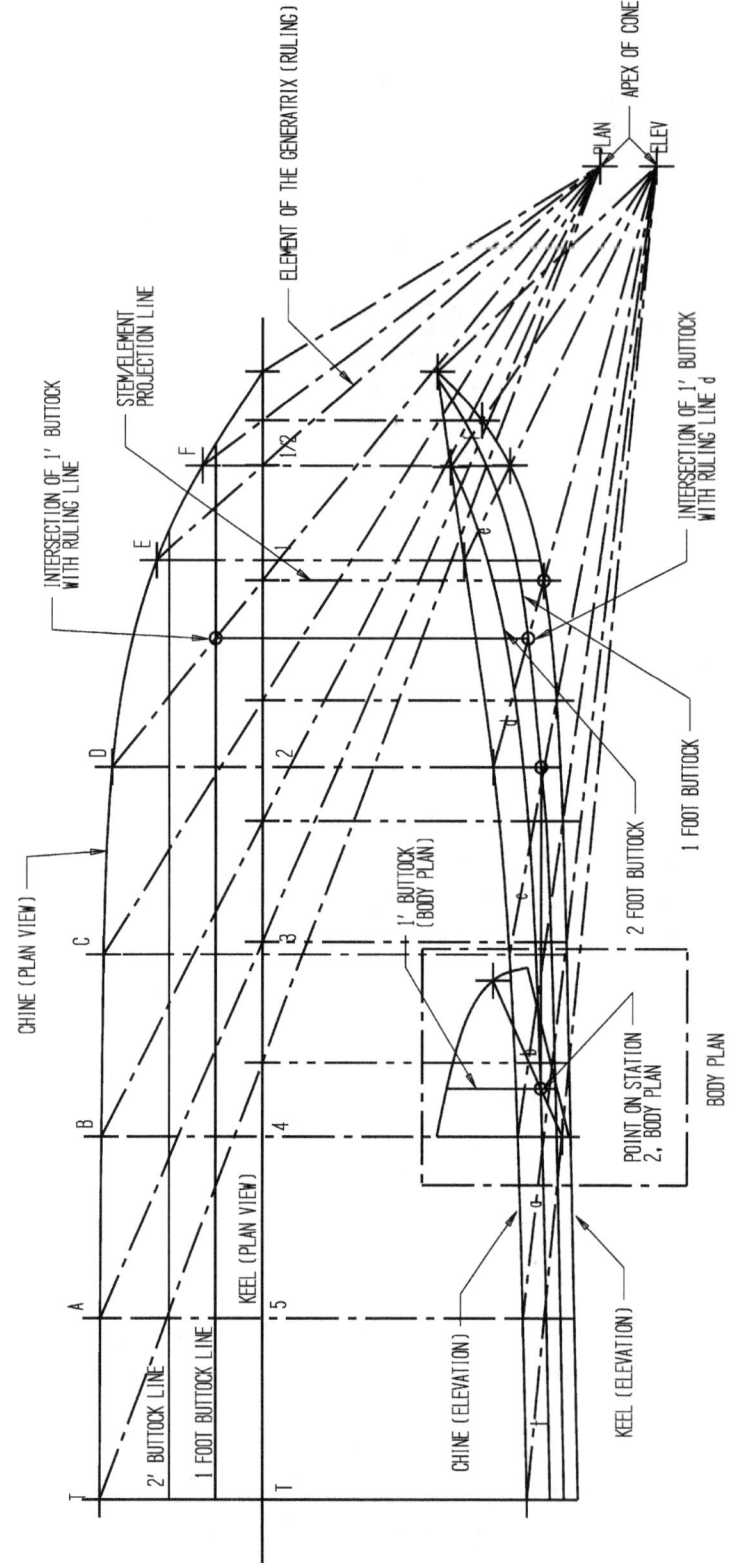

Figure C-3. Designer's method of laying out a developable hull bottom using single-cone development.

- The elements were then drawn in the plan view between the second apex point (marked Apex of a cone, Plan) and the chine line at each station and were designated by capital letters.
- The stem is located on the centerline in the plan view. The intersections of the elements with the centerline in the plan locate the stem outline when projected to corresponding elements in the profile view. A vertical line was then drawn between the intersection of the ruling D and the boat centerline (stem) in the plan view to intersect with ruling d in the profile view and marked Stem/Element (Figure C-3). This process was repeated to obtain sufficient points to draw in the stem in the profile view.

A similar process is used to locate buttock lines and waterlines. The resulting lines drawing will conform to a conical bottom development with the apex of the cone used for development as noted above and the stem and chine conforming to the cone geometry.

Development of lines defining a cylindrical surface requires the rulings to be parallel in both plan and profile. Multicone development involves a series of cones that share at least one common portion of a straight-line element.

CHECKING AN EXISTING DESIGN FOR A DEVELOPABLE SURFACE

It's not always practical to find a completed hull and lay a straightedge on the plate to find the location of the rulings (Figure C-4). In almost all cases, the loftsman has only the lines drawing, but from that he should be able to determine if the shell plate is developable.

A fast and sufficiently accurate method to locate rulings is to construct a simple scale model that will allow positioning a straightedge on the model's simulated shell plate. Once a number of rulings are located and drawn on the model's shell plate, they can be located on the existing lines drawing and used to confirm that the hull plate is developable. If the buttock lines and waterlines of the existing lines drawing conform to these straight-line rulings, then the surface is developable. If they don't, the hull form must be modified to be developable.

Construct the model without any framing that could interfere with the model's shell plate conforming naturally to a developable surface. Lay out the model to allow some stiff material, such as file-folder cardboard, to be wrapped around the two directrix curves, as shown in Figures C-5 and C-6.

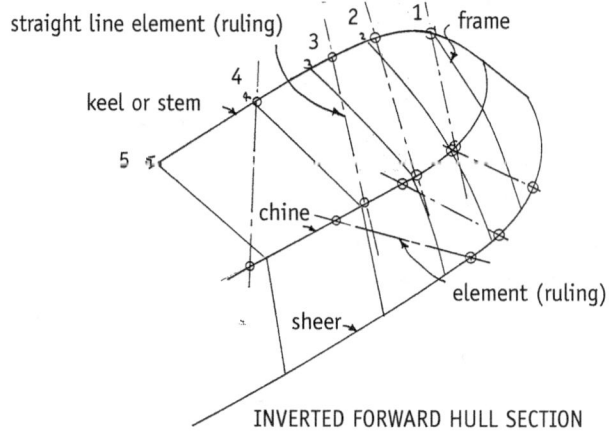

Figure C-4. Locating rulings (elements) on a completed hull.

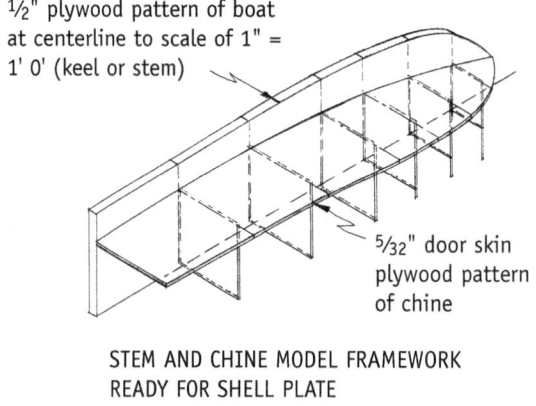

Figure C-5. Stem and chine model framework.

The simulated shell plate may require some pulling to fit snugly to the stem and chine—the directrixes for the developed bottom shell plate. After the shell plate is attached (usually with Scotch tape), a flat plane, simulated by a piece of plate glass, is laid on the bottom in contact with one point on each directrix (stem and chine). These are the tangent points between the plane and the directrix

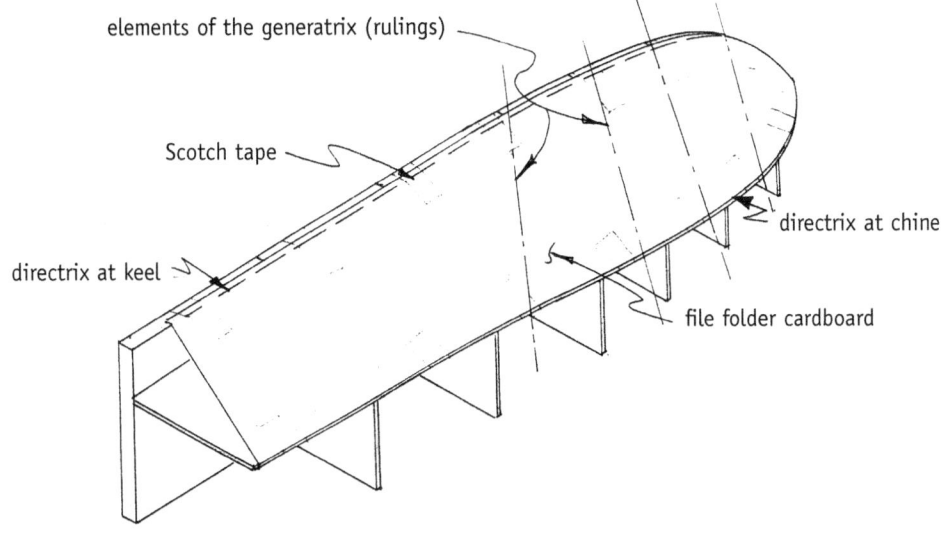

Figure C-6. Model to locate generatrix elements.

Figure C-7. Using a flat pane of glass to locate elements of the generatrix.

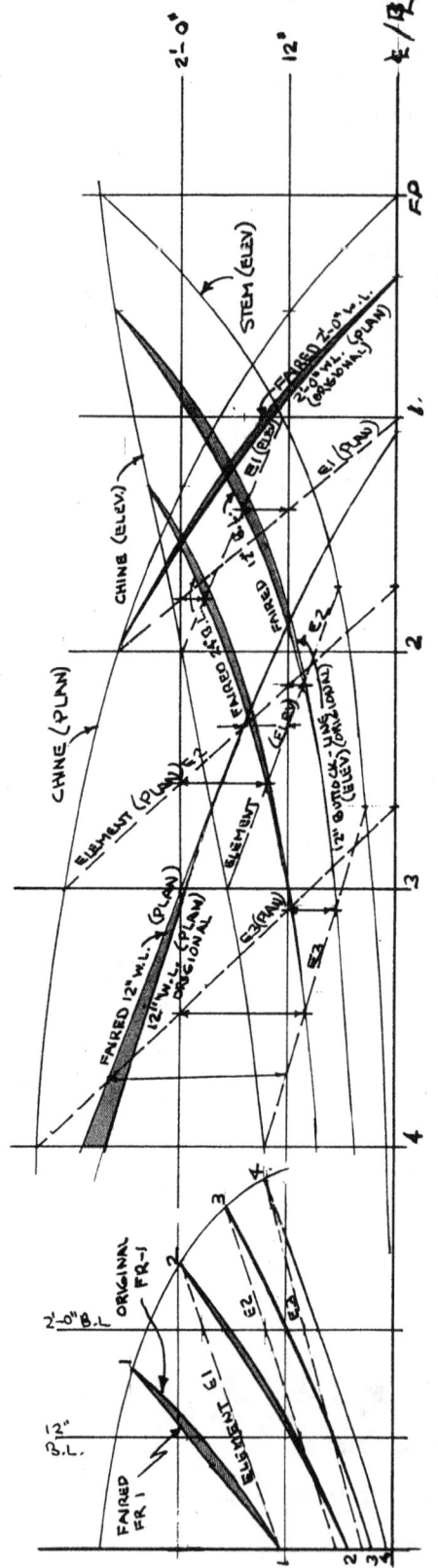

Figure C-8. Correcting the boat lines to conform to elements of the generatrix.

curves, and a straight line connecting these two tangent points is the location of one ruling. Locate a number of these rulings to fair in the bottom (one ruling crossing each station line is usually sufficient).

A simple method to locate the end points of each ruling on the model is to slide a thin piece of paper between the model and the glass, as shown in Figure C-7. The edge of the paper will stop at the line of contact between the model and glass and will assist in locating the rulings.

The procedure to fair the lines is similar to the conical development described previously, except you're working backward to adjust water lines, buttock lines, and stations to conform to the developable surface, as follows:

- Carefully pick the locations (from the model) of the ruling end points at the chine and stem, and locate them on the lines drawing in the profile view. Draw in the straight-line rulings as shown in Figure C-8.
- Project the ruling end points at chine and stem to the plan view. Draw the straight-line rulings in the plan view.
- Fair in the buttock lines and waterlines to conform with the straight ruling lines.
- Check the new developable-surface buttock lines and waterlines to the existing lines for conformance.

If the original lines do not conform to the rulings of the developable surface, then you must make a decision—either modify the original lines to conform or construct the boat without the benefit of a fully developable surface. The new locations of the waterlines and buttock lines for a developable surface are shown in Figure C-8.

The developable surface defined by the faired lines in Figure C-8 is probably multiconic, as evidenced by the apparent lack of a single apex point when projecting the elements. This is more likely to be the case when working backward from two known directrix curves, as multiconic development allows more latitude in hull design.

APPENDIX D

Line Fairing with a Flexible Batten

Fairing is a process in which a thin wood strip, called a batten, is used to smooth a curved line between points. Battens are different sizes and lengths and should be sized to best fit the intended application: Use short, limber battens for tight curves and long, stiff battens for long and gentle curves. A number of wood battens are normally found on a working loft floor, from 1/16 inch by 1/4 inch by 3 feet for short, tight-radius curves to 1/2 inch by 2 inches by 20 feet for long curves. A flexible draftsman's spline or a French curve (Figure D-1) is helpful in some situations.

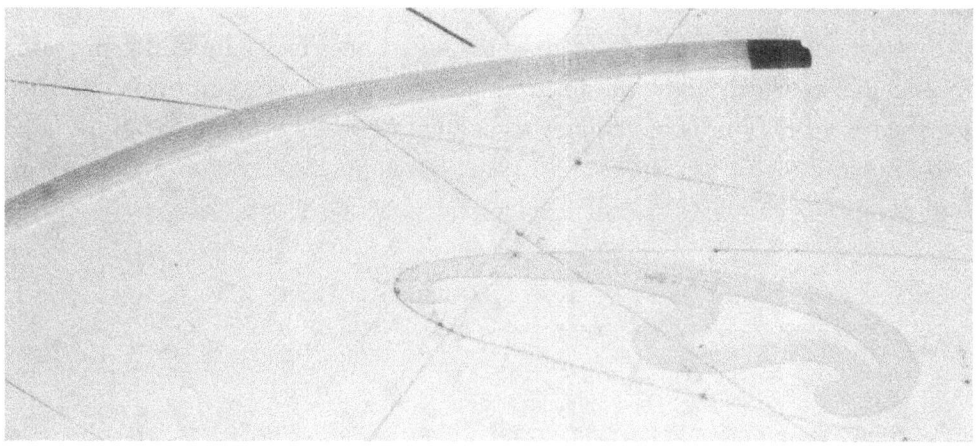

Figure D-1. A draftsman's spline and a French curve.

Line Fairing with a Flexible Batten

A good-size batten, which will fit most applications, is ¼ inch by 1½ inches by 16 feet made from tight-grained spruce. This batten can be used on edge for fairly tight curves or laid flat for long curves.

USING A BATTEN

To draw a long curved line (such as for a chine) using a batten, first locate points on the curve on the loft floor from the table of offsets or by other means. To provide a guide for the batten, drive finish nails into the loft floor at each known point. Place the 16-foot batten against these nails, and secure it in position with additional nails driven alongside it at each end. Grip one end of the batten and gently pull it to increase the curve—using the nail driven at the end of the batten as the fulcrum—until the batten just lifts off the nails immediately behind the fulcrum point (Figure D-2).

Now slowly release the pressure on the batten until it once again just touches the nails, and secure it in this new position by driving nails alongside. This better approximates the true curve of the line and eliminates a flat spot in the curve near the end of the batten. You will use this process repeatedly during the lofting process. When satisfied that the batten forms a fair line passing through the points, use it as a guide and draw a line with a sharp pencil.

It will be unusual if all points fall exactly on the line. Realize that the naval architect was working to a scale of 1 inch = 1 foot (or even smaller) when he developed the lines drawings; the offsets can be off a little bit at each point because of

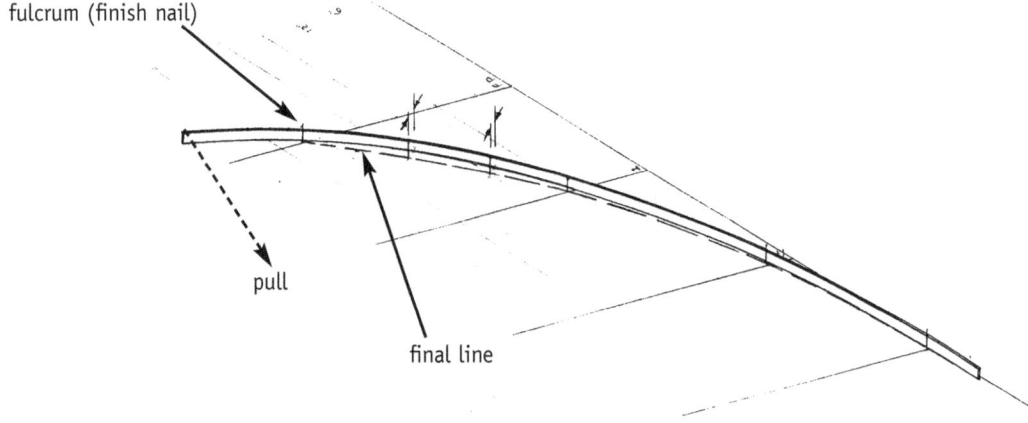

Figure D-2. Using a flexible batten.

the difficulty of absolute accuracy when reading a scale rule. Be alert for errors, even those as small as 1 inch. This is caused by the architect miscounting tick marks on the inches scale. Part of the fairing process is smoothing out the lines from the table of offsets by using a flexible batten and good judgment. Small errors in lifting scale dimensions from the lines drawing will usually be found during fairing of the lines full size on the loft floor.

STRAIGHT LINE TO CURVE TRANSITION

Often a curve requires a smooth transition from a straight line. Hold your batten straight for at least 2 feet prior to the start of curvature, and secure it with finish nails on each side of it. Now use the technique described above to complete the curve.

APPENDIX E

Conventional Drivetrain Installation

A *conventional drivetrain*—defined as an inboard engine with transmission gear, a propeller shaft, and a propeller—requires considerably more attention to install than other drive-train systems, such as I/Os or water jets. Because aluminum hulls shrink when welded, follow a set routine for strut alignment to minimize error caused by weld heat.

PROPELLER-STRUT ALIGNMENT

The alignment of the propeller strut with the main engine gear output flange can be a problem if the high rate of weld shrinkage associated with the aluminum structure is not taken into consideration. By following a careful procedure, you can minimize the effects of weld shrinkage, and install the strut without the use of line-boring equipment.

To install the strut, obtain a reasonably straight piece of round stock or pipe of a similar diameter as the required shaft—use it as a dummy shaft. Machine temporary bushings to fit within the strut-bearing housing to make the dummy shaft fit snugly into the housing. Position the dummy shaft, with the strut bearing housing on it, in the proper location in the boat (determined from the loft floor). Fit the strut legs to the hull and bearing housing, and tack-weld them to the hull. Next tack-weld the bearing housing to the strut legs to establish the correct angular relationship between housing and strut legs. At this point, the strut should be very close to the final alignment position.

Break loose the tack-welds holding the strut legs to the hull, and remove the strut assembly from the boat. Apply the final weld between the strut legs and the strut-bearing housing. The weld heat will cause some shrinkage and minor warping of the strut assembly.

The assembled strut is likely to be too large to be fit into a machinist's lathe for machine boring for the press-fit bearing. If it won't fit into the lathe, cut the strut legs approximately 6 inches up each leg from the bearing housing. Take the bearing housing assembly, with the attached stubs of the strut legs, to your machine shop for final boring for the light press fit of the shaft bearing. Also have the housing drilled and tapped for the bearing retainer set screws.

When the machined strut-bearing housing is available, you are ready for the final location of the strut. All weld shrinkage in near proximity to the shaft bearing has been corrected by machine boring the strut after welding. Again locate the strut legs on the hull, put the strut-bearing housing on the dummy shaft, and position the dummy shaft and strut-bearing housing on the boat. Securely tack-weld the strut legs to the stubs on the bearing housing, then tack-weld the strut legs to the hull. Remove the dummy shaft and final weld the strut legs into the hull. Wait on the final weld to join the strut legs to the machined bearing housing until after the fitting and final alignment of the actual propeller shaft.

This procedure of welding, then machining, then welding again compensates for weld shrinkage so that only the final strut-leg welding shrinkage affects the final alignment, and this shrinkage is usually insignificant and disregarded.

INBOARD ENGINE INSTALLATION

Once the propeller strut and shaft log are finish-welded to the boat, the location of the propeller shaft is fixed and cannot be changed. Therefore, to align the engine with the propeller shaft, you must move the engine. To do this, first make contact between the engine and shaft coupling flanges; use a feeler gauge to precisely check the gap between the flanges.

Put the propeller shaft into position in the boat and fit it with half the gear coupling; attach the other half of the coupling to the transmission. Check the mating faces on the flanges to be sure they're clean and flat. With both halves of the coupling in contact, adjust the engine mounts to obtain the proper height alignment. Shift the engine laterally for alignment. All four mounts must be positioned properly. Verify the coupling centerline alignment by butting the propeller-shaft coupler against the transmission output flange: The shoulder on the propeller flange should engage the recess on the transmission output flange with no resistance. Keep adjusting the engine position until the coupling faces are parallel and the boss is seated, as shown in Figure E-1. (This applies to both solid and flexible couplings.)

Install the mounting bolts between the adjustable mounts and the engine girders. (For full engine electrical isolation, these bolts must be fitted with isolation sleeves and washers of a nonconducting material.)

Check angular alignment by holding the coupling faces together tightly by hand and inserting a 0.003-inch feeler gauge between the coupling faces at 90-degree intervals (Figure E-2). Hand-rotate the propeller shaft a few times during the align-

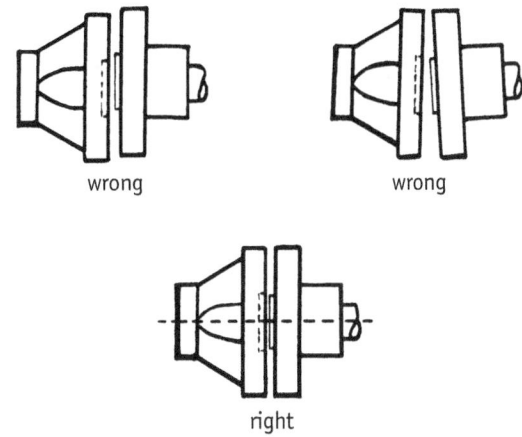

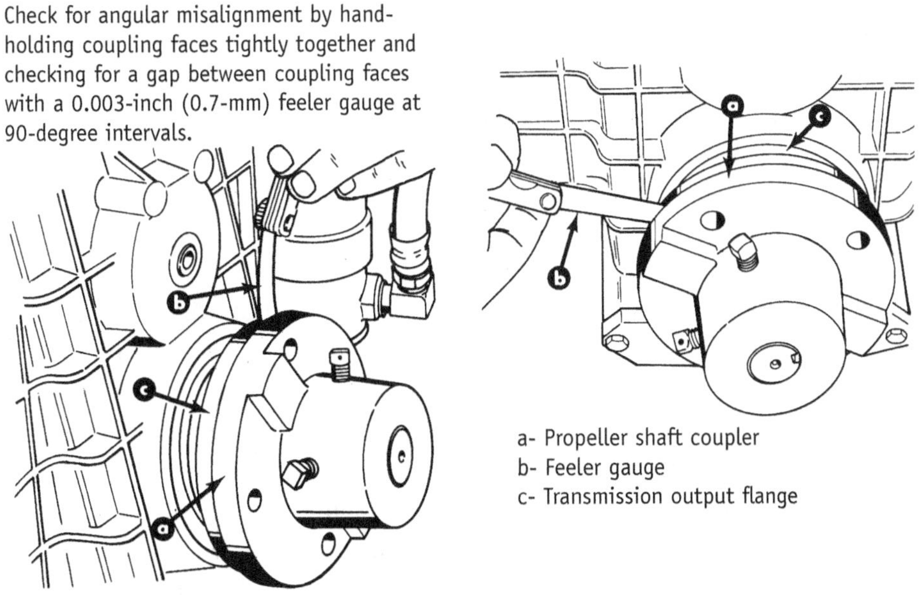

Figure E-1. Correct and incorrect alignment of the propeller-shaft coupling.

Check for angular misalignment by hand-holding coupling faces tightly together and checking for a gap between coupling faces with a 0.003-inch (0.7-mm) feeler gauge at 90-degree intervals.

a- Propeller shaft coupler
b- Feeler gauge
c- Transmission output flange

Figure E-2. Using a feeler gauge to align the shaft coupling.

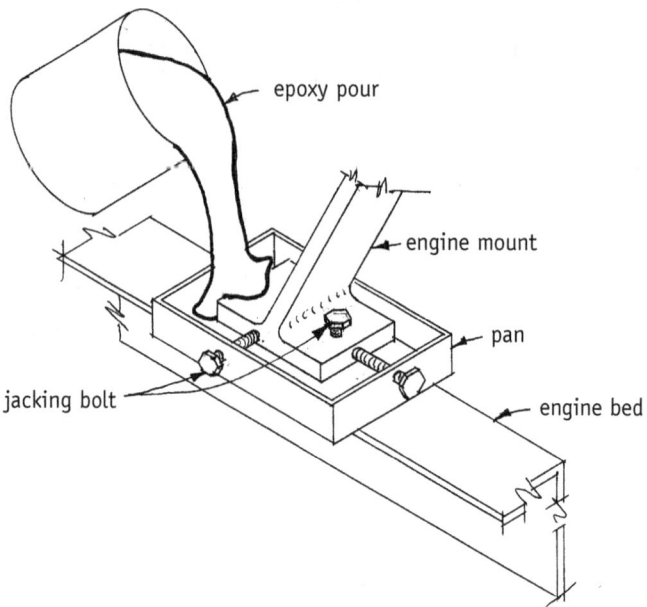

Figure E-3. Using the epoxy-pour method to align the engine.

ment, and adjust the engine mounts as necessary to obtain alignment within 0.003 inch. (Both front mounts or both rear mounts must be adjusted equally to keep the engine level from side to side.)

To adjust alignment left and right, loosen the mounting bolts and shift the engine as needed, then retighten the bolts.

To align larger engines located on rigid mounts, use shims or jacking bolts and an epoxy pour. The epoxy-pour method is much easier and faster than metal shims:

1. Install a stout metal pan, constructed of ½-inch aluminum plate, around the base of each engine mount (Figure E-3) to contain the liquid epoxy.
2. Drill and tap the outboard side of each pan for a jacking bolt (for lateral engine alignment).
3. Drill the engine beds and push stainless steel engine-mount bolts through from below. Hold them in place using a thin nut on the top side of the girder. Place an additional nut on the bolt to hold the weight of the engine and to serve as the jacking "bolt" to set engine elevation during alignment.

4. When the engine is in proper alignment, suspended on the jacking bolts, pour a special nonshrinking epoxy compound (e.g., Chock Fast from Philadelphia Resins) into the pan and up to the level of the base of the engine mounts. The hardened epoxy substitutes for the shims.
5. Once the epoxy hardens, add nuts to the top of the mounting bolts and tighten them to secure the engine in the desired position.
6. Remove the lateral jacking bolts, if possible, or simply cut them off.

APPENDIX F

Leveling a Structure Using a Water Level

A *water level* is nothing more than a water-filled, clear plastic tube. To determine the variation from level of two points of a structure, measure the difference in the water level inside the tube at each end.

To make a water level, obtain a piece of clear ¼-inch inside diameter flexible tubing about one and a half times the length of the structure being leveled. Fill the tube with water to within about 3 feet of one end and work the air bubbles out. Plug the ends of the tube with a ¼-inch bolt (about 1 inch long) and wrap with electrical tape to seal it until you are ready to use the level.

To use the water level:

1. Hold up one end of the level and have a helper hold up the other.
2. String the level between the two points that require leveling, and place the helper's end slightly above the starting point.
3. Hold the other end about level with the helper's end and remove the plugs from both ends of the tube. Hold the tube steady until the water in it has stopped moving.
4. If the water in the tube is below the starting point at the helper's end, slowly elevate your end of the tube, causing the water to rise in the tube, until the helper indicates the water is level with the starting point.

Leveling a Structure Using a Water Level

5. When the water stops moving in the tube and is level with the starting point, the water level in the other end of the tube is also level with the starting point. (See Figure F-1.)
5. Move the structure up or down as needed to be level. Mark the elevations obtained.
6. Repeat these steps as necessary until the water level is the same at all checkpoints. Mark the elevations at each checkpoint.

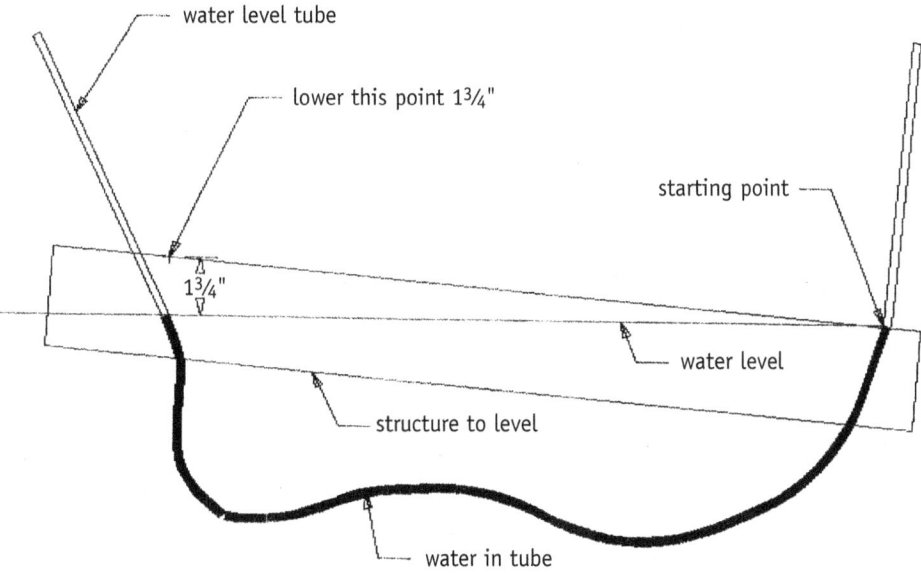

Figure F-1. Leveling a structure with a water level.

GLOSSARY

This glossary is provided to clarify boatbuilding terms used in this book, which are based on the author's everyday experience in boatyards in the U.S. Pacific Northwest. Other areas may have other terms for the same application. A glossary of shipbuilding terms can be found on the Internet under http://groups.msn.com/WoodenBoatBuilder/glossary.msnw.

Abaft. Behind or toward the rear.

Abeam. Some point alongside a ship; used to define a position relative to the ship.

ABL. Abbreviation for above baseline.

Above baseline. Designated dimension above the baseline of the vessel.

ABYC. American Boat and Yacht Council. An organization that writes and maintains voluntary standards for small craft.

Arc radius. The radius used to draw an arc of a circle.

Back chipping. Removing unwanted weld metal between welding-bead passes. Back chipping is accomplished by a chisel or other mechanical means; a power saw is often used on aluminum welds.

Baseline. The common reference line for all elevations; parallel with the design waterline (DWL) and generally the lowest point of the keel.

Batten. A long, slender, straight-grained wood stick used to fair lines on the loft floor.

Batten holder. A cut piece of material, usually wood, used to hold a flexible batten in place during the pickup of loft-floor lines for template making.

Beam. Width of a vessel at a specific point; generally used to describe the maximum width of the vessel.

Bearding line. The line formed by the intersection of the inside face of the planking and the face or side of the keel.

BL. Common abbreviation for baseline.

BLKD. Abbreviation for bulkhead.

Body plan. Lines-drawing view of stations at 90 degrees to the centerline; commonly located at center of lines drawing with stations forward of midships on the starboard side and those aft of midships on the port side.

Boot top. A narrow painted band at or slightly above the DWL to some distance (up to about 6 inches) above the DWL; a clearly defined parting between the bottom and topside paints.

Breakwater. A vertical bulkhead located forward on the main deck to deflect the force of water that may wash onto the deck.

Bulkhead. A solid vertical dividing structural member that may be watertight; nautical term for wall.

Bulwark. A section of the hull side extending above the main deck.

Butt line. Short for buttock line.

Butt weld. Weld joining two pieces of plate edge to edge.

Buttock line. An edge-on view of a plane parallel with the vertical plane at the boat's centerline. Buttock lines are straight lines in the plan and body plan views, normally equally spaced port and starboard of centerline.

CAD. Computer-assisted design.

Camber. The arch of a surface, usually a deck; a 3-inch camber means the center of the deck is 3 inches higher than the edges at its maximum beam.

Ceiling. Longitudinal planking placed on the inboard face of the frames.

Centerline. An imaginary line running down the center of the vessel in the plan and body plan views.

CFR. Code of Federal Regulations.

Chine. The intersection of the bottom and side of a hull. A hard chine (normally associated with powerboats) has an abrupt change of direction; a soft chine displays a rounded transition from bottom to side plate.

Chord. The straight line used to join the end points of an arc.

CL. Abbreviation for centerline.

Collar. A filler at a bulkhead penetration around an angle or a T-bar that makes the bulkhead watertight or is used for structural purposes.

Compound curvature. Description of a surface that is curved in more than one axis, such as the surface of a ball.

Conical developed surface. A surface that consists of a section of a cone or sections of a number of cones; straight-line rulings will point to the apex of the cone.

Construction drawing. Drawing prepared by the boatbuilder or naval architect to define details of construction.

Cumulative measurement. Laying out a series of dimensions by adding all dimensions together to obtain a total measurement, then laying out only one dimension.

Curve of areas (also curve of sectional areas). Developed by the naval architect for hydrostatic calculations; a curve plotted from a straight baseline representing the length of the ship, the ordinates of which represent the areas of the vessel's immersed cross sections. Found on lines drawings (not used during the lofting process).

Cylindrical developed surface. Surface that consists of a portion of a cylinder; ruling lines are parallel on a cylindrical developed surface.

Deadrise. Change in elevation in relation to a horizontal plane, similar to slope. The difference in height between the keel of a boat and the chine is an example of deadrise. A boat's cambered deck has a deadrise at centerline as compared to the deck edge.

Deck. Floor or walking surface; commonly parallel with the waterline, but decks may be sloped fore and aft and have camber.

Deck plan. Drawing looking down on the deck of a boat.

Declivity. Slope of a deck or vertical surface; used in conjunction with tumblehome found in a deck house side. Normally described in rise over run or in degrees.

Design waterline. The plane defined by the hull at the surface of the water; located by the naval architect during the design phase.

Developable surface. Any surface that can be constructed from a flat plate. Hull surfaces are defined as developable or undevelopable. A cylinder, which can be rolled from a flat sheet of material, is a developable surface; cones and flat planes are also developable. Surfaces such as spheres and ovoids are not developable; any attempt to construct these or other undevelopable surfaces from a flat sheet will result in wrinkles or stretching.

Diagonal. When used in lofting, a diagonal is similar to a waterline or buttock line but is located in a plane other than flat or vertical; commonly found in sailboat lines to assist in defining round-bilge geometry.

Directrix. A line or plane that guides the generatrix of a surface.

Displacement. Actual weight of a vessel; defined by the weight of water displaced by the vessel.

Doubler. See **hull doubler**.

Ductile. Easily bent or formed. Lead is more ductile than steel.

DWL. Abbreviation for design waterline.

Element. Term used to describe a specific location of the generatrix at any one position; in lofting, often called a ruling.

Elevation view. View on an engineering drawing looking from the side, or in elevation.

Engine bed. Girders, generally parallel with a boat's centerline, upon which the main propulsion engines are attached.

Fair line. A continuous natural curve, free of bumps or kinks. A fair line can be a straight line but is usually used in conjunction with a chine, stem, or gunwale line. Developed by spanning at least three reference points with a thin strip of straight-grained wood.

Fairing. Smoothing a curved line or surface; fairing a line is smoothing out the high and low points on a curve and averaging out the bumps—more art than science.

Faying surface. Mating surfaces of two adjoining materials.

FDN. Abbreviation for foundation.

Fillet weld. A weld joint where the edge of one piece of metal butts the flat surface of another piece of metal.

FL. Abbreviation for folding line.

Flair. Sloping outboard; opposite of tumblehome.

Flat-plate development. The process used to make a flat pattern of the surface of a three-dimensional object.

Floor. Horizontal part of transverse frame connecting the keel to the frame. Often used as a deck support.

Folding line. A 90-degree change of direction of a line of sight as associated with views of drawings. If a drawing of a boat were to be folded with a sharp crease so that the plan view was 90 degrees to the profile view, the crease would represent the folding line.

Foundation. Structure attached to hull or house for mounting items or machinery, such as generators, stoves, life rafts, etc.

FR. Abbreviation for frame.

Frame. A structural member, usually in the same plane as a station (they generally do not line up with the stations); in some cases, longitudinal frames run fore and aft.

Freeboard. Height of the hull side above the DWL at midships or some other designated position.

Freeing port. A hull opening on a weather deck to allow deck water to escape overboard.

Generatrix. Line guided by the directrix to generate a surface. For a developable surface, the generatrix must be a straight line. Various locations of the generatrix are called elements.

Girth. The measurement around a curved surface or arc; used in expanding views into flat patterns.

Good boatbuilding practice. Standard of quality commonly accepted by boatbuilders and boatowners based on experience and tradition.

Grid. In boat lofting, the basic straight layout lines representing the baseline, waterlines, buttock lines, and station lines.

Gunwale (also gunnel). Where topside and deck meet; also called the shear.

Half-breadth. Horizontal measurement from centerline to some point port or starboard; half the distance from gunwale to gunwale is a half-breadth.

Hard corner. The theoretical corner between two surfaces that actually meet in a rounded corner.

Heights. Vertical measurements above the baseline.

House. A ship's cabin or deckhouse.

Hull doubler. A plate welded to the surface of another plate to provide additional thickness in that area; often used to strengthen specific areas of a deck, such as attachment points for deck machinery.

Inboard profile. Elevation drawing showing ship cut along the longitudinal axis, looking outboard.

Intercostal. An intermittent framing member abutting adjacent framing, as compared to a through-passing member.

Jig. Tooling used to hold parts in position during fabrication.

Keel. Backbone of ship at base of hull; usually sits on the baseline. Also called the *stem* when located forward.

KNU. Abbreviation for knuckle.

Knuckle. A change in direction between two abutting surfaces.

Ladder. Nautical term for stairway; often quite steep.

Ladder riser. Vertical portion of a ladder, as compared with the step or rung, which is the horizontal portion.

Laying out. The act of measuring and locating a line or point.

Level. As used on large ships, a specific distance above the baseline; levels are commonly associated with decks, such as the 01 level on a large ship being the first deck above the main deck.

Lightening hole. A hole, commonly circular, where material has been removed to reduce weight.

Limber hole. Drainage hole cut through a structural member to allow fluid to drain by gravity.

Lines. Abbreviation for lines drawing.

Lines drawing. Drawing showing hull geometry of a ship or boat; normally includes plan, elevation (or profile), and body plan views defining the hull form by use of waterlines, buttock lines, and stations.

LOA. Abbreviation for length overall.

Loft floor. The actual drawing surface where the lines are drawn full size.

Lofting. Drawing of the boat hull full size; drawing full-size bulkheads, frames, and girders, and the layout and construction of templates from the lofted lines.

Loftsman. Individual who draws boat lines full size and makes templates.

Long. Abbreviation for longitudinal.

Long ton. 2,240 pounds.

Longitudinal. In the fore-and-aft axis; used to describe a long structural member, such as a T-bar hull stiffener.

Lvl. Abbreviation for level.

Margin plate. Strip of metal, typically about 10 inches wide, welded continuously to the inside edge of the shell plate and used as the attachment surface for a wood deck.

Midships. Toward the center of a ship in the fore-and-aft axis.

MIG. Standard abbreviation for Metal Inert Gas welding process, which uses a consumable electrode and an inert shielding gas.

Mold loft. The area where lines are laid down on the floor; usually a designated area of a shipyard.

Molded line. The line to which all layout dimensions are given. Since the thickness of the material affects dimensions, the molded line is used to determine which side of the surface to lay out. On metal boats, the molded line is the inside of the boat's shell plate, the underside of decks, and the inboard face of longitudinal bulkheads. The molded line on transverse members can vary but is usually the forward face in the forward portion of the boat. Notes on the molded line should be found on the construction drawings.

Molded surface. Similar to molded line, but referring to a surface; normally the underside of decks, the inboard surface of longitudinal surfaces, and either the forward or aft face of bulkheads, as specified.

Mullion. Slender bar or post that separates windows.

Nontight. Structural members not required to be watertight.

Offsets. Dimensions from centerline or above baseline.

Oilcan. Term used to describe distortion of plating, usually caused by excessive welding heat, as compared to a dented 5-gallon can.

Outboard profile. Elevation drawing showing the boat from the side view.

P. Abbreviation for port.

Pad eye. Any small metal plate with a hole in it attached to a structure and used as an attachment point for lifting or lashing; also a lifting eye welded to a base.

Panel breaker. Similar to stiffener; commonly used to break up a vibration in a panel or to provide additional stiffness.

Passageway. A hallway or access route.

Plug welding. Process of welding two plates, one on top of the other, by welding through holes in one plate to fuse the two together in a number of spots.

Port. Left in nautical terminology; also a hull opening above the waterline.

Portlight. Nautical term for window.

Profile. View from the side; elevation view.

Pulse-arc welding. A refinement of the MIG welding process involving rapid on and off of the welding current.

Rabbet. A longitudinal groove in a member used to receive another piece. Rabbet line is similar to the bearding line in metal boat construction.

Radial. One of a number of layout lines starting at a common point and radiating outward like the spokes of a wheel.

Rake. Forward or aft slope.

Rat hole. A cutout in a structural member for access to a welded seam.

Ray. A radial.

Ruled surface. A surface that may be generated by a straight line; a straightedge may be laid on the surface so that it will touch the surface for its entire length.

Ruling. An element of the generatrix.

Scale. Ratio of size in relation to actual size; a drawing showing a scale of ½ inch = 1 foot means ½ inch on the drawing equals 1 foot on the actual vessel.

Scantlings. Thickness of plates and sizes of structural members used to construct the hull.

Scribing in. Drawing a line using an adjacent surface as a guide; marking a cutting line to fit a surface.

Shaft horsepower. Output horsepower at the propeller shaft.

Sheer. A line in the profile view defined by the top of the ship's side and the main-deck intersection.

Shell. A boat's exterior skin or hull plate.

Shroud. A wire laterally supporting a mast.

STA. Abbreviation for station.

Stanchion. A vertical column or post used for structural support.

Starboard. Right in nautical terminology.

Station. A vertical plane perpendicular to the baseline in the profile view and to the centerline in the plan view; commonly the DWL is divided into 10 equal spaces separated by station lines.

STBD. Abbreviation for starboard.

Stem. Forward portion of keel; sometimes term used for the entire keel.

Stiffener. Structural member used to stiffen a specific panel.

Strake. An exterior hull stiffener running in the longitudinal axis; also one width of plate or planking running the length of the hull.

Stretch. Bundle of electrical wires transmitting current and electronic information between the power source and the weld feeder. An inert-gas supply tube is sometimes included.

Stretch-out. The dimension of a piece of material that is laid out flat (similar to flat pattern). Also used to define the flat-pattern layout distance around a circular shape.

Stringers. Longitudinal members, usually running through a number of frames, used to support sheet or plate members.

Strongback. A temporary structural member used to hold parts in alignment during fabrication; usually removed after welding on the part is complete.

Stuffing box. A packing gland used at the penetration of a shaft, wire, or other item through the hull or other watertight surface to keep it watertight; specifically the packing gland where the prop shaft penetrates the hull.

T. Abbreviation for transom.

Table of offsets. A table of numeric data included in the lines drawings that gives dimensions for heights and half-breadths; usually provided by the naval architect and scaled from the drawings. Dimensions commonly shown in feet, inches, and eighths.

Temper. Heat treatment to increase the mechanical characteristics of heat-treatable aluminum alloys; also the work-hardened condition of non-heat-treatable aluminum.

Template. A flat pattern defining the geometric shape of a frame or other part; usually "lifted" directly from the loft floor or the structure for fabricating parts. Previously called molds.

TIG process. Stands for Tungsten Inert Gas welding process, which uses a non-consumable electrode and an inert shielding gas.

Transom. Aft-most transverse member of the hull forming a watertight bulkhead.

Transverse. At 90 degrees to the centerline, running across the boat (port to starboard).

Triangulation. Method of layout using arcs of circles to locate the corner points of a triangle.

True length. A component shown on a drawing or loft floor in its actual length.

True size. A component shown on a drawing or loft floor in its actual size, such as a flat pattern for a curved surface.

Tumblehome. Slope of a surface in relation to a vertical surface; commonly used in conjunction with declivity.

Undevelopable surface. See **developable surface**.

Waterline. A plane parallel with the plane at which the vessel floats; waterline defines hull geometry at specific heights above the baseline.

Watertight. Describes any structure that will not allow water to pass under flooding conditions. All hull and deck shell plate should be watertight.

Weathertight. Describes any structure that can withstand a hose test without excessive leakage, such as a cabin door or window.

Wheel. The propeller.

Whip. Bundle of conduit, tubes, and electrical cables that provide filler wire, shielding gas, electric power, and electronic information to the welding gun from the welding-wire feeder.

WL. Abbreviation for waterline.

W.T. Abbreviation for watertight.

INDEX

Numbers in **bold** refer to pages with illustrations or tables

4043 filler wire alloy, 96
5000 series alloy, 22, 23–25
5052 alloy, 39
5052-H32 alloy, 25
5083 alloy, 39
5083-H112 alloy, 25
5086 alloy, 39
5086-H116 alloy, 17, 24–25
5356 filler wire alloy, 96
6000 series alloy, 25–27
6061-T6 alloy, 22, 25, 27, 39, 183, 184
6061-T651 alloy, 183
6063 alloy, 22
6063-T4 alloy, 27, 39

A

ABYC. *See* American Boat and Yacht Council (ABYC)
"AC and DC Electrical Systems on Boats" (ABYC), 254–56
AC electrical systems, 254–56
air bending, **84, 85**
air-wand tests, 179–80
alloys. *See* marine aluminum alloys
aluminum boat construction
  advantages, 16–20, **17, 19**
    extrusions and, 8–**9**
  origins, 6–7
  trends, 13–16, **14, 15**
  welded-aluminum boats, **9–11**, 13
Aluminum Boats (Kaiser Aluminum), 52
Aluminum Welder's Training Manual (Aluminum Association), 107
American Boat and Yacht Council (ABYC), 30
  design guidelines, 67
  sea trial guidelines, 66
  Standards and Recommended Practices for Small Craft, 30, 233
amperage calculations, 247–49
angle grinders, 81
annealing, 26, 112
antifouling paint, 271, 275–76
assembly. *See* construction sequence
assembly platforms, 159–65, **162, 164**
Awlgrip Marine Coatings, 273, **274,** 275

B

back chipping, 101, 102–3, 177
ballast keels, **198–204**
band saws, 78–79
battens, **297**–98
batteries, 252
Baywood, Inc., 220
bending rolls, 85–**86**

315

boatbuilders
  evolution of shops, 7
  Pacific Northwest, 8
boatowners, 7
Boatowner's Mechanical and Electrical Manual (Calder), 252
bonding DC systems, 253
bottom plate thickness, 53
bulkhead paneling, 266–**68**
bulkhead stiffeners, **173**
burn sheets, **157**–58
buttock lines, 44
butt welds, 62, **105, 109**–10

C

C. W. F. Hamilton, 223
CAD lofting programs, 13, 40, 41, 152–58, **154, 157**
camber curves, 277–**80**
cathodic protection, 253–54
ceilings, 265–66
chines, 26, **28**, 56–**57**
circular saws, 69, 73–78, **74, 76, 77**
Coast Guard regulations. *See* United States Coast Guard
compound curvature, 33–34, **87**–88
computer-guided cutting, **10,** 13
conical development, 34, 36–**37**, 288–91, **289, 290**
consoles, center-mounted, 52
construction drawings, **46**–49
construction sequence
  assembly platforms, 159–65, **162, 164**
  erecting framework, 168–70, **169**
  fabricating frames, **165**–68, **166, 167**
  fairing, 170
  final metal work, 180
  framing end connections, 172–**74**
  hull weld-out, 177–78
  limber holes, 171
  rat holes, 171
  shell plate fit-up, 175–77
  turning boat over, 179
  watertight weld-testing, 179–80
  welding framework to shell plate, 178
contract drawings, 40
corner welds, 63, **65**
corrosion, 53, 199

cost effectiveness, 19–20, 32
cost of materials, 39
crater cracking, 101–3, **102**
cutting systems
  band saws, 78–79
  circular saws, 69, 73–78, **74, 76, 77**
  laser cutters, 73
  plasma arc cutters, **72,** 73
  power saws, 73
  power shear, 79
  water jet, 73
cylindrical development, 34–**36**

D

DC electrical systems, **246**–53
deadrise, **31**
decks, 60, 265, 277–**80**
deep-V hulls, 31–32
delta pads, 56
design drawings
  about, 39–41
  construction drawings, **46**–49
  lines drawings, 41–46, **42, 43, 45**
designers, boat
  credentials, 29
  and design modifications, 51
developable surface hulls
  about, 6–7, 287–**88**
  CAD lofting, 155–56
  checking for, 291–95, **292, 293, 294**
  manual lofting, 124–25
  types, 33–39, **36, 37, 38**
diagonals, 44
die grinders, 80
diesel engines, 206–9, **207, 208**
directrixes, 287
drafting equipment, **296**
drawings. *See* design drawings
drivetrain systems, 213, 299–303, **301, 302**
durability, 18

E

East Teak Trading Group, Inc., 266
economic feasibility, 30, 32
elasticity, 18
electrical systems
  about, 245

Index

AC systems, 254–56
cathodic protection, 253–**55**
DC systems, **246**–53
lightning protection, 254
The Elements of Boat Strength (Gerr), 52
engine beds, 60–61, 151–52, **302**–3
engine compartments, 238–**41,** 264
engines. *See* propulsion methods
entrapped water, 53
E-Paint Company, 276
Eventide, **10, 16**
Everything You Need to Know about Propellers (Mercury Marine), 229–30

F

fabricating techniques
   cutting systems, 72–81
   forming techniques, 82–88
   general, 69
   marking for cutting, 71–72
   planing, 81–**82**
   shop size and climate, 70
   tools needed, 70–**71**
fairing, **296**–98
fatigue issues, 66–67
fillet welds, 63, **65,** 110–**14**
floating transverse framing, **59**
folding lines, **135**–38
forming techniques
   air bending, **84- 85**
   bending rolls, 85–**86**
   pipe bending, 86
   press brakes, 65, 82–85, **83**
   stretch-forming process, 87
framing, **59,** 156
fuel systems
   diesel fuel systems, 240–43
   gasoline fuel systems, 233–**41**
fuel tanks, **283**–85
furring out, **258**–61

G

galley units, **267**–**68**
galvanic corrosion, 199
gasoline engines, 209–**11**
gasoline fuel systems, 233–40, **234, 237, 239**
generatrix, 287, **293**

gunwales, **58**–59

H

hand nibblers, 81
hard-chine hulls, 34–35
headliners, 265–66
hull bottom, 54–56, **55**
hull design and form
   about, 5–7
   chines, 56–**57**
   combination surfaces, **38**–**39**
   conical development, 36–**37**
   cost of materials, 39
   criteria, 29–30
   cylindrical development, 35–**36**
   decks, 60
   delta pads, 56
   design drawings, 39–49
   design modifications, 49–50
   ease of construction, 62–63
   engine beds, 60–61
   engineering principles, 54–62
   framing, **59**
   gunwales, **58**–59
   hull bottom, 54–56, **55**
   parameters, 30–32
   preforming, 65–66
   ruled surface hulls, 34–35
   sailboats, 181
   sea trials, 66–67
   stock designs, 51
   strakes, 56
   structural considerations, 52–54
   superstructures, 49, 61–62
   transoms, 57–58
hull stiffeners, 53–54

I

impact resistance, 18, **19**
inboard engines. *See also* engine beds; engine compartments
   drivetrain installation, 299–303, **301, 302**
   propeller shaft assembly, **212**
   shaft and propeller, 213–19, **214, 215, 218**
inboard-outboard (I/O) drives, 219–21, **220**
inert shielding gas, 95–96
instrument panels, **209**

insulation, 262–64, **263**
International Marine Coatings, 276

J

jet sleds, 8
jigs, 159–65, **162, 164**

K

keels, ballast, **198–204**
Key Creator (software), 153
kit boats, 161

L

lap joints, 62
lead ballast, **200–203**
limber holes, 171
lines drawings, 41–46, **42, 43, 45**
lofting
    about, 123–25
    burn sheets, **157**–58
    CAD lofting programs, 41, 152–58, **154, 157**
    calculated distances, 140
    drift boat (sample), 127–34, **130, 131, 132, 133**
    engine bed, 151–52
    folding lines, **135**–38
    girths, 138–40, **139**
    laying down lines, 126–27
    loft floor, 123, 125–26
    loftsmen, 124
    molded lines, 124, 130–**32**
    scaling, 156–57
    side shell development, 142–45, **144**
    templates, 145–51, **146, 147, 149, 150**
    triangulation, 140–**43**
    true-size views, 134–**45**
longitudinal framing, **12**
longitudinal members, stitch-welded, 53

M

maintenance, 19
marine aluminum alloys
    4043 filler wire, 96
    5000 series, 22, 23–25
    5052, 39
    5052-H32, 25
    5083, 39
    5083-H112, 25
    5086, 39
    5086-H116, 17, 24–25
    5356 filler wire, 96
    6000 series, 25–27
    6061-T6, 22, 25, 27, 39, 183, 184
    6061-T651, 183
    6063, 22
    6063-T4, 27, 39
    alloying process, 21–**23**
    mechanical properties, **23**
    purchasing, 28
    special extrusions, 27–28
    stock sizes, 27
    welding filler wire, 96
masts, aluminum: about, 181–83, **182**
    cross-sections, **182**–83
    cutouts, **187–188**
    internal wiring, **193**–94
    loads, 183
    masthead fittings, **194**
    peripherals, 196–98
    splicing, 183–**84**
    spreader attachments, **188–192**
    stepping, 196–97
    tang attachments, 192–**93**
    tapering, 184–**86**
McKenzie River drift boat, **11**–12, 35–**36, 42–43**
Mercruiser MIE 5.7 L engine, 213–**14**
MIG (metal inert gas) welding, 18, 90–96, **93**
Millermatic GMAW 251 welding machine, **89,** 92
Miller Spoolmatic 1-pound-spool gun, 92, **94**
molded lines, 124, 130–**32**
motor wells, 52
multiconic hull surfaces, 35

N

naval architects, 29
noise control, 70
nondevelopable surfaces, 33–34, 181
Nyalic coating, 276

O

outboard propulsion systems, 13–14, 224–26

P

Pacific Northwest boatbuilding, 8
paint systems

Index

about, 13, 271–72
    antifouling paint, 275–76
    hull preparation, 275
    marine coatings, 274–75
    small welded production boats, 272–74, **273**
paper calculator tape, 129, **130**
performance criteria, **31**
Pettit, 276
pickup sticks, 129
pipe bending, 86
planes, power hand, 69, 81–82
planing hulls, 17, 52
plate thickness, 52
plywood construction, 6
power shear, 79
precut boats, 13
preforming, and design, 65–66
press brakes
    about, 65, 82–85, **83**
    material stretch-out, 281–**86**
production boats, **9–**12
propeller shaft assembly, inboard, **212**
propeller shafts, 215–17
propulsion systems
    about, 13–14
    controls, 226–27
    diesel engines, 206–9, **207, 208**
    drivetrain systems, 213, 299–303, **301, 302**
    engine selection, 205–6
    exhaust systems, 230–32, **231**
    gasoline engines, 209–**11**
    inboard-outboard (I/O), 219–**20**
    outboards, 13–14, 224–26
    propellers, 228–30
    shaft and propeller, 213–19, **214, 215, 218**
    steering, 227–28
    turbine engines, 211
    water jets, **8,** 13, 221–24, **222**
ProSurf 3 (software), 153
prototype boats, 51
pyramid bending rolls, 85–**86**

R

rat holes, 171
reciprocating saws, 80–**81**
regulations, design, 67–68
repair ease, 19
resale value, 20
routers, 80
ruled surface hulls, 34–35, 50, 288–**289**
runout tabs, **110**

S

sailboats, racing, 17
scallops, 171
scantlings, 52
sea trials, 66–67
semi-V hulls, 32
shaft and propeller propulsion, 213–19, **214, 215, 218**
size considerations, 31, 50–51
Specmar, Inc., 40
sportfishing, offshore, 14–**15**
Standards and Recommended Practices for Small Craft (ABYC), 30, 233
station lines, 41, 126
steel alloys, 215
steel construction, 19
stock designs, 51
strakes, 56
strength-to-weight ratio, 16–18, **17**
stretch-forming process, 87
strongbacks, 116–**17**
structural considerations, 52–54
stuffing boxes, **218**
style, design, 32
superstructures, 49, 61–62

T

table of offsets, 40, 44
tanks, fuel, **234**–35
Tar Bucket, **6,** 10
Thermax Marine, 268
tools needed, 70–**71**
trailering, 14, 20
transmissions, 214
transoms, 57–58, 133–34, 220
tripping, 172, **174**
tumblehome, 62
turbine engines, 211

U

United States Coast Guard regulations, 67–68, 233
upright construction, **10**

use, intended, 31

V

ventilation, 233, 238–**41**
Venturosa, 33–34
vibrations, panel, 67
Volvo D6-310 engine, 206–**8**
Vortec 5.8 L engine, **211**
Vortec 6.0 L engine, **210**

W

water-jet propulsion, **8**, 13, 221–24, **222**
water levels, 304–**5**
waterlines, 44, 126
welded-aluminum boat types, **9**–13
welding processes
    back chipping, 101, 102–3, 177
    butt-welding sequence, **105, 109–10**
    corner *vs.* fillet, 63, **65**
    crater cracking, 101–3, **102**
    fillet welds, 63, **65**, 110–13, **111, 113, 114**
    fit-up, **107–09**
    grinding flush, 121–22
    heat distortion, 103–4, 177
    hull weld-out, 177–78
    inert shielding gas, 95–96

MIG, 90, 91–96, **93**
Millermatic GMAW 251 welding machine, **89,** 92
Miller Spoolmatic 1-pound-spool gun, 92, **94**
one-sided hull seams, 53
power supply factors, 70, 89, 94–95
pulse-arc, 90
shop setup, 97–100, **99**
stitch-welded longitudinal members, 53
symmetric order, 120
technique, 100–101
TIG, 90
watertight weld-testing, 179–80
weld cleanup, 121
weld groove preparation, **105**–7
weld-induced distortion, 113–20, **115, 117, 118, 119**
welding filler wire, 96
welding personnel certification, 68
welding skill, 18
welding wire feeders, 92–**94**
windows, 268–70
wiring, protection and conductors, 249–**52**
woodwork
    decks, paneling, and furniture, **265**–70
    furring out, 257–**61**

www.ingramcontent.com/pod-product-compliance
Lightning Source LLC
Chambersburg PA
CBHW082030300426
44117CB00015B/2417